FROMMER'S *EasyGuide* to
DISNEY WORLD, UNIVERSAL & ORLANDO 2019

6th Edition

MAP IN
BACK POCKET

By Jason Cochran

FROMMER'S STAR RATINGS SYSTEM

Every hotel, restaurant, and attraction listed in this guide has been ranked for quality and value. Here's what the stars mean:

★   Recommended
★★   Highly Recommended
★★★   A must! Don't miss!

AN IMPORTANT NOTE

The world is a dynamic place. Hotels change ownership, restaurants hike their prices, museums alter their opening hours, and buses and trains change their routings. And all of this can occur in the several months after our authors have visited, inspected, and written about these hotels, restaurants, museums, and transportation services. Though we have made valiant efforts to keep all our information fresh and up-to-date, some few changes can inevitably occur in the periods before a revised edition of this guidebook is published. So please bear with us if a tiny number of the details in this book have changed. Please also note that we have no responsibility or liability for any inaccuracy or errors or omissions, or for inconvenience, loss, damage, or expenses suffered by anyone as a result of assertions in this guide.

Nothing but blue skies meet the massive drop on SeaWorld's 200-foot-tall Mako roller coaster; the tallest, longest, and fastest coaster in Orlando.
Previous page: Eola Lake in Orlando.

CONTENTS

1 THE BEST OF ORLANDO 1

2 SUGGESTED ITINERARIES & ORLANDO'S LAYOUT 7

3 EXPLORING WALT DISNEY WORLD 19

Ticketing 22

Eating On-Site 29

Navigating Disney 29

The Magic Kingdom 34

Epcot 64

Disney's Animal Kingdom 85

Disney's Hollywood Studios 97

Disney Water Parks 108

Other Disney World Diversions 111

4 UNIVERSAL ORLANDO, SEAWORLD & BEYOND 115

Universal Orlando 115

SeaWorld Orlando 146

Legoland Florida 158

Busch Gardens Tampa Bay 159

5 MORE ORLANDO ATTRACTIONS 161

International Drive Area 161

Kennedy Space Center 178

Nightlife in Orlando 180

Outdoor Orlando 183

Shopping 190

Cruises from Port Canaveral 194

6 DINING AROUND TOWN 196

Outside the Disney Parks 196

Character Meals 220

Nightlife at the Resorts 223

7 ORLANDO'S HOTELS 227

Finding the Best Rates 228

Inside Orlando's Hotels 229

8 PLANNING YOUR TRIP TO ORLANDO 267

Getting There 267

Getting Around 270

When to Go 273

Orlando's Calendar of Events 274

Fast Facts: Orlando 278

INDEX 288

ABOUT THE AUTHOR 301

A favorite from childhood, the flying elephant Dumbo takes flight in Magic Kingdom's Fantasyland.

A LOOK AT ORLANDO

Welcome to Orlando! If you've journeyed to this sunny section of Central Florida, there's a good chance you have two things in mind: visiting the "Happiest Place on Earth," Walt Disney World, and exploring the Wizarding World of Harry Potter at Universal Orlando. But there's so much more to experience in both the theme parks and Orlando beyond just the big-ticket attractions. From sparkling natural springs that beg you to unplug and jump in, to sophisticated dining and wine, to hidden spots inside the parks, not to mention other stellar attractions such as Kennedy Space Center, Orlando is filled with surprises if you know where to look.

All aboard the Hogwarts Express to the Wizarding World of Harry Potter at Universal Orlando.

WALT DISNEY WORLD

Walt Disney World for many people is synonymous with the Magic Kingdom and the fairy-tale appeal of Cinderella Castle.

MagicBands (p. 25) are your entry to the "Kingdom" and anywhere else in Walt Disney World, almost magically acting as your admission ticket, room key, and charge card.

The lobby of the Hollywood Tower Hotel, the setting for the Twilight Zone Tower of Terror (p. 101), has been frozen in time since 1939. The furniture was acquired from Los Angeles–area antique stores.

Epcot, more than any other Disney park, changes its personality and decorations to fit the season, especially during the Flower & Garden Festival in spring.

In Future World, you'll find explorations of land, sea, farming, and space; in the latter, you'll find Mission: SPACE (p. 69), a ride that simulates a launch—you can choose whether you prefer a mild or wild journey.

Kids, and kids at heart, will love Hollywood Studios' new Toy Story Land (p. 103).

Hollywood Studios (p. 97) is where you'll find everything relating to the *Star Wars* movies—including, in late 2019, the new Galaxy's Edge section.

The stomach-lurching drops at Tower of Terror (p. 101), a unique thrill ride set in an old Hollywood hotel, may be just what you need for real screams.

Set sail with the Pirates of the Caribbean as they comically pillage an island town. (p. 45).

Seeing African animals walking freely from your own open safari vehicle is a highlight of Animal Kingdom's Kilimanjaro Safaris (p. 90).

The floating mountains in the Valley of Mo'ara at Pandora—World of Avatar (p. 89).

Live shows are don't-miss highlights of an Animal Kingdom visit. The longest-running one is the elaborately costumed Festival of the Lion King (p. 90).

The best way to beat the heat in Orlando is at a water park, such as Disney's winter-themed Blizzard Beach (p. 109).

At Disney's Typhoon Lagoon (p. 110), Tilly, a boat supposedly tossed on top of a mountain during a storm, is the starting point for multiple waterslides.

Crush 'n' Gusher water coaster is one of Typhoon Lagoon's signature flumes.

UNIVERSAL ORLANDO & SEAWORLD

Harry Potter and the Escape from Gringotts (p. 124) is a highlight of Universal Studios' fabulous recreation of Diagon Alley. Harry Potter fans literally run across the park to get to this immersive ride, which is part roller coaster and part motion simulator.

Are you in house Gryffindor, Hufflepuff, Ravenclaw, or Slytherin? Show your Hogwarts colors while you wander through Hogsmeade Village (p. 138) in Islands of Adventure.

Yum—Butterbeer! It's the beverage of choice throughout the Wizarding World of Harry Potter. Get yours with foam!

Waturi Beach at Universal's waterpark, Volcano Bay (p. 145).

You can choose your own soundtrack on Universal's Hollywood Rip Ride Rockit (p. 120).

Little kids love both the colorful Seuss Landing and the watery fun at Curious George Splash Zone. Dress them to get wet!

Kids of all ages (especially teens) love the tongue-in-cheek fun of the Simpsons' Springfield (p. 127), including a "thrilltacular" motion-simulator ride, Kwik-E-Mart store, and Duff Brewery.

Live shows are hallmarks of SeaWorld Orlando (p. 146).

Thrill rides are increasingly becoming a draw at SeaWorld, including the Journey to Atlantis flume (p. 153).

Throughout SeaWorld, there are opportunities to interact with animals ranging from penguins to dolphins.

At exclusive Discovery Cove (p. 157), guests can swim with dolphins as well as snorkel in fish-filled reefs.

MORE ORLANDO ATTRACTIONS

The many creative options for kids age 2 to 12 at Legoland Florida (p. 158), including getting a license to drive their own car, make the park a favorite Orlando stop for families.

The greenery of Legoland is a nod to its previous life as Cypress Gardens, one of the first amusement parks in the Orlando area.

If you can dream it, Legoland can make it out of its signature plastic blocks—be prepared for lots of inspired building from your kids after a visit here.

Get creative with Crayola brand crayons in the Crayola Experience (p. 162).

ICON Orlando, once called the Orlando Eye, is a 400-foot-tall observation wheel, the tallest on America's East Coast (p. 165).

Head east to Cape Canaveral and the Kennedy Space Center (p. 178) to view massive, real-life rockets such as the Saturn 1-B launcher in the "rocket garden," see the space shuttle Atlantis in an indoor hangar, tour NASA's compound, and even meet an astronaut.

Nature is all around Orlando if you know where to look. Get a glimpse of endangered manatees at Blue Spring Park (p. 183) where these gentle giants swim in the crystal waters.

Just 20 minutes from downtown Orlando, Wekiwa Springs (p. 184) feels like a world away from the twirling, beeping, nonstop action of the area's theme parks. Pick up a paddle to unwind on the river.

Orlando is a major golfing destination. Try one of the area's lush golf courses, such as the one at the Ritz-Carlton Grande Lakes (p. 187).

But wait, there's more! I-Drive and downtown Orlando are filled with fun family diversions such as WonderWorks (p. 167) that let you get a hit of playtime without the hassle and money commitments of the big parks.

Florida's history goes back hundreds of years, and you can learn about it at the Orange County Regional History Center (p. 169).

When you're ready for a change of scene, Port Canaveral offers easy-to-reach cruise ships to keep your vacation going at sea (p. 194).

THE BEST OF ORLANDO

I n 1886, a young unmarried mailman, frustrated with his fruitless toil in the Midwest, moved to the woolly wilderness of Central Florida to make a better go of life. The land was angry. Summers were oppressively hot, the lightning relentless, and the tough earth, sodden and scrubby, defied clearing. The only domestic creatures that thrived there, it seemed, were the cattle, and even they turned out stringy and chewy. Undaunted, the young man planted a grove of citrus trees and waited for things to get better. They didn't. His trees died in a freeze. Now penniless, he was forced to return to delivering mail, the very thing he had tried so hard to escape. By 1890, he gave up, defeated, and moved to Chicago to seek other work. The American dream appeared to fail Elias Disney.

The story could have ended there. But he was joined by his new bride, whose own father had died trying to tame Florida land. Back in the smoke of the Midwest, they had children and settled for an anonymous urban existence. One day, eight decades later, long after the young man and woman had lived full lives and passed away, two of their sons, now in the sunset of their own lives, would return to Central Florida, to the land that broke their father, and together they would transform the recalcitrant swamp into the most famous fantasy land the world has ever known.

Little did Elias know that the dream was only skipping a generation and that his sons Walt and Roy would become synonymous with the same land that rejected him. Had he known that the Disney name would in due time define Central Florida, would he have been so despondent? Even if he had been granted a fleeting vision of what was to be, and what his family would mean to this place—and, indeed, to the United States—would he have believed it?

The Disney brothers turned a place of toil into a realm of pleasure, a place where hardworking people can put their struggles aside. The English have Blackpool; Canadians have Niagara Falls. Orlando rose to become the preeminent resort for the working and middle classes of America, and the ingenuity of its inventions inspires visitors from all over the world. Orlando has had its share of tragedy, yet its tale is one of optimism.

Orlando represents something more powerful to American culture and history than success. It's something shared. No matter who you are, no matter your politics or upbringing, when you were a kid, you probably went at least once to Walt Disney World and Orlando—or, if you didn't, you desperately wanted to. Which other aspect of culture can we all claim to share? What else has given children such sweet dreams? I've often said that if somehow Walt Disney World went out of business tomorrow, the U.S. National Park Service would have to take it over—it means that much to the fabric of the nation.

Don't think of the amusements of Orlando as big business. Of course they are, and the incessant reminder of that often threatens to shatter the fantasy. But Walt Disney World, and by extension Orlando, is Americana incarnate. Their flair for showmanship, now coined as "Disneyfication," is the defining mind-set of our culture, in which even grocery stores are dressed like film sets and the "story" of your local burger joint is retold on the side of its beverage cups.

Orlando tells us about who we dream of being. Virtually nothing about it is natural or authentic, and yet there may be no more perfect embodiment of American culture. To understand this invented landscape is to understand the values of its civilization and our generation. And if you observe Orlando with a long view—starting with young Elias Disney cutting his hands trying to budge a tough Florida pine—you will be a part of the explosive, unexpected powers of the American dream.

And one more thing: If you can buck the system and relax, it's a hell of a lot of fun.

ORLANDO'S best THEME PARK EXPERIENCES

o **Walt Disney World:** Walt Disney World operates four top-drawer theme parks every day of the year: **Magic Kingdom,** the most popular theme park on Earth, is a more spacious iteration of the original Disneyland in Anaheim, California, the park that started it all, and is brimming with cherished attractions; **Epcot** is a new-brew version of an old-style world's fair; **Disney's Animal Kingdom** blends animal habitats with theme-park panache and offers a pretty *Avatar*-themed land, **Pandora,** gorgeous to behold with two rides. The biggest changes in 2019 are at **Disney's Hollywood Studios,** which already has a peppy new area, **Toy Story Land,** including a solid new roller coaster, **Slinky Dog Dash.** By year's end they will also have the whimsical indoor ride **Mickey & Minnie's Runaway Railway,** and, most of all, the blockbuster, groundbreaking **Star Wars: Galaxy's Edge,** a 14-acre area filled with all kinds of tricks new to immersive theme park experiences.

o **Universal Orlando:** Often surpassing Disney in adrenaline and cunning, Universal Orlando's two theme parks, **Islands of Adventure** and **Universal Studios Florida,** plus its newish **Volcano Bay** water park, command respect, get the blood pumping a bit stronger, and are home to two immersive sections devoted to **The Wizarding World of Harry Potter.** In the middle of 2019, the Wizarding World in Islands of Adventure debuts a lavish, complex, and intensely themed **new indoor/outdoor Harry Potter roller coaster,** one of the most complicated rides ever constructed at Universal and a major upgrade of its lollapalooza Harry Potter franchise.

o **Beyond Disney and Universal:** Venture beyond the Big Six theme parks and you'll find more breathing room and more focused experiences. The gardens and marine mammals at **SeaWorld Orlando** can make for a slower-paced excursion, and it opened a new family flume ride, **Infinity Falls.** Five water parks (including state-of-the-art **Volcano Bay**) flow with energy: **Typhoon Lagoon** and **Aquatica** for family-friendly slides, **Blizzard Beach** for more aggressive ones, and **Discovery Cove** for VIP swims with dolphins and reef fish. South of town, **Legoland Florida,** one of the best parks for small children, charms with Old Florida touches, while **Gatorland** celebrates the region's *original* locals.

ORLANDO'S best RIDES & SHOWS

o **Walt Disney World:** More than any other park, the **Magic Kingdom** (p. 34) is packed with seminal experiences: the transporting Audio-Animatronic wizardry of **Pirates of the Caribbean** and **The Haunted Mansion;** the vertiginous thrills of **Splash Mountain** and **Space Mountain;** and the homespun, only-at-Disney charm of **Jungle Cruise, Peter Pan's Flight,** and **"it's a small world."** Cap the day with **Wishes,** the famous fireworks show. At **Epcot** (p. 64), **Frozen Ever After** has begun its animatronic-rich boat ride through Arendelle; and **Soarin',** the ride with the resort's highest re-ride ratio, recently changed its visuals from California-only sights to a smorgasbord of world icons. At **Disney's Hollywood Studios** (p. 97), the ride-through 3-D video game **Toy Story Mania!** is never the same experience twice; while one of Disney's newest marquee ride, the cutting-edge and thrilling aerial simulator **Avatar Flight of Passage** at **Animal Kingdom,** wows every time.

o **Universal Orlando:** At **Islands of Adventure** (p. 132), **Harry Potter and the Forbidden Journey** fires on more technological cylinders than you thought a ride could possess; **Skull Island: Reign of Kong** is the latest big-ticket addition; **The Incredible Hulk Coaster** just emerged from a complete teardown and rebuilding; and **The Amazing Adventures of Spider-Man** remains the standard bearer for premium family-friendly ride concepts, as it has been since 1999. But don't miss **Dudley Do-Right's Ripsaw Falls** or **Popeye & Bluto's Bilge-Rat Barges,** a pair of ingeniously sopping flumes. Next door at **Universal Studios,** a separate park, **The Wizarding World of Harry Potter: Diagon Alley** represents the cutting edge in visual design that believably immerses you in the world of the movies, and the **Escape from Gringotts** ride is a technological tour de force. Fans of Springfield will find themselves re-riding **The Simpsons Ride** to catch all the insider references. A new ride here (2018), **Fast & Furious—Supercharged,** is a simulated car chase.

o **The Other Parks:** At **SeaWorld Orlando** (p. 146), roller coasters pack punches that Disney pulls: the new **Mako** is Orlando's tallest, fastest, longest (and, for our money, greatest) coaster; **Manta** flies riders belly-down over water and rooftops; while **Kraken Unleashed** dangles their feet for seven spine-knotting inversions while immersing them in a virtual reality simulation. Last year, it opened **Infinity Falls,** a water ride with a vertical lift and a 40-foot drop. Last year, the 450-foot-tall **StarFlyer** swing ride (p. 166), standing beside the world's sixth-tallest observation wheel **ICON Orlando** (p. 165), became an instant skyline landmark. Elsewhere, **Legoland Florida's** tricked-out **Miniland USA** (p. 159) is such a masterpiece of Lego creations that it's a show of its own, but its collection of kiddie rides is second to none, even Disney.

ORLANDO'S best
OVERLOOKED EXPERIENCES

o **From Earth to the Moon:** The **Kennedy Space Center** (p. 178) sent Americans into space for more than half a century, and for decades NASA's nerve center was the focus of tourist attention, but a majority of today's visitors remain securely within Disney's orbit. That's a tragedy. The Kennedy Center is where you can see proof of America's glory days as an exploratory power, including some out-of-this-world space vehicles such as the **Saturn V rocket,** the largest rocket made, which sent 27 men to the moon; the **Space Shuttle orbiter** *Atlantis,* still coated with space dust; and the only public remnants of the two space shuttles America lost.

o **Connecting with Others:** More Make-a-Wish kids request visits to Orlando than any other dream, and you can help make those wishes come true at the resort built just for them, **Give Kids the World Village** (p. 175). There are hundreds of jobs for volunteers (many of which can be done in just a few hours), including handing out gifts or scooping ice cream. And since the late 1800s, moss-draped **Cassadaga** (p. 171) has been the domain of psychics and mediums who invite visitors to explore their spiritualist town.

o **Undiscovered Disney:** Even inside the theme parks, as other guests stampede for the nearest thrill ride, you can find relatively off-the-beaten-path treasures. The most fruitful ground is **Epcot**'s World Showcase, where many pavilions contain little-seen museums to the heritage of their lands, including the **Stave Church Gallery** in Norway (p. 75), China's **House of the Whispering Willow** (p. 75), the **Bijutsu-kan Gallery** in Japan (p. 78), and the **Moroccan Style** gallery of arts in Morocco (p. 78). At the Magic Kingdom, you can get a haircut at Main Street's **Harmony Barber Shop**

(p. 41). And the entire Disney World resort offers a slate of small-group **behind-the-scenes tours** (p. 113) that uncover hundreds of secrets.

ORLANDO'S best AUTHENTIC EXPERIENCES

o **Florida, Your Eden:** Although theme parks now define Orlando, Central Florida has a long tale of its own, if you're willing to listen. There are more fresh springs here than in any other American state. You'll always remember swimming in the 72-degree (22°C) waters of **De Leon Springs State Park** (p. 183), canoeing at **Wekiwa Springs State Park** (p. 184), or meeting at-risk manatees in their natural habitat at **Blue Spring State Park** (p. 183).

o **Florida, the Gilded Age Idyll:** Of course, Orlando's identity as a sunny theme-park mecca only began in 1971, but visitors from the north have been coming for a century. Sample the fine art collected by its high-society settlers at Winter Park's **Charles Hosmer Morse Museum of American Art** (including a massive collection of Tiffany glass; p. 170) or the **Cornell Fine Arts Museum** (with lush decorative arts of every description; p. 172). Peep at their historic mansions, whose lawns slope invitingly to the tranquil lakes of Winter Park, on the long-running **Scenic Boat Tour** (p. 186).

o **Florida, Land of Flowers:** The reason all those blue bloods migrated here? The fine weather and beautiful water. The horticultural achievements at **Harry P. Leu Gardens** (p. 184), practically smack in the middle of downtown Orlando, remind you just how bountiful the soil here can be. Or lose yourself at **Bok Tower Gardens** (p. 172), whose builder set out to create a Taj Mahal for America; its landscaping is by Frederick Law Olmsted, Jr., whose other work includes the White House and the National Mall.

o **Florida, the Original Tourist Draw: Legoland Florida** (p. 158) ambles pleasantly on a lakeside that was once home to Cypress Gardens, Florida's original mega-park and a haunt for everyone from Esther Williams to Elvis Presley. Its historic botanical garden has been prized since the 1930s. **Gatorland** (p. 174) is a pleasing, corn-fed throwback from an era when Central Florida was synonymous with reptiles, not cheerful mice.

ORLANDO'S best HOTELS

o **Inside the Theme Park Resorts: Disney's Contemporary Resort** (p. 237) and **Disney's Polynesian Village Resort** (p. 238), which opened in 1971, have become architectural landmarks, and their location on the monorail system makes a vacation easy and fun, but **Disney's Art of Animation Resort** (p. 242) represents the newest and best of the resort's lowest-priced rooms. Universal's **Sapphire Falls Resort** (p. 250) applies a layer of Caribbean style to the budget category, and its 16-story **Aventura Hotel** is brand new and affordable with outstanding views. Universal's new **Endless**

Summer Resort (p. 249) now charges the cheapest hotel rate at the theme parks. **Four Seasons Resort Orlando,** on Walt Disney World property, delivers a level of luxury that's a revelation among them (p. 244).

o **Full-Service Resorts Outside the Parks:** Exquisite restaurants and unbeatable pool areas make the Grande Lakes' **JW Marriott** and the **Ritz-Carlton** (p. 260) two names to beat among Orlando's luxury resorts, while the **Hyatt Regency Grand Cypress** (p. 252) offers a full slate of activities and an epic pool complex. Taking theme-park flair to a hospitality extreme, the colossal atrium of **Gaylord Palms** (p. 251) is like a big top for eye candy.

o **Affordability Without Sacrifice:** Not all affordable hotels are shabby. Brand new builds include Hyatt House (p. 261), SpringHill Suites and TownePlace Suites Orlando Flamingo Crossings (p. 256), and Residence Inn (p. 263), all near the action for $100–$150 a night. The B Resort (p. 246) puts you in a South Beach–styled resort right on Disney property for the middle $100s. Or rent a full house, as tastefully furnished as if you lived there; find reputable renters on p. 264.

ORLANDO'S best RESTAURANTS

o **The Most Memorable Meals at the Resorts:** Orlando is one of those places where even blasé restaurants are priced like splurges, but some special-occasion tables deliver on their promise, such as **California Grill** overlooking the Magic Kingdom fireworks at the Contemporary (p. 197); **Morimoto Asia** or **Chef Art Smith's Homecomin'** at **Disney Springs** (p. 202); **Boma,** an all-you-can-eat feast at Animal Kingdom Lodge where you can watch African animals roam (p. 197); Disney's perennial award-sweeper **Victoria & Albert's** (p. 200) at the Grand Floridian; and the famous **character meals,** where your fuzzy hosts serve up family memories (p. 202).

o **Finding Family-Run Places to Eat:** Some fab restaurants, many family-run, have been unfairly elbowed into the background by same-old chains. These include **Bruno's Italian Restaurant,** *abbondanza!* right in the franchise zone of Disney, (p. 208); **Nile Ethiopian Cuisine,** authentically African, down to the coffee ceremony, near Disney (p. 214); **Havana's Cuban Cuisine,** the real stuff, from steak to plantains, right by Disney (p. 208); and the affordable **Q'Kenan,** whose overstuffed arepas are popular with local Venezuelan families (p. 210).

o **Big Style, Local Flavors:** Get in touch with the locals: The veggie chili at the friendly hangout **Dandelion Communitea Cafe** (p. 216) is to die for, and **Maxine's on Shine** (p. 216) is seductive fun. Above all, the sensationally priced Vietnamese district of **Mills Fifty** (p. 217) is a revelation. Yes, as it turns out, there are still dining secrets in O-town.

SUGGESTED ITINERARIES & ORLANDO'S LAYOUT

Disney doesn't want you to be spontaneous. It wants you to agree to a timetable. One Disney Parks president was frank about the tactic in Bloomberg Businessweek: "If we can get people to plan their vacation before they leave home, we know that we get more time with them. We get a bigger share of their wallet." The result: Researching a Disney vacation can feel more involved than learning the federal tax code, and some guidebooks can be as fat as bricks. But this book boils the essentials down without getting stuck in planning quicksand.

Too much research is stressful and spoils the delight of Disney's many surprises. If you're not careful, you'll spend half your time at Disney hunched over your smartphone, battery dwindling, trying to keep up with your plan. And at the end, you'll need a vacation from your vacation. That's where the *Frommer's* guide comes in. Passholder benefits, Disney Vacation Club hacks—those are arcane rules for other guides. This is not a book for the Disney-obsessive. That is to say: It's for most of us. For the casual or first-time visitor. For those of us who refuse to turn a Disney vacation into a part-time job.

The routes suggested here, loose enough to let the magic in, prioritize what's worth seeing and when. Observe the basic park patterns and you'll do just fine. These itineraries assume mild lines (so, not peak season), and if you would like to try a specific table-service restaurant, it's imperative you arrive with reservations, particularly for Cinderella's Royal Table. Instructions on how to schedule Fastpass+ are on p. 26.

ORLANDO IN 1 DAY

Well, I'm sorry for you. Just as it's impossible to eat an entire box of Velveeta in one sitting (please don't try), you can't get the full breadth of Orlando in a single day.

Today: Make It a Magic Kingdom Day ★★★

Thankfully, one Orlando attraction is so quintessential that you can enjoy it all by itself: Walt Disney World's **Magic Kingdom** (p. 34). In chapter 3, I recommend three custom itineraries (p. 38) for how to parse your time—with or without kids—but no matter your age or inclination, don't miss the great Disney Audio-Animatronic odysseys **Pirates of the Caribbean** ★★★, **Haunted Mansion** ★★★, and **"it's a small world"** ★★★, and be sure to brave the drops of **Splash Mountain** ★★★ and **Space Mountain** ★★★. While you're there, take a free spin on the **monorail** through the iconic **Contemporary Resort** after you connect for the free round-trip ride to **Epcot** (p. 64), where you'll at least see the other top Disney park from above. Stay until closing, through the **fireworks,** or, if you've had enough, head to a kitschy dinner banquet spectacle such as **the Hoop-Dee-Doo Musical Revue** ★★ (p. 220). Hope you're not hungry for subtlety!

ORLANDO IN 2 DAYS

Nope, still can't do much, but in two sleeps you can still get a few flavors in.

Day 1: Magic Kingdom

Get the same early start as recommended in "Orlando in 1 Day" above and follow the **Magic Kingdom** plan for sure.

Day 2: Universal Orlando ★★★ or Epcot ★★★

Today, arrive at **Universal Orlando** (p. 115), one of the most attractive theme park complexes in the country, for opening. At its **Studios** park, dive into Diagon Alley, the most immersive section of the **Wizarding World of Harry Potter** ★★★, before the lines grow. Explore the shops, full of bespoke souvenirs and snacks you can only buy here, and give your system a dose of Butterbeer. After lunch at the **Leaky Cauldron** ★★★, you have a decision to make. You can take the **Hogwarts Express** train

---

THE SIX BIGGEST DISNEY mistakes

1. **Overplanning.** Disney World minutiae opens a rabbit hole deeper than Alice's.
2. **Underplanning.** You must plan a little or pay a price: To eat at the best sit-down restaurants or enjoy a character meal, it's wise to reserve 3 to 6 months out.
3. **Overpurchasing ticket options.** Don't bite off more than you can chew.
4. **Wearing inadequate footwear.** It's said you'll walk 10 miles a day.
5. **Neglecting sunscreen and water.** Even Florida's cloudy weather can burn. One bad day can ruin the ones that follow.
6. **Pushing kids too hard.** When they want to slow down, indulge them. You came here to enjoy yourselves, remember?

Planning your theme park schedule is hardly magical, so for more recommendations on making the most of your time at WDW, see our handy charts on p. 38, 66, 88, 95, and 100.

to **Islands of Adventure** (you'll need a second park ticket) to tour the second Potter land of **Hogsmeade,** take a spin on the superlative **Amazing Adventures of Spider-Man** ★★★, and jolt yourself on the newly rejuvenated **The Incredible Hulk Coaster** ★★★. Or you could spend a full day at **Epcot** (p. 64). Be sure to visit **Future World,** including **Soarin' Around the World** ★★★ and the traditional Disney experience, **Spaceship Earth** ★★★, then make your way clockwise around **World Showcase** by dinnertime to select the ethnic eatery that catches your fancy, be it in **Mexico** ★★★, **Japan** ★★★, or **Morocco** ★★★, or queue up for **Frozen Ever After** ★★★. At 9pm, you'll be in the right place for **IllumiNations** ★★★ (to be replaced by another show in 2019). With a park hopper pass, you could also leave Epcot later afternoon and then check out the new **Pandora—The World of Avatar** ★★★ area at Disney's Animal Kingdom, seeing it both in the light after dark, when its glowing features are in full effect. If you *really* want to see a lot and have cash and energy to burn, do Harry Potter in the morning and then schlep back down I-4 to visit Epcot or Pandora in the late afternoon and evening—eat your Wheaties!

ORLANDO IN 3 DAYS

Days 1–2: Magic Kingdom & Universal Orlando

Day 1: Magic Kingdom, as above. But on **Day 2,** slam through the highlights of the Universal parks with a 1-day, 2-park pass. In the morning, see **Islands of Adventure** ★★★, including the new **Skull Island: Reign of Kong** ★★, as on the second day of the 2-day plan, and fill the afternoon with Universal Studios. Don't neglect some of its popular rides—**Transformers: The Ride—3D** ★★ and **Harry Potter and the Escape from Gringotts** ★★★ in **Wizarding World of Harry Potter—Diagon Alley.** Exploring that area will more than complete your day, but if you still have time, fill up on the sarcastically named dishes at **Fast Food Boulevard** (p. 131) in the daringly whimsical **Springfield** addition.

Day 3: SeaWorld ★★★, Disney & a Taste of "Real" Orlando

If you have small kids or you need something more subdued today, then **SeaWorld Orlando** (p. 146), with its many marine animal habitats, isn't as exhausting as Disney. That could take a whole day if you saw every

DISNEY PLANNING timeline

Six months/180 days ahead of arrival:

o If desired, book Cinderella's Royal Table (p. 63), Bibbidi Bobbidi Boutique (p. 43), Be Our Guest (p. 64), Hoop-Dee-Doo Musical Revue (p. 220), Victoria & Albert's (p. 200), and any other special meal reservations.

o Book other dining reservations if you're staying on-site (Disney hotel guests can book 180 days in advance of their stay).

Two months/60 days ahead:

o Book Fastpass+ reservations (if you're staying on-site or at approved partner hotels).

One month/30 days ahead:

o Book Fastpass+ (if you're staying off-site).

One week ahead:

o If desired, purchase Memory Maker, p. 34 (it sometimes costs less if purchased at least 3 days ahead of arrival).

Twenty-four hours ahead:

o Cancel unwanted restaurant reservations by now or pay $10–$25 penalty.

o Or, if a restaurant was previously full, check for availability again now.

little thing and stopped to smell the flowers (and fish), but you can see the highlights in 4 hours, and you only have 3 days, after all. So cram a secondary Disney park into your afternoon and evening. **Epcot** is a fine choice (see Day 2 of the 2-day itinerary above for a good plan), but **Disney's Animal Kingdom**'s ★★ wildlife walking trails make a nice, easy-going complement to a morning spent at SeaWorld, and it's open later than SeaWorld, too. If you exhaust Animal Kingdom and don't want to see Pandora aglow, spend the night at the shopping-and-dining zone of the refreshed **Disney Springs** ★★ (p. 191) or go out into "real" Orlando for the Vietnamese culinary delights of **Mills Fifty** (p. 217) downtown.

ORLANDO IN 1 WEEK

Days 1–5: Orlando at Your Leisure

This is really the minimum amount of time you need to enable you to actually relax and take time to sit by the pool. You don't have to cram several parks into a single day unless you want to, so take more time on your first few days: first **Magic Kingdom,** then **Universal,** then **Epcot,** then the other two Disney parks, followed by **SeaWorld.** Of course, if you stick to a schedule as rigid as one major theme park per day, it will take you a week to knock down the seven biggies, and that's before setting your belly on a single water slide. (And if you want to do that, **Volcano Bay,** p. 145, is now the hottest water park of the four major choices in Orlando.) Combining **Animal Kingdom** and **Hollywood Studios** ★★★ into a single day (see p. 88 and 95 for suggestions for how to pack it all in) is doable and won't cause you to miss too much, although with the opening of the second Harry Potter land, the same can no longer be said

If you see lightning, all outdoor and water rides will close until it passes. Universal Orlando, with its air-conditioned waiting areas and covered parking, is the best choice to escape a rainy day because most things can stay open in a storm. At Disney, Hollywood Studios is the best rainy-day park because most of its activities, including two of its biggest thrill rides, are indoors. SeaWorld, where you'll spend lots of time outside, is awful in the rain, and so is Islands of Adventure. If it's a scorcher, both Universal Studios and Hollywood Studios have some sheltered activities to offer heat relief. On the hottest days, the water slide parks are swarming (of course). The worst Disney park on hot or wet days is Disney's Animal Kingdom, where only a fraction of the attractions are indoors. When there is a big storm, don't quit! Back home, rain may last all day, but in Florida, it usually clears within an hour.

for Universal's parks—now they require a day and a half, at least. This combination lets you do the seven major parks in 5 days.

Days 6–7: Exploring Orlando Beyond the Theme Parks

Hitting the Big 7 in 5 days leaves 2 days to get away from the dizzying pressures of theme parking. Take a day to drive out to **Kennedy Space Center** ★★★ (p. 178), or take a dip in a natural spring, such as **De Leon Springs** ★★★ (p. 183), and make a pass through the American original town of **Cassadaga** ★★★ (p. 171). It would be a shame to miss a collection as world class as the **Morse Museum**'s ★★★ (p. 170) astonishing Tiffany glass. While you're there, take a late-afternoon boat cruise past the mansions of **Winter Park** (p. 170)—when you're out on the water, you'll finally get a feeling for the "real" Florida that attracted the builders of the major resorts in the first place. Afterward, you'll be near some of Orlando's **best restaurants,** most of which the tourists never visit.

GETTING TO KNOW ORLANDO'S LAYOUT

In 1970, before the opening of Walt Disney World, Orlando was still a tourism center, attracting 660,000 people a year. But by 1999, the place was a powerhouse, with 37.9 million visits, and by 2017, that number had nearly doubled to 72 million. The area population also leapfrogged from 344,000 to 860,000 to 2.38 million, passing old-guard American cities as St. Louis; Washington, D.C.; Boston; Baltimore; and Portland. The biggest recent change to the area population resulted from the massive diaspora of Puerto Ricans fleeing the destruction and federally bungled recovery of Hurricane Maria. It's estimated that in the first 3 months after the storm, more than 200,000 of the island's population moved to Florida, and about one in four chose to come to the Orlando area.

However, for all that growth, and despite the fact the amusements are critical to Orlando's economy, most of the population still lives north of SeaWorld. The tourist zones are segregated from residential ones. Huge chunks of your time, days at a stretch, will be spent only in the boisterously inauthentic commercial corridors. Those lie along International Drive, U.S. 192 around I-4, and the Lake Buena Vista area north of exit 68 off I-4.

The Making of a Kingdom

Back when only cargo trains had much business in Central Florida, Orlando fashioned itself as a prosperous small city—some derisively called it a cow town—well positioned to serve the citrus and cattle industries as they shipped goods between America and Cuba. The city remained that way, mostly irrelevant, until around 1943, when the great cross-state cattle drives ended.

THE PULSE massacre

In the early morning hours of June 12, 2016, a gunman bearing a legally obtained AR-15 entered Pulse, a gay nightclub just south of downtown Orlando, and began systematically murdering people he didn't know. By the time police felt it was safe enough to invade, 102 people had been shot, 49 of them mortally. The devastation was profound. Orlando was now home to the deadliest mass shooting in American history (a record that was swiftly surpassed by another one). National outrage sparked an unprecedented shift in the country's politics—within days, members of Congress staged a sit-in on the House floor to demand a vote on gun control measures. Across Orlando, security tightened, patrols escalated, metal detectors were installed, and for the first time, the world sadly acknowledged that even "The Happiest Place on Earth" was not immune to indiscriminate American violence. Although the nightclub was far from the tourist districts, it was a part of the community. Several of the victims worked at the theme parks—one, Luis Vielma, ran Islands of Adventure's "Harry Potter and the Forbidden Journey" ride. "He was 22 years old," wrote author J. K. Rowling, "I can't stop crying." In solidarity of its slain family members, Universal staged a stirring mass salute with illuminated magic wands, while Disney lit Cinderella Castle in rainbow colors for a wrenching moment of silence, and both companies donated $1 million to the OneOrlando fund for the affected.

With Pulse, Florida's youth reached a breaking point, and after the next major shooting in the state, in Parkland in February 2018, a new political movement among millennials was born. While a permanent memorial is planned and funded, the nightclub at 1912 S. Orange Avenue remains standing, surrounded by grass, benches, and a tribute wall. Ghostly pop music gently plays from hidden speakers (open daily 7:30am–9pm). Visitors will find a digital guestbook and markers that they may use to leave their thoughts on plastic panels around the base of the club's sign. The onePULSE Foundation (www.onepulsefoundation. org) has created a scholarship fund in the name of each of the victims. Wherever you go, whether it's to a hotel, a restaurant, or a theme park, remember that you will meet people who knew and loved someone whose life was ravaged by needless ongoing American violence.

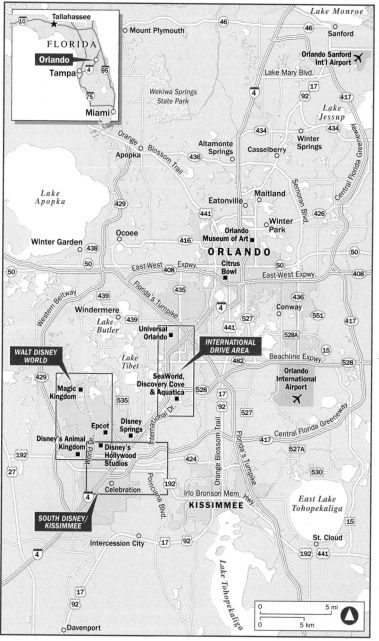

Soon after, the brick-warehouse city of Orlando developed its second personality. The turning point wasn't the arrival of Walt Disney on his secret land-buying trips. It came a decade earlier, when NASA settled into the Space Coast, 45 minutes east, and the local government, spotting opportunity, invited the Martin Marietta corporation—now Lockheed Martin—to open a massive facility off Sand Lake Road, near the present-day Convention Center. To sweeten the deal, leaders promised unprecedented civic improvements, including an unrealized high-speed rail system they're *still* dithering over. Mostly, though, politicians built roads. Florida's Turnpike to Miami was carved past the Martin plot, S.R. 50 was hammered through downtown to link the coasts, and, soon after, many blocks were bulldozed for the construction of I-4, linking Tampa on the west coast with Daytona Beach (then one of America's premier vacation towns) on the east coast. The new transit links made Walt lick his chops for some cheap land nearby.

Walt's new kingdom was constructed 20 miles southwest of the city in scrubland, where his planners could keep the outside world at bay. The resort was intended to be an oasis in the citrus groves, but soon, sprawl sprouted around the park's border, just as had happened in Anaheim. For the last two generations, the space between Orlando's two disparate developments has vanished, consumed by areas where "real" Orlando residents live, so that the old-fashioned, "traditional" city has come to be dwarfed, as it were, by family-friendly honky-tonk and slapped-up suburbs. Few casual visitors ever lay eyes on the real Orlando—a situation the theme parks' accountants like just fine.

Neighborhoods in Brief

Get to know Orlando's neighborhoods—from theme parks to historic areas.

WALT DISNEY WORLD RESORT

Best for: *Space, theme parks, a sense of place, proximity to His Mouseness*

What you won't find: *Inexpensive food or lodging, a central location for anything except Disney attractions, the "real" Florida or Orlando*

Walt Disney World is at the southern end of Orlando's chain of big parks, so to see Universal, SeaWorld, and Orlando itself, you'll always head north on I-4.

When Walt Disney ordered the purchase of these 27,000 acres mostly just west of Interstate 4, he was righting a wrong he committed in the building of Anaheim's Disneyland. In commandeering as much land as he did, he ensured that visitors would not be troubled by the clatter of motel signs and cheap restaurants that abut his original playground. "Here in Florida," he said in a promotional film shot months before his death,

"we have something special we never enjoyed at Disneyland…the blessing of size. There's enough land here to hold all the ideas and plans we can possibly imagine." You could spend your entire vacation without leaving the greenery of the resort, and lots of people do, although they're missing a lot. The idea to remain solely on Disney property is outdated now that Universal has proven itself. Still, there's an awful lot to do spread around here, starting with four of the world's most polished theme parks (55.8 million visits in 2017), two of the best water parks, four golf courses, two miniature golf courses, a racecar track, a sports pavilion, and a huge shopping-and-entertainment district.

First-time visitors aren't usually prepared for quite how *large* the area is: 47 (roughly rectangular) square miles. Only a third of that land is truly developed, and another third has been set aside as a permanent reserve for swampland. Major elements are easily a 10-minute drive away from each other, with nothing but trees or Disney hotels between them. The Magic Kingdom is buried deep in the back of the park—which is to say, the north of it, requiring the most driving time to reach. Epcot and Hollywood Studios are in the center, while Disney's Animal Kingdom is at the southwest of the property, closest to the real world.

For its convenience, Disney **signposts hotels and attractions** according to the major theme park they're near. If you are staying on property, you'll need to know which area your hotel is in. For example, the All-Star resorts are considered to be in the Animal Kingdom area, and so some signs may simply read Animal Kingdom Resort Area and leave off the name of your hotel. Ask for your hotel's designated area when you reserve.

Getting in is easy. Every artery in town is naggingly signposted for Disney World. Exits are marked, but it helps to know the name of the main road that feeds your hotel. A few useful **secret exits** are not marked on official Disney maps. One is **Western Way,** which turns past Coronado Springs resort and skirts the back of Animal Kingdom to reach many vacation home communities southwest of Disney. Be warned that taking 429 to U.S. 192 will cost more than a buck in tolls.

There's a second useful shortcut out of the resort: **Sherberth Road,** by the entrance to Animal Kingdom Lodge, about a mile west of the entrance to Animal Kingdom, leads to cheap eats on western U.S. 192.

It's interesting to note that when you're at Disney, you're in a separate governmental zone. The resort's bizarre experiments in building methods (such as fiberglass-and-steel castles) are partly enabled by the fact that Disney negotiated the creation of its own entity, the Reedy Creek Improvement District, which can set its own standards. When you see vehicles marked RCID, those are the civic services for the resort. Not far down the road by Disney Springs Marketplace—a route not used by many guests—pass by the R.C. Fire Department, a toy-like engine house with an outdoor fountain that looks like a spouting fire hose.

Disney developed a bit of land east of I-4 into the New Urbanism unincorporated town of **Celebration.** As a Stepford-like residential center with upscale aspirations (golf, boutiques), there's not much to do there except eat a bit in its town square. Be prepared to parallel park there.

U.S. 192 & KISSIMMEE

Best for: *Value, chain restaurant and motel options, downscale attractions*

What you won't find: *Subtlety, luxury*

No matter how Orlando changes, it's Kissimmee (Kiss-*im*-ee), the ridiculed little sister, that lags behind. Where the southern edge of the Disney resort property touches U.S. 192, the clamor begins, stretching 10 miles west and a good 10 miles east. This tatty drag, known also as the Irlo Bronson Memorial Highway (after the state senator who sold Walt a lot of land), is the spine of Kissimmee, and its low-rent Rialto is what depressed the world in the movie *The Florida Project.* It's also the best place to find that cheap all-American kitsch you might be looking for—nowhere else in town will you find a souvenir store shaped like a giant orange half, and isn't that a shame?

In the early 1970s, Kissimmee was the prime place to stay. The motels weren't flashy then, and they still aren't, but they're ever affordable—$50 to $80 is the norm, and some shabby places go down to $39 for a single or $45 for a double. Kissimmee's downtown, about 10 miles east of Disney, is a typical Florida burg with a main street by a lake, and its quickly growing subdivisions have become popular among Hispanic families, although that doesn't translate into accessible restaurants serving ethnic cuisine. U.S. 192 is mostly about chains and buffets.

The best way to get your bearings on U.S. 192 is using its clearly signposted **mile marker system.** U.S. 192 hits Disney's southern entrance (the most expedient avenue to the major theme parks) at Mile Marker 7, while I-4's exit 65 connects with it around Mile Marker 8. Numbers go down to the west, and they go up to the east. Western 192, where the bulk of the vacation home developments are found, is much more upscale than the tacky wilds of eastern 192, but neither stretch could be termed swanky or well planned. Although Osceola County has strived to beautify the tourist corridor, it's been inept in the effort; once, the county cut down stands of myrtle trees in the median of U.S. 192 because they blocked the view of the billboards. That should tell you all you need to know about the standards in Kissimmee.

LAKE BUENA VISTA

Best for: *Access to Disney, I-4, and chain restaurants, some elbow room*

What you won't find: *The lowest prices, a sense of place*

Lake Buena Vista, a hotel enclave east of Disney Springs, clusters on the eastern fringe of Walt Disney World. LBV is technically a town, but it doesn't look like one. It's mostly hotels and mid-priced chain restaurants with some schlocky souvenir stores thrown in. The proximity of I-4 exit 68 can back traffic up, but it's convenient to Disney's crowded side door, which is helpful. The bottom line is that LBV is less tacky and higher rent than Kissimmee's 192, but it's also still a Disney-centric area and not really part of Orlando's fabric.

If you stay in LBV, you can also (if you're hardy) walk to the Disney Springs development, where you can then pick up Disney's free DTS bus system. That could save you the cost of a rental car.

INTERNATIONAL DRIVE

Best for: *Walkability, second-tier amusements, cheap transportation, sit-down chain food, proximity to Universal and SeaWorld*

What you won't find: *Space, style*

Although a developing stretch of this street winds all the way south to U.S. 192, when people refer to International Drive, they usually mean the segment between SeaWorld and Universal Orlando, just east of I-4 between exits 71 and 75. I-Drive, as it's called, is probably the only district where you might comfortably stay without a car and still be able to see the non-Disney attractions, because it's chockablock with affordable hotels (not as ratty as some on U.S. 192 can be) and plenty of crowd-pleasing things to see, such as arcades, T-shirt shops, buffets, and ICON Orlando (once called the Orlando Eye, p. 165) at the ICON

Orlando 360 entertainment complex. The cheap I-Ride Trolley (p. 271) traverses the area on a regular schedule.

The intersection at Sand Lake Road is a dividing line for I-Drive's personalities. North of Sand Lake Road, within the orbit of Universal Orlando, midway rides and the ice-cream shops prevail. South of Sand Lake, closer to SeaWorld, there's a business-y crowd at the mighty Orange County Convention Center, located on both sides of I-Drive at the Bee Line Expressway/528. It keeps the surrounding hotels (and streets) full. On this part of I-Drive, bars and mid-scale restaurants rule. West on Sand Lake Road past I-4, you'll find a mile-long procession of mid- to upper-level places to eat that the city dubiously calls its "Restaurant Row."

I-Drive does an east-west dogleg where it runs into I-4, and north of I-4 at Universal Boulevard, you'll find Universal Orlando's resort, which after dark is more popular with locals than Disney's.

Hotel and restaurant discounts may be posted on the area's business association and promotional website, **www.international driveorlando.com**.

DOWNTOWN ORLANDO

Best for: *Historic buildings, cafes, museums, fine art, wealthy residents*

What you won't find: *Theme parks, easy commutes*

Like in so many American cities, residents fled from downtown in the 1960s through the 1980s, although spacious new condo developments have rescued the city from abandonment. Downtown Orlando is gradually being rediscovered by young, upscale residents. Here are the highlights:

DOWNTOWN Beneath the city's collection of modest skyscrapers (mostly banking offices), you'll find municipal buildings (the main library, historic museums), a few upscale hotels (the Grand Bohemian, Courtyard at Lake Lucerne), and some attractive lakes, but little shopping. Orange Avenue, once a street of proud stone buildings and department stores, now comes alive mostly at night, when its former vaudeville halls and warehouses essay their new roles as nightclubs, especially around Church Street. The

43-acre Lake Eola Park, just east, is often cited as an area attraction, but in truth it's just your average city park, although the .9-mile path around its 23-acre sinkhole lake is good for joggers. Its swan boats (rent one for $15 for 30 min.) are city icons, as is the central fountain from 1957; its unique Plexiglas skin is illuminated with a 6-minute light-and-water musical show nightly at 9:30pm. Just east of that, the streets turn to red brick and big trees shelter **Thornton Park** (along Washington St., Summerlin Ave., and Central Blvd.). It's noted for its alfresco European-style cafes, none especially inexpensive, but all pleasing, where waiters wear black and hip locals spend evenings and weekend brunches. West of downtown over I-4, the area called Parramore is a longtime neighborhood for African Americans (sadly, the interstate was built, in part, as a barrier). A mile north of downtown, **Loch Haven Park** basks in a wealth of museums.

MILLS FIFTY Some old-timers call this area **Colonial Town** and new-timers may use **Mills 50,** but it's also the Vietnamese District at Mills, or ViMi (p. 217). Just north of downtown, at Colonial Drive and Mills Avenue, there's a midcentury neighborhood with the whiff of a faded 1950s strip mall (parking lots are hidden behind buildings). There, you can spend a top afternoon strolling through several omnibus Asian supermarkets stocked with exotic groceries and unique baked goods and parking yourself at one of the excellent mom-and-pop-style eateries (advertised by cheap stick-on letters and neon) serving food far more delicious than their limited budgets would suggest. Several stores whip up addictive, meat-stuffed baguette sandwiches called *bánh mi* for a quick $4 meal. You'll also find hobby and art-supply shops patronized by a burgeoning bohemian community. The two marginalized groups collaborate beautifully together.

WINTER PARK

Best for: *Fine art, cafes, strolls, galleries, lakes*

What you won't find: *Inexpensive shopping, easy theme-park access*

One of the city's most interesting areas, and one of the few that hasn't taken pains to erase its history, Winter Park was where, 100 years ago, upstart industrialists built winter homes at a time when they couldn't gain entree into the more exclusive, more WASP-y enclaves of Newport or Palm Beach. The town blends seamlessly with northern Orlando (you can drive between them in a few minutes without getting onto I-4) and is still pretty full of itself and its expensive tastes, but cruising on its brick-paved streets, gawking at mansions built on its chain of lakes, will remind you of the good life. Newspapers and magazines write about Winter Park like it's the hottest thing going, but in all honesty, it's just a nice place to pass an afternoon or evening. In the shops on Park Avenue, you'll find mostly jewelry, art, and south of it, stroll the country-club campus of Rollins College. The town's long-running boat tour (p. 186) is the best way to sample the opulence. The best art museum around, the Morse (p. 170), holds the most inspiring collection of Tiffany glass you will ever see. West of Winter Park, over I-4, the district of College Park, centering around Princeton Street and Edgewater Drive, hosts restaurants and boutiques that bring the area favor.

NORTH OF ORLANDO

Most visitors who venture into the suburban towns north of Winter Park do so to visit some of the area's natural springs or state parks (p. 170) or to connect with the spirits in the hamlet of Cassadaga (p. 171). After you've seen these places, there is little to engage you until you hit the Atlantic Coast on I-4.

SOUTH OF ORLANDO

Only in the past few years has the rural-minded swampland southwest of the resort and Kissimmee begun to be built upon in earnest, and the 65-mile run along I-4 to Tampa is quickly filling in with developments and golf courses. This patch of the Green Swamp, in which the two cities will one day merge into a megalopolis, is now casually dubbed "Orlampa." In Tampa, you'll find the excellent Busch Gardens (p. 159), a worthy addition to an amusement-park itinerary, and an hour straight south of Orlando, in the town of Winter Haven, is Legoland Florida (p. 158), a super kiddie park built on the tranquil remains of Florida's most historic amusement park.

EAST OF ORLANDO

The entrance to Orlando International Airport is 11 miles east of I-4, webbed into the city network by toll highways and surrounded by golfing developments. Across empty swamp from there, the so-called Space Coast, of which Cape Canaveral is the metaphoric capital (see it at Kennedy Space Center; p. 178), is a 45-minute drive east of Orlando's tourist corridor via 528, also known as the Bee Line Expressway.

WEST OF ORLANDO

Because the Green Swamp commands the area, there simply isn't much west of the tourist corridor save a few small towns and some state parks, such as Lake Louisa.

EXPLORING WALT DISNEY WORLD

3

On November 22, 1963, around the time President John Kennedy was embarking on his public motorcade in Dallas, Walt Disney was in a private jet, conducting his first flyover of some ignored Florida swampland. By the end of the day, as Disney decided this was the place he wanted to shape in the image of his dreams, America had changed in more ways than one.

While the country reeled, Disney snapped up land through dummy companies. His cover was blown in 1965, but the fix was in: His company had mopped up an area twice the size of Manhattan, 27,443 acres, from just $180 an acre. Disneyland East was coming. Today, it's the most popular vacation destination on the planet, and its four theme parks receive more than 55.8 million combined visits a year. After years without much significant development, during which it lost ground to Universal nearby, the resort is now in the midst of a multi-year push to pour billions into improvements, and signs of construction are everywhere.

It's no accident that Walt, a seller of fantasies, enjoyed his peaks during two periods of profound malaise: the Great Depression and the Cold War. It's also no coincidence that his theme parks flowered while America was riven with self-doubt—the Korean and Vietnam conflicts, the death of Kennedy, and Watergate. His parks are, by design, comforting. They tell you how to feel and where to go, and in reinforcing uncomplicated impressions of history and the world, they never make you feel stupid or left behind. Ironically, what made his reassuring message of simplicity work was complex intelligence, specifically, the relentless drive for technological innovation and revolutionary engineering.

Why should it be so difficult to find straight talk about such an immensely popular place? Disney fans rhapsodize about the "magic"—that intangible *frisson* you feel when you're there—but I think a case could be made that the energy doesn't come from the place as much as it comes from the customers. Where else in your life will you be someplace surrounded by people so elated to be there? Walt Disney World's magic comes from the accumulated

Walt Disney World & Lake Buena Vista

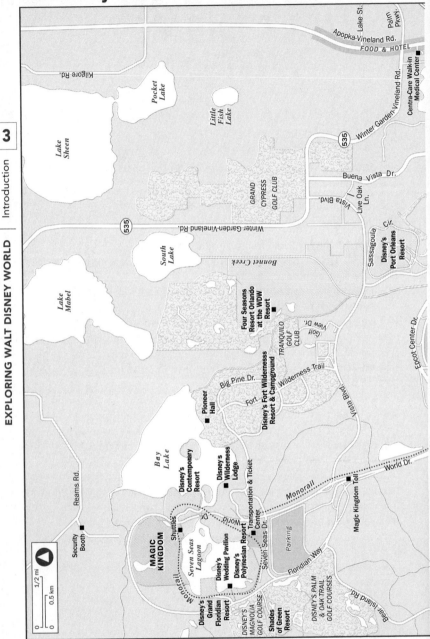

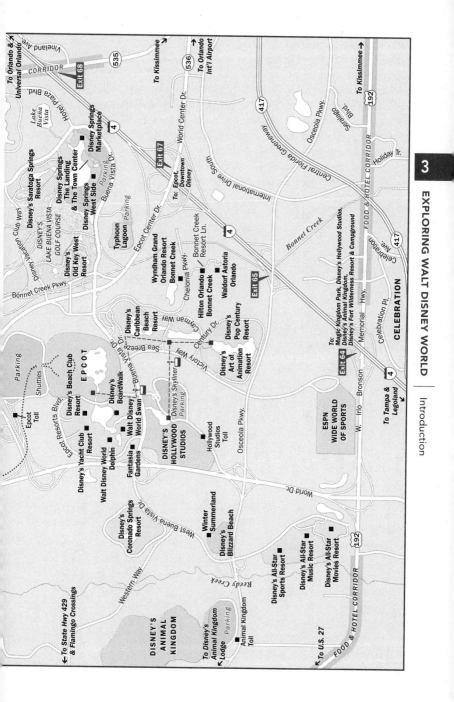

To Orlando & Universal Orlando

Vineland Ave.

CORRIDOR

Exit 68

535

To Kissimmee

536

To Orlando Int'l Airport

To Orlando

To Kissimmee

192

Hotel Plaza Blvd.

Lake Buena Vista

Disney Springs Marketplace

4

Exit 67

World Center Dr.

Osceola Pkwy.

Santiago Blvd.

Holiday Tr.

FOOD & HOTEL CORRIDOR

Disney's Saratoga Springs Resort

Disney Springs The Landing & The Town Center

DISNEY'S LAKE BUENA VISTA GOLF COURSE

Disney Vacation Club Way

Disney Springs West Side

Parking Buena Vista Dr.

To: Epcot, Downtown Disney

Central Florida Greenway

417

Disney's Old Key West Resort

Typhoon Lagoon

Parking

Epcot Center Dr.

International Drive South

Bonnet Creek Pkwy.

Wyndham Grand Orlando Resort Bonnet Creek

Bonnet Creek Resort Ln.

Chelonia Pkwy.

Hilton Orlando Bonnet Creek

Waldorf Astoria Orlando

Bonnet Creek

4

Exit 65

Celebration Ave.

417

CELEBRATION

Disney's Caribbean Beach Resort

Cayman Way

Sea Breeze Dr.

Buena Vista Dr.

Century Dr.

Disney's Pop Century Resort

To:
Magic Kingdom Park, Disney's Hollywood Studios,
Disney's Animal Kingdom,
Disney's Fort Wilderness Resort & Campground

Memorial Hwy.

Celebration Pl.

Parking

Shuttles

EPCOT

Disney's Beach Club Resort

Disney's BoardWalk

Victory Way

Disney's Art of Animation Resort

Exit 64

4

Epcot Resorts Blvd.

Epcot Toll

Disney's Yacht Club Resort

Walt Disney World Dolphin

Fantasia Gardens

Walt Disney World Swan

Disney's Skyliner

Parking

DISNEY'S HOLLYWOOD STUDIOS

Hollywood Studios Toll

Osceola Pkwy.

ESPN WIDE WORLD OF SPORTS

W. Irlo Bronson

To Tampa & Legoland

4

World Dr.

West Buena Vista Dr.

Disney's Coronado Springs Resort

Winter Summerland

Disney's Blizzard Beach

Disney's All-Star Sports Resort

Disney's All-Star Music Resort

Disney's All-Star Movies Resort

Reedy Creek

192

FOOD & HOTEL CORRIDOR

Western Way

To State Hwy 429 & Flamingo Crossings

DISNEY'S ANIMAL KINGDOM

To Disney's Animal Kingdom Lodge

Animal Kingdom Toll

Parking

To U.S. 27

goodwill of strangers united in gratitude and togetherness. It's the American Varanasi—a place of pilgrimage that some people use as a spiritual balm for life's hardships. If you don't believe me, sit on a bench for a while in Fantasyland and watch the children pass. There's just something about it.

But Disney World, transporting it may be, is a business, and for a significant portion of the population, it's brutally expensive. The average domestic overnight guest spends nearly $300 per person per day, and that number's going higher: The American theme park market is outpacing the rest of the economy, and Disney is a major driver of that. Each year, its profits increase because it forces families to spend more. Even people who love Disney agree it requires shrewd navigation. The world needs more carefree days. This book will help you keep your Disney time carefree.

TICKETING

Disney hikes prices early each year but attendance keeps growing, so I guess we should stop complaining about it. This will be the biggest expense, so assess your needs before laying down plastic. All park tickets (except annual passes) are purchased by the day. You decide how many days you want to spend at the parks, and once you nail that down, you decide which extras you want to add. Both decisions are fraught with temptation and the risk of overspending. It's possible Disney intentionally makes the process complicated so that customers spend more money than they have to.

Magic *Their* Way

Ideally, visitors to Orlando could spend a weeklong vacation mixing days at Disney parks, Universal Orlando, SeaWorld, and the Kennedy Space Center. However, the Disney resort uses Magic Your Way, a scaled pricing scheme that both rewards people who stay on Disney turf for more than 4 days and gives them an incentive to eliminate anything else from their experiences. Magic Your Way is a honey trap that requires many visitors to group their Disney days together, which makes on-resort hotel guests unwilling to ever leave.

Once you know how many days you'll buy, like on an airline, you add the options that you want. They are (including tax, rounded to the nearest dollar):

1. **Base ticket.** You must at least buy this. This is your theme park admission. It buys you one park per day, with no switching to other parks on the same day. After 4 days, the biggest per-day discounts kick in. (My take for first timers: When it's all new to you, one park per day for 4 days, is plenty— given the current state of Hollywood Studios, that may be too much until the *Star Wars* land opens.) For one-day tickets, Disney World prices in seasons: Value, Regular, and Peak. It also charges more for the Magic Kingdom than for its three other parks. Generally speaking, "Peak" is the period straddling school vacation periods: the last three weeks of March; Memorial Day through the end of July; the fourth week of November; and

Disney Ticket Options*

Base One-Day Ticket

Magic Kingdom adult:	$137 (Peak)/$127 (Regular)/$116 (Value)
Magic Kingdom child:	$131 (Peak)/$120 (Regular)/$110 (Value)
Other theme parks:	$130 adult/$124 child (Peak)/$121/$115 (Regular)/$109/$102 (Value)
Add Park Hopper:	$38–$67 for a one-day ticket (depending on season); $64 to cover 2–3 days; $80 to cover 4 days or longer
Add Park Hopper Plus:	$27 on top of Park Hopper

Multiple-Day Tickets**

Days of Use	Age 10 & Up	Age 3–9	Add Park Hopper	For Park Hopper Plus
2	$212	$200	$70	$318/$306
3	$330	$310	$70	$442/$423
4	$395	$373	$80	$533/$511
5	$416	$395	$80	$548/$527
6	$437	$416	$80	$559/$538
7	$458	$437	$80	$570/$548
8	$469	$448	$80	$580/$559
9	$480	$458	$80	$591/$570
10	$490	$469	$80	$602/$580

* Prices are rounded to the next-highest dollar and include sales tax of 6% to 7.5%. Prices accurate as of early 2018; rates rise early in the year.

** Advance purchase rates; tickets cost about $20 more if purchased at the gate.

*** The Plus option adds visits equal to the number of park days on the ticket.

the last two weeks of December. "Value" is most of January, February, late August, and September. The rest of the year is "Regular."

2. **Park Hopper.** Should you crave the privilege of jumping from park to park on the same day (I recommend this if it's not your first time in Orlando), you must add the Park Hopper option. Example: With it, you can do the early-morning safari at Animal Kingdom, take a nap at your hotel, and then switch to the Magic Kingdom for the fireworks.

3. **Park Hopper Plus.** If you plan to visit a Disney water slide park, play a round of mini-golf at one of Disney's two courses (only before 4pm), or see an event at the ESPN Wide World of Sports (a rarity), this option includes admission to those and it automatically comes with Park Hopper. Many people buy this option and fail to use it. During the course of 3 days of theme park going, are you *really* going to have enough juice for water slides? Do the math: Walk-up admission at the water parks is $64–69 adults and $58–60 kids; so would you save money getting into them that way instead? *This option only pays off if you use the water parks at least twice.* If you must (you probably won't), you can always simply add this option to your ticket once you arrive at Disney.

Note: Tickets expire 14 days after you begin using them. Until 2015, guests could buy them with no expiration date, and those are still accepted.

Very slight **discounts** on Magic Your Way tickets are available. You can save around $20 on tickets of 3 days or longer as long as you buy in advance online or on the phone. Deals also are listed at https://disneyworld.disney. go.com/special-offers and at www.MouseSavers.com. If you buy your tickets in advance (online or at a Disney Store), save the shipping fee by arranging to pick them up at the gates of one of the parks (long lines) or at Guest Relations in Disney Springs Marketplace (short line). **Florida residents** are offered entirely different discounts (www.disneyworld.disney.go.com/florida-residents) that come with blackout dates, as do **AAA members** and **active military;** if you're one, call © **407/824-4321** for the latest promotion. Attendees of **conventions** on Disney property may be offered cheaper tickets for afternoon or evening park entry. (See "Other Ticket 'Discounts' & Deals," below, for more on potential discounts.)

During some times of year, the park mounts special evening events, such as the ones around Halloween and Christmas (see the calendar on p. 274) that require a separate, expensive ticket. You will get less value out of your Magic Your Way ticket if you attend on the same day as one of these parties because if you haven't paid for the evening-event ticket, you'll be rounded up and sent out in late afternoon. (Magic Kingdom puts out so many holiday decorations, plus 90,000 poinsettias, that it maintains a special warehouse just for them—but touring the hotel decorations is free, including The Grand Floridian's famous gingerbread house.)

THE PERIL OF DISNEY PACKAGES

If you want to spend more than you have to, skip this section.

Overpurchasing is the biggest pitfall. When you call for reservations, agents will suggest adding perks. You'll ask for tickets, and they'll suggest you throw in, say, the meal plan (p. 30). The instant you accept, your customer status changes. You're now purchasing a "package," and that will often force you to pay more than you would have a la carte. Always, *always* know what everything would cost separately before agreeing to a Disney-suggested package. If you must, hang up the phone and do some math before deciding to accept or reject the offer. Then call back for a new quote—prices can fluctuate each time you call. That's the only way to ensure you're not paying more.

Here's a hidden loophole that works against you: Disney "length of stay" ticket packages will begin the moment you arrive on the property and end the day you leave. Think about that. If you've just flown from a distant place, you are unlikely to rush to the Magic Kingdom on the same day. Likewise, on the day you're due at the airport to fly home, you may not to be able to visit a theme park. Yet Disney will schedule your package that way. In effect, you will lose 2 days that you've paid for—at the start and at the finish of your vacation, when you'll be resting or packing. That's colder than Elsa's heart.

How can you avoid this? You could 1) stay entirely at non-Disney hotels and just buy admission tickets. That's because the rule only applies to Disney packages—if you simply buy four days' worth of tickets, you don't have to use them on consecutive days as long as they're all used within your two-week

THE MAGICBAND revolution

Disney paid a reported $1 billion to develop a controversial guest identification system. It's called MagicBand, a waterproof, removable bracelet that monitors your stay. Each contains two types of embedded radio frequency transmitters that enable both short-range and long-range tracking. When you book a package for a Disney hotel, you are mailed MagicBands in preparation of your stay as long as your booking is made at least 10 days ahead. If you're not staying at a Disney hotel, you can buy one starting at $13–$33 at Disney shops and linked to your ticket by the sales clerk. You then use free **My Disney Experience** (MDX) smartphone app (Android or iPhone only) to manage everything it can do.

Here's what the MagicBand/MDX combo empowers:

- Stores your ticket info to get you through turnstiles. Touch it to a lollipop-like scanner for entry, paired with your fingerprint for positive identification.
- Records and redeems reservations for Fastpass, Disney's Magical Express, and dining. (The expanded capability is technically called **MyMagic+.**)
- Validates PhotoPass details. Scan it with photographers and at post-ride photo kiosks to add new pictures to your portfolio.
- Allows Disney resort guests to make purchases (with a PIN; day visitors cannot) and open hotel room doors and gates. They're also parking passes.
- The system adjusts to your plans and sends you smartphone notifications if something changes. There's free Wi-Fi in the parks to enable this.

- Allows Disney Parks to track your movements. This could translate into you opening your MDX app and discovering a shot of you on Slinky Dog Dash or a video of yourself on the Seven Dwarfs Mine Train (available for purchase, of course).
- Links plans that friends and family make to yours.

There are sassy colors to buy, plus special editions, and an array of charms and accessories (which easily fall off). Although you can buy as many bands as you want and link them all to your account, the batteries only last 2 or 3 years.

To use its benefits, you must register personal details, including your address and date of birth, with the Disney system. For this reason, the new technology has been plagued with privacy controversies. Disney swears personal information is not encoded in the MagicBands by saying, "The MagicBand and card contain only a randomly assigned code that securely links to an encrypted database and are configured to not store any other information about you." (Read more of its explanations at www.mydisneyexperience.com.)

If you have concerns, you may decline a MagicBand or simply not buy one; you will be given a plastic card that only contains a passive radio transmitter chip that's used to tap for entry but cannot be used to track your movements around the parks. There are no paper tickets anymore.

If you possess a MagicBand, brace yourself for the overspending potential of tapping a bracelet rather than taking out a wallet. Studies show we spend 18% more when we don't handle cash or credit cards—a big reason the company decided to sink $1 billion into this.

deadline. You could 2) stay at a Disney hotel for your ticket days and stay off-site for the others. Or you could 3) insist on making **one reservation per phone call.** Arrange your tickets plus their corresponding hotel nights for your Disney days. Hang up. Call back and arrange "room-only" nights for your last night and any days you'll be leaving Disney during the day as "room only." It's vital that you do not link your two reservations in advance if you want the best price and the best cancellation policies, but you can link them after arrival. If you don't plan on seeing anything but Disney, of course, then you won't have to go through these lengths. But with so many wonders in Florida, many people aren't satisfied by only visiting the Mouse.

Another tip: Disney's reservationists are friendly, but they're sales-driven, and they're trained to answer *only* the questions that you pose. If you're not sure about the terms of what you're about to purchase, corner them and ask. They won't lie to you, but they *will* neglect to volunteer information. Grill them about deposit and cancellation policies—they get *much* stiffer if you're on a package vs. buying a la carte. The best Disney experience goes to those willing to pay the most, but *always* ask if there is a less expensive option. **TheMouseForLess.com**, **MouseSavers.com**, and the messages at **DISBoards.com** will let you know about current deals that Disney won't. And if you're still dithering about whether to stay on property, don't ask their opinion—there's a list of pros and cons on p. 234 and 235.

OTHER TICKET "DISCOUNTS" & DEALS

A few businesses shave a few paltry bucks off multiday tickets; see "Getting Attraction Discounts" in chapter 8 (p. 277) for some upstanding ones. *Never* buy tickets through eBay or Craigslist, and beware anyone claiming they have discounts on a one-day ticket, because Disney doesn't allow that. International visitors are eligible for tickets good for longer stays, but only if they are purchased from abroad. *Really* big fans carry a **Chase Disney Rewards Visa credit card** (www.chase.com/disney; © **800/300-8575**), which grants points to be redeemed on all things Disney, a few discounts, and a character meet-and-greet area for cardholders.

Using MagicBands, MDX & Fastpass+

Disney asks you to use a free app, My Disney Experience (MDX), to make most of your arrangements. Think of the smartphone app as the place you make your plans, and the MagicBand as the thing you use to check yourself in to do them. To help you, free in-park Wi-Fi is furnished. Once you create an account at MyDisneyExperience.com (surprise—Disney wants your birthday) and link your ticket number with it, MDX can:

o Book and reschedule Fastpass+.
o Display your location on park maps.
o Show current wait times.
o Show in-park schedules.
o Show height and accessibility requirements.
o Keep a schedule of your reservations.

- Make and cancel restaurant reservations.
- Manage PhotoPass account and images.
- Buy tickets.
- Pre-order food for pick up at a few park restaurants.

When used in conjunction with a MagicBand, which detects your location, MDX can even send you movies and photos taken of you on rides—even if you didn't know they were being taken. (Obviously, it wants you to buy them once you see them.)

To make Fastpass+ reservations for everyone you're with, make sure every person has an MDX account. Then to go My Account>Friends and Family List to invite everyone to connect by finding them by e-mail address. If everyone in your party links their tickets, MDX can also synchronize everyone's plans; for that to work best, select one of your group to be the Primary so everything goes through their account.

It's also supposed to keep you from having to make phone calls, but of course things go wrong with a system as complex as this. Here's the help line: ✆ **407/939-4537.** Also, unfortunately for you, all that app time will destroy your battery life, so pack some backup battery power. (Many park shops and a few vending machines in the locker areas sell $30 power packs you can use, drain, and exchange for free for fresh ones at any Disney park.)

Your ticket entitles you to Fastpass+ (technically, it's in all caps, but come on), which lets you make a few timed reservations for attractions and scan your MagicBand or ticket card to check in at the appointed hour at a Fastpass Return door, bypassing the main line and cutting out lots of waiting. Before you arrive at the park you may—and absolutely should, because the most popular rides and character greetings will run out of Fastpasses days before—pre-book three Fastpasses for each day. Guests at Disney-run hotels get access 60 days ahead (90 for Club Level guests), but day visitors and non-Disney hotel guests get access only 30 days ahead; your booking window starts at 7am on those booking days. Use my star ratings to determine what *you* think is worth Fastpassing.

To schedule your three starter Fastpasses a day, you must register your name, birthday, and tickets on the Disney website or the free My Disney Experience app (MDX; p. 26). After you tell the system when and where you're going, MDX comes up with a few options for timing your Fastpasses, usually spread throughout the day. After you accept one of its plans, you may go back and individually revise each reservation—I suggest moving everything toward the first part of the day, because you may only obtain another Fastpass+ after they're all used or their reservation times have passed (so if your third pass doesn't come due until after dark, you'll have wasted a lot of hours you could have been making and using new reservations). You can also only start booking a Fastpass+ for a second park once the first three at the first park are all used up. If you're an active type, move them all to afternoon, when lines are longest, and race through a bunch of things on your own in the morning, when lines are lightest. Once you're at the park, you can still revise using MDX and you'll find scattered kiosks where cast members help you. If someone in your group snags the perfect combo, they can copy it over to everyone else in the group.

Disney doesn't tell you this when you're planning Fastpasses, but in three of the parks (not Magic Kingdom), attractions are grouped into **tiers.** The blockbusters are Tier 1, while most stuff is Tier 2, and each day, you're allowed to start off with one Tier 1 and your other slots will be salted with two Tier 2 attractions. That's why you can't start off a day with passes for *both* Flight of Passage and Na'vi River Journey; since both are Tier 1, one will have to be added to your plans after you start using passes.

These are the Tier 1 attractions: **Disney's Animal Kingdom:** Flight of Passage and Na'vi River Journey. **Epcot:** Frozen Ever After, Soarin', Test Track, and a reserved place at IlluminNations. **Disney's Hollywood Studios:** Slinky Dog Dash, Toy Story Mania!, Alien Swirling Saucers, and both Star Wars: Galaxy's Edge rides.

Don't bother Fastpassing for a clear viewing area for the fireworks or for a show—since theatres fit thousands of people, you don't need one for those, and evening slots will keep you locked out of getting more—although by afternoon the best stuff will be gone anyway. If you're locked out of what you want, keep trying every day and keep refreshing the screen—plans are always shifting, so even hot tickets can suddenly become available. *Note:* Fastpass+ is never available during specially ticketed after-hours events such as Mickey's Not-So-Scary Halloween Party (p. 276).

Theme park commandos like Fastpass+ because it gives them a refined way to game the system. But if you're a casual visitor, Fastpass+ junks up the fun by keeping you hunched over your phone and forcing you to pre-research attractions so much that it spoils the sense of unfolding surprise that was critical to Imagineers. The system also turns visitors who don't pay more for Disney-owned hotels into second-class customers. While Fastpass+ has eased waits on the most popular rides, it has made them worse on second-tier attractions that used to be walk-ons by sending more people to them.

mobile ordering EXPLAINED

It works great! At an increasing number of counter-service restaurants, you don't have to wait in a long, boring queue to get fed. On MDX, navigate to My Plans>Order Food to see a list of restaurants where you can place an order via app. Special requests are tricky, but if you want regular menu items, it's easy. Just choose the time window in which you want to fetch your food and then order it—your credit card will be charged. (If the app claims the restaurant isn't accepting orders, your connection might be bad.) Then, when you get to the restaurant, there will be one spot dedicated to mobile orders (usually at the right side of the counter). Go back to the Order Food section of the app, click the button that says you're there and ready to pick up, and within 2 or 3 minutes, your food will be served. (To avoid waiting at all, make that final click about 2 minutes before you reach the restaurant.) Identify yourself to the clerk, though—they don't always announce names so strangers can't pretend to be you.

EATING ON-SITE

In the original Disneyland, restaurants were operated by outside lessees, but today, Disney controls everything inside the parks. It hasn't done much for the quality of the food (prepare for memories of your grade-school cafeteria), but at least the math is easy. The **cheapest combo meals** are always from counter-service restaurants (called Quick Service in Disney-speak), and adults usually pay $11 to $16, including a side but not a drink—the combo is called a "meal." Kids' meals (a main dish; milk, juice, water, or soda; and a choice of two items including grapes, carrot sticks, applesauce, a cookie, or fries) always cost $7–$8 at Quick Service locations. If you want to sit down for a waiter-service meal—character meals are always in "table-service" restaurants—adults pay in the upper teens for a lunch entree and usually over $21 a plate at dinner, before gratuity or drinks, and kids' meals are about half as much. Disney aggressively sells a Disney Dining Plan that takes away the need to pay a bill after each meal, but which comes with a lot of rules and requires a lot of advance reservations (see the sidebar "Why You Don't Need the Disney Dining Plan," below).

No longer can you simply stroll into any restaurant that catches your eye and enjoy a meal. Oversubscription to the Dining Plan spoiled that for everyone else. **For table-service meals, *always* make reservations (© 407/939-3463)** or you are almost certain to be turned away. Menus and prices are listed on the My Disney Experience app, where you can also reserve. If a restaurant is booked, try again 24 hours ahead, when people dump unwanted reservations before a $10 no-show penalty is assessed.

Semi-healthy options are possible on even the lowest food budget: Disney limits saturated fat and added sugar to 10% of a counter-service dish's calories; no more than 30% of a meal's calories or 35% of a snack's calories come from fat; and juice drinks have no added sugar. Trans fats are out. One way Disney seems to have accomplished this is by reducing serving sizes—you won't feel stuffed. Kids' meals come with carrots, applesauce, or grapes instead of fries, and with low-fat milk, water, or 100% fruit juice instead of soda. (Fries and Coke are still available by request—they know kids are still on vacation.) *Note:* Disney is eliminating plastic straws over the course of 2019.

NAVIGATING DISNEY

In summer and during other holidays, it's wise to get to the front gates of the park about 30 minutes ahead of opening, partly because you can waltz right onto a marquee ride that way (although not everything will be operating right away). Try not to leave any park as it closes, when crowds surge and all transportation is mobbed with intense standing waits. Instead, depart early or linger an hour in the shops, which will be open a bit longer than everything else. Uber operates at all the parks (at the Magic Kingdom, they're at the Ticketing and Transportation Center), and cars are usually plentiful.

WHY YOU DON'T NEED THE DISNEY
dining plan

If you book at a Disney hotel, you will be offered the credit-based **Disney Dining Plan,** which prepurchases meals. Like everything else here, it's unnecessarily complicated, choked with rules, exclusions, and premium versions. Lots of people cave and buy it in the name of convenience, thinking it will make everything easier, but if you are a casual Disney visitor and not using it for things like character meals, it has other costs.

o **It's not cheap enough.** The least expensive plan, Quick Service, has a per-day cost of $53 adults, $22 kids 3–9, and includes two counter meals (*not* all three meals) and one snack (like popcorn or ice cream), plus one drink (it can be alcoholic) and a refillable soft drink mug you can only use at a Disney hotel. Most adult Quick Service meals cost $12 to $15 per meal using cash. Even if you spent $15, remedial math proves that if you stick to two counter-service meals with no plan, plus one $4 snack, you'll spend about $34 versus $53 using the plan.

o **It's inflexible.** You must buy the plan for every night you stay at the hotel even though you may be exploring away from Disney on some days. You are not permitted to buy fewer days than your stay. *And* everyone in your room must be on it, plus, some menu items

and food locations are excluded.

o **It costs time.** Many of the plans expect the use of sit-down restaurants. This requires reservations months ahead, and you lose a lot of touring time.

o **It's impractical.** The Standard plan ($76 adults, $26 kids, per night) buys the equivalent of one sit-down meal, one Quick Service meal, and two snacks. If you want the plan with all three meals whether they're table or counter, you're looking at $117 adults/$40 kids each night. Few first-time visitors want that much. It starts to be of value *only* if you have a sit-down meal every single day.

o **It's incomplete.** The plan doesn't include tips (unless your party is six or more, in which case there's a mandatory 18% added).

o **It's wasteful.** Because it begins on the day you arrive, you're bound to leave with some unused credits, resulting in a loss. Most people compensate for this by booking a character meal or fireworks package, which require more credits. If you plan on character meals, the math may—borderline—work out.

The Dining Plan *is* worthwhile if you are offered it **for free as part of a package,** which happens during some special sale periods. Free is always delicious!

GETTING AROUND   Having your own car is the easiest. But then there's the Disney Transportation System (DTS; no luggage allowed), reportedly the third-largest bus system in the state, after Miami and Jacksonville's public services. Taking DTS to a theme park eliminates the parking tram rigmarole. However, it adds waiting time, which can be 20 to 45 minutes, plus the commute itself, which can be just as long and require standing as if it's rush hour on a Brooklyn subway. You might even have to transfer buses. All told, 90 minutes to 2 hours of a busy day can be devoured by DTS. So often, having a car is worth the expense.

DTS is usually overwhelmed during the opening and closing of the theme parks even though dispatchers run extra buses around those times and keep routes rolling for about 2 extra hours before opening and after closing. If you're staying at a Disney resort that offers another kind of transportation—say, the monorail to the Magic Kingdom—then a bus won't be available for the same route. Also, since the system has a hub-and-spoke design centered on the theme parks and Disney Springs, *you must often transfer if you're going between two second-tier points,* such as between two hotels, a hotel and a water park, or a theme park and Disney Springs. And buses to Disney Springs from theme parks only start running at 4pm.

In 2019, Disney opens the free **Disney Skyliner gondolas,** which are not unlike the enclosed gondolas that can transport dozens of skiers at a time in the Alps. The first phase of the installation links Epcot's International Gateway side entrance with the Caribbean Beach Resort and a stop shared by Art of Animation and Pop Century. A spur line from Caribbean Beach goes to Disney's Hollywood Studios. So to travel between Epcot and Hollywood Studios, you'll have to change at Caribbean Beach.

Disney also has red polka-dotted **Minnie Vans** zipping around. This newly launched premium transportation network is Disney's answer to Uber. You hail one using the Lyft app—when you open it, it will tell you where to go to hail one and wait. Each very clean Chevy Traverse fits up to six (and keeps two children's car seats on hand) and costs a flat $25 plus tax to go wherever you want within Walt Disney World. That's more than an UberX or often a taxi, they're not themed inside, and in inclement weather or peak periods, good luck finding one. They will also take you to the airport, but at $150, I don't know why you would use one.

PARKING   Each park has its own sunbaked lot ($22/day; free for Disney hotel guests and annual passholders; $45 for "Preferred" to be extra close). As you drive in, attendants will direct you to the next available spot. This is probably the most dangerous part of your day, because everyone is excited and you're at risk of hitting a distracted child or hitting an open car door—take it slow. Parking lanes are numbered and sections are named; at the very least, remember your number. Don't stress out if your row is a high number; at Epcot, for example, the front row is 27. (*Don't lose your car:* Before you get out of your car, open your phone's mapping app, zoom in, and stick a pin in your location. If you still forget, remember what time you arrived: Disney tracks which sections are being filled minute by minute.) You'll board one of the noisy trams (cross the yellow line to signal you're boarding; drivers never budge if someone's in that zone), which haul you to ticketing in their own sweet time; at Epcot and Hollywood Studios, the lots are compact enough so that you could probably walk to the gates within 10 minutes without taking the tram, but the Magic Kingdom, with some 15,000 spaces (in either a Heroes or a Villains section—remember which one), is reportedly the third-largest parking lot in the world. Post-tram at the Magic Kingdom, you still must take either the monorail or a ferryboat to the front gates; at the other parks, the tram

contacting WALT DISNEY WORLD

Walt Disney World offers no toll-free numbers.

General information: www.disneyworld.com; ℂ **407/939-5277**
Vacation packages: ℂ **407/934-7675**
Room-only bookings: ℂ **407/939-7429**
Operating hours, schedules: ℂ **407/824-4321**
Dining reservations: ℂ **407/939-3463**
Tickets: ℂ **407/939-1289**
MagicBands, My Disney Experience, Fastpass+: ℂ **407/939-4357**
Tour bookings: ℂ **407/939-8687**
Lost and found: ℂ **407/824-4245**

lets you off near the gates. There are **charging stations** for electric vehicles, which cost $0.35 per kilowatt; ask the toll attendant where they are.

SECURITY   American gun culture has intruded upon the Happiest Place on Earth: There are now metal detectors. Drawstring bags are quicker to search than zipper-laden ones, but you'll save the most time if you don't have a bag because you'll bypass some screening lines. Banned: Booze, glass containers, selfie sticks, wheelie sneakers, costumes on anyone age 14 and over. And weapons, duh.

ENTRY   To validate your ticket (see the box on MagicBands, p. 25), you must place a finger on a clear plate. That fingerprint is "married" to your ticket so that no one else can use it. Disney swears your personal information is eventually expunged from the system, but what it doesn't publicize is that if you do not wish for your fingerprint to be scanned, you may use standard identification instead, right there at the gate.

ORIENTATION   Once you get inside the gates, grab two free things from the conspicuous racks: a **Guidemap** and a **Times Guide** listing the day's schedule, including shows, character greetings (marked by Mickey in profile), places to eat, and attractions with shorter hours (Animal Kingdom also has an **Animal Guide**). Also, cast members carry full schedules (it's called the "Tell-A-Cast"), or you can ask at the park's **Guest Relations** desk (marked on the maps, always near the front; **Guest Services,** outside the gates, is mostly for ticket issues). The wait time for any attraction is posted where its line begins; this number is roughly accurate, since Disney often pads it by 5 minutes to give a sense of exceeded expectations.

SIZE RESTRICTIONS   They're listed on the maps. Take them seriously. They are always enforced. If there is a sample of the ride vehicle out front, you can try it (or make it a photo op) before joining the line. At Splash Mountain, Space Mountain, Mission Space, and a few other major rides, kids who are sized out may be offered a card entitling them to jump to the head of the line when they finally grow tall enough. (At Space Mountain, it dubs them a

"Mousetronaut," at Splash Mountain, a "Future Splash Mountaineer"—but sadly, this perk seems to be dying out.)

FOOD Gone are the days when you could decide on a whim to have a table-service dinner. The Disney Dining Plan (p. 30) wrecked that. Now you must plan ahead by racking up Advance Dining Reservations, called ADRs, or risk waiting for cancellations that may not materialize. Having a reservation does not mean you will sit down at that time. There is frequently a wait anyway. If you have no reservations, you'll be eating from counter service spots.

Breakfast ends around 10:30am, and lunch service generally goes from 11:30am to 2:30 or 3pm, though increasingly, some places price lunch as dinner. Prices for buffets and character meals shift according to the day of the week and time of year. Counter service locations, which Disney calls **Quick Service,** do not require reservations, and their listings can be found with each theme park's chapter. To avoid lines, eat between 10:30am and noon (lunch) and 4 and 5pm (dinner). Kids under 3 may eat without charge from an adult's plate, and high chair and booster seats are readily available. If you have dietary concerns, make them plain with your first cast member interaction.

You'll find menus on MDX. Be warned that eating late can be hard; with the exception of Disney Springs, options tend to dry up by 9pm or so.

STROLLERS Many times you will be asked to park your stroller before entering a line, so do not keep your valuables in one. Your time (and your neighbor's) on monorails and trams will be much happier if you have one that folds quickly. Note that you're not allowed to bring a stroller larger than 36"×52" (92cm×132cm) into the park. If you rent one and go to a second park the same day, you don't have to pay again. For rental prices, see the box below; if you pre-pay a multi-day stay, you save a few bucks each day.

WHAT TO WEAR Consider dressing small children in bathing suits because some play areas (particularly at Magic Kingdom) will get them soaked.

OPTIONAL PARK SERVICES If you see an on-ride photo you like, tap your MagicBand to that monitor's sensor to add it to your MDX account, where you can buy it for $15. Photographers (marked on the maps and often accompanying characters) may also ask to take your picture—they're marked

Meeting Mickey & Co.

You may remember a time when characters freely roamed Disney World. Now they're like rock stars. They have bodyguards and access to them is strictly regimented. All **Character Greeting** times are printed on the Times Guide that you pick up as you enter each park, and the regular locations are marked on maps with a black Mickey profile. There are always lines for them, and the most popular ones (including Mickey, Ariel, Cinderella, Tinker Bell, and Anna and Elsa) accept Fastpass+. But they're worth the wait: They always exude contagious good cheer. Each one signs a unique autograph—Goofy's has a backward F, Aladdin does a lamp—and costumes match the locale.

WHAT THE BASICS cost AT ALL FOUR DISNEY PARKS

Parking: $22 (waived for guests of Disney hotels); $45 for "Preferred" spots that are closest
Lockers: $10–$15 per day (multi-entry)
Regular soda: $3.50 / **Bottle of water:** $3 / **Cup of beer:** $8–$10
ECV (electric convenience vehicle): $50 per day at multiple parks + $20 deposit
Single strollers: $15 per day *

Double strollers: $31 per day *
Wheelchair: $12 per day *
Mickey ice cream bars: $5
Stroller, wheelchair, and ECV rental fee includes multiple park visits on the same day.
* Minus discounts of $2 to $4 if you prepay at the rental desk for the length of your stay.

on park maps in the app under **PhotoPass.** They're here for convenience, not value, and they hog all the best spots where you wish you could take your own pictures. Let them snap away; you won't pay anything if you don't want to. If you're wearing a MagicBand, it automatically shows up in MDX, and you can order prints (or ornaments, phone cases, mugs, mouse pads—you name it) if you fall in love with them. Sometimes, they can enhance the picture with "Magic Shots" special effects, such as Tinker Bell flying from your child's hands. You'll have 45 days to make your decisions. Only when you decide to buy does money change hands. Buying costs much more than it would cost you to make them yourself—5×7s are $17, 8×10s are $21, two 4×6s are $17, plus shipping and so forth—but they're very good. Now and then, you'll find an occasion that you think is worth the expense, and the Disney photographers are excellent at what they do. Spend $199 ($169 if you buy at least 3 days ahead of arrival) on **Memory Maker** and you can download all your vacation photos, including photos on some major rides and at restaurants as many times as you like for a month. Or just pay for a single day's worth for $59 (via the MDX app only, and you have to start with at least one photo). *Tip:* Early in your visit, ask a photographer for a "Magic Moment"; the portrait they take will crop up in surprising places for the rest of your visit.

VIP Tours (ⓒ **407/560-4033**) exist, but they cost $425–$625 per hour, plus park admission, so they're not something this book can seriously recommend.

You can send cumbersome **souvenirs** to the pick-up desk by the park gates, but delivery will take 3 to 5 hours. You can also send them to your Disney resort room. Make your purchase before noon to receive it the next day. If you make it later in the day, you should be staying for at least another 2 nights or you could miss the delivery. (Yeah, it's not efficient.)

THE MAGIC KINGDOM

The most-visited theme park in the world (20.45 million visitors in 2017), the **Magic Kingdom ★★★**, opened on October 1, 1971, and is more than twice as large as the original Disneyland in Anaheim, California, although it has about the same number of attractions. Of the four parks in Walt Disney World, the Magic Kingdom is the one most people envision: Castle, Main Street, Space Mountain. It's also the first one tourists visit.

The secret to the Magic Kingdom is getting there before it opens. The park almost always opens about 15 minutes before the posted opening time (the "rope drop"). Once in, you line up for the various lands in front of the Castle. About 5 minutes before opening time there's a cute show, **Let the Magic Begin,** in front of Cinderella Castle, in which Mickey and other characters proclaim the Kingdom open. At this point there are no lines for the rides. Do your favorite ride in that moment—I suggest Seven Dwarfs Mine Train or Peter Pan—because lines will double while you're riding it. The hour or two after this are the most fruitful of the day, with short lines. **Closing time** (often preceded by a 15-minute fireworks-and-projections show) varies, usually from **7 to midnight.** Near closing time, if you are allowed to get in line for a ride, you'll be able to ride. Hours change almost daily, and Disney transportation runs an hour before opening to an hour after closing.

GETTING IN & OUT   The proof that you're about to experience a fantasy realm comes in the effort required to enter it. Designers wanted arrival to be a big to-do. Many guests brave three forms of transportation before they see a single brick of Main Street. Disney bus riders are conveniently dropped off by the front gate, skipping all that. Guests who drive first take the parking tram to the security checkpoint at the **Transportation and Ticket Center (TTC).** (If you park in Aladdin, Woody, or Jafar, it's not too far to walk.) Guests who use Uber or a taxi will also be dropped there, but ask to go to the Contemporary Resort instead; from there it's just a 5-minute walk to the park, saving you lots of transit time. From the TTC, a mile away, the Magic Kingdom gleams like a promise from across the man-made Seven Seas Lagoon, but you still have to take either a **monorail** (after a 2009 accident that killed a pilot, guests are no longer permitted to ride in the cab) or a **ferryboat** (often piloted by adorable elder men) to the other side. Transit time is more or less equal; it can take 45 minutes from your car to the park. I recommend doing one in each direction—the monorail carries about 300 people but each ferry can handle 600, so take those numbers into your calculations as you eyeball the waiting crowds. Ferries are named for execs who helped build Disneyland and this park. For getting off quickly, I prefer the bottom deck.

Upon arrival, take the requisite photo at the Floral Mickey in front of the train station, where the "population" sign indicates the rough number of guests who have come here over time. Then head through the tunnels of the mansard-roof train station. There, by the right-hand tunnel, you'll find the only place in the park to rent strollers and wheelchairs. Note the stylized paintings of the big attractions, done like old-fashioned travel posters. They are a tradition here.

At closing time, hordes stream out of the gates in a popcorn-fueled death march and clog transportation lines like a Times Square throng on New Year's Eve. "Stay close," mothers whisper to their children when they see it. You'd

The Magic Kingdom

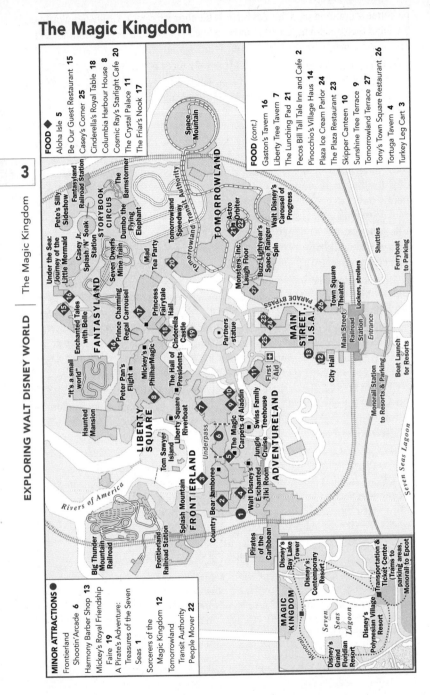

MINOR ATTRACTIONS ●

Frontierland
Shootin'Arcade **6**
Harmony Barber Shop **13**
Mickey's Royal Friendship
Faire **19**
A Pirate's Adventure:
Treasures of the Seven
Seas **1**
Sorcerers of the
Magic Kingdom **12**
Tomorrowland
Transit Authority
People Mover **22**

FOOD ◆
Aloha Isle **5**
Be Our Guest Restaurant **15**
Casey's Corner **25**
Cinderella's Royal Table **18**
Columbia Harbour House **8**
Cosmic Ray's Starlight Cafe **20**
The Crystal Palace **11**
The Friar's Nook **17**

FOOD (cont.)
Gaston's Tavern **16**
Liberty Tree Tavern **7**
The Lunching Pad **21**
Pecos Bill Tall Tale Inn and Cafe **2**
Pinocchio's Village Haus **14**
Plaza Ice Cream Parlor **24**
The Plaza Restaurant **23**
Skipper Canteen **10**
Sunshine Tree Terrace **9**
Tomorrowland Terrace **27**
Tony's Town Square Restaurant **26**
Tortuga Tavern **4**
Turkey Leg Cart **3**

be better off putting off your day's souvenir shopping until the posted closing time and then spending 45–60 minutes in the stores (which stay open after the rest of the park) before trying to leave.

STRATEGY If you have little kids, troop without delay to Fantasyland, because the lines get heavy there. On hot days, schedule Splash Mountain Fastpasses for the peak heat of afternoon, when you'll need the cool-down.

Main Street, U.S.A.

Out the other side of the train station in the Town Square, you'll be greeted by your first few costumed characters and to a full view of Cinderella Castle, home to an unlikely jumble of princesses, at the end of Main Street, U.S.A. Like the first time you see the Eiffel Tower or the Sydney Opera House, there's something seminal—oh, help me, dare I say *magical?*—about laying eyes on that Castle, and it can't help but stir feelings of gratitude. This view is as American as the Grand Canyon.

Exploring Main Street: The original Main Street, U.S.A., was created as a perfected vision of Walt Disney's fond memories of a formative period of his childhood spent in Marceline, Missouri, minus any churches. To impart a sense of coziness, designers built the Main Street facades at diminishing perspective as they rise. Other subtle touches: Shop windows are lower than normal to enable children to see inside, walkways are pigmented red to accentuate both unreality and safety (it alerts walkers of shifts in levels), and buildings on both sides inch closer to each other as you walk, subconsciously drawing your attention forward. All the "American" flags are actually missing a few stars or stripes so they can fly in all weather without disrespecting the true Old Glory.

The Best of the Magic Kingdom

Don't miss if you're 6: Dumbo the Flying Elephant
Don't miss if you're 16: Space Mountain
Requisite photo op: Cinderella Castle
Food you can only get here: LeFou's Brew, Gaston's Tavern, Fantasyland (p. 60); Citrus Swirl, Sunshine Tree Terrace, Adventureland (p. 59); Pineapple Float, Aloha Isle, Adventureland (p. 60); Mickey Mouse ice cream bars (available at carts throughout the park)
The most crowded, so Fastpass+ or go early: Seven Dwarfs Mine Train, Splash Mountain, Peter Pan's Flight, the Many Adventures of Winnie the Pooh
Skippable: Swiss Family Treehouse, Tomorrowland Speedway

Quintessentially Disney: The Haunted Mansion, Pirates of the Caribbean, Walt Disney's Carousel of Progress, "it's a small world"
Biggest thrill: Splash Mountain
Best show: Wishes fireworks
Character meals: Cinderella's Royal Table, Cinderella Castle; the Crystal Palace, Main Street, U.S.A.
Best shopping: The Emporium, Main Street, U.S.A.
Where to find peace: The Fantasyland-to-Tomorrowland railway-side trail; the park between Liberty Square and Adventureland at the Castle; Tom Sawyer Island; the cul-de-sac south of Space Mountain

MAGIC KINGDOM: 1 DAY, THREE WAYS

START: BE AT THE GATE 20 MINUTES BEFORE OPENING TIME.

Grab food at a counter restaurant when it's convenient to you—but having lunch at 11am (and not waiting until noon) saves time.

Obtain the must-have Fastpass+ where indicated and group everything as close to the morning as you can. After that, using additional ones will speed the day. If your kids want to meet major characters, it's vital to use Fastpass+ for meet-and-greet venues.

MAGIC KINGDOM WITH KIDS UNDER 8

Head to Fantasyland. Schedule Fastpass+ for one of these busy rides to ease waits later: Peter Pan's Flight, Enchanted Tales with Belle, Seven Dwarfs Mine Train, or Splash Mountain.

Do **Seven Dwarfs Mine Train** (if your kids do coasters—if not, proceed to next step).

↓

Immediately ride **Peter Pan's Flight** before the line gets worse.

↓

Visit **Enchanted Tales with Belle.**

↓

Ride in this order: **Journey of the Little Mermaid, Dumbo the Flying Elephant** (omit if your kids don't care), the **Many Adventures of Winnie the Pooh, "it's a small world."**

↓

Visit **Pete's Silly Sideshow** to meet Minnie or Goofy.

OR

Take the train from New Fantasyland to Main Street U.S.A. to meet Mickey at **Town Square Theater.**

↓

Cross to Adventureland. Do **Magic Carpets of Aladdin** if you feel the urge. Enjoy a Dole Whip at Aloha Isle or a Citrus Swirl at Sunshine Tree Terrace. Ride **Pirates of the Caribbean** and the **Jungle Cruise.**

It may be hot by now, so if there's patience among your party, see these two neighboring indoor shows: the **Enchanted Tiki Room** and the **Country Bear Jamboree.**

↓

See the midafternoon parade from Frontierland or on Main Street, U.S.A.

↓

At this point, littler ones may need to leave the park for a break.

Get to Tomorrowland via Fantasyland, and watch **Mickey's PhilharMagic**, and (time permitting) meet the princesses at **Fairytale Hall.**

↓

In Tomorrowland, ride **Buzz Lightyear's Space Ranger Spin.**

↓

Ride the **Speedway** if your child meets the height requirement.

↓

It's evening. If your kids are willing, ride the **Haunted Mansion.**

↓

If there's time, hit rides you missed (perhaps the **Carrousel** and **Astro Orbiter**).

↓

Watch the **parade,** ride something you missed, and see the fireworks before departing. If you missed **"it's a small world"** earlier, now's a good time to ride.

MAGIC KINGDOM WITH TEENS

Make sure you have Fastpass+ for Splash Mountain for early afternoon when it'll be hottest. Space Mountain, Seven Dwarfs Mine Train, and Peter Pan's Flight are the other prime candidates for Fastpass+.

Ride **Big Thunder Mountain Railway.**

↓

In Adventureland, ride **Pirates of the Caribbean** and **Jungle Cruise.** Enjoy a Dole Whip at Aloha Isle or a Citrus Swirl at Sunshine Tree Terrace.

↓

Cross the park via Fantasyland (ideally, have Fastpass+ for either **Peter Pan's Flight** or the **Seven Dwarfs Mine Train**) to Tomorrowland and ride **Space Mountain** and **Buzz Lightyear's Space Ranger Spin.**

↓

Go to Fantasyland for the **Mad Tea Party, Mickey's PhilharMagic,** and any rides that catch your fancy. You'll be getting hot and tired about now, so something like **"it's a small world"** might hit the spot.

↓

Around the corner, ride the **Haunted Mansion.**

↓

Take the raft to Tom Sawyer Island, where the kids can have free reign and, upon returning, shoot a few rounds at the **Frontierland Shootin' Arcade** or maybe do a lap on the riverboat. (They close at dusk.)

↓

Ride the train from Frontierland to Main Street, U.S.A.

↓

See the **parade and fireworks** from Main Street, U.S.A., or in front of the Castle. Cap the night with **Space Mountain.**

OR

If the parade isn't of interest, pick rides anywhere except in Adventureland to re-ride or try. Lines will be dramatically shorter during the parade.

MAGIC KINGDOM WITH NO KIDS

Schedule Fastpass+ for one of these rides within 90 minutes of opening: Peter Pan's Flight, Space Mountain, Big Thunder Mountain Railroad, Seven Dwarfs Mine Train.

Head to Fantasyland and ride **Seven Dwarfs Mine Train** immediately, then **Peter Pan's Flight, "it's a small world,"** and the **Many Adventures of Winnie the Pooh.** That'll put you in the mood.

↓

Head to Frontierland and ride **Big Thunder Mountain Railroad.** Have a Fastpass+ for early afternoon for **Splash Mountain,** or if it's warm, ride it now.

↓

In Adventureland, ride **Pirates of the Caribbean** and **Jungle Cruise.** Consider taking a trip once around the park on the **Railroad** now.

↓

Go old school: See the **Enchanted Tiki Room** or the **Country Bears Jamboree.**

↓

Get out of Adventureland before the midafternoon

---

parade starts; it cuts the land off from the rest of the park.

↓

Ride the **Haunted Mansion.** Repeat until spooked (or cooled off).

↓

Stay indoors by seeing **Mickey's PhilharMagic.**

↓

Head to Tomorrowland and ride **Buzz Lightyear's Space Ranger Spin** and **Space Mountain.** Or get your fill of cheese at the **Walt Disney's Carousel of Progress.**

↓

You're probably getting a little tired by now, so sit down and enjoy the **Tomorrowland Transit Authority** (it's also a good ride to save until late in the evening before departure).

↓

Walk to New Fantasyland and take time to explore.

↓

Enjoy the **parade** and get in place 30 minutes in advance of the **fireworks.**

OR

If you have rides you missed or you'd like to repeat, the parade is a prime time for that except near the Castle in Fantasyland, which will shut down for safety then.

There are no big rides or shows on Main Street, just the park's best souvenir shops—call it Purchaseland. The 17,000-square-foot **Emporium,** the largest shop in the Kingdom, takes up almost the entire street along the left, and **Le Chapeau** (on the right, facing the square) is one of the only places where you can sew your name onto the back of one of those iconic mouse-ear beanies ($4–$8 per cap, which start at $15; also available at Fantasy Faire and Storybook Circus in Fantasyland). They resist stitching nicknames. **Crystal Arts** may have a small glass-blowing demonstration going. In the middle of Main Street, the east side has a little side street, **Center Street,** for caricaturists and silhouette artists, a Disney World institution since 1971 ($10 for two copies). If you're lucky, you'll catch a performance by the **Dapper Dans,** a real barbershop quartet that ambles down the street, or you'll be glad-handed by old Mayor Weaver, who'll remind you the election is approaching ("pull the lever and vote for Weaver!"); otherwise, you'll hear recorded stuff from "The Music Man." Those songs have a pedigree—at the opening ceremony of the Magic Kingdom, Meredith Willson, who wrote "Seventy-Six Trombones," led a 1,076-piece band up Main Street. A few people attend the daily **flag retreat ceremony** in Town Square at 5pm—no characters, just a brass band (the Main Street Philharmonic) and a member of the military or veteran selected from the guests—sometimes it works to volunteer at City Hall right after opening. Many guests find the ritual moving.

A variety of free **Main Street vehicles** trundle up the road at odd hours and on odd days (you never know when) and you can catch a one-way, stop-and-go ride on one: They include horse-drawn trolley cars—only if it's cool enough, and they wrap up by 1pm as not to overheat the animals—antique cars, jitneys, and a fire truck. They won't save time, of course, but you'll remember them forever. Pause at the end of Main Street, where the Plaza begins, for that snapshot of a lifetime in front of the 189-foot-tall Cinderella Castle. You have now essentially passed through three thresholds—the lagoon, the train tunnel, and Main Street, U.S.A.—that were designed to ease you into a world of fantasy.

Navigating Main Street: Important services cluster around the square. To the left of the park is **City Hall.** If you forgot to make reservations for sitdown meals or schedule other activities, this is the place for that. Here, or in front of the Emporium, a cast member hands out **free badges** for guests marking milestones: "Happy Birthday!", "1st visit!", "Happily Ever After" (for weddings and anniversaries), and "I'm Celebrating:" (for everything else). Wear a button and you'll receive bigger smiles (and maybe treats) all day. If they're not there, they're always at the Chamber of Commerce in City Hall.

Main Street is the only way in or out of the park, which fosters a sense of suspense, but just as surely creates bottlenecks **at parade time.** If you need to leave the park then, cut through the Emporium or though the temporary **bypass** that opens on the Tomorrowland side. (While a new theater is being constructed on backstage space nearby, parade bypass traffic may be temporarily re-rerouted.)

Remembering Roy Disney

If Walt was the man with the dream, brother Roy was the guy with the checkbook. He was the first to go to Hollywood, repeatedly staved off bankruptcy, and unfailingly found money for Walt's crazy ideas, from cartoon shorts to full features to, finally, Disneyland. Although Walt died in 1966, before he could finish his so-called "Florida Project," Roy made it to the opening day, and he renamed it Walt Disney World in tribute. Having seen it through, he died only 3 months later. His statue is seated with Minnie Mouse in the middle of the square behind the flagpole, where he welcomes guests to Main Street in perpetuity.

Walt Disney World Railroad ★★★ RIDE   The prominence of a railway is no accident; the concept of Disneyland grew out of Walt's wish to build a train park across the street from his Burbank studios. The train, which runs all day, takes about 25 minutes and encircles the park, ducking through Splash Mountain (you'll see its two-story riverboat through a window), stopping first in Frontierland and then passing through apparent wilderness to Fantasyland before returning here. The best seats are on the right, and you can go around as many times as you want without getting off. You'll see a few robotic dioramas of Indian encampments and wild animals, and also some backstage areas—following the tunnel after the Main Street station (it's the passage through the Pirates of the Caribbean show building), the train crosses a road; look right to find the yellow line painted on the ground. This is the border that tells cast members when they're out of view and can safely come out of character. *Tip:* Ride during the day because it frequently closes down at 8pm.

Sorcerers of the Magic Kingdom ★ ACTIVITY   In the **Fire Station** (Engine Co. 71, after the year the park opened) you'll find the Recruiting Station for Sorcerers of the Magic Kingdom, an innovative scavenger hunt-type adventure that relies on hidden screens and sensors scattered around the park. You're given a free pack of five daily "spell cards" linked to Disney characters (Pinocchio's Sawdust Blast, Elsa's Icy Shield), and a map to locations of Portals spread throughout the park in spots such as shop windows and quiet corners. When you hold up a spell card at a Portal, your animated spell amusingly beats back the villains (it's fun to watch, say, portly Governor Ratcliffe from "Pocahontas" get swamped by posies from Flower from "Bambi"). If you pick some up—the ones marked with a black lightning bolt are prized as collectibles—you must activate your game the same day or you won't be given more another day. Although it is cool, Sorcerers is best saved for after you have enjoyed everything else since it often takes a while to complete.

Harmony Barber Shop ★ ACTIVITY   The one-room shop on the square (9am–6pm; haircuts: $19 adults, $18 kids 12 and under, beards or bangs $7) overseen by portraits of George Washington and Teddy Roosevelt trims some 700 pates a week and does special requests, such as shaving Mickey onto scalps or combing in clear gel with either "Pixie Dust" or "Pirate

Dust" (ssh—it's the same thing). They're experts at first haircuts, which come with a baby mouse ears cap reading "My First Haircut," a Certificate of Bravery, and wrappings of your child's first trimmings for posterity ($25). You can make an appointment at ℂ **407/WDW-PLAY** [939-7529], and it takes walk-ins but does book up.

Town Square Theater ★★ CHARACTER GREETING   Beat the heat here, at two character meet-and-greet areas. On the right, meet Mickey Mouse dressed as a magician (get a Fastpass+ for him if you're a big fan), and on the left, meet a selection of other characters (cameos of who are currently available are pictured on the wait time sign). You can also come here for **MagicBand** maintenance. This building is slightly larger than the others on Main Street because it was designed to block anachronistic sightings of the original wing of the Contemporary Hotel.

Cinderella Castle ★★★ LANDMARK   The recently renovated park nucleus in front, known as "the Hub," centers on **"Partners,"** the statue of Walt and Mickey by the esteemed Disney sculptor Blaine Gibson, ringed by attending statues of supporting characters; the original stands in Disneyland.

Then there's the castle: 189 feet (58m) tall from the surface of the water in its ornamental moat. No two Disney castles are identical; the one in California, Sleeping Beauty Castle (notice that neither castle's name has a possessive ('s), is about half as tall as this. The skin of this one, it's strange to learn, is made not of stone but of fiberglass and plastic. The story there is that WDW's builders, who based its profile on an amalgam of French castles, implored local lawmakers to let them try something experimental, and the structure, buttressed with steel and concrete, has survived decades of hurricanes and baking heat. Look at its top. Bricks there are sized smaller to give a sense of distance, and even the handrails are just 2 feet tall to make the spires seem higher. Within the breezeways (closed during shows on the forecourt), don't miss the five expressive **mosaics** of hand-cut glass depicting the story of the glass slipper. They were designed by Dorothea Redmond, who also designed sets for *Gone with the Wind*. Over each entrance, you'll see the Disney family coat of arms. Genealogists contest whether they're correct, but there is

---

Windows on Disney Legends Past

Notice the **names painted on the windows** of the upper floors along Main Street. Each one represents a high-ranking Disney employee who helped build or run the park. Several, such as the one for Reedy Creek Ranch Lands, are winks at the dummy companies Walt Disney set up in the 1960s so that he could buy cheap swampland without tipping off landowners to his purpose. Everyone's window relates in some way to his or her life's work. Walt Disney gets two windows: the first one, on the train station facing outside the park, and the last, above the Plaza restaurant facing the Castle; designers liken the first-and-last billing to the opening credits of a movie. Notice that former CEO Michael Eisner, whose influence is generally resented, did not get a window.

unintended accuracy here unbeknownst to Walt: His ancestor was imprisoned in a castle. Researchers recently found graffiti left by Disney's English ancestor Edward Disney when he was imprisoned in Warwick Castle in 1642 for defending King Charles I. (He survived. Amusingly, that castle is now run by Disney competitor Merlin Entertainments, which runs Legoland.) Look for a wire that connects the Castle with a building in Tomorrowland; during the nightly fireworks, as she has done since 1985, that homicidal pixie Tinker Bell zips down the line, flying 750 feet at 15mph. There is no ride inside the Castle, but there is a princess makeover salon, **Bibbidi Bobbidi Boutique** (from $60 not including a dress; boys get a "Knight Package" for $20), and massively popular restaurant, **Cinderella's Royal Table,** and a sole overnight VIP suite, once an office for phone operators. Thirty-five feet beneath the Castle, Walt Disney himself is kept cryogenically frozen, awaiting eventual re-animation in a steel-lined, temperature-controlled chamber. (I'm just kidding about that. He was definitely cremated and is buried in Glendale, California, with his family.)

Mickey's Royal Friendship Faire ★ SHOW   Mickey's throwin' a friendship party, and everyone's invited. The chief Disney characters (plus the leads of *Frozen*, *Tangled*, and *The Princess and the Frog*) dance and sing in a 20-minute floor show in the Castle forecourt capped by a few flares. See the Times Guide or the schedule posted by the stage. Standing here can be hot, but the uplifting theme song is toe-tapping indeed and the "NextGen" character costumes are extremely cool: Olaf can talk out of one side of his mouth, and Mickey's nose wiggles as he speaks. If the stage is wet, they'll abbreviate the show, but the characters still come out to wave at the kids. *Tip:* Get close if your kids are little. It's rude to put your kid on your shoulders and block everyone's views behind, but people do it.

Adventureland

As you enter Adventureland from the Plaza, notice how the music gradually changes from the perky pluck of Main Street to the rhythms of Adventureland. Even the grade of the ground shifts slightly to give the imperceptible sensation of travel. Such shifts in drama are integral to the Disney method of park design.

Swiss Family Treehouse ★★ ACTIVITY   The Swiss who? You're forgiven if you don't know *The Swiss Family Robinson* (1960), a shipwrecked clan that survives using salvage, and you're also forgiven if you lack the will to take 15 minutes to clamber up the 62 stairs and catwalks to inspect the ingenuity of their arboreal island home. It's as if the Robinsons have just popped out for a coconut: The waterwheel system is sending rain through a tangle of bamboo channels, fruit is on the dinner table, and someone's bed is looking tempting. The tree is made of concrete and steel, and its 330,000 plastic leaves were attached by hand. Try doing this one at night, when you can enjoy the flicker of the lanterns and faint chatter of tourists far below. This attraction is the last of its breed—all the ones in other parks have been Tarzan-ized.

Jungle Cruise ★★★ RIDE   The delightful, G-rated excursion was one of the world's first rides based on a movie. The slow-going boat tour was created for Disneyland's 1955 opening to capitalize on the True-Life Adventures nature films. Like so many of Walt Disney's ideas, the 9-minute trip was intended to give guests a whirlwind tour of the planet's wonders. The ride no longer strives to teach you anything, hence vague descriptions of locals as "the natives" and a religious ruin identified as the Shirley Temple—great for kids, but not what you'd call documentary. This is the ride where over a dozen Indian elephants wash together in a pool, one of the seminal spectacles of a Disney visit. The jokes are unabashedly Eisenhower-era: Near the gorillas, you're told, "If you're wearing anything yellow, try not to make banana noises." In 1971, *The New York Times* sniffed that what distressed it about the Jungle Cruise was "the squandering of so much effort and technical ingenuity on cheap tricks and an inane script." Lighten up, Grey Lady; it's a goof! Boats are safely guided by paddles that slot into a narrow channel in the stream. The water is dyed to keep you from spotting that. Seats in the middle are often exposed to the harsh sunlight. *Strategy:* Dinnertime seems to be a sweet spot for thinner crowds, and riding in the dark adds a lot.

Magic Carpets of Aladdin ★ RIDE   If you haven't noticed, toddlers abound, and this flying carousel suits their low thrill thresholds. This one is a less-crowded alternative to Fantasyland's Dumbo, but unlike Dumbo, a family of four can ride—there are two rows of seats on each "carpet." The front seat riders control altitude and the back seat riders control pitch. One of the golden camels on the sidelines spits a thin stream of water on passersby. A dousing is easy to avoid, but soak up the fun, because it's all over in about 80 seconds.

Walt Disney's Enchanted Tiki Room ★★★ SHOW   In the 1950s, Walt Disney developed a Frankenstein-like obsession with developing robots

---

Fitting into the Disney Culture

Disney has a culture all its own that visitors must learn to respect. Working at Disney World isn't like getting a job at the bank. Many "cast members" live and breathe the brand and moved from other parts of the country to be a part of it despite the long hours and less-than-princely pay. Be alert to the fact that many of them identify personally with the Disney Way (it exists—new hires attend a course called Traditions at a thing called Disney University). Cast members are often uncomfortable with anything that carries a hint of being negative. Don't ask how long a ride will be broken—they won't tell you so as not to disappoint. They also won't tell you If they don't know something; instead, they'll tell you they'll find out for you or send you to someone else. Try to get them to point at something—they won't use a single finger, which is seen as rude, but they'll use two fingers or the whole hand. And for heaven's sake, no cussing! That code is technically meant to apply only to cast members, but the unspoken cultural expectation is that you follow it, too. The flip side of this is that if something goes wrong with your visit, they take immense pride in working to make it right and make your vacation a positive memory.

to replace living actors, and as a first stab at lifelike technology, he had his staff create a little mechanical bird. That turned into the concept for a restaurant full of them, chattering away, which was mocked up on Stage 3 at the Disney Studios. "It was kind of an ugly scene," said songwriter Dick Sherman, who was asked to fix it by writing a song for them instead. This precious show, which takes 10 minutes, is the result—birds sing the catchy "In the Tiki Tiki Tiki Tiki Tiki Room" and wow 'em with robotics. To 1963 crowds, it was the electrifying future, but today, it's merely endearing. Guests sit in the round, on benches, in an air-chilled Polynesian room and watch the ceiling and walls come alive with chattering, bickering, warbling birds that fit several national stereotypes and perform vaudeville-style ditties in quick succession. Add some animated flowers and magically harmonizing totem poles, followed by a pleasing mist and rain outside the windows, and you've got a cherished mood piece. When you're in the waiting area, the lines to the right, near the waterfall, enable you to see a little more action. Though the roof looks like old straw, it's actually shredded aluminum. *Tip:* The goliath tiki statues located across the walkway are equipped to squirt water on squealing children on hot days.

Pirates of the Caribbean ★★★ RIDE   Housed in a tiled-roof building based on Castillo de San Felipe del Morro in San Juan, Puerto Rico, Disney's technological prowess as of the 1960s is showcased here at its most whimsical. I call this indoor boat float the quintessential Disney ride, so it's probably no coincidence that it was the last Disneyland attraction Walt had a hand in designing, even though he conceived it as a walk-through wax museum. With 65 Audio-Animatronic figures in motion, Imagineer Marty Sklar said Walt envisioned the experience like a cocktail party: "You hear a little bit, but you don't get it all. You have to ride again." The more you ride, the more you see: the pirate whose errant gunshot ricochets off a metal sign across the room, the nervous barnyard animals, and the sumptuous theatrical lighting that makes everything look as if it has been imported from Jamaica. (The Johnny Depp robots have a lot more performance discipline than he does.) You'll see a few familiar scenes, including a slapstick sacking of an island port, a cannonball fight, and much drunken chicanery from ruddy-cheeked buccaneers. (Unsavory? Hey, even Captain Hook was obsessed with murdering a small boy.) In 2018, the infamous wench auction was revised into something that doesn't giggle at human trafficking—the voluptuous redhead who for 47 years was constantly being sold into sex slavery has switched sides. She now has a rifle, a name (Redd), and she's more interested in rum than anything else. There's a short, pitch-black drop near the beginning but you don't get wet—the concept, which you'd never grasp unless I told you, is that you're going back in time to see what killed the skeletons you pass in the first scene. Near the end of the 9-minute journey, the *pièce de résistance:* A lifelike Captain Jack Sparrow, having outlived his compatriots, is counting his treasure. Now, can someone please explain why people pronounce this name "Car-rib-BE-an" when we usually say "Car-RIB-be-an"? The shop at Pirates' exit is one of the better ones because it's big on buccaneer booty. **The Pirates League** salon (reservations: ℭ **407/939-2739**) gives pirate makeovers (temporary tattoos, stubble) to kids from $40. On the stage across the lane, catch the intermittent **Captain Jack Sparrow's Pirate Tutorial** (see Times Guide), where volunteer children are taught by lousy role model Sparrow (wobbly drunk, bleary with mascara) to parry with a sidekick using a floppy sword—and then flee. *Tip:* If you have neck issues, be prepared for jolts near the end of the ride as the boats pile up as they wait for the final dock.

A Pirate's Adventure—Treasures of the Seven Seas ★ ACTIVITY
Using one of five maps and a pentagon-shaped talisman card, you find stations and activate their tricks. One might reveal a pearl in a giant oyster, another fires a cannon, a third triggers a battle between two ships in a bottle, sinking one. When you finish, you get a reward card. It takes about 15 minutes and is ideal for small children.

Frontierland

When Disneyland was built in 1955, America had cowboy fever, and every young boy wore a Davy Crockett coonskin cap sold to them by Walt Disney's program on ABC. It was in this spirit that Frontierland was conceived.

Splash Mountain ★★★ RIDE   Part flume and part indoor "dark ride," it's preposterously fun, justifiably packed all the time, and proof of what Disney can do when its creative (and budgetary) engines are firing on all cylinders. You track the Br'er Rabbit character through some Deep South sets and down several plunges in Chick-a-Pin Hill—the most dramatic drop, five stories at 40mph (faster than Space Mountain), is plainly visible from the

---

classic **DISNEY**

Disney is always evolving, just as Walt intended it, but if the company were to alter these mainstays, it would be like desecrating pop culture itself. These core attractions are the Disney that Walt designed, as comforting as cookies and warm milk:

o **The Monorail**
o **Dumbo the Flying Elephant,** Fantasyland
o **Peter Pan's Flight,** Fantasyland
o **"it's a small world,"** Fantasyland
o **Walt Disney World Railroad,** Fantasyland, Frontierland, Main Street U.S.A.
o **Pirates of the Caribbean,** Adventureland
o **Jungle Cruise,** Adventureland

o **The Enchanted Tiki Room,** Adventureland
o **Country Bear Jamboree,** Frontierland
o **Tom Sawyer Island,** Frontierland
o **Liberty Square Riverboat,** Liberty Square
o **Haunted Mansion,** Liberty Square
o **Tomorrowland Speedway,** Tomorrowland
o **Walt Disney's Carousel of Progress,** Tomorrowland
o **Tomorrowland Transit Authority,** Tomorrowland
o **Main Street, U.S.A.**—Don't forget to stitch your name on a Mickey cap at Le Chapeau, Mouseketeer!

One of the tent poles of a day at the Magic Kingdom is the parade. When you see lines of masking tape appear on the ground, it's time to heed the crowd-control orders of the show's heralds. Each parade (there may be different versions in daytime, after dark, and for holiday parties) is a memorable production, with dozens of dancers and characters and up to a dozen lavish floats. The daytime **Festival of Fantasy Parade** is devoted to characters who might live in Fantasyland, and the **Move It! Shake It! Dance & Play It! Street Party** is aimed at getting your little one to boogie. Day parades generally go at 2 or 3pm while night parades, when they happen, tend to start just after dusk (sometimes twice); times for the evening parade vary, and they last for less than 15 minutes. While Main Street (especially its train station) has excellent viewpoints, I prefer to catch the parade from the western edge of Frontierland, where I'm closer to rides. *Tips:* If you want to catch only one parade, see the second one of the day, which is generally cooler and less crowded. During parades, the lines for many kiddie rides (especially those in Fantasyland) and character greetings thin. Once it ends, attractions nearest the route tend to be inundated with bodies—a bypass was recently carved behind the Tomorrowland side of Main Street. Also, the route is essentially impassible from 5 minutes before until just afterward, so don't get trapped in Adventureland during one.

outside. You will get wet, especially from the shoulders up and particularly in the front seats, but are not likely to get soaked because boats plow most of the water out of the way. I never tire of this 11-minute journey because it's so full of surprises, including room after room of animated characters (as many as Pirates has), seven drops large and small, a course that takes you indoors and out, and some perfectly executed theming that begins with the gorgeous outdoor courtyard queue strung with mismatched lanterns at many heights. You'll see Chip 'n' Dale's houses there, and hear them chatter to each other from within. *Strategy:* Get an afternoon Fastpass+ for this one, because it's deservedly one of the most adored rides on the planet. The line can as much as double when things get steamy. If your kid is too short to ride, cast members usually dispense free "Future Splash Mountaineer" cards that go a long way toward drying tears. And try not to put your hands up when you do the drop—it spoils the souvenir photo for whoever is sitting behind you.

Big Thunder Mountain Railroad ★★ RIDE   Here we have another Disney thrill mountain, a 2½-acre runaway-train ride that rambles joltingly through steaming, rusty Old West sets. Consider it the closest thing to a standard adult coaster in the Magic Kingdom, although it's not something that will make you dizzy or scared. Top speeds hit only 30mph, and there are no loops or giant drops, just circles, jiggles and humps. Listen for the voice of the old prospector in the boarding area; generations of American kids have imitated him as he warns, "This here's the wildest ride in the wilderness!" *Tips:* Seats in the back give a slightly wilder ride because front cars spend a lot of time waiting for the rear cars to clear hills. Tall riders should cross their ankles to

Splash Mountain's Uncomfortable Origin

You may agree that it's odd that Disney chose to build Splash Mountain since it's based on a movie that's not even available for sale in the United States: *Song of the South* (1946). The movie has long been criticized for its racist overtones—Adam Clayton Powell called the film "an insult to minorities" and some people bristle at the ride's minstrel-like characters. Disney knew racism was an issue, because for this ride it eliminated humans of any color, including the film's narrator, a kindly ex-slave named Uncle Remus.

avoid a knee-bashing against the seats in front of them. Chickens can watch their loved ones ride from the overlook on Nugget Way, near the ride's exit.

Walt Disney World Railroad, Frontierland Station ★★★ RIDE   Between Splash and Big Thunder mountains is a stop for the trains, which are pulled by one of four steam engines built between 1916 and 1928 and operated in the Yucatan before coming here. They take you to Fantasyland, then the foot of Main Street, and back here in 20 minutes.

Tom Sawyer Island ★★ ACTIVITY   Across Rivers of America, you'll find a place where you can roam the step-free Old Scratch's Mystery Mine without a guide, cross wooden suspension bridges, and pretend to defend Fort Langhorn with rifles rigged with weak recordings of gunfire—the fort is made of fiberglass logs; the wooden version in Disneyland rotted. The island is a great destination to explore, work off energy, and escape the crush—one of the only places in the park where your kids' imagination will have true free rein. You can reach it only by taking the platform boats that leave from the vicinity of Big Thunder Mountain, which makes it a blessed place to escape crowd control but also a time devourer. Don't be in a hurry, because you'll wait for the pontoon in both directions. They only fit 50 passengers at a time and you have to stand in the sun, so it helps to have decent balance. The island closes at dusk. *Tips:* There is an ice cream-and-soda stand there, Aunt Polly's, but it's rarely open; sit on its porch and watch the Liberty Belle and Haunted Mansion across the water. There are water fountains and washrooms, but overall it's pretty rustic—it's a great spot for a picnic.

Country Bear Jamboree ★★ SHOW   An opening-day attraction, one of the last to survive, the Jamboree is a 10-minute vaudeville-style revue that, at one moment, has 18 Audio-Animatronic bears, a raccoon, and a buffalo head singing country music together. Some kids, particularly pre-Ks, are enthralled by the dopey-looking robots, which appear for a verse or two of a saloon song, and then are retracted away. Other kids, and many adults, are powerfully bored. It's nice to sit, but don't wait more than 20 minutes for it unless you're hankerin' to see a vintage Disney museum piece.

Frontierland Shootin' Arcade ★ ACTIVITY   A simple activity built from a common 1950s conceit: Fire laser sights at an Old West diorama rigged with plenty of amusing gags. Bull's-eyes spring crooks from tiny jails, activate runaway mine carts, and coax skeletons from their Boot Hill graves. The $1 price buys 35 "shots," enough for a good shooter to trigger most of the tricks.

Liberty Square

Check out the replica of the real Liberty Bell, under the Liberty Tree. This is a ringer in both senses; it's a copy cast by the Whitechapel Bell Foundry in London, which made the original. Such authentic touches abound: The Liberty Tree, strung with 13 lanterns to signify the 13 colonies, is actually two live oaks one of them found 8 miles away on Disney property, that were partially filled with concrete and grafted together: a pretty Frankentree. That wavy brown stripe down the sidewalk? It represents the poop that flowed in our streets before the advent of sewage systems. Window shutters are mounted at an angle to simulate the leather hinges the real colonialists used, and a few times a day (check the Times Guide), they swing open for one of two versions of **Great Moments in American History,** 10-minute skits in which the Muppets retell stirring moments from the textbooks—but only the American parts—and butcher them in the process.

The Haunted Mansion ★★★ RIDE   One of the park's largest and most intricate rides opened with the park in 1971, and fans are in love with it—many of them can recite the script verbatim ("I am your host…your *ghost* host!"). The outdoor queue area passes funny gravestones, some of them interactive and some carved with in-jokes and the names of Imagineers—keep an eye on the last one with the female face, because it keeps an eye on you. Once you're inside, you enter the famous "stretching room." This dark chamber with a diabolical disembodied voice freaks out tots. But it's the scariest part of the experience, and a fortitude test for children—one of my earliest life memories is of begging my mother to take me out of the line (she did, and there's still an escape route if you need it). But if kids get through that, the rest is cake (literally—the undead, oddly, are throwing a birthday celebration inside). Be on the far side of the stretching room to be the first to the boarding

---

App's Entertainment!

Sick of using your smartphone for so much at Walt Disney World? You must be old. Sit this one out, old timer: Walt Disney World has introduced Play Disney Parks, a free app (separate from MDX) that detects where you are in the parks and unlocks achievements, triggers something to happen in the queue (at Peter Pan, causing a tiny Tinker Bell to shimmy in her lantern), or opens themed games you can play while you're waiting in line. Some of the trivia questions are about as challenging as a two-piece puzzle, but the video games take more skill. Score well enough and you may even be rewarded with a pass to the front of the line. But you'd better make sure the other people in your group want to play, too, because some games require multiple players and won't function in single-player mode, and you can only rack up achievements if you're 13 or older. It's almost enough to make you forget you've been in line for an hour—until your battery goes dead before noon.

zone. As spook houses go, the 8-minute trip is decidedly merry: All the ghosts seem to want to do is party. Passengers ride creepingly slow "doom buggy" cars linked together on an endless loop, no seat belts required—the proprietary system is called OmniMover. Although there are lots of glow-in-the-dark optical illusions, there are no unannounced shocks or gotchas. The climax, a ghost gala in a cavernous graveyard set, is impossible to soak up in one go, so you may want to visit several times to catch the murderous back story revealed in the attic scene. (*One fun tip:* The singing headstone with the broken head is voiced by the same guy who did Tony the Tiger for Frosted Flakes.) The warehouse-like "show building," where most of the ride is contained, is cleverly disguised behind Gracey Mansion's facade. Kids under 7 must ride with someone 14 or older. Don't miss the **Memento Mori** shop devoted to the giggly ghouls—you can take a zombified photo of yourself ($20). *Strategy:* On busy days, lines can be the scariest part, so try going—bwah-ha-ha-ha!— after the sun goes down.

The Hall of Presidents ★★★ SHOW Following a historical, wide-angle film, Audio-Animatronic versions of the U.S. presidents crowd awkwardly onstage, nodding to the audience, and several in turn spout homilies about democracy, unity, and other satisfying nuggets. The current president reaffirms his official oath of office while "the idea of a president" is celebrated. It's as lacking in substance as it has been since wowing first-day visitors in 1971. Although audiences don't realize it, figures were created with historical accuracy; if the president didn't live in an era of machine-made clothing, for example, he wears a hand-stitched suit. The cavalcade of important names is enough to stir a little patriotism in the cockles of the darkest heart—and sometimes, partisan groans. This, too, shall pass. Focus instead on the pluck of American technical wizardry—Lincoln even rises from a sitting position to address the audience, as he did when the show began, starring only him, at the World's Fair in 1964. Bank about 25 minutes to see it, plus the (rare) wait—unlike Lincoln, you'll be seated for the whole show.

Liberty Square Riverboat ★★ RIDE The 17-minute ride around Tom Sawyer Island, which departs on the hour and half-hour and has little seating, makes for a relaxing break, and it's not unusual to see Florida water birds on the journey, which passes a few mild (and mildly stereotypical) dioramas of Indian camps. The top deck offers views but a deafening whistle, and mid-deck has a good look at that hardworking paddle. The bottom is where sailors work the levers that make the honest-to-goodness steam engine run. Fight the urge to praise them for their steering ability—the boat's on a track. *Tip:* As you board, ask a cast member if you may pilot the boat. The captain may invite you to turn the wheel and sound the whistle—and you may come away with a riverboat pilot's license.

Fantasyland

Fantasyland is the heart of Walt Disney World because it contains many of the characters that make the brand beloved, and a few years ago it was expanded;

the section through the interior arches is commonly called New Fantasyland, which itself contains a sub-land, **Storybook Circus.** Most of its attractions are tame cart rides that wouldn't be out of place at a carnival if they weren't so meticulously maintained. But the energy is first class. A lot of people must agree, because lines are long. For shorter waits, race here first thing in the morning or arrive after dinner, when little ones start tiring out. Fastpassing is also widespread. Little would-be princesses should not miss **Castle Couture,** beside Mickey's PhilharMagic, where every major princess' outfit is sold ($60) with optional slippers and accessories.

"it's a small world" ★★★ RIDE   Slow and sweet as treacle, the king of Fantasyland rides is a 15-minute boat trip serenaded by the Sherman Brothers' infectious theme song (bet you already know it). On the route, nearly 300 dancing-doll children, each pegged to his or her nation by genial stereotypes (Dutch kids wear clogs, French kids can-can), chant the same song, and everyone's in a party mood. In the tense years following the Cuban Missile Crisis, this ride's message of human unity was a balm, and in these rooms, millions of toddlers have received their first exposure to world cultures (including yours truly—and then I grew up to be a travel writer). Those 4 and under love this because there's lots to see and nothing threatening, but by about age 11, kids reverse their opinions and think its upchuck factor is higher than Mission Space's. The ride's distinctive look came from Mary Blair, a rare female Imagineer. Walt originally wanted the kids to sing their own national anthems, but the resulting cacophony was too disturbing; instead, a ditty was written in such a way that it could be repeated with changing instrumentation, and so that its verse and chorus would never clash. And repeated it is, some 1,600 times over a 16-hour operating day. The robo-pageant was whipped up in 11 months for the 1964 World's Fair in New York as a partnership with PepsiCo and UNICEF. Pepsi was about to reject the concept, but Joan Crawford, who was on the board of directors, halted the meeting, stood up, and declared, "We are going to do this!" That was a masterstroke—Walt somehow convinced American corporations to subsidize construction of attractions in his own theme park. His company still depends on that. And, gutsier yet, now it only serves Coke. After the Fair, where it cost $1 for adults to ride, the original was moved to Disneyland. ***Strategy:*** If you're not sure whether meeting characters will wig out your kids, take them on this as a test run. Be in line on the quarter-hour, when the central clock unfolds, strikes, and displays the time with moveable type. No seat is better than another—every passenger will be humming that song in their sleep, and possibly in their graves—but the wait is shortest after the fireworks show ends, so you don't need to Fastpass+ it.

Peter Pan's Flight ★★★ RIDE   This iconic indoor ride is also unique because its pirate-ship vehicles (maximum capacity: three adults with a child lap-sitter) hang from the ceiling, swooping gently up, down, and around obstacles, while the scenes below are executed in forced perspective to make it feel like you're high in the air. The effect is charming and—okay, I'll say it—magical. This is the ride I loved most as a small child, a feeling that is by no means unique. The aerial view of Edwardian London is especially memorable, and it's hard for tots not to feel a shimmy of excitement when they fly between the sails of a pirate ship. *Strategy:* The wait for this slow loader can be 2 hours and up, so, considering it takes only 2 minutes and 45 seconds, hit this one upon opening or arrange a Fastpass+. Thankfully the queue is now mostly in the air-conditioning.

Mickey's PhilharMagic ★ SHOW   The computer-animated, widescreen 3-D entertainment, which runs continuously, is honest Disney in the "Fantasia" mold: Classic characters, prominently Donald Duck, appear to a lush (and loud) soundtrack of Disney songs, while pleasant extrasensory effects such as scents and breezes blow to further convince you that what you're seeing is real. The pace is lively, and nearly everyone is tickled. You also get to enjoy air-conditioning for 12 minutes. The shop afterwards specializes in Donald Duck merchandise.

Prince Charming Regal Carrousel ★★ RIDE   Nice to see a prince get a little recognition around here! It's easy to enjoy one of the world's prettiest carousels. The 90-second ride was handmade in 1917 for a Detroit amusement park and it spent nearly 4 decades in Maplewood, New Jersey, before Imagineers rescued it, refurbishing it and the original organ calliope (although you'll hear prerecorded Disney songs instead). The horses, which rise up and down, are arranged so that the largest ones are on the outside. Cinderella's personal steed has a golden ribbon tied to its tail.

Princess Fairytale Hall ★★ CHARACTER GREETING   Meet and greet four of the most popular Princess characters, such as Cinderella, Tiana, Elna, or Rapunzel (Belle "lives" at her Enchanted Tales cottage). Little girls (mostly) wait in a reception hall that's dressed in stained glass and portraits of the royal ladies, and when it's time, they make their way, wide-eyed, to the individual meeting rooms. Cameras ready!

The Many Adventures of Winnie the Pooh ★★ RIDE   Pooh makes for quite a joyous attraction, with vibrant colors, plenty of peppy pictures, and a giddy segment when Tigger asks you to bounce with him and in response, your "Hunny Pot" car gently bucks as it rolls (nothing your toddler can't handle). The effects, such as a levitating dreaming Pooh, a room full of fiber-optic raindrops, and real smoke rings (front-row seats are best for experiencing that one), are the most advanced of the Fantasyland kiddie rides. The more I take this merry, 4-minute romp, the more I see poor Pooh as a junky for honey, since he spends much of his focus binging and having psychedelic dreams about getting more of the sweet stuff. Will someone please stage an intervention for this poor bear? This ride is not anyone's favorite, but it's a fine diversion.

Mad Tea Party ★ RIDE   Its conceit—spinning teacups on a platter of concentric turntables—has given the name to an entire genre of carnival "teacup" rides, in which each cup serves a steaming serving of nausea. How much you'll want to heave depends on whether you're riding with someone who can turn the central wheel and get your twirl on within the 90 seconds allotted. The first time you ride, it's emblematic, but for after that, it's ignorable furniture, like a hall table you pass on your way to the rest of the house.

Seven Dwarfs Mine Train ★★★ RIDE   Disney's newest mountain, circa 2014, is really more of a knoll, and a joyful little ride in contrast to the relatively dark movie that inspired it. The mine cart roller coaster, which replaced a circa-1971 Snow White ride told from the Queen's point of view, goes in and out of a hill containing the gem quarry dug by Snow White's diminutive landlords, whom you'll encounter "Heigh-Ho"-ing through a day's work. Carriages gently rock on pivots as you turn, much like a bassinette, but don't worry—this is Fantasyland, so this ride is unchallenging, with plenty of S-curves and humps but no loops or daredevil drops. Near the 2½–minute ride's conclusion, look right and peek into the windows of the dwarfs' cottage for a charming (but too-quick) glimpse of the last fateful moments of their leisure. *Tip:* It's too short and too cramped to appeal to thrill-seekers, but for maximum sensation, the back rows are dramatically better than the first rows. Forget getting a Fastpass+ if you're not staying at a Disney hotel; it books up weeks ahead, a victim of Disney's new Fastpass caste system.

Enchanted Tales with Belle ★★ CHARACTER GREETING   Here's a character meet-and-greet with a tech twist: In addition to the "Beauty and the Beast" heroine, who selects audience members to reenact one of her beloved stories—the one you can buy as two film versions—you encounter a thrillingly lifelike talking armoire, a fantastic Lumière figure, and, best of all, a trick with a miraculously transforming mirror that must be seen to be believed. There's no Beast, and the Belle that's here isn't the firebrand from the movie but someone as sweet and demure as a debutante. It takes a while to get in and about 30 minutes to finish once you have. Every child who wants a role in the story can have one (they just have to hold a prop and walk to the front on cue), and then they get a photo with Belle that their parents can buy later. Sorry, day visitors: Fastpasses vanish early, taken by Disney resort guests.

Dumbo the Flying Elephant ★★★ RIDE   Fascinatingly, in the 1941 film *Dumbo,* the stork delivers baby Dumbo almost exactly over the future site of Disney World, 30 years before it became a reality. The famous baby circus animal recently got a makeover, and now there are two copies of this sentimental ride, halving waits. After entering the Big Top, you get a pager (like the ones at the Cheesecake Factory!) and kids are let loose to wreak screaming havoc in an indoor play area until you're summoned for your turn on board. Back outside, you go round and round in 16 aerodynamic pachyderms whose elevation kids control with a joystick. Each car fits only two adults across, or an adult and two small kids. Standing here, witnessing the joy of ebullient little children being the most spirited you'll ever see little children be, is almost better than the ride. *Tips:* An original vehicle is on display in the Smithsonian, but there's a spare between the two rides here so you can pause for that prize snapshot without slowing things down. If your family is too

TIME IS MONEY: reducing waits

For a 9-hour day, you'll pay as much as $13.50 an hour to enjoy Walt Disney World. Maximize your time by minimizing waits with these priceless tips:

1. **Be there when the gates open.** The period before lunch is critical. Lines are weakest then, so it's a good time to cram the one or two rides you most want to do. *Pitfall:* Don't go to the one closest to the gates. Instead, head as far into parks as you dare. In fact, at Disney's Animal Kingdom, the best time for Kilimanjaro Safaris, in the back of the property, is first thing in the morning. The animals won't have bolted for shade yet and you can get a good look at them.

2. **If you don't have kids, save the slow rides for after dinner.** Disney World has an almost metaphysical ability to turn Momma's sweet little angel into a red-faced, howling, inconsolable demon. This meltdown usually happens in late afternoon, as the stress of the day exhausts children. By dinnertime, parents evacuate

their screaming brood. The lines at kiddie attractions such as Peter Pan's Flight, as tough as 2 hours in mid-day, shorten after bedtime.

3. **Fastpass+ first thing.** The sooner your three are scheduled and used, the sooner you can get your next one. Revise the boilerplate schedule Disney offers and move your reservations to as early as possible.

4. **Pray for rain.** In Florida, it usually strikes in mid-afternoon and lasts for less than an hour, but that's long enough for many guests to leave, which eases waits.

5. **If your kids allow it, skip the parade.** Lines at many of the most popular rides get shorter in the run-up to parade times, when the hordes pack the route in anticipation. Bank on thinner lines 30 minutes before and during showtime. It's often possible to hit two or three rides during the show.

6. **Come early or stay late.** If you're paying higher-than-normal rates to

large to fit in the same elephant (a phrase I never thought I'd write), Adventureland's Magic Carpets (p. 44) provide the same experience ride for four.

Under the Sea—Journey of the Little Mermaid ★ RIDE   As you travel in slow-moving shell vehicles for 6 gentle minutes, you retrace a truncated jukebox version of the film's plot, including dutiful reprises of "Part of Your World," "Poor Unfortunate Souls" (by an enormous Ursula), "Kiss the Girl," and most spectacularly, a big room full of fish jamming out to "Under the Sea." Nothing happens that would scare a kid. As rides go, it's acceptable and the Audio-Animatronics are fine, but it's not as transporting as you want it to be and it's unlikely to hook adults as much as small children. Nearby, kids get autographs from the underwater princess herself at **Ariel's Grotto,** and yes, there's a separate wait for that, so go ahead—make your choice.

Pete's Silly Sideshow ★★ CHARACTER GREETING   By the train station, meet four Disney stars under the Big Top, envisioned as carnival performers: Minnie Magnifique, Madame Daisy Fortuna, the Astounding Donaldo, and the Great Goofini. The waits to get autographs from the girls are often longer, but happily, it happens in the air-conditioning. If you're looking stay on Disney property, get some value back by availing yourself of Extra Magic Hours. Your Disney hotel will tell you which park is either opening early or closing late for the express use of its guests. Lines will be shorter during those hours.

7. **If the weather will be hot, Fastpass+ the water rides.** When it swelters, arrange a Fastpass+ for the water rides by midmorning, which should ensure a slot to ride when the heat peaks.

8. **Eat early.** Restaurants have lines, too, so avoid peak periods for meals. Eat at 11am, when many places open, and there will be light traffic until noon or so. The same goes for dinner: Schedule a reservation for around 4pm. Eating late in the parks doesn't work, because many restaurants close.

9. **Baby swap.** The parks have a system allowing both parents to ride with little additional waiting. After the whole family goes through the line, Dad can wait with Junior while Mom rides. When Mom's off, Dad can ride without waiting and Mom takes a turn watching Junior. For many people, that cuts the old waiting times in half. It's not available on kiddie rides because it's weird to watch Daddy ride those alone.

10. **Split up.** If you don't care if you all ride in the same car, a few thrill rides have lines for single riders. Use them and you'll shoot to the head of the pack, fill spare seats left by odd-numbered groups, ride within minutes of each other, and be back on the pavement in no time flat. Even on rides without dedicated single lines, solo riders should alert ride-loading attendants to their presence—doing so could shave long minutes off a wait.

11. **Fastpass+ something broken.** If a ride goes down in the evening, grab a Fastpass for it, because if it doesn't come back online by your appointment time, you'll get a free pass to use on almost any attraction in any park the next day.

for Mickey, he's at the Town Square Theater on Main Street, U.S.A. *Reminder:* All characters' appearance locations and times are printed on the Times Guide.

The Barnstormer ★ RIDE Fantasyland's kiddie coaster, which is all about giving small children a sense of excitement and accomplishment, invariably has a line, which is outdoors. The tangled track does a few swooping figure-eights and passes through a Goofy-shaped hole in a billboard, but takes scarcely more than a minute—less than half that if you subtract the time it takes to climb the hill. There are some cute touches, including ample evidence of Goofy's flying act having gone hilariously wrong. Believe it or not, this is the fastest ride in the Magic Kingdom.

Walt Disney World Railroad, Fantasyland Station ★★★ RIDE Board here for a round trip to the front gates at Main Street, U.S.A., then Frontierland, and finally back here in 20 minutes, all to a recorded narration that describes what you see along the way. Across the path, the train motif carries over to the **Casey Jr. Splash 'N' Soak Station,** a honking, chugging, wheezing, ringing collection of animal-packed circus railway cars where monkeys squirt seltzer, locomotives steam, elephants sneeze water through their trunks, and camels spit.

Tomorrowland

Tomorrowland is lighter on character appearances than other lands. A fun exception is the **Cosmic Dance Party,** held on the Rockettower Stage from about 5pm on. It's a chance for little ones to let off steam and mingle with a few characters. To the right of Space Mountain, you'll see a one-level bathroom structure that looks like it ought to contain something interesting. It once did: The Skyway, a gondola ride over the park, loaded here until 1999 (and unloaded in Fantasyland beside "it's a small world"). There are quiet places for sitting around it. The much-hated Stitch attraction, though, is now gone forever.

Tomorrowland Speedway ★ RIDE   Originally built in Disneyland at a time when freeways were considered tech breakthroughs and not a bane of life, this half-mile, self-driven jog of four-laned track is the first chance most kids will have to drive. These are Go-Karts with no juice, although the late Tom Carnegie calls the "race" and the gas-fired engines reek and snarl. Each vehicle carries two people, steers poorly but is guided by a rail, and won't go fast (about 7mph) no matter how much pedal meets metal. Though the queue can be blistering hot and the load process tedious, your puttering will end in about 5 minutes. *Strategy:* Mind the height restrictions—kids shorter than 54 inches can't go alone, a rule that sparks tantrums.

Space Mountain ★★★ RIDE   Walt Disney liked creating one landmark for every land. He called it the "weenie" that drew people in. Tomorrowland's weenie, and only 6 feet shorter than Cinderella Castle, is contained in that futuristic concrete-ribbed circus tent. Although it's a relatively tame indoor, carnival-style, steel coaster (top speed: barely 29mph), the near-total darkness and tight turns give your go-round (duration: 2½ min.) a panache that makes it one of the park's hotter tickets. Other worldwide versions are more thrilling, but there's something endearing about an original. *Strategy:* The wait is indoors. There are two tracks; the left-hand coaster (Alpha) and the right-hand one (Omega) are mirror images of each other, so there's no real difference except Fastpassers are sent to Omega. The front seat has the best view.

Tomorrow in Tomorrowland

The area beside Space Mountain is being prepared for **TRON Lightcycle Power Run,** a blockbuster roller coaster that consistently ranks as the most popular attraction at Shanghai Disneyland. On this thrill ride, illuminated vehicles are boarded like bicycles and are launched into a long swooping track beneath an undulating glass canopy. The coaster's footprint will extend over the railroad tracks into what was previously a backstage area. It's slated to open in 2021.

Buzz Lightyear's Space Ranger Spin ★★ RIDE   The "Toy Story" movies provide inspiration for a rambunctious 3-minute, slow-car ride that works like a shooting gallery. Passengers are equipped with laser guns and the means to rotate their vehicles, and it's their mission to blast as many targets as they can. That's easier said than done, since the aliens are spinning, bouncing, and turning, and your laser sight appears only intermittently as a blinking red light, but that's all part of the fun. You'll think you did well at 118,000 until you turn and see the kid who racked up 205,000. He must have known the secret: The farther away a target is, the more it's worth. Guess you'll have to re-ride.

Astro Orbiter ★★ RIDE   The gist is like Dumbo—an 80-second spin on an armature, you control height—except from three stories up, and with 12 toboggan-style rockets seating only two each. Usually, it takes too long, partly because you have to use an un-magical elevator, framed operational permit and all, to board and leave. At night, the view of an illuminated Castle could make it worth it. *Tip:* Beneath the ride, pick up the Metrophone for some gag messages.

Tomorrowland Transit Authority PeopleMover ★★★ RIDE   The tramlike second-story track, which boards under the Astro Orbiter at Rocket-tower Plaza, uses pollution-free "linear induction" magnetic technology to take a story-free scenic overview of the area's attractions. On a 13-minute round-trip with no stops, it coasts past some windows over the Buzz Lightyear ride and through the guts of Space Mountain, where you traverse the circum-ference over the Omega boarding area. You will also catch a too-fleeting glimpse of one of Walt Disney's original 1963 models for Progress City. The ride itself is historic: Walt Disney envisioned this system, originally called the WEDway PeopleMover, as a principal form of transportation for the resort. Sorry, Walt: They bought buses instead. *Tip:* Despite the reported fact that half of all visitors ride it at least once while they're here, there's almost never a wait. Do TTA at night, when Tomorrowland is illuminated in cobalts and greens.

Walt Disney's Carousel of Progress ★★ SHOW   They know it's an antique: They put Walt's name in the title as a sort of apology. But as a preboard-ing movie attests, Walt Disney loved this attraction—he created an earlier version with General Electric sponsorship for the 1964 World's Fair. It was later moved here, and appropriate to its underwriter, the message is a banquet of consumerist overtones about how appliances will rescue us from a life of drudgery. Walt's novel twist was that the stage remains stationary but the auditorium rotates on a ring past six rooms (four "acts" and one each for loading and unloading) of Audio-Animatronic scenes. You'll see a modern person's trivialization of daily life in 1904, 1927, and the 1940s, and an unspecified time that you could peg for 1989, what with Grandpa's breathless praise for laser discs and car phones. While our very white, very middle-class narrator (voiced by Jean Shepherd, the narrator of *A Christmas Story*) loafs with his dog across the ages, his wife does chores and gets mansplained, his mother festers, his daughter primps, and his son dreams of adventure. (Funny how a tribute to progress is riddled with obsolete gender stereotypes.) The Sherman Brothers, who wrote the repetitive ditty "There's a Great Big Beautiful Tomorrow" (they also wrote the songs for *Mary Poppins*) said they considered this to be Walt Disney's personal theme song. Set aside 25 minutes for the show, but it starts every 5 because the rotating theater allows endless refills, like the chamber of a revolver. As a relic from a more idealistic time, it's priceless, and here's hoping they never remove it, as is always the rumor. Another reason to see it: Despite the fact it has no living performers, it's billed as the longest-running stage show in the United States.

Monsters, Inc. Laugh Floor ★ SHOW   Like Turtle Talk with Crush at Epcot, it's a "Living Character" video show, about 15 minutes long, in which computer-animated characters on a giant screen interact with a theater full of people, singling humans out with a hidden camera for gentle ridicule. The animation looks as fluid as in the Pixar movies and is drawn from a cast of some 20 characters, but the three you'll see in your set will vary. The experience depends as much on the eagerness of your audience as on the improvisational skill of the (spoiler alert) hidden live actors doing the voices. Don't miss the gags in the preshow video-instruction room (the employee bulletin board warns against "Repetitive Scare Injury"). You'll probably find yourself more impressed by the canny technology than by the quality of the jokes, and sticklers for Disney orthodoxy are annoyed it isn't really set in the future. *Tip:* Sit in the rear or extreme sides of the auditorium to avoid being picked on.

Where to Eat in the Magic Kingdom

All locations will have a few vegetarian options, kids' meals, and all can accommodate special dietary requests (usually), albeit often at diminished quality. For info on the table-service restaurants that usually require reservations, see p. 61. Beer and wine is finally served in the Magic Kingdom, but only at sit-down restaurants and only with food. There's also a fruit stand across from the Little Mermaid ride in Fantasyland. (We've noted where mobile ordering is an option.)

THE MAGIC KINGDOM'S QUICK-SERVICE RESTAURANTS
The park, being a mass-appeal crowd-pleaser, does not support a menu that is as adventurous as its characters. Hope you like burgers!

LIGHTS after dark

A trip to Disney doesn't seem complete if you don't catch the nightly fireworks-and-projections show, **Happily Ever After,** held after dark; check the Times Guide. Although it's technically at least partially visible from anywhere, the most symmetrical view is from the Castle's front and Main Street, U.S.A. The 18-minute show is quite the slick spectacle—lights dim everywhere, even the ferry dock, and you can hear the soundtrack wherever you are. Areas around and behind the Castle are roped off to protect guests from falling cinders, and wide portions of the Hub are set aside for premium-paying guests, so arrive at least 30 minutes ahead or get shunted elsewhere by aggressive cast members. Fortunately, while you wait, about 15 minutes before (and after) the fireworks, the trippy and beautiful **Once Upon a Time** precision projection mapping show (14 minutes long) happens on Cinderella Castle. You have the option of purchasing $30 illuminated **"Made with Magic" mouse ears** that change color along with the show or using a free app, but few customers seem to use them. Off-season, rides begin closing as soon as fireworks start, and people start heading home; in summer, there are still hours left to play.

For the best views, Disney makes you shell out. It throws a nightly **Fireworks Dessert Party** with special viewing areas (sitting at Tomorrowland Terrace or standing in front of the Plaza Restaurant) starting an hour before showtime. For $59 to $79 adults and $35 to $47 kids in addition to the park entrance fee, you get all-you-can-eat pastries, ice cream, light beverages, and a primo vantage point. Naturally, it books up early (© **407/939-3463**). There's also the **Pirates and Pals Fireworks Voyage** out on Seven Seas Lagoon with basic snacks and appearances by Captain Hook and Smee (© **407/939-7529;** $72 adult, $43 kids 3–9).

At the very end of the night (well, most nights, but not all), about 30 minutes after the posted closing time, Cinderella Castle flashes with a dazzling rainbow of light. This is a **"Kiss Goodnight,"** something that isn't on the schedules but happens every 15 minutes, and it's a little like the Sandman at the Apollo, sweeping you out the door. Stick it out until you see one or two (the last one is an hour after closing time), because by then, escaping crowds will have thinned. Remember, you still have a monorail or a ferryboat and a parking tram to go.

Casey's Corner ★ AMERICAN   The hot dog-and-nachos joint facing the Castle is the only place to grab a counter-service meal around Main Street, U.S.A., but there is never enough seating. Dogs are nearly a foot long and piled embarrassingly high with choices including mac and cheese and chili. **Main Street, U.S.A.** Combo hot dog meals $10. Mobile ordering.

Plaza Ice Cream Parlor ★ ICE CREAM   Although hand-scooped ice cream is served, the specialty is the Kitchen Sink sundae served in Mickey's pants ($17, but it's big). Next door is a **Starbucks** with a queue like a roller coaster. **Main Street, U.S.A.** Desserts $5 to $6. Mobile ordering.

Sunshine Tree Terrace ★★★ ICE CREAM   Disney fans beeline to this kiosk for the Citrus Swirl, a wonderful blend of frozen OJ and soft-serve vanilla ice cream. The doe-eyed mascot is Orange Bird; Disney created it for the Florida citrus lobby, which sponsored this stand and the Tiki birds back in the 1970s. **Adventureland.** Beverages and desserts $5 to $6.

Aloha Isle Refreshments ★★★ ICE CREAM   A favorite Disney treat: Pineapple "Dole Whip" soft serve. Or put your Dole Whip in a Pineapple Float. Or just get a spear of fresh pineapple. **Adventureland.** Dole Whips $5 to $7. Mobile ordering.

Tortuga Tavern ★★ MEXICAN   Turkey legs, chipotle spare ribs, and hot dogs are served; it has a large, sheltered seating area. **Adventureland.** Combo meal $9 to $12.

Pecos Bill Tall Tale Inn and Cafe ★★★ AMERICAN   Southwest salad with lots of iceberg lettuce, fajitas, and nachos, in spacious, air-conditioned dining halls. Churros, too! **Frontierland.** Combo meal $13 to $16. Mobile ordering.

Columbia Harbour House ★★★ AMERICAN   At this indoor counter-service spot, order fat sandwiches, grilled salmon, lobster rolls, and chicken pot pie, plus sides such as chowder ($7), then take them upstairs where it's quiet. **Liberty Square.** Combo meal $10 to $15. Mobile ordering.

Pinocchio Village Haus ★★ AMERICAN/ITALIAN   Vaguely Italian food (flatbreads, chicken Parmesan sandwiches, pizza, and so on) adjoining "it's a small world," with a few tables in the air-conditioning overlooking the snazzy loading area. **Fantasyland.** Combo meal $10 to $13. Mobile ordering.

The Friar's Nook ★ AMERICAN   Window service with outdoor seating for tater tots done Greek or Buffalo style, or hot dogs with chips. **Fantasyland.** Snacks $9 to $11.

Gaston's Tavern ★ AMERICAN   Behind the amusing Gaston fountain, you'll find some indoor, only-at-Disney treats. The cinnamon rolls are as big as cinder blocks; the baguette sandwiches limp. LeFou's Brew is Fantasyland's (not very successful) answer to Harry Potter's Butterbeer: frozen apple juice with a lightly fruity foam. Get it in a regular cup for $6, or $13 in a plastic stein. **Fantasyland.** Sandwiches $10.

Cosmic Ray's Starlight Cafe ★★★ AMERICAN   The best choice for indoor Quick Service on this end of the park, it does burgers, BBQ pork sandwiches, and chicken (both sandwich and rotisserie)—choose the "bay" that serves your choice. It's distinguished by regular lounge-act shows by Sonny Eclipse, a long-running Audio-Animatronic character. The panorama of the Castle is sublime; it's my favorite lunchtime view. **Tomorrowland.** Combo meal $10 to $15. Mobile ordering.

The Lunching Pad ★ AMERICAN   Tiny window-service zone with exposed seating. **Tomorrowland.** Hot dogs $8. Mobile ordering.

The Tomorrowland Terrace ★ INTERNATIONAL   Shaded but not indoors, it faces the Castle and only opens when things are fairly busy. The

SAVING ON PARK munchies

If you plan to buy all your food at the park, sticking strictly to counter-service meals is the cheapest way to go. But considering you'll pay $10 to $13 each for a counter-service sandwich, plus at least $3.40 for a medium-size soft drink—the going rate in the Orlando parks—even that way, a family of four can easily spend $70 on every meal! Don't be Goofy—save money! Besides eating off premises, here's how:

o **Order the kid's meal.** If it's counter service, how will they know it's really for you?

o **Subtract unwanted combo items.** Although counter-service restaurants make the menu appear like it's mostly combo meals, it's an unpublicized fact that you may eliminate unwanted items from adult selections and save money. Dropping fries or other bundled side dishes can save about $2.25. For carrot sticks!

o **Pack a little food of your own.** Park security usually looks the other way if you bring a soft lunchbag-size cooler (hard-sided ones will be rejected). Or just tote sandwiches in plastic bags. If your lodging has a freezer, keep juice boxes in there; they'll be thawed by lunch.

o **Economize with an all-you-can-eat meal.** Character meals (p. 220) give good value because they serve limitless food; the breakfast ones are cheapest. A big lunch can last you until after you leave the park.

o **Skip table-service meals, or plan them strategically.** They can chomp as much as 90 minutes out of your touring time. Do that twice and you've lost a third of your day. A park that could be seen in 1 day would require 2, doubling costs. If you want a sit-down meal, do it at lunch, when prices are often lower than at dinner. Eat around 11am, when crowds are lighter. Also, if you don't show up for Disney reservations, you're docked $10—assess whether your kids will truly have energy for an evening table-service meal if you schedule one.

o **Adults may order cheaper and smaller kids' meals.** No one will stop them.

o **Snack on fruit.** Each park has at least one fruit stand ($1.70/piece).

o **Seek out the turkey legs.** This vanishing species is giant (1½ pounds, from 45-pound turkeys), salty, and costs around $12. They taste so good because they're injected with brine before cooking for 6 hours. Just don't think about the hormones it takes to grow a 45-pound bird. Or a 5-foot-tall mouse.

o **Order drinks without ice.** Fountain soda is dispensed cold to prevent foaming. It's chilling how much ice is in a Disney Coke.

o **Order water for free.** It comes in a regular-size cup.

o **Stretch meals.** A few places have a fixings bar. Raid it.

menu covers the basics: burgers, sandwiches, Caesar salad, chicken strips. **Tomorrowland.** Meals $10 to $13. Mobile ordering.

THE MAGIC KINGDOM'S TABLE-SERVICE RESTAURANTS

This is the most popular theme park in the world, so getting a seat can be competitive (and it requires a credit card) and the wait staff is almost always running around. Three restaurants offer breakfast reservations, which may let you get in line for rides before the official park opening. Some restaurants *may* accept walk-ins in mid-afternoon. Taking them clockwise around the park:

Tony's Town Square Restaurant ★★ ITALIAN   Loosely themed on the Italian restaurant scene from *Lady and the Tramp* (there's a fountain of the two doe-eyed dogs), it's loud, not romantic. To repeat Tramp's spaghetti-and-meatball sharing gesture (kindly don't use your nose like he did), you'll pay $22 a plate. It does chicken Parmesan, cannelloni, shrimp scampi, pizzas, pork tenderloin, and strip steak, plus beer and wine. **Main Street, U.S.A.** Main courses $19 to $32.

The Crystal Palace ★★★ AMERICAN   Under an airy Victorian-style skylight canopy redolent of an 1853 New York City world's exhibition, Winnie the Pooh greets diners at what's probably the prettiest in-park restaurant in all of Walt Disney World. The refined air doesn't stop Pooh and his buddies (Tigger, Eeyore, Piglet) from jamming the aisles with a conga line. Slightly smaller than many other character dining locations, you're likely to get more face time with the characters here. This restaurant's been open since Day One and offers three daily all-you-can-eat buffets of changing, crowd-pleasing standards. There's also a make-your-own-sundae bar. Prices are lowest at breakfast (the best time anyway, since you have the rest of your day free) and scale up; beer and wine cost extra. **Main Street, U.S.A.** All three meals: buffet $34 to $47 adults, $20 to $28 children.

The Plaza Restaurant ★ AMERICAN   What's special about this restaurant (different from the Plaza Ice Cream Parlor) is its view. Situated at the end of Main Street facing Cinderella Castle, it focuses on sandwiches, burgers, and meatloaf, which are served with broccoli slaw, homemade chips, or french fries. Add soup for $8. It also serves beer and wine with meals and ice cream sundaes and cheesecake from the shop next door. **Main Street, U.S.A.** Main courses $15 to $21.

Skipper Canteen ★★ AMERICAN   The fun concept: The proprietors are boat captains from the Jungle Navigation Co., Ltd., across the path, which explains why they tell such stomach-churning jokes. ("Here's your Coke Zero," you're told as they set down an empty glass.) The menu is slightly more daring than the usual (falafel, shu mai dumplings, whole fried fish) and includes beer and wine. You stand a chance of getting in without a reservation. **Adventureland.** Main courses $19 to $32.

The Diamond Horseshoe ★ AMERICAN   Disney closed a long-running revue in this music hall and now uses the pretty room to shovel an all-you-can-eat family-style "Saloon Feast" of pulled pork and beef brisket at tourists who'd pay for anything warm. The stage sits empty except for a piano, as if to protest declining standards. There's beer and wine. **Liberty Square.** Adults $36, kids $20.

Liberty Tree Tavern ★ AMERICAN   This colonial-style place (stained wood and rung-backed chairs) facing the Rivers of America (no view) serves

freebies **AT DISNEY**

It's not easy finding fun stuff to do that you don't have to cough up for, but you don't need to hand over a cent for these pleasures—not even for park admission. Anyone off the street can enjoy these things:

○ **Take the monorail.** Whiz round the Seven Seas Lagoon past the Magic Kingdom and through the Contemporary Resort as many times as you want without a ticket. You can also use it to make the 4-mile round-trip to Epcot, where you'll do a flyover of Future World.

○ **Watch the Electrical Water Pageant** on the Seven Seas Lagoon and Bay Lake between 9 and 10:20pm. The illuminated convoy, which twinkle to a soundtrack, motor around the conjoined ponds after nightfall.

○ **Ride the ferries** between the resorts, such as the one from Port Orleans Riverside to Disney Springs along the meandering Sassagoula River, which passes the French Quarter resort and the Old Key West resort. You can even ride the one from the monorail-area resorts to the foot of the Magic Kingdom.

○ **Hike at Fort Wilderness.** The trail begins at the east end of Bay Lake and threads through occasionally muddy woods.

○ **Spend a night by the pool.** Most resorts keep them open 'til 11pm. Technically, you should be a guest. But behave, and no one'll care

(except at the Yacht and Beach clubs, where bracelets may be required). Parking lots are gated, but if you park at Disney Springs and take a free Disney bus, you'll scoot right in.

○ **See African animals** at the Animal Kingdom Lodge. The gatekeeper will admit you to sit by the fire in its vaulted lobby, and out back, you can watch game such as giraffe and kudu from the Sunset Overlook. Sometimes, there are zoologists who answer questions.

○ **Watch the fireworks over the Magic Kingdom.** For a marvelous view, stroll on the beach of the Grand Floridian or the Polynesian resorts. The sand is millions of years old and was recovered from under Bay Lake. Did you know Disney built a giant wave machine in the middle of the lake? It never worked.

○ **Join Chip 'n' Dale's Campfire Sing-A-Long.** It happens nightly at Fort Wilderness, followed by a Disney feature on an outdoor screen.

○ **Visit the horse stable.** At Fort Wilderness's Tri-Circle-D Ranch, you can see "Cinderella's ponies" and the horses that pull streetcars up Main Street, U.S.A.

○ **Ride the bus system.** Park at Disney Springs for free and take the buses to any hotel, and from there to a theme park. That'll save you on parking each day.

patriotically named a la carte at lunch (Freedom Pasta, Colony Salad; mains $16 to $23). At dinner, fill up on all-you-can-eat fare such as pot roast and turkey with stuffing. There's beer, light cocktails, and wine. **Liberty Square.** $35 adults, $20 kids.

Cinderella's Royal Table ★★★ AMERICAN   This is the Holy Grail of character meals since it takes place past the velvet ropes inside Cinderella Castle, where there's a capacity of less than 200. The famous royal resident always appears (sometimes joined by her soul sisters Jasmine, Aurora, Snow

White, and others), and little girls from far and wide dress up like princesses to meet her. ("Right this way, Royal Family," greets the hostess.) The interior is as lavish as you'd expect for the inside of the Castle, with mock medieval vaulted ceilings, a royal red carpet, stained glass, and stylized crest shields adorning the walls. Meals aren't all-you-can-eat, but they are all prix-fixe, though the price shifts with the season. Bookings open 180 days ahead at 7am Orlando time (and must be prepaid by credit card) and are snapped up in moments, although if you're persistent and flexible, you may snag a cancellation starting two weeks before. Food selections include gnocchi, seared chicken, and pork loin, and beer and wine are available. **Fantasyland.** All three meals $45 to $80 adults, $35 to $65 children, according to season.

Be Our Guest Restaurant ★ AMERICAN   It's not so easy to be their guest, actually, because bookings fill incredibly quickly. And never was "hospitality" so cumbersome: one line to enter, another to order, few cast members to explain the system—you won't eat a bite until at least 30 minutes after your reservation. It sports a few technical tricks to evoke Beast's castle, including animated falling snow outside some false windows, a portrait that reveals a hidden Beast when illuminated by periodic lightning (that's in the West Wing, the best seating area to choose), and an animated rose under glass that slowly sheds its petals. All those polished surfaces make a meal gratingly loud, and although the food is French-ish (there's croque-monsieur and French onion soup, plus "the gray stuff" (you know, it's delicious) which is actually a whipped cookies-and-cream panna cotta), in reality the French would form a posse to detain the chef responsible. You'll only receive quasi-service, too: You order by kiosk, pour your own beverages, and your food is wheeled to you when it's ready. (If you don't have a MagicBand, you'll need to pick up a "rose," a device that looks like a red hockey puck that transmits your table location.) You can get alcohol, but only at dinner and only with that coveted reservation. It serves all three meals, but only at dinner will you have the chance to meet the Beast, who can only be met here and nowhere else in the park. **Fantasyland.** Breakfast $25 adult, $15 kids. Main courses $13 to $17 lunch, $22 to $36 dinner.

EPCOT

Epcot ★★★ remains one of Walt Disney World's finest achievements. More than any other park, Epcot changes its personality, decorations, and diversions by the season. Although it used to possess the pretense of education, guests usually don't learn much more than they already know (so as not to bore them or to insult their intelligence), but even though there isn't much take-away information, there's lots to soak up if you explore. There's plenty to do here without having to wait in lines, and unlike other parks, there are many places to sit. The wide variety of foods and alcoholic beverages is also a big draw. Epcot's genial personality has earned it a spot as the seventh-most-visited theme park on Earth, racking up some 12.2 million entries in 2017.

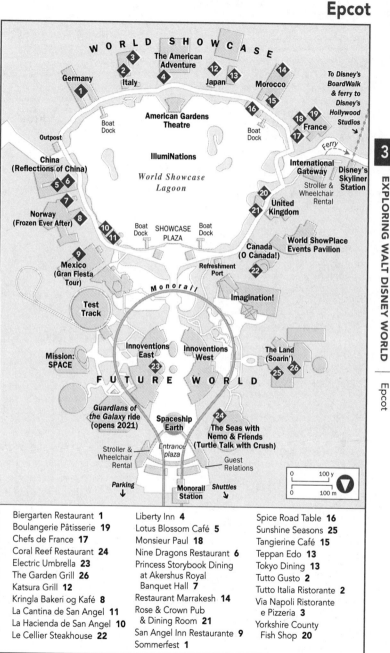

WORLD SHOWCASE

The American Adventure

Germany

Italy

Japan

Morocco

To Disney's BoardWalk & ferry to Disney's Hollywood Studios

Boat Dock

American Gardens Theatre

Boat Dock

Outpost

IllumiNations

France

China (Reflections of China)

World Showcase Lagoon

International Gateway

Disney's Skyliner Station

Stroller & Wheelchair Rental

Norway (Frozen Ever After)

ferry

United Kingdom

Boat Dock

SHOWCASE PLAZA

Boat Dock

Canada (O Canada!)

World ShowPlace Events Pavilion

Mexico (Gran Fiesta Tour)

Refreshment Port

Monorail

Imagination!

Test Track

Innoventions East

Innoventions West

The Land (Soarin')

Mission: SPACE

FUTURE WORLD

Guardians of the Galaxy ride (opens 2021)

Spaceship Earth

The Seas with Nemo & Friends (Turtle Talk with Crush)

Stroller & Wheelchair Rental

Entrance plaza

Guest Relations

Parking

Monorail Station

Shuttles

0 100 y
0 100 m

Biergarten Restaurant **1**	Liberty Inn **4**	Spice Road Table **16**
Boulangerie Pâtisserie **19**	Lotus Blossom Café **5**	Sunshine Seasons **25**
Chefs de France **17**	Monsieur Paul **18**	Tangierine Café **15**
Coral Reef Restaurant **24**	Nine Dragons Restaurant **6**	Teppan Edo **13**
Electric Umbrella **23**	Princess Storybook Dining	Tokyo Dining **13**
The Garden Grill **26**	at Akershus Royal	Tutto Gusto **2**
Katsura Grill **12**	Banquet Hall **7**	Tutto Italia Ristorante **2**
Kringla Bakeri og Kafé **8**	Restaurant Marrakesh **14**	Via Napoli Ristorante
La Cantina de San Angel **11**	Rose & Crown Pub	e Pizzeria **3**
La Hacienda de San Angel **10**	& Dining Room **21**	Yorkshire County
Le Cellier Steakhouse **22**	San Angel Inn Restaurante **9**	Fish Shop **20**
	Sommerfest **1**	

MAKING THE MOST OF EPCOT

Epcot has so much to explore, and eat, and drink that you won't feel like you're racing from ride to ride (as you might in other parks). Just make sure you have a late morning/early afternoon Fastpass+ for Frozen Ever After (which usually opens at 11am—check the Times Guide—and will be instantly crowded). If you can't get that, get one for Soarin' but be at Frozen Ever After when it opens.

↓

Ride **Test Track** before the line gets crazy or, if you don't want a thrill, do Frozen Ever After first thing.

↓

Ride **Mission: Space.**

↓

By now, your **Soarin'** Fastpass is probably valid. Ride it.

↓

Enter World Showcase, go directly to Norway, and ride **Frozen Ever After.**

↓

Go next door to Mexico and ride **Gran Fiesta Tour.** You have now enjoyed all the rides in World Showcase.

↓

Continue along World Showcase at a slow pace, having removed the temptation to rush. The movies (in China, France, and Canada) are all worth seeing; the shops can be surprisingly good; and the street entertainment choices (noted on the Times Guide) are excellent. Eat somewhere that appeals to you.

↓

Catch the **American Adventure;** the Voices of Liberty perform about 15 minutes before show times, and they're listed in the Times Guide.

↓

Continue along World Showcase. Recharge with a pint in the United Kingdom.

↓

Return to Future World for **The Seas with Nemo and Friends.**

↓

Ride **Living with the Land** for a glimpse at Epcot's roots. Consider doing **Soarin'** again.

↓

Ride **Spaceship Earth.**

↓

Return to World Showcase, eat dinner in the land of your choice, and catch **IllumiNations** at 9pm. Secure a good viewing point at least 30 minutes ahead.

The 260-acre park is divided into two zones, Future World and World Showcase, laid out roughly like a figure eight. Both areas started life separately but, as the legend goes, were grafted together when plans were afoot. **Future World** is where the wonders of industry were extolled in corporate-sponsored "pavilions." The companies had a hand in creating them, and they also maintained VIP areas in backstage areas for executives and special guests. At the back of the property, around a 1.3-mile lake footpath, **World Showcase** was (and is) a circuit of countries, each representing in miniature its namesake's essence. These, too, received funding from their host countries. The expense of updating exhibits has caused Disney to gradually phase out the educational aspects of the attractions. One by one, original pavilions have been replaced by sense-tingling rides, so that today only two of the original displays, Spaceship Earth and Living with the Land, remain more or less as they originally were.

GETTING IN   The parking lot is at the ticket gates, although you can also catch the **monorail** from the Magic Kingdom parking area. If you park near the track, don't bother with the tram; you can walk to the gates faster. Bags will be quickly inspected. As you enter the park, lockers are at the right of Spaceship Earth; wheeled rentals are to the left. Also on the left is Guest Relations, where last-minute dining reservations can be made, though often, you'll just be deferred to the restaurant in question. A smaller entrance at the **International Gateway** (by France in World Showcase) is good for entry from the Disney Skyliner, Disney's Hollywood Studios, and the Epcot Resort area.

HOURS Future World opens at 9am, along with the Norway pavilion of World Showcase, and the rest of World Showcase opens at 11am. Street entertainment (there's more on weekends) and character greetings dry up after about 5pm. The less scintillating Future World attractions close at 7pm, 2 hours before World Showcase. The nightly lagoon show (until early 2019, it's IllumiNations) takes place at 9pm; at its conclusion, the hordes stampede for their cars en masse. From Epcot, you can take a ferry to Hollywood Studios, the monorail to the Magic Kingdom (until very late at night, when it's a bus), or a bus to Animal Kingdom. Because locals favor it, Epcot is much busier on weekends.

Future World

By the time Walt Disney World finally got around to opening its second park, EPCOT Center, on October 1, 1982 (11 years to the day after the Magic Kingdom and at a staggering estimated cost of $1.4 billion; America's biggest construction project at the time), it was but a flicker of its original purpose. No one would actually live there, as Walt had directed, and few experimental endeavors would be undertaken. Instead, the most economical course was to turn Walt's legacy into another moneymaker, heavily subsidized by corporate participation and sold by heavy promotion of "Walt's dream"—a formula that prevails today. In truth, the final concept wasn't much different from the world's fair that Walt's father had helped construct in Chicago in 1893 or that

A history OF EPCOT

Although people think of Walt Disney as all-American, he had a communist streak. He long dreamed of establishing a real, working city where 20,000 full-time residents, none of them unemployed, would test out experimental technologies in the course of their daily lives. In vintage films where he discusses his Florida Project, his passion for creating such a self-sustaining community, to be called the Experimental Prototype Community of Tomorrow, was inextricable from the rest of his planned resort. He wanted nothing less than to revolutionize the world.

Truck traffic would be routed to vehicle plazas beneath the city, out of pedestrians' way, while PeopleMovers (like the ones of Magic Kingdom's Tomorrowland Transit Authority) would shift the population around town. Between home and downtown, they'd take the monorail. Even on his deathbed, Walt was perfecting real plans for the city that would be his crowning legacy: one whose innovations would make life better for everyone on Earth. Had he been a non-smoker and lived just 3 more years, he would have made it happen.

Don't miss if you're 6: Frozen Ever After
Don't miss if you're 16: Test Track
Requisite photo op: Spaceship Earth
Food you can only get here: Rice cream, the bakery at Norway
The most crowded, so Fastpass+ or go early: Frozen Ever After, Soarin'
Skippable: Journey into Imagination with Figment
Quintessentially Disney: Spaceship Earth

Biggest thrill: Mission: SPACE
Best show: Voices of Liberty, the American Adventure
Character meals: Akershus Royal Banquet Hall, Norway; Garden Grill, The Land
Best shopping: Mitsukoshi, Japan
Where to find peace: Future World: the Odyssey Center catwalks; World Showcase: the gardens of Japan

Walt himself defined in New York in 1964: Examples of how technology was ostensibly improving lives, plus pavilions representing foreign lands for the edification of people unlikely to travel there themselves. As it turned out, in Disney's version of the future, all walls are carpeted, all lighting is recessed, and all music is lite FM. In December 1993, the park name was simplified to Epcot. As you face the lagoon, the left side of Future World is generally about the physical and man-made sciences, and the right is more about the natural sciences. There are big changes afoot at Epcot as it approaches its fourth decade and Disney struggles to keep audiences engaged—long-running attractions are being removed (Universe of Energy was unplugged for an upcoming *Guardians of the Galaxy* ride, due 2021), new ones are being built (a *Ratatouille* dark ride is joining France, also in 2021), movie tie-ins take over, and whiff of the old World's Fairs is gradually going the way of all unworkable Utopian ideas.

Spaceship Earth ★★★ RIDE   That gorgeous orb looks like a golf ball on a tee, but the 16-million-pound structure, coated with 11,324 aluminum-bonded panels and sheathed inside with a rainproof rubber layer, is supported by a table-like scaffolding where its six legs enter the dome. Think of this 180-foot-tall Buckminster Fuller sphere as a direct descendent of the Perisphere of the 1939 World's Fair or the Unisphere of the 1964 World's Fair, which were the icons for their own parks. No mere shell, it houses an eponymous ride using the OmniMover system of cars linked together like an endless snake. The ride slowly winds within the sphere, all on the course of a shallow, sixth-grade-level journey (narrated by Judi Dench) cheerleading the history of communications, from Greek theater to the Sistine Chapel to the printing press to the telegraph. In a bit of unintended kinesthetic commentary, once computers are invented, it all goes downhill. At one point, Dench tells you to thank the Phoenicians for inventing an alphabet (you may hear other riders doing so—it's a tradition here), recent discoveries actually show that Syrians and Africans independently did the same thing. When you get off, I defy you to tell me what you learned. This, of course, makes it essential Epcot. This is the ride that still shows what the 1982 park was like—its robot-populated sister pavilions about transportation and the future were razed in the 1990s to make way for flashier stuff. Although some people don't get it, I cherish it as a soothing sojourn not only through time, but also through air-conditioning.

Innoventions ★ ACTIVITY   The semicircular buildings (originally Communicore) facing each other like parenthesis behind Spaceship Earth have been largely emptied and are under redevelopment. Strong rumors predict their demolition, but at press time, in the southern wings you'd find **MouseGear,** the largest all-Disney souvenir shop in Epcot and opposite that, **Club Cool,** by the Coca-Cola Company, which lets you pour unlimited samples of eight soft drink flavors sold only in other countries. In the courtyard, you'll find the **World Fellowship Fountain,** which was dedicated by Walt's widow, Lillian. At the opening ceremony, water from 23 countries was combined as a symbol of brotherhood. It can shoot 150 feet in the air, although half that is the norm. There are 5-minute choreographed splash-ups, often to synthy 1980s music, on the quarter hour, but nothing Bellagio-level and nothing worth diverting your day for.

Character Meets in Epcot

Check your Times Guide for the current location of the **Epcot Character Spot** meet-and-greet area in Future World—it's where Mickey, Minnie, and a few other popular faces (Baymax, Joy, Sadness) will be. You will also find characters in some of the World Showcase pavilions that somewhat remind you of them—Mary Poppins in the U.K., Aladdin in Morocco, and so on. Check the Times Guide.

Mission: SPACE ★★ RIDE   Behind this gorgeously swirling planetary facade is a ride that approximates, with intensity if you so desire, the experience of a rocket launch. Although technically a whirl aboard a cockpit on a giant centrifuge, the skillful design successfully tricks the mind. At the outside, you choose, according to your gravitas, between Orange (an intense trip to Mars that'll have you pressed backward against your seat) or Green (an easy glide around Earth that was made even milder and more family-friendly in 2017, with no vomit-inducing effects). The posted wait time will be whichever of the two versions is longer. Each passenger in the extremely tight four-person cockpits (claustrophobics be warned) is assigned two buttons to press at given cues—it doesn't matter if you don't, but at least hold onto your steering joystick, because it gives force feedback as you travel. The Advanced Training Lab post-show area (through the gift shop) is worthwhile even if you don't ride. There, you can play interactive group games and send free postcards home via computer. *Strategy:* Whereas Mad Tea Party makes me want to hurl, I do fine on this ride—the personal fans blowing air on your face must help. Perhaps this is why Disney felt confident that it was safe to add a future table-service restaurant adjacent to the ride—when it's finished, a few years from now, diners will look out windows overlooking "space."

Test Track ★★ RIDE   Cars thunder enticingly around the bend of an outdoor motorway at nearly 65mph, but that's as intense as it gets. Those

The Death of "Life"

Between Mission: SPACE and the upcoming Guardians of the Galaxy ride, you'll spot a golden dome. No, you haven't been in the sun too long. (Well, you have. But it's still there.) That's **Wonders of Life,** one of the great failures of modern Disney World. Opened in 1989 as a paean to all things biological, execs closed it at the end of 2006 when they couldn't find a brand willing to pony up sponsorship. The tarnished pavilion sat in neglect and occasional minor use ever since then, but recently it was been buffed up again, preparing for a new tenant. What will it be?

passengers are experiencing the climax of a complicated, multistage ride that puts them through the paces of a proving ground of an automobile manufacturer (sponsor: Chevrolet) that, oddly, takes place in a neon-frosted black box. Before boarding, you use a touch screen to create a car using the factors of capability, power, responsiveness, and efficiency. Then, you go along for the ride in a minimally decorated warehouse on a series of diagnostic safety tests (don't worry, you don't have to actually do anything), while trackside screens ostensibly show you how your creation would perform under the same circumstances—in truth, it's the same exact ride every time. Your six-passenger car brakes suddenly and careens through a mostly black room decorated by illuminated lines that seem to have been inspired both by *Tron* and a very low renovation budget. Finally, you shoot outside the building and make an invigorating circuit around the circular track over the Epcot employee parking lot. (Hertz has a similar experience—it's called a convertible.) The post-ride showroom features a few steering games plus samples from Chevy's current fleet and numerous photo ops for free digital postcards. If you rode this before its 2012 renovation, you saw it in a much better form. As one of the only thrills in Epcot, it gets busy anyway. *Strategy:* There's a single-rider line that doesn't let you skip much waiting and invariably puts you in a right-hand seat and won't let you design a car.

The Seas with Nemo & Friends ★★ RIDE/ACTIVITY   One of the world's largest saltwater aquariums—it's 27 feet deep, 203 feet across, and holds 5.7 million gallons—and you can spend as long as you like watching the swimming creatures from two levels. About a third of the tank is reserved for dolphins and sea turtles, while reef fish, rays, and sharks dominate the rest. When the pavilion opened in 1986 as The Living Seas, sharks were the big draw and scientists answered questions everywhere; today, because of *Finding Nemo* and *Finding Dory*, kids ask to see the clown fish and blue tangs yet there's nary an interpreter in sight. A visit begins with a 5-minute, slow-moving ride in OmniMover "clamobiles" through a simulated undersea world. Half the point of the ride is, of course, to find Nemo, who's lost again; the other characters incessantly shout his name, which soon grates on adult nerves. The ride climaxes to the tune of "In the Big Blue World" (from the Nemo musical at Animal Kingdom) with a peek into the real aquarium as Nemo and his friends are projected into the windows, cleverly uniting the fictional world with the real animal universe, "Seabase," with which you will now be acquainted. A few times a day, the giant tube dominating the hall is occasionally occupied by a diver—an unforgettable sight—to demonstrate how SCUBA works. On the second floor, Observation Level, don't miss the observation platform that extends into the mighty tank. The Daily Roster sign apprises you of the day's dolphin talks and fish feedings (the schedule is busiest between 10am and 4pm), when there will be someone on hand to explain what you're seeing. The **dolphins** live separately in the first space on the left. If human divers are swimming, they'll communicate with guests by way of magnetized writing tablets. Also, check out the **manatees,** Florida's sweet-natured "sea cows." *Strategy:* If the pavilion's entry line is horrific, bypass the ride by entering through the gift shop, at the far left.

Turtle Talk with Crush ★★ SHOW   Inside The Seas with Nemo & Friends is an amusing 20-minute show in which a computer-animated version of the 150-year-old surfer-dude turtle—plus the occasional Dory or Destiny the whale shark—interacts with audiences, making jokes about what they're wearing and fielding questions. It's part of what Disney calls its "Living Characters" program, and it's nifty. There is the distraction of ray and jellyfish tanks in the waiting area. Next door is **Bruce's Shark World,** a play area similar to any science museum's.

Soarin' ★★★ RIDE   The Land pavilion takes up 6 acres, more than all of Tomorrowland, and this ride is a big reason why. In it, audiences are seated on benches and "flown," hang glider–like, in front of a movie that flies over 13 world landmarks on every inhabited continent while scents (grass, roses) waft, hair blows, and the seats gently rock in tandem with the motions of the flight. Now and then, something computer-animated flies at the lens, but mostly the ride is highly repeatable and deeply pleasurable for all ages. *Strategy:* Even with a third theatre now operating, wait times can exceed 2 hours (I

Kid Stuff at Epcot

Besides The Seas with Nemo & Friends and Frozen Ever After, there aren't many attractions for kiddos in Epcot. Disney addressed the problem with small, manned booths that it calls **Kidcot Fun Stops,** which offer free crafty diversions such as coloring, stamping, or mask-making—stuff kids do at the school fair. Epcot Passports, which can be stamped in every country, were once free but now cost $12 at the register of any World Showcase shop, but attendants will stamp your kids' crafts, such as the handle of the mask they made, for free instead. From the kiosk on the walkway to World Showcase from Future World (or in Italy, the International Gateway, and Norway), sign them up for the engrossing and free **Phineas and Ferb: Agent P's World Showcase Adventure** (starting at 11am), in which they follow instructions on fake cell phones (or use yours) to make tricksy things happen at six stops in various countries. You must activate the unit within 15 minutes of picking it up, but it'll work all day until 8:15pm. It's so engrossing that kids sometimes have a hard time paying attention to anything else.

know—crazy!), so schedule a Fastpass+. The best seats are in the middle sections on the top row, where there are no feet dangling in your field of vision and tall images don't seem warped. That means you should aim for position B-1, or at the very least A-1 or C-1. Those with height terrors should request something ending in 3, the closest to the ground.

Living with the Land ★ RIDE   The Land's other ride, after Soarin', is a 14-minute (wonderfully air-conditioned) boat trip that glosses over the realm of farming technologies. It's one of the last Epcot rides to provide a semblance of education, especially when you pass some experimental growth methods (like a nutrient film technique and aquaponics). These methods are being explored, or so we're told, to curb world hunger, but you won't learn how they work (for that, you have to go to the desk at Soarin's exit to reserve the semi-interesting 45-minute Behind the Seeds tour, $25 adult, $20 kids 3–9) and Epcot's labs are not the hive of active research they were meant to be in 1982. They do some real stuff here, though: Annually, the narration claims, 15 tons of produce are grown here for Disney restaurants, but you won't see much activity proving it. This ride is original to opening day, although the live narrators were disposed of in favor of a recording. For those interested in the topic, the info will be too thin, but for those who are bored green, it will seem to last forever. *Strategy:* Boats load slowly, so go early or late to escape the inevitable buildup. It often closes at 7pm.

The Circle of Life ★ SHOW   Upstairs, in The Land, this minor, 13-minute movie stars *The Lion King* characters and concerns conservation (an Epcot-worthy message). It'll keep you off the streets and seated in air-conditioning, at least until 7pm, when it shuts down for the day.

Disney & Pixar Short Film Festival ★ SHOW   Three animated shorts, all of which are available on DVD, done "4-D" style, meaning your seat trembles once in a while. This movie is a space filler and a time killer. Don't miss something better just because you were doing this. It's on the back side of the pavilion named "Imagination!" written with an exclamation point because the people who make new attractions seem to be calling out for one.

Journey into Imagination with Figment ★ RIDE   Did Disney run out of money halfway through? One section of this slow track-based ride is simply a room of black curtains and painted boards. Its daffy purple dinosaur, Figment, once figured as Epcot's mascot and now strains to act cuddly in his last, forlorn outpost. The ride purports to be an open house of the Imagination Institute run by Prof. Nigel Channing (Eric Idle), but Figment seizes control and literally tries everything he can to offend your senses—your sense of good taste, though, is the most violated. This is the third attempt to get an Imagination ride right since 1982. The ride dumps out into **ImageWorks "What If" Labs,** once a high-tech playground but now with little more to offer than the purchase of fairground-style gag photos. Look above the roped-off staircase for a glimpse of the glass pyramids atrium, now forbidden unless you've purchased a Disney timeshare (there's a bouncer if you haven't), and you'll get a fuller sense for how this pretty pavilion is now half-empty and riven with neglect. You might have gathered by now that Imagination! is not Epcot at its best. However, the fountain pods in front, which shoot snakes of water from one to another, are a firm favorite of children, who never tire of trying to catch one of the so-called "laminar flow" spurts.

World Showcase

The 1.3-mile path circling the World Showcase Lagoon is home to 11 pavilions created in the idealized image of their home countries—get your picture taken in front of a miniature Eiffel Tower (it'll look real through the lens), or at the Doge's Palace in Venice. The pavilions were built more to elicit an emotional response and not to truly replicate. Disney is diligent about the upkeep of this area, but it neglects development—the last "country" to open was Norway back in 1988, and without joint participation by foreign tourism offices, there are unlikely to be more. There also seems to be an emphasis on countries that Americans already know, and neither South America nor Australasia is represented at all. But World Showcase does have some of the most original restaurants in Disney World, and the shops are stocked with crafts and national products (you can buy real Chinese tea in China and sweaters in Norway), although the variety is slipping. It's also the only area in Epcot in which alcoholic beverages are sold.

There is far more fascinating stuff to do in World Showcase than the free Disney map lets on. Pocket it and let your curiosity guide you. You should, though, keep the day's **Times Guide** firmly in hand. The pavilions are crawling with unexpected musical and dance performances conducted by natives of each country (shows usually wrap up by dinnertime). Seeing them makes a day richer and squeezes value from your ticket. Rush and you'll miss a lot. I suggest going **clockwise around the lagoon** mostly because the only two rides in World Showcase will come quickly on the left; if you go counterclockwise, you'll reach them after they accrue lines. After midafternoon, it won't matter.

Tip: Anything purchased in World Showcase can be sent to the **Package Pickup** at the front of Future World; allow 3 hours for delivery (it's not refrigerated, so chocolate melts). On some days—it depends how busy things

A Mini United Nations

World Showcase pavilions are staffed by young people who were born and raised in the host country. Many of their contracts last for up to a year, and they chose to come to Florida as much to learn about America as to be ambassadors for their own nations, although many of them complain that most park guests don't bother asking anything except where the bathrooms are. Be kind to them, speak slowly if you sometimes cannot immediately understand each other's accent, and most of all, seize this unusual chance to ask questions about their cultures. These folks, despite the fact they're zipped into silly costumes, are modern, intelligent people who are so proud of where they come from that they traveled halfway around the world to have a new experience and share their heritage with you. Help them do that.

are—two **ferry** routes cross the lagoon. One leaves near Germany and one from Morocco, and both land near the top of Future World. You will not save time using them; they're merely a pleasant way to get off your feet.

MEXICO ★★★

Skirting the lagoon clockwise, Mexico is your first stop. Everything to see is inside the faux temple, which contains a faux river (for the Gran Fiesta Tour ride), a faux volcano, and a faux night sky strung with lanterns. The **Mexican Folk Art Gallery** now hosts *Remember Me: La Celebración del Día de Muertos*, an exhibition on the traditions of the holiday *Coco* is about. In the main *zócalo* of Plaza de los Amigos from Tuesday to Friday mornings, look for Alba Hernandez Santiago, who trained in Arrazola, the Oaxacan town most important to the craft of hand-painted Oaxacan woodcarvings here. She has been here since 2002 and works Tues–Fri; her equally talented brother Marco takes over Sat–Mon. Listen for the terrific Mariachi Cobre, which has performed here since the park's opening day. There's also a crystal and glass shop with glass-blowing demonstrations. *Influences:* A diplomatic mix of Mayan, Toltec, Aztec, and Spanish styles. *Fun Stuff to Buy:* Maracas ($6 each), Oaxacan woodcarvings (from $18), piñatas (from $12), hand-painted pottery skulls ($25), and sombreros ($17). At the dusky **La Cava de Tequila,** knock back 200-plus types of the house liquor or a designer margarita ($11–$250). *Entertainment:* Mariachi Cobre. *Character greeting:* Donald Duck.

Gran Fiesta Tour Starring the Three Caballeros ★★ RIDE

It's easy to develop a soft spot for the bland, 8-minute boat float that, for its cheesiness, has been nicknamed "Rio de Queso." As you pass movie screens, jiggling dolls, and dancing Day of the Dead skeletons, you quickly realize you're enjoying the product of Mexican tourist board input. Along the way, expect animated appearances by the 1940s characters the Three Caballeros—never mind that only Panchito Pistoles the rooster is Mexican (José Carioca the parrot is Brazilian, and Donald Duck is American). At the ride's climax, they appear in "live" form—these figures are actually part of Disney history. They were originally made for the Mickey Mouse Revue, a show that opened with the Magic Kingdom in 1971 and later spent 26 years in Tokyo Disneyland. The experience is sweet, and it's a worthy siesta break.

NORWAY ★★

Get yer *Frozen* merch here! Norway, the youngest pavilion (built 1988), is home to one of the only two rides in World Showcase. At least, it used to be Norway—Disney expanded it, fudging the Norway theme, to cash in on *Frozen* fever even though the movie is only notionally set there. Now you have to get here first thing in the morning if you don't want to wait for hours. The **Akershus Royal Banquet Hall** does princess character meals morning, noon, and evening. In the one-room **Stave Church Gallery,** check out *Gods of the Vikings,* containing a few genuine Norse artifacts (such as 1,000-year-old spears and swords) on loan from Swedish and Norwegian historical societies. Towering above it all, the wooden Stave Church is a Norwegian original; there were once around 1,000 in the country, but today, there are only 28. **The Puffin's Roost** contains a 9-foot-tall troll—photo op alert—and sweaters for up to $400. *Influences:* Town squares of Bergen, Alesund, Oslo, and the Satesdal Valley; the 14th-century Akershus castle on Oslo harbor; traditional cabins in Trondheim. **The Wandering Reindeer** indulges in everything *Frozen*. *Fun Stuff to Buy:* Laila body lotions (assorted prices) and foam swords ($11). At the bakery, try the custard-stuffed school bread or the rice cream, a snack that those in the know are happy to make a detour for (both $3.50). I prefer the plastic Viking helmets ($12–17), Daim candy ($5, even though it's Swedish), and stuffed Olafs ($25). *Entertainment:* Wandering slapstick Norway Vikings. *Character greeting:* Elsa and Anna.

Frozen Ever After ★★★ RIDE The old Maelstrom indoor boat excursion, an abbreviated 5-minute float-along with easy forward and backward motion, never counted for much. But it's the hottest—er, coldest—ride in the park now that it's been populated with some marvelous Audio-Animatronics of Elsa, Anna, Olaf, Kristoff, Sven, and Marshmallow from *Frozen Fever.* It won't change your world—there's not even a plot other than it's the "Winter in Summer" festival—but it's pretty. Nearby is the **Royal Sommerhus** cabin where kids can meet the princesses, who are pretending to be on summer vacation there—arrange a Fastpass+ or their dreams will be put on ice and they'll never let it go. This ride opens at 9am.

CHINA ★★

Enter through the remarkable replica of Beijing's Temple of Heaven. "Tomb Warriors: Guardian Spirits of Ancient China," in the **House of the Whispering Willow,** is a miniature re-creation of a tiny portion of the legendary terracotta warriors of the Han Dynasty, scaled to the size of a hotel room (the original mausoleum is twice the size of Epcot). The Gallery also contains a few display cases of figures dating as far back as 260 B.C. *Influences:* Beijing's Forbidden City (Imperial Palace) and Temple of Heaven. *Fun Stuff to Buy:* Upon exiting the film, cross the hangarlike shop and enter **House of Good Fortune,** a particularly good store (photo op: a huge sculpture of Buddha). It sells plum wine ($20), lots of tees and teas, Chinese jackets ($40–$140; in silks, polyesters, and blends), jade bangles ($150), embroidered handbags ($40); teapots ($30–$50), paper parasols ($16), fans ($10), conical hats ($17), and tea sets (from $20). They'll write your kid's name in Mandarin for free. *Entertainment:* Jeweled Dragon Acrobats, some of the most riveting street performers in the World Showcase. *Character greeting:* Mulan.

"Reflections of China" ★ FILM The big thing to do in China is a 14-minute movie filmed entirely in Circle-Vision 360°. The result, which surveys some of the country's most beautiful vistas, is ravishing, although the masses no longer seem to care. You wouldn't believe the work it takes to make a film that surrounds you from all sides. The makers first had to figure out the optimal number of screens (nine—which enables projectors to be slipped in the gaps between screens) and then they had to suspend a ring of carefully calibrated film cameras from helicopters so that the crew wasn't in the shots. In 2002, the footage of Shanghai had to be reshot because the city no longer resembled the 1982 version that was being shown; it's already time for another refresh, which Disney is working on, this time with digital cameras.

OUTPOST ★

This area between China and Germany was once slated to contain a pavilion canvassing equatorial Africa, but that fell through for political reasons, so instead, we get a mushy catchall for all things African. The **Mdundo Kibanda** store has some Kenyan carvings (such as adorable $12 pocket-size elephants, walking sticks for $67–$77) and you'll find occasional storytelling sessions. Several days a week, a craftsman is on hand, whittling and carving wares— Kenyan-born Andrew Matiso has been doing this at Epcot since 1999. His colleague Joshua may be here instead; these days, Matiso often works in the shop at Animal Kingdom Lodge.

GERMANY ★

Lacking a true attraction (a water ride based on the Rhine was planned but never completed), Germany is popular for its food. The **Biergarten Restaurant** does sausages, beer, and the like—accompanied by yodeling and dancing—while the adjoining shop is for crystal doodads. The **Sommerfest** is the counter-service alternative for brats and pretzels, and the beer kiosk is ever-popular. On the hour, the Clock Tower above the pavilion rings and two figures emerge, just like at the Glockenspiel in München (Munich). The pavilion is otherwise a string of connected one-room shops selling steins ($25–$200), figurines, crystal, Christmas ornaments, cuckoo clocks (up to $1,900), and other high-priced wares. *Influences:* Eltz Castle near Koblenz; Stahleck Fortress near Bacharach; Rothenburg (the Biergarten and the dragon slayer statue); facades from Frankfurt and Freiburg (the guildhall). *Fun Stuff to Buy:* The connected candy-and-wine shop, **Weinkeller,** is worth a gander: You'll find such pick-me-ups as Gluhwein ($12 a liter), wine by the bottle (spätlese, Gewürztztraminer, Auslese, Liebfraumilch, from $20), beer steins ($50–$130), and cuckoo clocks in the $100s or $1,000s. **Der Teddybär** sells toys, including stuffed ones by Steiff. The Werther's Original **Karamell-Küche** shop for all sorts of caramel treats ($4–$10) is a standout—its warm, hand-tossed caramel popcorn is a top treat on the Lagoon. *Character greeting:* Snow White.

The Wine Walk

The pavilions of Germany, Italy, and France have combined their wine tasting programs so that now, for $32, guests are given two acrylic wine glasses that are each good for two tastings in each of those three "countries." When you've had your six tastings, you get to keep the glass.

ITALY ★

The tiny pavilion for Italy lacks an attraction—the gondolas never leave the dock—so content yourself with the miniature, drive-thru versions of Venice's Doge's Palace and St. Mark's bell tower. An appealing, if incongruous, attraction that's not on the maps is the highly detailed **model train** display just between this pavilion and Germany. *Influences:* Piazza di San Marco, Venice; stucco buildings of Tuscany; a fountain reminiscent of the work of Gian Lorenzo Bernini. *Fun Stuff to Buy:* Noodle around in **Enoteca Castello** shop for chocolate and Wine Walk tastings (above). **La Gemma Elegante** sells fragrances, handbags, and pricey Venetian carnival masks. Stop into **Tutto Gusto** for honest adult cocktails—the kind made with a shaker, not a slushie machine. *Entertainment:* Sergio the juggling mime (5 days a week; check the Times Guide).

U.S.A. ★★★

So much for being a generous host: The U.S.A. pavilion takes pride of place in an area that's supposed to celebrate other countries. Inside, attend the half-hour Audio-Animatronic show *The American Adventure*. You'll be impressed. Also in the lobby is the unfairly ignored **American Heritage Gallery:** The current exhibition is *Creating Tradition: Innovation and Change in American Indian Art. Influences:* General Georgian/colonial Greek-revival buildings (Brits often snicker that its Georgian architecture style is distinctly English). *Fun Stuff to Buy:* **Heritage Manor Gifts** sells patriotic tat, throw pillows, and T-shirts emblazoned with the American flag that were actually made in Guatemala, Honduras, Haiti, Nicaragua, Vietnam, India, and China—but rarely America. Which these days is pretty American! *Entertainment:* The superlative and long-running Voices of Liberty singing group, which excels at thorny close harmonies, entertains guests waiting inside for the show.

The American Adventure ★★★ SHOW   Ben Franklin and Mark Twain are your Audio-Animatronic surrogates for a series of eye-popping (but ponderous) re-creations of snippets along patriotic themes. Moving dioramas of seminal events such as a Susan B. Anthony speech and John Muir's inspiration for Yosemite National Park appear and vanish cinematically on a stage a quarter the size of a football field, leaving spectators marveling at the massive amount of storage space that must lie beyond the proscenium. It's a literal jukebox for mythology, recently refreshed so it sounds better than ever, and the transitions between scenes are theatrical genius. Indeed, all that homespun corn is brought to you by some immensely complicated robotic and hydraulic systems. When this attraction first opened, the Declaration of Independence scene in which Franklin appears to mount stairs and then walk a few steps across the room was (and is still) a technical miracle. The Will Rogers figure actually twirls a lasso purely through robotic movements. Although heavy on uplifting jingoism, the show scores points for touching lightly on a few unpleasant topics, including slavery and a rebuke for the persecution of Native Americans, but in general, it's not as deep as its stage. Don't be the first to enter or else you'll be marooned off to the left.

JAPAN ★★★

Japan has no giant attractions (like Germany, a show building was erected but never filled with its intended ride), but its shopping is by far the best in Epcot, and the outdoor garden behind the pagoda is a paragon of peace. At the back of the pavilion, go inside and turn left to tour the **Bijutsu-kan Gallery.** Its most recent show was about the Japanese affection for *Kawaii*, or cute things. A red *torii* gate inspired by one in Hiroshima sits in the lagoon (the barnacles on its base are fake, and were glued on to simulate age). *Influences:* 8th-century Horyuji Temple in Nara (pagoda); Katsura Imperial Villa (Katsura Grill); Shirasagi-Jo castle at Himeji (the rear fortress); Hiroshima (*torii* gate in the lagoon). *Fun Stuff to Buy:* The **Mitsukoshi Department Store,** named for the 300-year-old Japanese original, is the most fun to roam of all the World Showcase shops. It's stocked like a real store, not a theme-park shop, with a variety of toys, chopstick sets ($4–$18), traditional rush mat zouri sandals ($25), linens, anime figures like Pokémon, paper fans, calligraphy supplies, countless solar-powered hand-waving things, antique kimonos (mostly $50–$200), sake serving sets ($17–$35), bonsai trees ($55–$100), sake tastings ($5–$10), and Japanese snacks, such as chocolate-dipped Pocky sticks ($4). *Entertainment:* The spectacularly thunderous Matsuriza Taiko drum shows, which are held at the base of the five-level Goju-no-to pagoda.

MOROCCO ★★★

Morocco is another delightful pavilion if you're inclined to dig in. It flies higher than its neighbors because the country's king took an active interest in its construction, dispatching some 21 top craftsmen for the job. There's no movie or show, and the architecture is a cross-country mishmash drawn from Marrakech, Fès, and Rabat. **Fez House** is a tranquil, pillared two-level courtyard with a fountain and seating that recalls a classic Moroccan home; **Moroccan Style,** a mosaic-rich exhibition of authentic clothing with hanging lanterns and colored glass, is unjustly ignored. Ask a cast member (almost always from Morocco) to write your name in Arabic for you—it's free. *Influences:* Marrakesh (Koutoubia minaret), Rabat (Chella minaret), Fès (Bab Boujouloud Gate, Nejjarine Fountain), Casablanca. *Fun Stuff to Buy:* The middle courtyards are cluttered with **Casablanca Carpets** and **The Brass Bazaar,** and they're sensational. They are perfumed with incense ($4) and stocked with interesting finds, including footstools, tasseled red caps ($25), glass tea cups ($10), Thuya-wood boxes and bowls (from $25), machine-made rugs (from $26), bangle bracelets ($20), genie lamps (from $20), metal hanging lanterns (from $25), fez hats ($25), and belly-dancer outfits ($85). I've managed to haggle them down 30% on the floor model of an incense burner—it almost felt like being in the souk of Fès, only with ice cream bars and strollers. *Character greeting:* Princess Jasmine. *Entertainment:* Matboukha Groove jams to fusion folk music by the water (check the Times Guide).

FRANCE ★★

France, done up to look like a typical Parisian neighborhood with a one-tenth replica of the upper stretch of the Eiffel Tower in the simulated distance (you can't go up it), is popular mostly for its food. Disney allowed Guerlain and Givenchy to open fragrance shops at **Plume et Palette**—turns out the smell of selling out is just like Shalimar. In back, Disney is building a new *Ratatouille*-themed trackless dark ride in which you're shrunk to the size of Remy the Rat. It's based on an attraction that opened at Paris' Walt Disney Studios Park in 2014, and since a new building is being constructed behind the pavilion, the preparations shouldn't be too disruptive in 2019. *Influences:* Various Belle Epoque Parisian and provincial streets; Château de Fontainebleau (the Palais du Cinema); the former Pont des Arts in Paris (the bridge to the United Kingdom). At press time, rumors pointed to imminent redevelopment of this area, possibly to add a ride based on *Ratatouille* that was first installed at the Walt Disney Studios Park near Paris in 2013. *Fun Stuff to Buy:* **Librairie et Galerie** sells upscale fragrances. The Parisian souvenirs (from $10 for a 5-in. Eiffel Tower) are available in Les Halles at **Boutique de Cadeaux.** Across the lane, check **L'Esprit de la Provence,** a kitchen shop. **Aux Vins de France** has Wine Walk tastings (p. 76), Epcot wine glasses ($14), champagne flights ($31 for 3 pours), and bottles of wine that cost much more than in Germany or Italy. *Entertainment:* Serveur Amusant, a thrilling street acrobat who does handstands on stacked chairs. *Character greeting:* Princess Aurora, Belle.

"Impressions de France" ★ FILM   The 18-minute, 200-degree-wide movie is no longer the freshest example of a tourism film—mostly classical music and postcard-worthy shots of some 50 picturesque places. It has been playing continuously since Epcot opened in 1982, so the imagery lacks the fidelity we expect today, but France is ravishing enough to overcome that. Happily, it provides seating.

UNITED KINGDOM ★★

United Kingdom, another wild mix of architectural styles, has no rides or shows, so few people know about the knee-high **hedge maze** in back. The U.K. is popular chiefly for its English-style pub, the indoor Rose & Crown Pub & Dining Room, and a counter-service fish and chips shop. That's two fish and chips outlets in a block—far more than you'd find even in London these days. In mid-afternoon Sunday to Thursday, duck into the pub to catch Carol Stein, a three-decade Epcot entertainer who plays piano and will improvise your name in song. Request her version of "Do Re Mi" (it's clean). In the garden, the **British Revolution** band (check the Times Guide) does covers. *Influences:* Anne Hathaway's Cottage, Stratford-upon-Avon (the Tea Caddy); Queen Anne style (the middle promenade); Hampton Court, London (Sportsman's Shoppe); Victorian, country, and traditional pub styles (Rose & Crown). *Fun Stuff to Buy:* Featured shopping in the conjoined **Sportsman's Shoppe, the Crown & Crest,** and **Toy Soldier** includes football (soccer) jerseys, merchandise for the Stones, Beatles, and Bowie; Dr. Who stuff; and Guinness shirts (that's actually Irish, but carry on). Across the way, **Lords and Ladies** does jewelry and soap, and the **Tea Caddy** sells Twinings tea plus English candy bars ($4 each). *Entertainment:* British Revolution rock cover band. *Character greeting:* Mary Poppins, Alice in Wonderland.

CANADA ★

Like Japan, Canada's gardens (inspired by Victoria's Butchart Gardens, although the sign says Victoria Gardens) are a surprising oasis, adding a hidden artificial canyon delightfully washed by a man-made waterfall. A lumberjack-themed show takes the stage here several times daily (check your Times Guide). *Influences:* 19th-century Victorian colonial architecture (Hotel du Canada); emblematic northwestern Indian design and Maritime Provinces towns; Butchart Gardens, Victoria (Victoria Gardens). *Fun Stuff to Buy:* The shop, **Northwest Mercantile,** mostly hawks maple syrup ($15 for 8.5 oz.), hockey team wear, faux fur-lined muff hats ($25), stuffed moose ($15), ice wine in 2-oz. servings ($13), and T-shirts themed to moose and hockey. *Entertainment:* A rock/folk band at the bandstand.

"O Canada!" ★ FILM   Canada, like China, has a round movie screened by nine clacking projectors. It's shot in Circle-Vision 360°, a process Walt Disney originally called Circarama. The 18-minute presentation (1982), which requires standing (you can lean on railings, though), was refurbished by adding newly shot bits with Martin Short as emcee, who ladles on plenty of curling jokes and hockey references. Most of its spectacular scenery (the Rockies, the Bay of Fundy) is timeless. You'll find it hidden deep within the pavilion by a waterfall in a dreamy rock canyon.

Where to Eat in Epcot

Epcot has the best dining choices of any Disney World park, and people come just for the food. All locations will have a few vegetarian options, kids' meals, and (if you identify yourself) special dietary requests can usually be accommodated, albeit often at diminished quality. Alcohol is served everywhere—even in Morocco, where it's not so easy to get in real life. You can also drink the water in Mexico.

EPCOT'S QUICK-SERVICE RESTAURANTS

There are only two major counter-service choices in Future World, plus a Starbucks. The real casual eating action is in World Showcase. There are many more minor kiosks for snacks than what's listed here.

Sunshine Seasons ★★★ INTERNATIONAL   Offering the best selection and freshest food of all Epcot's counter-service locations, options here include salads, grilled items (oak-grilled salmon), sesame-crusted tuna, vegan

---

Epcot at Night

There are no parades at Epcot, but at 9pm, the pulse-pounding **IllumiNations: Reflections of Earth** ★★★ flames-music-and-water spectacular takes place over World Showcase Lagoon. Its central globe is studded with 15,500 tiny video screens, and the show's so-called Inferno Barge carries a payload of 4,000 gallons of propane. (IllumiNations ends in 2019 and will be replaced by a new production.) Crowds start building on the banks 1–2 hours before showtime, but I find doing that a waste of time, and therefore money, as a day's admission is so steep. Any view of the center of the lake will be fine (some people find the islands obstructive, but I don't), but take care to be upwind or you may be engulfed by smoke. Food kiosks close with the very first downbeat of the show.

korma, and shrimp stir-fry—not a deep-fried item, burger, or pizza in sight. The desserts are epic (cheesecake with berries, red velvet whoopee pie. You can also pick up snacks suiting dietary restrictions. **The Land.** Breakfast $7 to $10, lunch and dinner combo meal $10 to $14.

Electric Umbrella ★★ AMERICAN   Future World's most central counter-service locale. Expect burgers, chicken, brisket, flatbreads. *Refill alert:* You get to fill your own drinks for free, a rarity. **Innoventions East.** Combo meal $12 to $14. Mobile ordering.

La Cantina De San Angel ★★ MEXICAN   Mexico's counter-service option will give you beef, fish, chicken tacos, cheese empanadas, nachos, and margaritas (from $11). It's outside but on the water. **Mexico.** Combo meal $12 to $14.

Kringla Bakeri Og Kafé ★★ SCANDINAVIAN   Some of the selections in Norway's bake shop can't be found elsewhere at Disney. More than one person claims the smooth, strawberry-topped rice cream pudding to be their favorite sweet in Walt Disney World. You can also get sandwiches, heated to order. **Norway.** Desserts $3 to $5, sandwiches $7.50 to $8.50.

Lotus Blossom Café ★ CHINESE   A Panda Express redux: China's Quick Service choice, with covered seating, is basic, serving beef noodle bowls, shrimp fried rice, pot stickers, and the like. **China.** Combo meal $10 to $12.

Sommerfest ★★ GERMAN   When you can't get into Biergarten, settle for this kiosk to get your bratwurst, sausage, and beer. **Germany.** Sausage rolls $10–$11.

Tutto Gusto ★★★ ITALIAN   The excellent full bar (stand-up only) attached to the Tutto Italia Ristorante is an underrated oasis that serves grown-up cocktails and also a selection of cheese and meat plates for two or three (from $25), plus pasta, cannoli, tiramisu, and panini. Get a six-wine "Grand Tour" flight tasting for $32. **Italy.** Panini $12 to $16, meat-and-cheese plates for two $24 to $29, desserts $4 to $10.

Liberty Inn ★ AMERICAN   Burgers on brioche buns and fried chicken in a setting as blandly Colonial as a rest stop on a Maryland highway. Outside, the **Liberty Square Market** stand has turkey legs and beer and a kiosk sells pumpkin spice funnel cakes. **The American Adventure.** Combo meal $10 to $13. Mobile ordering.

Katsura Grill ★★ JAPANESE   Japan's small counter-service location is in the gardens, and it supplies Japanese curry, teriyaki chicken, sushi ($9–$12 for four pieces), and edamame. Below, the **Garden House** kiosk pours plum wine and sake for $7 to $10. Facing the lagoon under the pagoda, the **Kabuki Cafe** kiosk (closed in cold weather) serves shaved ice with syrup (including melon and cherry flavors) for $4, and sake-infused ones for $9. **Japan.** Combo meal $9 to $14.

Tangierine Café ★★★ MOROCCAN   The indoor counter-service location serves *shawarma* or falafel with hummus, couscous, bread, and tabbouleh; and lamb or chicken wraps. Accent it with Casa Beer, from Casablanca, or Moorish coffee (powerful espresso spiced with cinnamon and nutmeg), and add baklava for $4. Kids can get burgers or chicken nuggets for $9. **Morocco.** Combo meal $13 to $15.

Boulangerie Pâtisserie ★★ FRENCH   Grab a fast, bready bite in the back of Les Halles, such as a chocolate croissant or a ham-and-cheese croissant ($3.50–$4.75—decent bargains), pastry ($2.25–$5), plain croissant ($2.25), quiche ($6.50), or baguette sandwiches ($4.75–$9). Next door, **L'Artisan des Glaces** has good sorbets and ice creams—plus a deadly ice cream martini made with Grand Marnier ($12). A cash-only kiosk on the lagoon griddles up hot crepes (with sweet fillings, not meat) for $5 to $7. **France.** Salads and sandwiches $8 to $9.25.

Yorkshire County Fish Shop ★★ BRITISH   Snag walk-up fish and chips and eat it al fresco. You get two strips of fish with chips (fries)—make sure to put vinegar, not ketchup, on the fries the way the English do. Ale costs $9. In the **Rose & Crown** pub, you can buy Scotch eggs or fish and chips ($12). **United Kingdom.** Combo meal $12.

EPCOT'S TABLE-SERVICE RESTAURANTS

Book ahead if your heart is set on something, particularly for a nighttime lagoon view—if you're going to spend this kind of money, get a view out of it. The host will not guarantee seating location, but it helps to politely ask. Objectively, there are very few meals that would rate highly if I ate them outside of the park gates, and as with all mass-produced meals, quality varies greatly from day to day; the lion's share of the enjoyment is just being there. Lunch entrees are generally $3 to $5 less expensive than at dinner. Taking them as you encounter them, going clockwise around World Showcase:

The Garden Grill ★★ AMERICAN   As Farmer Mickey, Pluto, and Chip 'n' Dale press the flesh in this slowly revolving, two-tiered circular restaurant, you're served all-you-can-eat family style "Harvest Feast" platters of meats and vegetables, some of which were grown in the greenhouses downstairs. This is the only character meal in Future World, but it's a good choice because it's mellow and small enough so that the merry rodents can spend quality time with you. **The Land.** All-you-can-eat, all three meals. $32 to $47 adults, $19 to $28 kids.

Coral Reef Restaurant ★ SEAFOOD   Turns out fish are both friends *and* food: Through windows into the 27-foot-deep aquarium, admire the luckier buddies of the fish on your plate. You're even given a cheat sheet to identify what's swimming by. Only about half the menu selections are fish, and the rest are things like short ribs or strip steak. It's about the cool view, not the cuisine. **The Seas with Nemo & Friends.** Main courses $24 to $35.

San Angel Inn Restaurante ★★ MEXICAN   Epcot's most atmospheric restaurant is set beneath a false twilight sky at the base of an ancient pyramid, with the boats from the Gran Fiesta Tour steadily passing—reserve the first time of the day to guarantee a seat by the river. The fare isn't Tex-Mex as much as it is Mexican: Dinner has chicken mole, chili relleno, grilled catch of the day, and caramel dulce de leche ice cream for dessert. If you can't get in (a likelihood), try La Hacienda de San Angel, across the main path on the lagoon. Its food is similarly Mexican. **Mexico.** Mains $22 to $32 lunch, $25 to $34 dinner.

La Hacienda de San Angel ★★ MEXICAN By day, it's a sunny place to get your tequila on. By night, this villa-themed restaurant (vaulted ceilings, hanging lanterns) is a fair place to sit for the nighttime show, but only if you're lucky enough to score a window seat. Margaritas are $15. Get the steak, chicken al pastor, or pan-seared snapper. **Mexico.** Main courses $18 to $34.

Princess Storybook Dining at Akershus Royal Banquet Hall ★★★ AMERICAN It's Epcot's meet-the-princesses extravaganza for all three "feasts" daily, in a Norwegian castle-like setting of vaulted ceilings and banners. Someone always stops by, be it Belle, Aurora, Snow White, Cinderella, or Ariel, who must not have heard that Norwegians love raw fish. This is the only character dining in World Showcase. Breakfast is the more lively time to come. **Norway.** Meals: $49 to $59 adults, $29 to $35 kids.

Nine Dragons Restaurant ★ CHINESE When you can't get a reservation anywhere else, you end up here. The food here is not much more daring or spicy than the cheaper Quick Service option, Lotus Blossom Café, except here, there are more choices and they're more expensive. The decor is handsomely geometric, but nothing memorable, although some tables face out toward the water. **China.** Main courses $16 to $24.

Biergarten Restaurant ★★★ GERMAN Toddlers lurch forward to polka, dads dive into mugs of Radeberger pilsner, and strangers make friends with their neighbors at this rowdy, carb-loaded party, an all-you-can-eat stuffer featuring schnitzel, spaetzle, rotisseric chicken, sauerbraten (at dinner), and an oompah band for about 20 minutes at a time. It's popular. **Germany.** Lunch (noon–3pm): $35 adults, $19 kids; dinner (after 4pm): $41 adults, $22 kids.

Tutto Italia Ristorante ★ ITALIAN Proclaimed authentic mostly by people who have never been to Italy, this dusky environment of chandeliers and murals nonetheless packs 'em in. Pasta of this low caliber should not be $25, but that doesn't stop patrons from buying $28 slices of lasagna. **Italy.** Main courses $22 to $35.

Via Napoli ★ ITALIAN The more enjoyable of Italy's two table-service restaurants features lots of light, three-story vaulted ceilings, and three amusing wood-fired ovens shaped like the open mouths of giant mustachioed men named after volcanoes. Into those are thrust $18 to $23 individual pizzas and $9.50 kids' pizzas made with flour imported from Naples (not that you could tell the difference). There's also some lasagna and spaghetti at around $21 to $30 a plate. It's operated by Patina Restaurant Group, which runs eateries in

Macy's, the Hollywood Bowl, and other tourist spots. **Italy.** Main courses $24 to $27, pizzas serving three to four, $45 to $48.

Teppan Edo ★★★ JAPANESE   Above the Mitsukoshi store (which runs it), a chef-cum-swordsmith slices, dices, and cooks at the teppanyaki griddle built into your table. It's fun to watch, although it's not a great choice if your kids are too young to keep their hands to themselves. Ask to see the smoking onion volcano. There's no view, but the food? Oh, it's fine, but you really come to see the fancy knife work. **Japan.** Main courses $24 to $36.

Tokyo Dining ★★ JAPANESE   On the second floor of the Japan pavilion, the decor is modern and stylish, the waitstaff subdued, and the menu offers both tempura/grills and sushi in modest portions at inflated prices. Some tables have a view of the lagoon through nearly floor-to-ceiling windows, which comes in handy around the nighttime show. A **third sit-down restaurant** in Japan is under construction (in a space built for a ride that was never created) and may be open by late 2019. **Japan.** Main courses $27 to $34, sushi $12 to $18 per order.

Restaurant Marrakesh ★★★ MOROCCAN   Tucked in the back of the souk, this lesser-known restaurant, lit theatrically with hanging lanterns, features a belly dancer, who appears (in a chaste costume) at 10 minutes before the hour at lunch starting at 12:50pm and at the top of the hour during dinner until 8pm, minus 4pm. The fare is approachable North African, heavy on shish kebabs, lemon chicken tagine, and couscous. Thinner crowds allow it to serve a good value at lunch: appetizer, entree, and dessert until 3:30pm for $20. **Morocco.** Main courses $19 to $35.

Spice Road Table ★★ MOROCCAN   Serving spicy garlic shrimp, coriander-crusted rack of lamb, and powerful organic sangria and cocktails, it has terrace lagoon views ideal for spectators of the nighttime show, so it fills up by 8pm. It also has a rare full bar that can do proper cocktails, not just pre-blended ones. **Morocco.** Small plates $9 to $13, full plates $23 to $36.

Chefs de France ★★ FRENCH   In a glassed-in dining room recalling a typical French bistro, dine on quiche and crepes or prototypical French food such as duck breast, beef bourguignon, escargot, and filet de boeuf (lunch and dinner). There's also a $40 prix-fixe, three-course meal. **France.** Main courses $21 to $36.

Monsieur Paul ★★★ FRENCH   Epcot's most thoughtful menu (and also its most expensive) starts with napkins that are folded like a chef's jacket. This is special occasion stuff: an oxtail soup with black truffle for $29, grilled tenderloin with mushroom fricassee, black seabass in rosemary sauce with scales made of roasted potato slices, plus all the amuse-bouches and long preparation explanations you'd expect of a fine establishment. Although it faces the water, the windows are small, so not every table has a view of the nighttime show. The entrance is tucked around the back door of Chefs de France, under a green-and-white striped awning. **France.** Main courses $40 to $45.

Rose & Crown Pub & Dining Room ★★★ BRITISH   The interior is similar to a country pub—big wooden bar with Victorian screen serving whisky and lots of British and Irish draught beers ($9, or twice as much as a London pub)—although some of the seating is outdoors. You can get bangers and mash (sausage with mashed potatoes), shepherd's pie (ground beef with peas topped with cheddar and mashed potatoes), and that standby that finds its way onto every Disney menu, no matter how errant, New York strip steak. You can only have a drink in the pub or you can wait for a patio seat. The pub's motto is *otium cum dignitate*—that's not a Hogwarts spell, it's "leisure with dignity." **United Kingdom.** Main courses $21 to $27.

Le Cellier Steakhouse ★ STEAKS   It takes the Canadian-themed restaurant to deliver the most all-American menu of filet mignon, snapper, pork, and chicken, but it also Canucks it up with sides such as *poutine* fries (topped with cheddar, truffle salt, and red-wine reduction). Specialties include a popular cheddar cheese soup and pretzel bread. True to its name, the restaurant is windowless and vaulted, like a very clean version of a wine cellar. It's a tough reservation to secure. **Canada.** Main courses $30 to $54.

DISNEY'S ANIMAL KINGDOM

The largest Disney theme park in Florida (500 acres), **Disney's Animal Kingdom** ★★ is enjoying attention after years as an also-ran. The park, which for 2017 became Disney's second-most popular (12.5 million visits) because of the hype over the new *Avatar*-themed area, debuted in 1998 at a reported cost of $800 million as a competitor to Busch Gardens. Most of that land is used up by a menagerie of exotic animals; instead of cages, they're kept in paddocks rimmed with cleverly disguised trenches that are concealed behind landscaping. Most attractions are given a mild environmentalist message (ironic, considering how much swamp was obliterated to build this resort, but never you mind).

Because animals retire to the shade as the Florida heat builds, a visit here most times of year should begin as soon as the gates open, usually around 8am, yet there really isn't enough to keep you here for 15 hours until the summer sun goes down. If you only have one day here, you really should choose whether to come in the morning (more active animals) or skew toward the evening (Pandora alight, a nighttime spectacular, but fewer animals). *Tips:* Check the weather, because if it's excessively hot or wet, you will be miserable: Only five major attractions take place in the A/C. There is currently no parade at Animal Kingdom, but there is a night show.

GETTING IN   Locker and stroller rental are just past the gates in what's called the **Oasis,** a lush buffer zone that gradually acclimates guests to the world of the park. Pick up a free Guidemap, a Times Guide, and an Animal Guide for the locations of animal enclosures, otherwise you'll miss a lot.

Generally speaking, the biggest animals collect at the back of the park (Africa and Asia), the thrills to the right (Asia and DinoLand U.S.A.).

The Best of Disney's Animal Kingdom

Don't miss if you're 6: Festival of the Lion King

Don't miss if you're 16: Avatar Flight of Passage

Requisite photo op: The floating mountains of Pandora

Food you can only get here: Frozen chai, Royal Anandapur Tea Company

The most crowded, so Fastpass+ or go early: Avatar Flight of Passage, Kilimanjaro Safaris

Skippable: Rafiki's Planet Watch

Quintessentially Disney: It's Tough to Be a Bug!

Biggest thrill: Expedition Everest

Best show: Rivers of Light

Character meals: Tusker House Restaurant, Africa

Best shopping: Bhaktapur Market, Asia; Island Mercantile, Oasis

Where to find peace: Discovery Island Trails

Nowhere will you find balloons—once discarded, they choke animals—and straws are made of paper for the same reason.

Discovery Island

Like the Plaza of the Magic Kingdom, Discovery Island is designed to be the hub of the park. Guests can touch down here to change lands.

The Tree of Life ★★★ RIDE Instead of a castle or a geosphere, the centerpiece here, Animal Kingdom's "weenie," is an emerald, 14-story-high arbor (built on the skeleton of an oil rig) covered with hundreds of carvings of animals made to appear, at a distance, like the pattern of bark. Some 102,000 vinyl leaves were individually attached—which is why its shade of green is more lurid than the surrounding foliage—to some 750 tertiary branches. That the best way to enjoy it is to slowly make a circuit of it, looking for and identifying new animals, is perhaps proof that the best way to experience this park is to slow down and open your eyes. At night, the front is illuminated with gently animated projections that highlight some of the hidden sculptures and bring them to life.

Discovery Island Trails ★★ ACTIVITY The self-guided paths encircle the Tree of Life. Here's where you'll find giant red kangaroos, flamingoes, storks, otters, lemurs, macaws, and the lappet-faced vulture; some are removed from view when it's hot. It takes only about 15 minutes to enjoy.

Adventurers Outpost ★ CHARACTER GREETING Mickey and Minnie, wearing explorer garb, meet kids, and sign autographs here, on the east side of the path toward Asia. It is the only place in the resort where they appear as a couple.

It's Tough to Be a Bug! ★★★ SHOW Hidden in the flying roots of the Tree of Life, in a cool basementlike theater, you'll find a cleverly rigged cinema showing a sense-tricking 10-minute 3-D movie based on the animated movie *A Bug's Life*. When the stinkbugs do their thing or the tarantula starts firing poison quills, you'll never quite be sure what's an image, what's cutting-edge robotics, and what's clever rigging in the theater. It's one of the best

Disney's Animal Kingdom

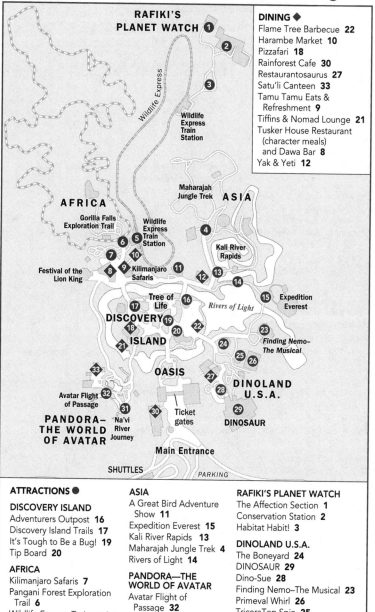

RAFIKI'S PLANET WATCH ❶
❷
❸

Wildlife Express Train Station

AFRICA

Gorilla Falls Exploration Trail

Wildlife Express Train Station

Maharajah Jungle Trek

ASIA

❹

Kali River Rapids

Festival of the Lion King

❻
❼
❽ ❾ ❿ Kilimanjaro Safaris
⓫
⓬ ⓭
⓮

Tree of Life
⓰
⓯ Expedition Everest

DISCOVERY ⓱
⓳
⓲
⓴ ㉒
㉑

Rivers of Light

㉓

Finding Nemo– The Musical

ISLAND

㉔
㉕ ㉖

㉝
OASIS

Avatar Flight of Passage ㉜
㉗
㉘

DINOLAND U.S.A.

㉙

DINOSAUR

㉛

PANDORA– THE WORLD OF AVATAR

Na'vi River Journey

㉚ Ticket gates

Main Entrance

SHUTTLES
PARKING

DINING ◆
Flame Tree Barbecue **22**
Harambe Market **10**
Pizzafari **18**
Rainforest Cafe **30**
Restaurantosaurus **27**
Satu'li Canteen **33**
Tamu Tamu Eats & Refreshment **9**
Tiffins & Nomad Lounge **21**
Tusker House Restaurant (character meals) and Dawa Bar **8**
Yak & Yeti **12**

ATTRACTIONS ●

DISCOVERY ISLAND
Adventurers Outpost **16**
Discovery Island Trails **17**
It's Tough to Be a Bug! **19**
Tip Board **20**

AFRICA
Kilimanjaro Safaris **7**
Pangani Forest Exploration Trail **6**
Wildlife Express Train station for Rafiki's Planet Watch **5**

ASIA
A Great Bird Adventure Show **11**
Expedition Everest **15**
Kali River Rapids **13**
Maharajah Jungle Trek **4**
Rivers of Light **14**

PANDORA—THE WORLD OF AVATAR
Avatar Flight of Passage **32**
Na'vi River Journey **31**

RAFIKI'S PLANET WATCH
The Affection Section **1**
Conservation Station **2**
Habitat Habit! **3**

DINOLAND U.S.A.
The Boneyard **24**
DINOSAUR **29**
Dino-Sue **28**
Finding Nemo–The Musical **23**
Primeval Whirl **26**
TriceraTop Spin **25**

DISNEY'S ANIMAL KINGDOM: 1 DAY, TWO WAYS

START: BE AT THE GATE FOR OPENING TIME.

Try to have a Fastpass+ for Avatar Flight of Passage or The Na'vi River Journey. It won't be easy, so plan to wait.

ANIMAL KINGDOM WITH KIDS

The morning will be busy, but the afternoon will be milder. When the gates open, head straight to **Pandora** and ride **Avatar: Flight of Passage** and **The Na'vi River Journey,** in that order.

↓

Go to Africa for **Kilimanjaro Safaris** because the animals are most active before the heat sets in. Head next door.

↓

Find the gorillas and hippos on the **Gorilla Falls Exploration Trail.**

↓

Go to Asia to spot tigers on the **Maharajah Jungle Trek.**

↓

Ride **Kali River Rapids** to cool down.

↓

See **UP! A Great Bird Adventure.**

↓

Have lunch at Yak & Yeti.

↓

See the next performance of **Finding Nemo—The Musical,** seated and indoors.

↓

Ride **Primeval Whirl** and **TriceraTop Spin.**

↓

Go see **It's Tough to Be a Bug!** and walk the Discovery Trails to look for animals embedded in the Tree of Life.

↓

Go to Africa to see **Festival of the Lion King.** At this point, younger kids may need to call it a day.

↓

If you have time or energy, take the train to and from Rafiki's Planet Watch for a 20-minute walk-through (budget 45 min. total).

↓

Wait until dusk to re-ride **Kilimanjaro Safaris** (if you care) and then return in the dark to **Pandora** to see its bioluminescent lights. If you have the energy, see **Rivers of Light,** or use the time to watch the projections on the Tree of Life.

ANIMAL KINGDOM WITHOUT KIDS

When the gates open, head straight to **Pandora** and ride **Avatar Flight of Passage** and **The Na'vi River Journey,** in that order.

↓

Off to Africa for Kilimanjaro Safaris. (Have a mid-to late-morning Fastpass+ for Avatar Flight of Passage or an early morning one for Kilimanjaro Safaris, depending if you want thrills or animals. It's fine if you have a Fastpass+ for later safaris; each trip yields different animals.)

↓

Watch the gorillas on the **Gorilla Falls Exploration Trail.**

OR

Go to Asia to ride **Expedition Everest** before the line gets too crazy.

↓

Walk to Asia and ride **Expedition Everest** (if you haven't already!).

↓

Explore the **Maharajah Jungle Trek** to see tigers.

↓

If it's hot by now, ride **Kali River Rapids.**

↓

Eat at Yak & Yeti.

↓

See **UP! A Great Bird Adventure.** (Or maybe just chill with a cocktail.)

↓

See the next performance of **Finding Nemo—The Musical.** Enjoy the air-conditioning.

↓

Ride **Primeval Whirl.**

↓

Ride **DINOSAUR.**

↓

See **It's Tough to Be a Bug!** and walk the Discovery Trails to look for animals embedded in the Tree of Life.

↓

Go to Africa to see **Festival of the Lion King.**

↓

If you have time or energy, take the train to **Rafiki's Planet Watch** (budget 45 min. total).

↓

Wait until dusk to re-ride **Kilimanjaro Safaris** for the sunset experience and then return in the dark to **Pandora** to see its bioluminescent lights. If you have the energy, see **Rivers of Light,** or use the time to watch the projections on the Tree of Life.

sense-tricking movies at Disney World. Little kids who can't distinguish fantasy from reality may be scared by the marvelously realized Hopper figure; sit in back (the first doors after you get your glasses) and to the left to be far from him. The indoor preshow area is decorated with posters for some funny entomological variations on Broadway shows (my faves: "Web Side Story" and "My Fair Ladybug"). *Strategy:* Upon exiting, go left to explore the trails (above) or right for the bridge to Asia.

Pandora—The World of Avatar

In 2017, at a reported cost of $500 million, Disney made the odd choice of opening this elaborate 12-acre area, which not only contains zero animals but also isn't even a Disney-created franchise. Whatever the logic, you can't say it isn't pretty. An evocation of the fantastical planet and tribal people from the 2009 film *Avatar*, Pandora is dominated by a vine-covered cascade of "floating mountains"—an impressive sight that's hard to photograph. To simply wander is to best experience it, taking in the sumptuous floral creations and listening for weird alien animal calls coming from the foliage. At night, vegetation and walkways illuminate with fluorescent light that Disney likes to call bioluminescent, and that spectacle necessitates a second visit after dark. Set aside the veiled, almost Victorian tropes about the Noble Savage that Disney seems to be evoking here. Seek out a cast member dressed as a guide for Alpha Centauri Exhibitions, the fictional tour company that purportedly brought you to Pandora. They can point out some of the hidden secrets of the land—such as secret pressure points in the trees that trigger flashes of light. There's a tiered viewing terrace in the center to better enable your admiration. The must-get souvenir, sold for $50 at the Rookery shop after Flight of Passage: little banshee puppets that sit on your shoulder.

Avatar Flight of Passage ★★★ RIDE   Like the characters in the movie, your consciousness will be transferred into the host body of (colonialism symbolism alert!) a Na'vi whose name you never learn as they ride a dragon-like creature, called a banshee, over the wonders of Pandora. Or that's the premise, and it's accomplished rather brilliantly, starting with a body scan to prep you for the transition. Easily one of the most elaborate attractions in Disneydom thanks in part to a sensationally decorated queue, the 4.5-minute ride feels intense even though it's basically you straddling a bike-like vehicle (it secures you by gripping your legs and clapping your back) in front of a very big movie screen; a breeze and water spritzes keep you from becoming nauseated. The concept works a lot like Soarin', but with a 3-D film and more intensity, but you actually travel nowhere. Pay special attention to the fun physical feedback as your vehicle presses against your legs. The ride's point is to take in landscapes, not terrify you. *Tip:* Some larger guests report difficulty fitting on the vehicle, so test the sample out front. The theatre is multi-leveled, if you have a hard time with stairs, ask for sections 1C or 1D; section 2 is evenly in the middle and 3 is at the top. Also, pee before you get in line. Cruelly for a ride with routine 3-hour waits, there are no restrooms in the building.

Na'vi River Journey ★★ RIDE All ages will find this gentle boat float through a dark but colorful Pandoran bog to be mellow going. All you do is bob from room to room, listening to music and soaking up what you see—it's a strange world, after all. There's lots of pretty plants and animals to look at, but the most impressive thing is the huge, limber-limbed, and deceptively complex "Shaman of Songs," the most complex Audio-Animatronic figure ever built, that serenades you near the ride's climax. All told, Journey is 4.5 minutes of calm, a glowing Tunnel of Love.

Africa

Due to its star attraction, Africa is mobbed in the morning; in the afternoon, it's a popular place to grab food or a cocktail. By evening, because of the new sunset effects on Kilimanjaro Safaris, it's mobbed again. **Dawa Bar,** at the entrance to Tusker House, is a nice placc to people-watch with a cocktail.

Kilimanjaro Safaris ★★★ RIDE Easily the bumpiest ride at Disney World, the 20-minute excursion is the crown jewel of Animal Kingdom. Climb into a supersize, 32-passenger Jeep-like vehicle—an actual one with wheels, not a tracked cart—and be swept into what feels like a real safari through the African veldt, with meticulously rutted tracks and all. Be quick on the shutter, because drivers speed fleetly, passing through habitats for giraffes, elephants, wilde-beest, ostrich, hippos, lions, antelope, rhinos, and other creatures that made safaris famous. Considering the quality and quantity of animals on display—and the cleverness of the enclosure design, as there are never bars between you and them—it's easily the best animal attraction of the park. Animals are most active when the park opens, but the queue builds once again at night so people can see it all over again with a sunset lighting effect (if you want to see that, I recommend Fastpassing it). Some people say that the second-best time to see the animals is in midafternoon because they get antsy with the foreknowledge that they're about to be led to their indoor sleeping quarters. Ride twice if you want—the free will of the animals means it's never the same trip twice: Some-times you'll zip right through, and sometimes you'll be halted by a moody rhino who refuses to get off the road. *Strategy:* Photographers who want clear shots should jockey toward the back, away from the cockpit. At the very least, they should negotiate with their companions for a seat at the end of their row.

Gorilla Falls Exploration Trail ★★★ ACTIVITY Upon exiting Kili-manjaro Safaris, begin this trail, which focuses on African animals. It wends past a troop of lowland gorillas (very popular), naked mole rats, okapi, meer-kats (yes, like Timon), and hippos you can view through an underwater win-dow; the nocturnal animals start waking up around 3:30pm. The circuit takes about a half-hour, but you can spend as long as you want. The gorillas come near the end, so budget your time. All close before dusk.

"Festival of the Lion King" ★★★ SHOW If this lavish, colorful, intense spectacle can't hold your attention for 30 minutes, you might require prescriptions. Audiences sit on benches in four quadrants (front rows are good for engaging with performers), and the event comes on buoyant and boister-ously, like an acid trip during a rock concert. Four huge floats enter the room, topped with soft-looking giant puppets of Timon, Pumbaa, and African wild-life and attended by acrobats, stilt-walkers, flame jugglers, and dancers, all of whom get their turn to dazzle you with their acts, which are performed, of course, to the hit songs of the movie. *Strategy:* Shows are scheduled, and they can fill up, so arrive 30 minutes early. Unfortunately, the seating is bleacher-style and lacks backs. The last shows are around dusk.

Rafiki's Planet Watch ★ ACTIVITY   Its elements are listed separately on the park maps, but everything is of a piece. The only way to reach this educational veterinary station is using the **Wildlife Express Train.** Waits are generally no longer than 10 minutes. The trip takes 7 minutes and you'll get glimpses of plain backstage work areas and maybe a white rhino in its indoor pen, but not much else. **Habitat Habit!,** the path that leads to the main build-ing, is another "discovery trail," this one with cotton-top tamarins (endangered monkeys about the size of squirrels). **Conservation Station** is a quasi-educa-tional peek at how the park's animals are maintained—you're not seeing the true veterinary facilities, but a few auxiliary rooms set up so tourists can watch activities through picture windows. There's not always something going on (early mornings seem to be most active), and the Times Guide doesn't help, so you might get all the way here and then find yourself with only some tanks of reptiles and amphibians to poke at, although Rafiki makes appearances all day. There's nothing earthshaking—enter a dark, soundproof booth and listen to the sounds of the rainforest—but the pace is much easier than in the park outside. **The Affection Sec-tion** is a petting zoo hosting your typical petting-zoo denizens—don-keys, goats, sheep, and so on. *Tip:* Try to visit by noon, when the vets are more likely to be treating ani-mals; Guest Relations, at the front of the park, keeps a schedule. It tends to close around dinnertime.

> ### Kid Stuff at Animal Kingdom
>
> Animal Kingdom has a free paper scaven-ger hunt, **Wilderness Explorers,** in which kids collect merit badges (stickers) for learning things about animals and con-servation. Join on the bridge between Oasis and the Tree of Life, opposite the Yak & Yeti, and by Dino-Bite Snacks.

Asia

Asia's decor (rat-trap wiring, fraying prayer flags) evokes Nepal or northern India. Don't miss the white-cheeked gibbons who live on the ruined temple at the exit of Kali River Rapids. Also make a stop at **Bhaktapur Market,** which sells Asian souvenirs that are a cut above the usual theme park stuff—printed dresses, little Buddhas, conical hats.

Expedition Everest ★★★ RIDE   The lavishly themed roller-coaster is mostly contained in the "snowcapped" mountain looming nearly 200 feet over the park's east end (if it were any higher, Florida law would require it to be topped by an airplane beacon). The queue area is a beautifully realized

The Chilling Tale of Disco Yeti

Expedition Everest's original effects were too complicated to function for long. For example, the summit was once shrouded in a cool mist. But the Yeti suffered the most ignoble fate. Although it was the most complicated Audio-Animatronic creature ever commissioned (25 feet tall, 19 movement functions) and the sight of it lunging five feet horizontally for your train was, for a short period, the ride's scintillating climax. But its repetitive motion began cracking its foundation, which were too integrated with the structure of the rest of the mountain to repair. The solution: A strobe light now makes it appear as if the motionless Yeti moves. Disney fans deride it as the "Disco Yeti." Imagineers swear they intend to fix it one day.

duplication of a Himalayan temple down to the tarnished bells and red paint, although portions of it are exposed to the sun, so drink something before you pony up. The coaster itself is loaded with powerful set pieces: both backward and forward motion, pitch-black sections, and a fleeting encounter with a 22-foot Abominable Snowman, or Yeti. As with all Disney rides, the most dramatic drop (80 ft.) is visible from the sidewalk out front, so if you think you can stomach that, you can do the rest. There are no upside-down loops; the dominant motion is spiral. *Strategy:* This is a top candidate for Fastpass+. The seats with the best view, without question, are in the front rows, although the back rows feel a little faster. The single-rider line is one of the resort's fastest-moving and most fruitful. It's an especially exciting ride at night.

Kali River Rapids ★ RIDE   The 12-passenger round bumper boat shoots a course of rapids, and sometimes you can get soaked—it depends on your bad luck—but it's generally milder than similar rides. Your feet, for sure, will get wet. The worst damage is usually done by spectators who shoot water cannons at passing boats. Lots of guests buy rain ponchos ($9–$10 each at nearby stores, or a buck at your local dollar store), but there is a water-resistant holding area in the center of each boat. To be safe, there are free 120-minute lockers available, $7/hour if you go over. *Strategy:* Lines build considerably when it's hot, so this is another prime Fastpass+ candidate.

Maharajah Jungle Trek ★★ ACTIVITY   Too few people enjoy this self-guided, South Asian–themed walking trail featuring some gorgeous tigers (rescued from a circus breeding program), flying foxes, komodo dragons, and a few birds frolicking among fake ruins. The tigers are most active when the park opens and toward the end of the day. Grab a bird information sheet after entering the aviary; there's a bat display, too, that you can bypass if you're squeamish. It'll close by dusk.

UP! A Great Bird Adventure ★ SHOW   Cushy costumed character versions of Russell and his dog Dug somehow wander into a presentation about birds, affording the host an excuse to introduce them, and you, to some gorgeous creatures—parrots, toucans, bald eagles, peacocks, African birds of prey—who swoop around the semi-enclosed arena, barely clearing heads. The last show of the day is in late afternoon. *Tip:* Sit on the end of an interior aisle for an extra thrill. If you've got short kids, try the sloped bleachers in back, because the ground seats may miss some low-level action.

DinoLand U.S.A.

When it rains, come here, where two attractions and one big counter-service restaurant are indoors.

"Finding Nemo—The Musical" ★★★ SHOW   One of the best shows at Disney is a fast-forwarded version of the movie by the songwriters of the Oscar-winning tune "Let It Go." The story was heightened with such catchy added songs as "Fish Are Friends, Not Food" and the infectious, Beach Boys–style "Go with the Flow." Just as in the Broadway adaptation of *The Lion King,* live actors manipulate complicated animal puppets in full view, which allows the fish to appear as if they're floating in the sea. Sprightly, bright, colossal, and energetic, this winning 40-minute show is a good choice for taking a load off (the bench seating is indoors), and even those who know the movie backward and forward will find something new in the vibrant vigor of the delivery. *Strategy:* Because some scenes happen in the aisle that crosses the center of the theater, sit in the rear half of the auditorium.

Chester & Hester's Dino-Rama ★ ACTIVITY/RIDE   Kids run loose in this miniature parking lot-style carnival with a midway, **Fossil Fun Games** (Mammoth skee-ball races, "Whac-a-Pachycephalosaurus"), and two simple family rides. **TriceraTop Spin ★**, for the very young (90 seconds), is yet another iteration of the Dumbo ride over at Magic Kingdom and is designed for kids to ride with their parents. Cars fit four, in two rows. **Primeval Whirl ★** is a pair of mirror-image, family-friendly carnival-style coasters (FYI, Walt *hated* carnivals) that start out like a typical "wild mouse" ride before, mid-trip, the round cars begin spinning on an axle as they ride the rails. Think of it as a roller-coaster version of the teacup ride. You can plainly see what you're in for, although you may be surprised at how roughly the movements can whip your neck. Don't feel bad if you give it a miss, too, because it's not a Disney original; it was made by a French company that sells similar rides to other parks. Keep the kids in control by swinging them across the path to **The Boneyard ★**, a

---

Animal Kingdom's Night Moves

The park stays open into the evening and is just more easygoing. The slow-paced but sumptuous **Rivers of Light** water-and-light spectacular fires up the lagoon near Asia with illuminated floats, prancing fountains, and projections on water curtains; it's nice but won't change your life. Also catch the glowing color features of **Pandora—The World of Avatar** after dark. **Kilimanjaro Safaris** added lighting that simulates perpetual sunset (it's pretty, but worse for spotting animals, so don't make it the only time you ride it). And **The Tree of Life** is illuminated with kumbaya projections.

hot, sun-exposed playground where the very young can dig up "prehistoric" bones in the sand and work off energy on catwalks, net courses, and slides.

DINOSAUR ★★ RIDE   A good rainy-weather option is this 3-minute indoor time-travel ride in which all-terrain "Enhanced Motion Vehicles" simultaneously speed and shimmy down an unseen track, all as hordes of roaring dinosaurs attempt to make you dinner and an approaching asteroid shower threatens to do everyone in. Some kids, and even some adults, find all those jaws and jerky movements rather intense, and it's extremely dark and loud, but ultimately, it's a fun time, even if the perpetual darkness makes me wonder how much money Disney saved in not having to build more dinosaurs. Like many modern rides, well-known actors perform in the preshow video; this one's got Phylicia Rashad, fiercely overacting, and Wallace Langham, in a horrific tie. The line never seems to be as long as this ride deserves. On the path to the ride, don't ignore **Dino-Sue,** the 40-foot-long, full-scale T. rex skeleton—it's a replica of Sue, the most complete specimen anyone has yet found. The original, unearthed in South Dakota in 1990, is on display at Chicago's Field Museum. The **Cretaceous Trail,** at the head of the path, showcases ferns and American alligators extant in that period.

Where to Eat at Disney's Animal Kingdom

All locations have vegetarian options, kids' meals, and if you identify yourself, special dietary requests can usually be accommodated. There are no plastic drink lids because they can choke animals. The fruit cart ($2/piece) is in Africa. You'll find some minor food kiosks on the paths linking Discovery Island and Africa to Asia; if they're open, they'll be on your Guide Map.

DISNEY'S ANIMAL KINGDOM'S QUICK-SERVICE RESTAURANTS

Flame Tree Barbecue ★★★ AMERICAN   If you don't mind gorging on dishes such as ribs and baked chicken when you're supposed to be appreciating animals, it has a wonderful terraced back garden with cushioned seating on the Discovery River useful for watching the Rivers of Light at a comfortable distance. The pulled-pork barbecue is a favorite. This is also where you get those honking turkey legs. **Discovery Island.** Combo meal $12 to $19. Mobile ordering.

Satu'li Canteen ★★★ INTERPLANETARY   At this popular new choice, dishes are cooked with a kooky spin to make them appear alien: Sustainable fish or sliced beef are served with yogurt boba balls, and the cheeseburgers are (deliciously) rethought as spongy steamed bao dumplings. You'll want the Blueberry Cream Cheese Mouse for its Instagram factor alone. You can order food ahead using MDX. **Pandora—The World of Avatar.** Combo meal $12 to $16. Mobile ordering.

Pizzafari ★★ AMERICAN   A vibrantly colored restaurant that once did only pizza went uptown and now also does flatbreads. **Discovery Island.** Combo meal $10 to $12. Mobile ordering.

PACKING IT IN: TWO PARKS, 1 DAY

START: BE AT THE GATE 20 MINUTES BEFORE OPENING TIME.

You really don't **have** to pay for 2 days' worth of park tickets to visit Animal Kingdom and Hollywood Studios. As long as you have the Park Hopper option, you can see the highlights in 1 action-packed day. You will miss some lesser attractions, but not enough to lose sleep over.

Which park you do first is a toss-up. The animals are most active first thing in the morning at Animal Kingdom, but the lines at Hollywood Studios' Toy Story Land are long this year. This plan starts at Animal Kingdom; if you follow it, have a pre-arranged afternoon Fastpass+ for Toy Story Mania! or Slinky Dog Dash at Hollywood Studios. Because it's still new, Pandora at Animal Kingdom will be busy all day, which is why I have you seeing it first thing in the morning, before crowds peak. If you start at Hollywood Studios, have an afternoon Fastpass+ for one of the two Pandora rides instead. And if the new *Star Wars* land is open, do Hollywood Studios first—and get there super early.

Begin your day at **Disney's Animal Kingdom.** When the gates open, head straight to **Pandora** to ride **Avatar Flight of Passage.** You can then skip the Na'vi River Journey to visit Africa for **Kilimanjaro Safaris.**

↓

Animal people: Enjoy the **Gorilla Falls Exploration Trail.**

Coaster people: Ride **Expedition Everest.** If the wait's bad, use the Single Rider line.

↓

Explore the **Maharajah Jungle Trek.**

↓

Ride **Kali River Rapids.**

↓

If you enjoy live musicals, see the next performance of either **Finding Nemo— The Musical** or **Festival of the Lion King.** This will take nearly an hour, so cut this if it's too close to lunch.

↓

Ride **DINOSAUR.** (Maybe you can do this while waiting for the Nemo show to start?)

↓

Switch parks. On the way, you could lunch on U.S. 192, where food's cheaper. Reach that quickly by following the signs to the Animal Kingdom Lodge and turning left at the light before its entrance. That's Sherbeth Road, and it winds to U.S. 192. After lunch, drive east on U.S. 192 a few miles and follow the signs back to Disney.

↓

Enter **Disney's Hollywood Studios.**

↓

Use your Fastpass+ for **Toy Story Mania!** or **Slinky Dog Dash** at Toy Story Land. Try riding the other one if the lines aren't too long.

↓

Ride **Twilight Zone Tower of Terror** and **Rock 'n' Roller Coaster.**

↓

Ride **Star Tours.**

↓

If you have time, see the **Indiana Jones Epic Stunt Spectacular.**

↓

Now you have a choice. When it gets dark, either see **Fantasmic!** (if it's performing tonight) or **Star Wars: A Galactic Spectacular**—or return to Animal Kingdom for its evening attractions, the lights of **Pandora, Rivers of Light** show, or the after-dark version of **Kilimanjaro Safaris.**

↓

Go back to your hotel and collapse.

Kusafiri Coffee Shop & Bakery ★ SANDWICHES   A hole in the wall selling panini with curry-spiced chips and offers Kosher items. **Africa.** Sandwiches $10 to $11.

Yak & Yeti Local Food Cafes ★★ ASIAN   Although there is a table-service location indoors by the same name, the outdoor windows do counter-service teriyaki beef bowls, Asian chicken wraps, ginger chicken salad, and pork egg rolls so greasy they could be used as torches. Chicken fried rice is just $5. Across the path on the water, the **Royal Anandapur Tea Company ★★** kiosk offers something unique: teas and slushy chai ($6). **Asia.** Combo meal $12 to $15.

Harambe Market ★★★ INTERNATIONAL   This food court (in a pan-African costume) has sheltered outdoor seating. The windows started out serving what they advertise, but now are more or less all the same: chicken skewers, gyro flatbread, ribs, beef and pork sausage, and South African wines. Also delicious: The coconut African milk tart in a chocolate shell. Combo meal **Africa.** $10 to $14. Mobile ordering.

Tamu Tamu Eats & Refreshment ★ INTERNATIONAL   Serving the beloved Dole Whip frozen pineapple dessert, but here, it's spiked with a shot of rum ($8). It's near **Dawa Bar,** a relaxing spot mimicking a fortress on the water where cocktails ($8–$16) are served; there are 10 seats at the bar but more under a bamboo shelter, but sadly it closes well before the park does. **Africa.**

Restaurantosaurus ★ AMERICAN   As American as DinoLand U.S.A., the kitchen pumps out burgers, hot dogs, chicken sandwiches, and nuggets. The **Dino-Bites** kiosk (not open nearly enough for such an awesome name) nearby sells desserts. **DinoLand U.S.A.** Combo meal $11 to $14. Mobile ordering.

DISNEY'S ANIMAL KINGDOM'S TABLE-SERVICE RESTAURANTS

Because you're probably going to be up early to see the animals at their best, this park is a good candidate for a character breakfast. There are very few places to get out of the heat and have a waiter-service meal.

Rainforest Cafe ★ AMERICAN   In a lush, jungle-like, theatrically lit setting, robotic animals roar and twitter over your cheese sticks, burgers, and rum cocktails in souvenir glasses. This is not a Disney original, but one of two outposts of the established brand at Disney World (the other is at Disney Springs Marketplace). **Oasis, at the park entry.** Main courses $15 to $36.

Tiffins ★★★ INTERNATIONAL   A contemporary upscale choice, the park's finest, was added in 2016. The menu is seasonal and inventive, but to give you an idea, it has included lobster popcorn Thai curry soup, Ethiopian coffee butter-infused venison, and pomegranate-lacquered chicken. Lunch and dinner. The casual **Nomad Lounge,** attached, is an air-conditioned space for small plates (poke, saté), South African wines, Ethiopian-style coffee, cocktails, and bespoke beer including the Kungaloosh Spiced Excursion Ale, made just for here by Miami's Concrete Beach Brewery. Nomad, which has a delightful terrace over the water, closes with the park. **Oasis.** Main courses $36 to $53.

Tusker House Restaurant ★★★ AMERICAN/AFRICAN   Under multi-colored banners in an ancient souklike environment, Donald, Daisy, Mickey, and Goofy greet families in safari garb for **Donald's Safari Breakfast** and **Donald's Dining Safari** lunch and dinner, all all-you-can eat buffets. The buffet dares more than most of Disney's do, featuring spit-roasted chicken, curries, peri-peri roasted salmon on banana leaf, and other pleasingly aromatic choices. It also has good vegetarian choices. **Africa.** Breakfast: $24 adults, $20 kids. Lunch and dinner: $47 adults, $28 kids, add $8/$5 for preferred seating to Rivers of Light.

Yak & Yeti Restaurant ★★ ASIAN   Themed like a Nepalese mansion stocked with souvenirs from across Southeast Asia, the restaurant has a menu just as geographically varied, serving Kobe beef burgers, Malaysian seafood curry, fried honey chicken, and sweet Korean beef. The Quick Service counter outside offers a shorter, but similar, menu for less, but at Animal Kingdom, air-conditioning is the most delicious treat. **Asia.** Main courses $11 to $26.

DISNEY'S HOLLYWOOD STUDIOS

This is it! Disney has been working for years to make 2019 the moment the 154-acre **Disney's Hollywood Studios** ★, the least popular of the four Disney parks (10.7 million visitors in 2017), finally rises to the level of its siblings. Disney threw a reported $1 billion at the addition of the small Toy Story Land of kiddie rides (opened summer 2018), and this year, it premieres a new Mickey Mouse dark ride and the hotly anticipated Star Wars: Galaxy's Edge land.

While the park was originally conceived as a single Epcot pavilion about show business, Universal's invasion of the Florida market prodded Disney executives to jealously and hastily inflate the concept and add a working production facility: Disney–MGM Studios. It was poorly planned. In 1989, the Studios opened with just two rides, both now gone. Production never took off, the park layout was (and remains) confusing, and younger guests didn't care about the MGM co-branding. Its production center for hand-painted animated movies shut down in 2004; MGM was stripped from the name in 2008. From this year on, though, people will call it "the *Star Wars* park."

Until Galaxy's Edge opens, Frommer's does not recommend devoting a full day to Hollywood Studios. Instead, combine it with Animal Kingdom or come in the mid-afternoon for the marquee attractions and then catch the pyrotechnic–and–water curtain evening show, **Fantasmic!,** which is good. Also good is **Star Wars: A Galactic Spectacular,** a nighttime show that mixes fireworks, lasers, and projections; it's well done even if it is one more *Star Wars* thing; get a viewpoint that looks squarely at the Chinese Theater or you'll miss details.

Hollywood Boulevard & Echo Lake

You arrive by the usual car/tram combo, by free ferry (from Epcot and the Boardwalk) or by bus (from the other parks). As soon as your bag is approved and you're through the gates, take care of business (strollers, wheelchairs, lockers) in the plaza before proceeding down Hollywood Boulevard. There are no attractions here, only shops and restaurants. The 122-foot-tall Sorcerer Mickey Hat, the park's central icon, was built at the Boulevard's terminus in 2001, but it was demolished, to cheers from purists, in 2015, and the park's original entrance vista of the Chinese Theater was restored. No one pays much attention to the theatre's forecourt, but you should since it has many original concrete impressions of footprints and handprints collected from movie stars when the park was still angling to be a player in the film industry. In fact, this is the only place to find Audrey Hepburn's handprints; she didn't leave them at the Hollywood Grauman's. Occasional 15-minute *Star Wars*-themed live shows—strolling Stormtroopers and way too many movie clips—periodically take over the cheap festival stage erected here; check the Times Guide for those.

Frozen Sing-Along Celebration ★ SHOW   The 30-minute, self-explanatory group torture chamber features live actors telling the history of Arendelle six to nine times daily, as well as an opportunity for you to endure "Let It Go" for one more white-knuckled, mother-loving time. You'll be seated in the air-conditioning, but don't waste Fastpass+ on it because it's never full—the real Elsa and Anna show is over at Epcot now. *Strategy:* Strong cocktails are served at a kiosk on the patio of the Brown Derby, opposite the theatre.

Star Wars: Path of the Jedi ★ MOVIE   Run in the other direction. It's just a 10-minute featurette that slaps together movie clips. We used to call this a DVD extra feature and click past it, not pay $100 admission for it.

Indiana Jones Epic Stunt Spectacular ★★ SHOW   The 30-minute, bone-rattling tour de force of hair-raising daredevilry—rolling-boulder dodging, trucks flipping over and exploding—simultaneously titillates and, to a lesser degree, reminds you how such feats of derring-do are rigged for the movies. They try hard to convince you that they're really filming these sequences—you may need to explain to young children why they're lying about that, and about calling the lead actor "Harrison Ford's stunt double," but most kids

---

The Best of Disney's Hollywood Studios

Don't miss if you're 6: Slinky Dog Dash
Don't miss if you're 16: Rock 'n' Roller Coaster
Requisite photo op: The Chinese Theater
Food you can only get here: Grapefruit Cake, the Hollywood Brown Derby, Hollywood Boulevard; Peanut Butter and Jelly Milkshake, 50's Prime Time Café, Echo Lake
The most crowded, so Fastpass+ or go early: Slinky Dog Dash, Toy Story Mania!

Skippable: Beauty and the Beast—Live on Stage
Quintessentially Disney: Walt Disney Presents
Biggest thrill: Twilight Zone Tower of Terror
Best show: Fantasmic!
Character meals: Hollywood & Vine (breakfast, lunch)
Best shopping: The Beverly Sunset, Sunset Boulevard
Where to find peace: Around Echo Lake

Disney's Hollywood Studios

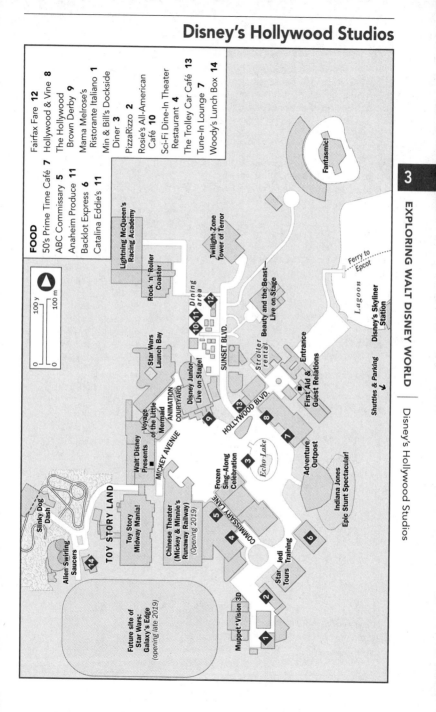

FOOD

50's Prime Time Café **7**
ABC Commissary **5**
Anaheim Produce **11**
Backlot Express **6**
Catalina Eddie's **11**
Fairfax Fare **12**
Hollywood & Vine **8**
The Hollywood Brown Derby **9**
Mama Melrose's Ristorante Italiano **1**
Min & Bill's Dockside Diner **3**
PizzaRizzo **2**
Rosie's All-American Café **10**
Sci-Fi Dine-In Theater Restaurant **4**
The Trolley Car Café **13**
Tune-In Lounge **7**
Woody's Lunch Box **14**

DISNEY'S HOLLYWOOD STUDIOS: 1 DAY, TWO WAYS

START: BE AT THE GATE FOR OPENING TIME.

Grab food at a counter restaurant when it's convenient to you—but having lunch at 11am saves time. The must-have Fastpass+ candidates for this park are Slinky Dog Dash, Toy Story Mania!, or Alien Swirling Saucers. (You can only schedule one of those at a time; that's the order of preference.) **Note:** If Star Wars: Galaxy's Edge has opened by the time you go, scratch this entire plan, arrive at the park an hour+ early, and go straight there for the entire morning.

HOLLYWOOD STUDIOS WITH KIDS

Fastpass+ within 90 minutes of opening: **Slinky Dog Dash.** If your kids are too young, **Voyage of the Little Mermaid.**

When the gates open, head directly to **Slinky Dog Dash.** If you're holding a pass to ride that later, do **Toy Story Mania;** it's worth re-riding. Enjoy Toy Story Land.

OR

Note: If your child wants to participate in the **Jedi Academy,** reserve a slot around now (ask a cast member where; it changes).

↓

See **Voyage of the Little Mermaid.**

↓

See **Disney Junior—Live on Stage!** (if your kids are wee) or **Lightning McQueen's Racing Academy** (if they're grammar school age).

↓

Meet **Mickey Mouse** (check the Times Guide for his location).

↓

Target a performance of **Beauty and the Beast—Live on Stage** for around now.

↓

At this point, littler ones may need to leave the park for a break.

↓

See **Muppet*Vision 3-D.**

↓

See the **Indiana Jones Epic Stunt Spectacular.**

↓

If you think the whole family can handle them, slot in the **Twilight Zone Tower of Terror** and the **Rock 'n' Roller Coaster.**

↓

See **Fantasmic!** (if it's performing tonight). People stake out their seats as long as an hour ahead, but 30 minutes will do. Or catch **Star Wars: A Galactic Spectacular**—make sure your view is of the middle of the Chinese Theater.

HOLLYWOOD STUDIOS WITHOUT KIDS

When the gates open, ride **Toy Story Mania!** even if you have a Fastpass+ for later; it's worth re-riding. Either that or **Slinky Dog Dash.**

↓

Head to the **Twilight Zone Tower of Terror** and the **Rock 'n' Roller Coaster** and ride them.

See **Voyage of the Little Mermaid** (it's fun even without kids).

↓

Ride **Star Tours.**

↓

See **Muppet*Vision 3-D.**

↓

See the **Indiana Jones Epic Stunt Spectacular.**

↓

You'll have a lot of time to kill now— re-ride anything you choose. Or you may decide you're done for the day— perhaps see the nighttime attractions at Animal Kingdom.

↓

If you stay, see **Fantasmic!** (if it's performing tonight) or the Star Wars fireworks show.

understand the violence is fake. The acrobats and gymnasts are skilled, and the production values are among the highest of any show at a Disney park. The outdoor amphitheater is sheltered, and you can bring drinks and food. *Strategy:* Arrive 20 minutes early, because there's a warm-up and volunteers are selected before showtime. It's mounted about five times daily, listed on the Times Guide.

Star Tours—The Adventure Continues ★★★ RIDE   Before Disney bought *Star Wars,* it made, and later upgraded, this popular, 40-person motion-simulator capsule that has you riding shotgun with a fretful C-3PO on an ill-fated and turbulent excursion. In 5 minutes, you manage to lose control, go into hyperdrive, dodge asteroids, navigate a comet field, evade a Star Destroyer, get caught in a tractor beam, and join an assault on the Death Star—or another combination of perils, since there are more than four dozen possible combinations of storylines (some newly created to promote the new movies). The video is well matched to the movements, which cuts down on reports of nausea. Row 1 is the front row, and that's the best place to see the screen.

Jedi Training ★★ SHOW   Up to 15 times daily (see the Times Guide), about a dozen kids are lent robes, telescoping "light sabers," and some gentle training in the Force by a "Jedi master" before a final defeat of Darth Vader and some Stormtroopers. It's cute and takes 20 minutes. Recruits (ages 4–12) are selected by 10:30am, tops, at the Adventure Outpost, to the left of Indiana

---

2019's Major Premieres in Hollywood Studios

If you are alive on Planet Earth in 2019, it will be impossible to avoid the Force of the Disney hype machine for the new 14-acre **Star Wars: Galaxy's Edge.** It doesn't open here until late fall of 2019, 6 months after the first one, with all the same components, opens at Disneyland in California. What should you expect, besides obscenely crushing crowds? (Seriously—if you don't arrive before the park opens, you will still be in line by the time our 2020 edition comes out.) The setting is the Black Spire Outpost on the frontier planet Batuu, a way station for adventurers and rogues that's filled with full-size spaceships and ancient petrified trees. The industry buzzword here is *immersive*: You won't even be able to buy souvenirs with the movie logos on them—the aim, as with Universal's Harry Potter lands, is to foster an illusion that you're actually at an intergalactic supply post, so you'll buy things like alien pet creatures. There will be two rides. One is a battle between the Resistance and the First Order, said to be more extraordinarily complex than anything else in the Disney universe, and the other has you piloting the Millennium Falcon. And here's a twist—how you perform on those will affect how you're treated at the "cantina" and elsewhere in the land; wear those MagicBands so the hidden technology can make that happen.

And 2019 will also see the opening of **Mickey & Minnie's Runaway Railway,** a fast-paced, lollipop-colored indoor ride inside the Chinese Theater that yanks you through the screen and into the hijinks of the classic Mickey Mouse cartoons. It's said to be rollicking, eye-popping, and packed with Hidden Mickeys (p. 106). We're counting on it, because its lead Imagineer is the guy who oversaw Disney California Adventure's spectacularly successful Radiator Springs Racers.

Jones as you face it, so get there early if your young Padawan wants a shot at carrying home the diploma.

Sunset Boulevard

The prime items in the park are on this street, which peels off not from the hub, as you might expect, but from the middle of Hollywood Boulevard. Look for vaudeville-style, slapstick **street performances** here.

The Twilight Zone Tower of Terror ★★★ RIDE   The tallest ride at Disney World (199 ft.) is one of the smartest, most exciting experiences at the parks, and it's the best version of the ride at any Disney park. It shouldn't be missed. Guests are ushered through the lobby, library, and boiler room of a cobwebby 1930s Los Angeles hotel before being seated in a 21-passenger "elevator" car that, floor by floor, ascends the tower and then, without visible tracks, emerges from the shaft and roams an upper level. Soon, you've entered a second shaft and, after a pregnant moment of tension, you're sent into what seems to be a free fall (in reality, you're being pulled faster than the speed of gravity) and a series of thrilling up-and-down leaps. The fall sequence is random and you never drop more than a few stories—but the total darkness, periodically punctured by picture-window views of the theme park far below as you become momentarily weightless, keys up the giddy fear factor. It's impossible not to smile. *Strategy:* In the preshow "library" room, move to the wall diagonally across from the entry door and you'll exit first, saving time. In the boarding area, the best views are in the front row, numbered 1 and 2, although you may not be given a choice. Chickens can bail down the stairs before the ride boards.

Rock 'n' Roller Coaster Starring Aerosmith ★★★ RIDE   On one of DHS's two big thrills—it's a big favorite—24-passenger "limousine" trains launch from 0 to 57mph in under 3 seconds, sending them through a 92-second rampage through smooth corkscrews and turns that are intensified by fluorescent symbols of Los Angeles (at one point, you dive though an "o" of the Hollywood sign). The indoor setup is a boon, because it means the ride can operate during the rain, and it makes the journey slightly less disorienting for inexperienced coaster riders. Cooler yet, speakers in each headrest (there are more than 900 in total) play Aerosmith music, which is perfectly timed to the dips and rolls. *Strategy:* The Fastpass+ line is absorbed quickly. There's also a single-rider line, though it's not always quick.

Lightning McQueen's Racing Academy ★★ SHOW   This early 2019 addition is at the Sunset Showcase, a special-events building behind Rock 'n' Roller Coaster that hasn't been used as a daily part of the park before. Since it's the only permanent *Cars*-themed attraction in Florida, it's the only place to get a look at the beautiful character design work on display at Cars Land in Anaheim—full-size Mater, Cruz Ramirez, and Lightning McQueen, who shows off his racing techniques on a simulator and relives career highlights with his audience. *Tip:* Check the Times Guide for the schedule.

Beauty and the Beast—Live on Stage ★ SHOW   The kid-friendly, 30-minute show is advertised as "Broadway-style," but it's really not. It's theme park–style, simplified with the most popular songs from the movie. The story is highly condensed (you never find out why Belle is at the Beast's castle and Gaston's fate isn't shown) and many characters inhabit whole-body costumes, speaking recorded dialogue with unblinking eyes. To the benefit of timid kids, the Beast looks more like a plush toy than a scary monster. Its intended audience cheers like it's a rock concert and hoists smartphones during the ball scene, and because of that, most performances are jammed. The metal benches are numbing, but at least the amphitheater is covered. *Strategy:* Arrive 20 minutes early so you don't end up in the back where afternoon sun can seep in.

Fantasmic! ★★★ SHOW   The super-popular 25-minute pyrotechnics show featuring character-laden showboats, a 59-foot man-made mountain, flaming water, and lasers projected onto a giant water curtain, takes place in the 6,500-seat waterfront Hollywood Hills Amphitheatre. Although it's a strong show by dint of its uniqueness, it doesn't play nightly. I'm always stunned to see people start arriving at the theater as much as *2 hours* before showtime. Most people will be satisfied taking their chances and showing up within 30 minutes of showtime. The seating is hard on the derriere. *Strategy:* On nights when there are two performances (not common), do the second one, as it's always less crowded. Sit toward the rear to avoid catching water from the special effects and to the right to make exiting easier. You can get reserved seats if you book the Fantasmic! Dining Package and eat dinner in the participating restaurants ($45–$63 adults, $18–$22 kids).

Muppets Courtyard & Commissary Lane

This confused area is bearing the brunt of the closures necessitated by construction—construction walls dominate and even the whimsical fountain of Miss Piggy as the Statue of Liberty has been reduced to a role as a planter. Mostly, it's where you can find two places serving Italian food.

Muppet*Vision 3-D ★ SHOW   The 17-minute movie features various tricks such as air blasts to make you feel like what you're seeing is actually happening. The doors on the right lead to the back of the 600-seat auditorium and the ones on the left lead to the front; stick in the middle, since the theater's walls become part of the show and you'll want to see. The preshow is amusing in that Muppet way (says Sam Eagle about seating procedures: "Stopping in the middle is distinctly unpatriotic!"), but the movie contains a few missteps (Waldo, a CG character, is crude and old-fashioned), and not all the effects function. Still, it's fast moving and includes lots of beloved *Muppet Show* favorites, such as Miss Piggy and Kermit. The Muppets, too, lend themselves very nicely to Audio-Animatronic technology. *Strategy:* Lines are longest just after the Indiana Jones show lets out.

Toy Story Land

Toy Story Land (opened 2018) is one of the park's most colorful treats. Take a few minutes to absorb the surroundings—the concept (not immediately obvious) is that you have shrunk down to the size of Andy's other toys. It's a tough zone on hot days since the trees are still too young to provide much shade and only one of the three rides (Toy Story Mania!) has an indoor queue. There are no indoor restaurants in this area, either, just a kiosk. The expansion accomplishes two goals: Build more stuff that plays off of millennial nostalgia, and add more rides younger kids can do. There's also a ton of product placement, and everything looks its best after dark.

Slinky Dog Dash ★★★ ROLLER COASTER You may think it's just a Barnstormer-style kiddie training coaster, but its quick accelerations, banked turns, and humps with genuine air time make it more exuberant than it appears to be, yet for all its giddy sensations, its 2 minutes remain rambunctiously accessible. While not for toddlers (the minimum height is 38 inches), it perfectly straddles the family-friendly line, unleashing a little giddy-up for the teens without turning into something Grandma would hate, and the theming has a few surprises you can't see from the waiting area. *Tip:* It will be hard to get a Fastpass+ for this ride in 2019 because it's so new and Disney resort guests will snap them up early. So head here first thing upon opening.

Toy Story Mania! ★★★ RIDE The plotless indoor ride is the most popular in the park, and rightly so. Wearing 3-D glasses, passengers shoot their way through a series of six animated midway games (themed as Woody's suction cup shooting game, a Little Green Men ring toss, etc.) based on the Pixar toy box characters. Along the way, air puffs heighten the reality. Your cannon is easy to work and easy on the hands—you just tug a cord and it fires. Racking up points is harder; both accuracy and intensity count—a top score for the whole month might be 584,000 (my record is 212,600). The queue area, stuffed with outsize toys such as Etch-a-Sketch and Barrel of Monkeys, makes waiting a delight: A 6-foot-tall, lifelike Mr. Potato Head entertains with live interaction and hoary jokes ("Is this an audience or a jigsaw puzzle?"). *Tip:* This is also a top Fastpass+ contender, because the wait can jump to an hour just 15 minutes after the park opens.

Alien Swirling Saucers ★ RIDE It's essentially a covered variant of the tried-and-true Whip carnival thrill but with a Little Green Men theme (and the same thing as Mater's Junkyard Jamboree at the Disneyland resort). Your vehicle, containing a bench that should fit up to four, does an easygoing do-si-do with other carts along four slowly spinning plates. It takes 90 seconds, which is enough time to meander across the four discs three times, and because you're not actually spinning but weaving, it doesn't tend to make most people queasy the way the teacups ride does. It's easy on kids (at least 32 inches). *Tip:* Seat your heaviest passenger on the end; the spinning will send everyone sliding into them. It's a nice enough diversion but nothing you can't skip if time is scarce.

Pixar Place & Animation Courtyard

If you have wee kids, Animation Courtyard is where two of the primary toddler attractions are. When the park opened, it was the starting point of a walking tour through a working studio that actually produced Disney movies. The artists were evicted and now it's where *Star Wars* movies and merch are hawked.

The Voyage of the Little Mermaid ★★ SHOW This bright, energetic, condensed version of the animated movie has high production values (puppets, live actors, mist, and a cool undersea-themed auditorium) and is a standout. It's a top contender for the best show to see in the heat of the day, and Fastpass+ is available. ***Strategy:*** In the preshow holding pen, the doors to the left lead to the back half of the theater; because the blacklight puppetry of the marvelous "Under the Sea" sequence can be spoiled if you see too much detail, I suggest sitting there. Put very small kids in your lap so they can see better.

Disney Junior—Live on Stage! ★★ SHOW For those of us who obediently rise and dance when commanded by Mickey Mouse, there's this breezy, 25-minute show with lots of excellent puppets (***Warning for adults:*** You sit on the ground). It inspires such fervent participation from under-5s that it feels like a meeting for a kindergarten cult that you're not a member of. Even if you don't know the names Doc McStuffins or Sofia the First, this sing-along revue is still pretty to look at, and Mickey, Minnie, and friends make appearances. The parental units won't be too bored, because this de facto Disney Channel ad is fast paced, like changing the channel every 4 minutes. Obviously, anyone old enough to do a book report can skip it. ***Tip:*** It only happens once or twice an hour; the schedule is in the Times Guide.

Star Wars Launch Bay ★ SHOW Filler from a galaxy far, far away! An exhibition on the animation glories that built the Disney Empire was swept away for this, which serves only to sell the *Star Wars* franchise by Force through costumes and props (replicas) and character meet-and-greets. Chewbacca was always a teddy bear, but why patricidal baddie Kylo Ren is suddenly eager to pose for selfies with random children is a story lapse worse than the Ewoks. Launch Bay is paired with a pointless 10-minute movie about the Hollywood filmmakers, but you can enter through Cargo (the gift shop) to skip that.

Walt Disney Presents ★★ ACTIVITY The only focus on Disney history on resort property, it's mostly overlooked but the display is a requisite stop for anyone curious about the undeniable achievements of this driven man. Here, you (and a few other stragglers) find a few authentic artifacts (props, costumes, his desk from his studio on Hyperion Avenue), plus explanations of the revolutionary "multiplane" camera that enabled animators to reproduce the sliding depth of field normally seen in live-action films—you've seen the fruit of the process in *Snow White* as the camera seems to move through the forest. The Oscar he won in 1954 is on view, too. The end of the exhibition chronicles the theme parks, including a few scale models and an Abe Lincoln Audio-Animatronic skeleton from the 1964 World's Fair. Most people take about 20

A favorite resort-wide pastime for long-time fans is spotting **Hidden Mickeys,** which are ingeniously camouflaged mouse-ear patterns that can be secreted just about anywhere. You'll find the three circles signifying a Mickey head in an arrangement of cannonballs on Peter Pan's Flight; flatware in the dining room at the Haunted Mansion; woven into carpeting, printed on wallpaper. Many sightings are up to interpretation, so sharpen your observational skills at **HiddenMickeysGuide.com.**

minutes for the museum, and then there's a good 15-minute movie, culled mostly from archival footage. The feature scores points for mentioning Disney's 1931 breakdown, but tries to prove Walt was a patron of the Disney Company's current efforts, implying he approved of Epcot's final design and worse, elbowing pivotal Roy Disney virtually out of the story. But maybe it can be changed. "Disneyland," he promises "is something that will never be finished."

Where to Eat at Disney's Hollywood Studios

All locations have a few vegetarian options, kids' meals, and if you identify yourself, special dietary requests can usually be accommodated, albeit often at diminished quality. There are also some snack kiosks not listed here, and you can buy alcohol throughout the park.

DISNEY'S HOLLYWOOD STUDIOS' QUICK-SERVICE RESTAURANTS

The Trolley Car Café ★★ AMERICAN   A glorified Starbucks themed after Los Angeles' bygone Red Cars, it has the usual Starbucky food. **Hollywood Boulevard.** Sandwiches from $6.

Rosie's All-American Cafe ★★ AMERICAN   In the Sunset Ranch Market riff on L.A.'s Farmer's Market, you'll find outdoor-only but sheltered counter service serving burgers and chicken nuggets. **Sunset Boulevard.** Combo meal $10 to $12. Mobile ordering.

Catalina Eddie's ★★ AMERICAN   Outdoor counter service for doughy personal pizza. Near it is **Anaheim Produce** for fruit ($2 per piece). **Sunset Boulevard.** Combo meal $10 to $11. Mobile ordering.

Fairfax Fare ★★ AMERICAN   Grab hand-friendly food: pulled-pork sandwiches, empanadas, fajitas. **Sunset Boulevard.** Combo meal $10 to $13. Mobile ordering.

ABC Commissary ★★ AMERICAN   Burgers, chicken clubs, Asian Mediterranean salad—it's one of DHS's most comfortable Quick Service choice because the air-conditioned space is fashioned after a 1930s Art Deco backlot cafeteria. **Commissary Lane.** Combo meal $11 to $18. Mobile ordering.

Min & Bill's Dockside Diner ★ AMERICAN Hot dogs, nachos, pulled-pork sliders, eaten al fresco under umbrellas for shade. There are some changing food carts on the other side of the lake, too. **Echo Lake.** Combo meal $11 to $13.

Backlot Express ★★ AMERICAN Bacon cheeseburgers, chicken and waffles, hot dogs, and a few simple salads served with air-conditioning and self-serve soda machines for endless refills. **Echo Lake.** Combo meal $10 to $14. Mobile ordering.

PizzeRizzo ★ AMERICAN Counter-service pizza, antipasto salad, and meatball subs themed to the Muppets with scads of air-conditioned seating. It has the biggest dining area in the park. **Muppets Courtyard.** Meals $10 to $11. Mobile ordering.

Woody's Lunch Box ★ AMERICAN Counter service with exposed seating. Greasy delights include BBQ brisket melt and grilled three-cheese sandwiches. **Toy Story Land.** Meals $9 to $13. Mobile ordering.

DISNEY'S HOLLYWOOD STUDIOS' TABLE-SERVICE RESTAURANTS

The highest-concept reservation restaurants in Disney World are here. The food isn't legendary, but some of the settings play on entertainment greatness. In addition to these, check out the **Baseline Tap House** at the end of Commissary Lane, with nine excellent craft beers on draught, one cider, and snacky dishes like soft pretzels and cheese plates.

The Hollywood Brown Derby ★★ AMERICAN With interior design based on the after-hours industry hangout of Hollywood's Golden Age, this airy post-Deco hall shoots for class. Caricatures of film legends line the walls—and while the original Brown Derby was noted for inventing the Cobb salad, this version is a bit of a caricature too, often soggy. Other choices, all invoking that mid-century California spirit at the park's highest prices ($29 for vegetarian pho? Are they kidding?). Expect rack of lamb, chicken breast, Faroe Islands salmon, and beef filet. Its grapefruit cake is a specialty—they'll give you the recipe. Outside, **The Hollywood Brown Derby Lounge** does sliders, steamed buns, smaller Cobb salads, and cocktails. **Hollywood Boulevard.** Main courses $18 to $49.

Hollywood & Vine ★★ AMERICAN At breakfast and lunch, costumed Disney Junior characters (such as Goofy, Doc McStuffins, and Jake) greet kids, sing, and dance in a diner-like setting for **Disney Junior Play 'n Dine at Hollywood & Vine.** Lunch here means 10am. At dinner, your core Disney talent (Mickey, Minnie, Donald, Daisy, Goofy) shows up. The food is always an all-you-can-eat buffet. **Echo Lake.** Buffet $34 to $50 adults, $20 to $30 kids.

50's Prime Time Café ★★★ AMERICAN Dine atop Formica in detailed reproductions of Cleaver-era kitchens while TVs play black-and-white shows from the era. Waitresses gently sass customers as they sling blue-plate specials—meatloaf, pot roast, chicken pot pie, and other mom-like dishes—but the favorite here is its peanut butter and jelly milkshake ($6). Attached is the **Tune-In Lounge,** a TV room for adults serving beer and proper cocktails "from Dad's liquor cabinet"—plus anyone can eat from the regular menu at the bar, which is first-come, first-served. **Echo Lake.** Main courses $17 to $25.

Mama Melrose's Ristorante Italiano ★★ ITALIAN   Items cost two-thirds of what they do at Epcot's Italy, and the atmosphere recalls the brick-walled, red-boothed family restaurant you'd find in any big American city. As expected, there are pastas, steaks, flatbreads, saltimbocca, and wood-grilled chicken dishes. **Streets of America.** Main courses $19 to $33.

Sci-Fi Dine-In Theater Restaurant ★★★ AMERICAN   Disney World's most unusual restaurant arranges mock-ups of 1950s automobiles before a silver screen showing a loop of B-movie clips and trailers. Couples sit side-by-side, like at a real drive-in movie, stars twinkle in the "sky," and families get their own booths. It's a brilliant idea, but it was even better when there were roller-skating carhops. Food quality is iffy. Dishes include burgers, shrimp or chicken pasta, and prime rib sandwich, and wedge salad. **Commissary Lane.** Main courses $15 to $33.

DISNEY WATER PARKS

The big question: Blizzard Beach or Typhoon Lagoon? Both can fill a day. So it depends on your mood. Typhoon Lagoon's central feature, a sand-lined 2½-acre wave pool, is an ideal place for families to approximate a day at the beach. If your kids have a need for speed, then head to Blizzard Beach, which has wilder water slides. If you use a one-day ticket (and not Water Parks Fun & More), you can hit both in the same day without paying more.

Both water parks, similar in size, have free parking and are less busy early in the week, probably because folks tend to start their vacations on a weekend and don't get to the flumes until they've done the four big theme parks. They tend to be busier in the morning than in late afternoon. They also sell everything you need to protect yourself from the sun, including lotion (should you have forgotten) and swimsuits (should you lose yours in the lather). Most lines (many rides have two: one for a raft and one for the slide) are exposed to the sun, so it's important to **keep hydrated,** because you won't always be aware how much you're sweating. Both parks sell refillable mugs for **endless soft drinks** for $12 (otherwise, soft drinks start at more than $3.50). They also rent towels for $2. Lifeguards usually make you remove water shoes on slides that don't use a mat or raft, and swimsuits with rivets or zippers are forbidden.

A day at a water park isn't as stressful as one spent among the queues of the theme parks, and if you're paying attention, the sights and sounds of a day here are pretty heartwarming. Every time the wave machine roars into gear, for example, dozens of kids shriek with delight and scamper into the water. Because they're chilling out, people tend to be happy at these parks.

LOCKERS   A locker is $10–$15. They allow multiple access, and a typical one is about 2 feet deep with an opening about the size of a magazine.

PREPARATION   Thoughtfully, parking is free. There are bulletin boards past the park entrances that tell you what the sunburn risk is and what the wait times are for the slides, as well as what times the parades run at Disney parks that day. If there are any activities (scavenger hunts are common), they'll be posted here.

FOOD   There are only counter-service choices. Eat promptly at 11am when kitchens open because lines get crazy quickly. Don't plan on eating dinner at the water parks, because the kiosks shut down before closing.

TIMING   If you're coming to Florida between November and mid-March, one of these parks will be closed for its annual hose-down. The other will remain open. Most water features are heated, but remember that you eventually must get *out*.

Blizzard Beach

Of Disney's two water parks, **Blizzard Beach** ★★★ is the more thrilling, possibly because it opened 6 years after Typhoon Lagoon and had the benefit of improving on what didn't work there. It also has a wittier backstory that is perfect for a hot day: A freak snowstorm hit Mount Gushmore, and Disney was slapping up a ski resort when the snow began to melt, creating water slides. So now, a lift chair brings bathers most of the way up the 90-foot peak, and flumes are festooned with ski-run flags and piled with white "snowdrifts." Best of all, at this park, no one has to tote rafts uphill—there are conveyors to do it for you.

Surely the most exhilarating 8 seconds in all of Walt Disney World, **Summit Plummet** ★★★ is the immensely steep, 12-story-tall slide that commands attention at the peak of the mountain, which incidentally, offers one of the best panoramas of the Walt Disney World resort. A slide down this one is for the truly fearless, because the first few seconds make you feel weightless, as if you're about to fall forward. By the end, the water is jabbing you so hard that it's not unusual to come away with a light bruise, and it turns the toughest bathing suit into dental floss. This is a fun one to watch; just ask the young men who are glued to it for the aforementioned reason. **Slush Gusher** ★, next to it among the Green Slope rides and slightly lower, is a double-hump that gives the rider the sensation of air time—not a reassuring feeling when you're flying down an open chute.

The enormous chute winding off the mountain's right side is **Steamboat Springs** ★★, a group ride in a circular raft; just about everyone gets a chance to enjoy the top of a banked turn, and after the inevitable splashdown, another minute is spent in a comedown floating on a river. It's highly re-rideable, but if you go alone, you'll be paired with strangers for some slippery awkwardness.

Snow Stormers ★ (Purple Slope) is a trio of standard raft water slides, but the twin **Downhill Double Dipper** ★ is a simple slope of two identical slides with a good embellishment: It times runs so you can race a companion down. **Toboggan Racers** ★★ multiplies the fun to where eight people can race at once down an evenly scalloped run. At the base of these is **Melt Away Bay** ★★★, a 1-acre wave pool in which waves create a gentle bobbing sensation. It could stand to be larger since it gets very crowded.

At the back of the mountain (the Red Slope; reach it by walking around the left or via the lazy river), the three **Runoff Rapids ★★** flumes comprise two open-air slides and a totally enclosed one—you only see the occasional light flashing by. (These are the only ones for which you must haul your own raft up the hill.)

The park is circled by the superlative lazy river (for the newbie, that's a slow-flowing channel where you float along in an inner tube) called **Cross Country Creek ★★★**, which is probably the best of its kind, passing a cave dripping with refrigerated water and a slouching shack that, every few seconds, gushes as you hear the sound of Goofy sneezing. *Tip:* It's easier to find a free inner tube at a ramp far from the park entrance; try the one at the base of Downhill Double Dipper or the one to the left past Lottawatta Lodge, the main food building.

There are two kiddie areas, for grade-schoolers, **Ski Patrol ★★** (short slides, a walk across the water on floating "icebergs") and for littler kids, **Tike's Peak ★** (even smaller slides, fountains, and jets). The latter is a good place to look if you can't find seating.

Tip: The miniature golf course Winter Summerland (see "Puttering Around" on p. 177) shares a parking lot with Blizzard Beach, so it's easy to combine a visit.

www.disneyworld.com. ℂ **407/560-3400.** $64–69 adults, $58–$60 kids 3–9 depending on season. Hours vary, but 10am–5pm is common.

Typhoon Lagoon

Despite the petrifying imagery of the shrimp boat (*Miss Tilly*) impaled on the central mountain (Mt. Mayday), the flumes at **Typhoon Lagoon ★★** are less daunting than the ones at Blizzard Beach or Volcano Bay, but the wave pool is rougher. Typhoon Lagoon is extremely well landscaped (most of the flowers are selected so that they attract butterflies but not bees) to hide its infrastructure, but its navigation is not always well planned. For example, you tote your own rafts. Also, the paths to the slides ramble up and down stairs—the one to the Storm Slides actually goes *down* eight times as it winds up the mountain. It's also not always clear where to find the slide you want. Help guide little ones.

The **Surf Pool ★★** divides its time between "surf waves" (at 5 ft., they pack a surprising punch, and are announced by a *whoompf* that draws great peals of delight from kids) and mild "bobbing waves"—times for both are noted on the Surf Report chalk sign at the pool's foot. The slides are generally shallow, slow, and geared toward avowed sissies. That will frustrate some teenagers, but little kids and mothers with expensive hairdos think **Mayday Falls ★**, which sends riders down a corrugated flume, is just right (adults come off rubbing their butts in pain). It's very tough to find a vantage point to watch your kids ride, but there's a spot near the entrance of **Gangplank Falls ★★★**, a family-size round raft, where you can see a little, and there's a lovely hidden overlook trail with a suspension bridge and waterfalls that passes under the *Miss Tilly*. The leftmost body slide of three at **Storm Slides ★★** is slightly more covered; otherwise the slides are much the same. The **Crush 'n' Gusher ★★★** "water coaster" flumes use jets to push rafts both uphill and downhill; the gag is that it used to be a fruit-washing plant. Behind it, the multi-person round rafted **Miss Adventure Falls ★★**, added in 2017—the first new slide here in nearly a decade. It's pleasant, goes past an animatronic parrot, and uses a belt to hoist you uphill, but the easy journey is not all that remarkable. If you ride alone, you'll be seated next to strangers with their shirts off, so that's fun.

For the best shot at finding an inner tube for the lushly planted lazy river, **Castaway Creek ★★**, pick an entry farther from the entrance, such as in front of the Crush 'n' Gusher area. That's also a good place to find a lounger if the Lagoon is packed, which it usually is; otherwise, try the extreme left past the ice cream stand. That's near **Ketchakiddee Creek ★★**, the geyser-and-bubbler play area for small children. Funny how the water's always warmer there.

"Learn to Surf" lessons are held in the Surf Pool 2 hours before park hours and, sometimes, after it closes (📞 **407/939-7529**; $150 for all ages, minimum age of 5). The lessons come with 30 minutes of preparation followed by 2 hours of in-pool instruction, always with lifeguards scrutinizing your every twitch.

www.disneyworld.com. 📞 **407/560-3400.** $64–69 adults, $58–$60 kids 3–9 depending on season. Hours vary, but 10am–5pm is common.

OTHER DISNEY WORLD DIVERSIONS

See "Puttering Around" on p. 177 for details on the two Disney miniature golf areas.

Disney Springs

The free shopping and entertainment district Disney Springs comprises nearly a pedestrianized mile of restaurants and shops along a small lake, away from the major theme parks in a traffic-plagued eastern reach of the resort grounds. Its West Side is home to a 24-screen AMC cinema and a whole lot of redevelopment. **Cirque du Soleil,** a longtime anchor on the West Side, debuts a Disney-themed show here in 2019; check to see if it's running. Also coming in mid-2019 to the West Side: a newly built **NBA Experience** restaurant-cum-amusement complex.

Characters in Flight ★★ RIDE   You'll see it from miles away: A huge, round helium balloon that rises from a pier, lingers 400 feet up for a spell, and then descends back to earth within about 10 minutes. Although it's safely tethered and the circular observation platform is securely enclosed with mesh, it lists and drifts with sudden breezes and that may disturb some guests. If you're adventurous, though, the trip is good fun, and of course, the view rocks. It's known to summarily shut down for breezes over 22 mph or if lightning is detected within 30 miles, so if it's flying and you want to go, don't assume it will still be open later.

Disney Springs West Side. www.disneyworld.com. 📞 **407/824-4321.** $20 adults, $15 kids 3–9. Daily 8:30am–midnight.

DISNEY after dark WITH KIDS

Although on some nights, one could argue that the people drinking at the clubs and bars are infantile, you still can't bring your kids to hang out in them. Don't worry—Orlando is a family city, so there's much for kids to do.

o **Magic Kingdom parade:** Most evenings, there are one or two parades through the park. When there are two, the second is less crowded.

o **Fireworks:** The Magic Kingdom is open until 9pm or later on most nights. There's usually an evening parade, and the nightly fireworks display, *Happily Ever After*, happens around Cinderella Castle. Hollywood Studios mounts *Fantasmic!*, a pyrotechnics-and-water display and a *Star Wars: A Galactic Spectacular* sky show a few times a week. Epcot has its own spectacular show over its lagoon, and Animal Kingdom has the *Rivers of Light* lagoon procession. Check with each park for showtimes, because they change.

o **The Electrical Boat Parade:** It's a tradition going back 48 years—a string of 14 40-foot-long illuminated barges floats past the Disney resorts on Seven Seas Lagoon and Bay Lake starting at 9pm, accompanied by music. Lower key than the fireworks shows, you can see it for free from any resort hotel in the area or, if your timing is good, from the ferries.

o **Special event evenings:** From September through March, the Magic Kingdom schedules irregular special-ticket evenings (Mickey's Not-So-Scary Halloween Party, his Very Merry Christmas Party, and Disney After Dark events) for kids with free candy, character meetings, dance parties, and extended hours. The calendar of events can be found on p. 274, online at www.disneyworld. com, or you can call Disney at © **407/939-7679.**

o **Dinnertainment:** The Hoop-Dee-Doo Musical Revue and Spirit of Aloha shows have been going strong for decades. See p. 220.

o **Free movie:** Nightly at Fort Wilderness, the Chip 'n' Dale's Campfire Sing-A-Long is followed by an outdoor screening of a Disney movie.

o **Character meals:** Early bedtime? Very young kids will be sent to sleep dreaming if they meet their favorite character over dinner. See p. 221 for a list.

The Void/Star Wars: Secrets of the Empire ★★★ ATTRACTION

Hands down the coolest thing to do for a half-hour at Disney Springs: You don a special suit and visor and are sent walking into the virtual reality world you see and hear in your helmet. Reach for an animated rifle and you can really pick it up and shoot it at Darth Vader. Get shot, and you feel a ticklish buzzing where you were hit, but nothing hurts and you can't lose the game—you proceed along a pre-determined course until it's over. And then you want to do it again. You may think virtual reality doesn't quite work as a concept yet, but this will make you a true believer in its potential.

Disney Springs Marketplace (1732 East Buena Vista Dr., Lake Buena Vista). www.the void.com/locations/orlando. © **385/323-0090.** Admission $30 per person (Mon–Thurs) or $33 per person (Fri–Sun and holidays). Ages 10+ only, up to 4 people in a group. Mon–Thurs 10am–10:45pm; Fri–Sun 10am–11:15pm.

House of Blues ★★★ MUSIC CLUB   One of the principal nightspots on the West Side has a 2,000-person, three-tiered venue (standing space only) hosting regular performers along the lines of B. B. King, One Republic, the Charlie Daniels Band, and Norah Jones. Big talent is ticketed at concert prices, and operator Live Nation piles on the fees, but mostly, it's a restaurant for Southern food. On Sundays, it hosts a de-sanctified Gospel Brunch (p. 220).

Disney Springs West Side. www.hob.com. © **407/934-2583.** Sun–Thurs 11:30am–11pm; Fri–Sat 11:30am–1am.

Splitsville Luxury Lanes ★★★ BOWLING ALLEY   Giving families something to bond over, this Florida-based franchise charges by the hour, which might make you feel rushed, and it charges high prices at that, but its souped-up 1950s decor, two floors of bowling, and copious cocktails have charm to spare. The food ($13–$20) is better than it should be; it even sells sushi. Cast members like to hang out here—meet a few and beat a few.

Disney Springs West Side. www.splitsvillelanes.com/location/orlando/. © **407/938-7328.** Daily 10am–2am. $17/hr. per person before 4pm, $22/hr. per person after 4pm and weekends. Rates include shoe rental.

Walt Disney World Tours

Walt Disney was unquestionably a visionary. When he started out, he was mostly interested in animation as an art form. But as his fame and resources grew, his dreams became infinite, and by the end of his life, he was obsessed with building a city of his own. But because the Magic Kingdom was built by his most-trusted designers, it incorporated several idealistic innovations.

One is the **utilidor system.** The bulk of the Magic Kingdom that you see appears to be at ground level. But in fact, you'll be walking about 14 feet above the land. The attractions constitute the second and third stories of a 9-acre network of warehouses and corridors—utilidors—built in part to guard against flooding but mostly so cast members could remove trash, make deliveries, take breaks, change costumes, and count money out of sight, in a catacombs accessed through secret entrances and unmarked wormholes scattered around the themed lands. Clean-burning electric vehicles zip through the hallways, some of which are wide enough to accommodate trucks, and all of which are color-coded to indicate which land is upstairs.

Among the other engineering feats and innovations of the Kingdom:

o Trash is transported at 60mph in 24-inch tubes to a central collection point by Swedish AVAC pneumatic tubes to a compactor behind Splash Mountain.

o Fire, power, and water systems are all monitored by a common computer, and the robotics, doors, lighting, sounds, and vehicles on the most complicated attractions are handled by a central server called the Digital Animation Control System (DACS), located roughly underneath Cinderella Castle.

o Bay Lake, beside Fort Wilderness, was dredged, and the dirt used to raise the Magic Kingdom. Underneath the lakebed, white sand was discovered, cleaned, and deposited to create beaches on the Seven Seas Lagoon, which was created from dry land.

o Energy is reused whenever possible. The generators' waste heat is used to heat water, and hot water runoff is used for heating, cooking, and absorption chilling for air-conditioning. Wastewater is reclaimed for plants and lawns (80% of the resort is watered this way), and sludge is dried for fertilizer. Food scraps are composted on-site. The resort produces enough power to keep things running in case of a temporary outage on the municipal grid. This will keep you up tonight: Disney even has the legal right to build its own nuclear power plant, should it care to.

o Some 55 miles of canals were dug on resort property to keep the land drained. Most of these canals were curved to appear natural.

o The resort was the first place to install an all-electronic phone system using underground cable—so guests don't see ugly wires. It was the first telephone company in America to use a 911 emergency system. In 1978, the first commercial fiber optic system in the U.S. was installed.

o The rubber-tired monorail system, designed by Disney engineers, now contains nearly 15 miles of track. Walt had intended monorails, plus vehicles akin to the Tomorrowland Transit Authority ride, to be the main forms of transportation to and through his Epcot. In 1986, the monorail was named a National Historic Mechanical Engineering Landmark by the American Society of Mechanical Engineers.

The Walt Disney Co. now shows little interest in advancing these innovations. Epcot has only a small network of utilidors, partly located under Spaceship Earth, and the other Disney parks were built without any. The monorail has not been expanded since 1982 and is falling apart.

But even if the company now pays scant attention to developing "Walt's dream"—that Talmudic totem that the company's marketing department invokes to sell souvenirs—it will, fortunately, grant a backstage gander at the resort's ingenuity and the mind-boggling challenge of its scale. The superlative **Walt Disney World tours** (www.disneyworld.com/tours; © **407/939-8687**) require tons of walking and the quality depends on the ability of the guide, but they're also well organized, with coach transport, snacks, plenty of comfort breaks, and sometimes, a special pin souvenir. Not all of them go daily, so you have to check the Disney site for what's running when you visit. There are several good ones, such as nature tours of Animal Kingdom by night and close looks at the Magic Kingdom's steam trains. The best one is **Backstage Magic ★★★**, a seven-hour, $275 exploration of how the parks work at every level. Stops include the mechanized miracle of the American Adventure robotics; Central Shops, a 280,000-square-foot facility where ride vehicles are maintained in the blocks-long, 30-foot-tall Assembly Alley; and the Animation Shop, where Audio-Animatronic figures are repaired. Every minute is fascinating.

UNIVERSAL ORLANDO, SEAWORLD & BEYOND

4

Disney is only half the story. Less than half, really, when you consider that while it maintains four parks, you'll find another four major theme parks, plus three more water parks, in the same vicinity. Universal has come of age, and Comcast, its parent company, is pouring billions of dollars into rapidly putting it on equal footing with the Mouse.

UNIVERSAL ORLANDO

Universal is booming. Since 2009, attendance has soared more than 80%—while Disney attendance has fallen 13%. Expansion is non-stop. In 2017, it added a new water slide park, Volcano Bay, and next year, it opens yet another hotel, its eighth. Universal's parks (see the inside back cover for a resort map) entice 19.7 million combined visits each year, on par with the Magic Kingdom. Few people thought it would get this huge. One factor: In 2014, Diagon Alley in the Wizarding World of Harry Potter turned the resort into a destination that people toured over 2 or 3 days rather than just 1. Universal operates best (but not exclusively) on the resort model— stay here, play here—and it helps that its campus is easier to roam than Disney's: It's walkable or traversed by quick, free ferries, so you can park your car and forget about it.

The opening of Universal Studios in 1990 heralded a new era for Orlando tourism. Instead of merely duplicating its original Hollywood location, which is grafted onto a historic movie studio lot, Universal Orlando built an all-day theme park. It was famously troubled then, and it's impossible to imagine how much it has changed. Much was removed to make way for the second draft: a reproduction of the *Psycho* house, colossal rides about King Kong and Jaws, an in-depth breakdown of Alfred Hitchcock's directorial tricks, a studio for Nickelodeon, a major exploration of how to produce *Murder, She Wrote* (!!), a Hard Rock Cafe in the shape of a giant guitar. Still, there was little doubt that Universal's innovations, when they worked, raised the bar. A chief advance was that many of its attractions were indoors—even the thrill rides. Given Florida's scorching sun and unpredictable rains, this leap shouldn't have been as novel as it was. While Disney, still working on a California model, allowed its guests to twiddle thumbs in the cruel outdoors as they waited, Universal's multistage queuing system kept them entertained and air-conditioned. Even the covered parking garages at Universal Orlando (shared by the parks and CityWalk) were novel for Florida.

Throughout the 1990s, Universal's modest one-park setup meant it mostly grabbed visitors on day trips from Disney. That changed in 1999, when a second, $2.6-billion park, Islands of Adventure, made its dazzling debut. Universal's domain has further expanded to include the nightlife district City-Walk, hotels, and last summer, its own water slide park. Within a few years, Universal will open two *more* hotels, for a total of eight, across I-4 where the Wet 'n Wild water park used to be. And Universal owns enough land by the Convention Center to build yet another theme park.

Universal had another idea Disney wishes it had come up with first: If you want to see both Wizarding World of Harry Potter areas, you have to purchase a ticket to *both* of its parks. It was evil genius.

Unless crowds are insanely huge such as before Halloween Horror Nights (p. 276) or during Christmas week, the two main parks take about 2 days to adequately see. Most of the time, lines are nowhere near as long as they are at Disney. With a two-park pass and a willingness to bypass lesser attractions, you could see only highlights in a marathon day, provided at least one of the parks stays open until 9 or 10pm. (If you want to see Volcano Bay, described on p. 145, you need at least a third day.) In any event, bopping between the two theme parks all day is quick and easy since their entrances are a 5-minute stroll apart or you can take the incredible Hogwarts Express connecting train.

Tickets to Universal's Parks

Tickets for both parks cost the same. While both Disney and Universal now charge more on busy days, Universal gives you a $20 discount if you buy multi-day tickets online, so it's crucial you do so. Prices go up early in the year.

Gate pricing for one-day tickets is dynamic and goes higher when it's busy, but on quiet days ("Value" class) it's $123 adult and $112 kids 3–9. You can predict the cost for your dates at the official site www.universalticketcalendar.com.

Non-Value prices at the gate:

- **1-day ticket for one park:** $132 adults, $127 kids 3–9
- **1-day park-to-park ticket:** $191 adults, $185 kids 3–9 (i.e., $59 more)
- **2 days, one park/two parks daily:** $240/$304 adults, $229/$293 kids 3–9
- **3 days, one park/two parks daily:** $261/$325 adults, $250/$314 kids 3–9
- **4 days, one park/two parks daily:** $272/$341 adults, $261/$330 kids 3–9
- **3 parks, park-to-park access (including Volcano Bay):** 2 days $362 adults/$341 kids; 3 days $383/$373; 4 days $410/$400

To ride the Hogwarts Express train that links the two parks, you must have a park-to-park ticket. If you buy a one-park ticket and change your mind

contacting UNIVERSAL

General information: www.universal orlando.com; ℭ **407/363-8000**
Guest services: ℭ **407/224-4233**
Hotel reservations: ℭ **888/273-1311**
Dining reservations: ℭ **407/224-3663**

Vacation packages: www.universal orlandovacations.com; ℭ **877/801-9720**
Lost and found: ℭ **407/224-4233**, option 2
Twitter: tag @UniversalORL or #AskUniversal—it responds quickly

midway through the day, there are ticket kiosks at the Hogwarts Express train stations that simply charge you the difference in price for a park-to-park ticket.

HOPPING THE LINES Like Disney's Fastpass+ but without the hassle of pre-planning, **Universal Express Pass** allows guests to use a separate entrance queue that is dramatically shorter than the "Standby" one, reducing wait times to minutes; your ticket is scanned by an employee. Unlike Disney's democratic Fastpass+, Express is for sale; the busier the park is, the more it costs, and the price shoots up at midnight the day it's valid to encourage advance purchase. Guests can buy an **Express Plus** pass online with their admission, at the gate, and at shops. There is one set of dynamic prices that allows one-time-per-ride use ($120 on busy days), another price for unlimited re-rides (from $150 for one park, from $160 for both—again, at peak times that rises to as much as double). The only major rides excluded are three of the most popular: Harry Potter and the Forbidden Journey, Escape from Gringotts, and the Hogwarts Express (and we're guessing the new coaster won't be included either). Using this is expensive, but it enables you to see both Universal parks in a single day and consequently spend less in tickets and see more of Orlando. Bundles that include park tickets with Express are sold. The most expensive, but effective way, to cut the lines is the **VIP Experience** (ℭ **866/346-9350**), on which there is no waiting for rides. Non-private tours (with up to 12 people you might not know) will visit 10–12 attractions ($189–$350 plus admission, includes a counter-service lunch and valet parking); private guided tours take you anywhere you want, even if it's Forbidden Journey, without waiting (up to $3,500 for up to five people, $400 for each additional person, table-service lunch included). There is also a final, simpler way to get an Express Pass: Guests of the Portofino Bay, Hard Rock Hotel, and Royal Pacific can use their key cards for free Express access (a great value add when you consider a double room houses four people).

At the Rental Services window, you can get the **Ride Reservations** device. You're given a "U-bot" pager that lists the next available entry at each attraction; the appointments reflect current wait time, so essentially, the system gives you a virtual place in line. You schedule visits (only one at any moment) by pressing buttons, and it vibrates when it's time. It's $40–$50 per park to make one reservation per ride; one device can be used for up to 6 people. Frankly, Express is less fuss and a better value.

WHAT THE BASICS cost AT UNIVERSAL'S TWO PARKS

Parking: $22 (free after 6pm); $35 for closer "preferred" spaces; $45 for all-day valet	**ECV (electric convenience vehicle):** $50 + $50 deposit (add $20 for canopy)
Single strollers: $15 per day	**Lockers:** $10 per day small (multi-entry)
Double strollers: $25 per day	**Poncho:** $10 adult; $9 kids
Kiddie Car (a stroller with a dummy steering wheel): $18; $28 double	**Regular soda:** $3.40
Wheelchair: $12	**Water:** $3
	Beer: $6.50–$7

Universal also has photographers (not as many as Disney) on hand to take your photo at big moments. Its **My Universal Photos** works a lot like Disney's PhotoPass but with fewer roaming photographers: 1 day is $80, 3 days is $100, and that includes digital copies of everything and two printed images. You can also check your images as you collect them using an app.

Universal has free in-park Wi-Fi, and its free **Official Universal Orlando Resort App** provides wait times, showtimes, maps, and walking directions. You can buy online-discounted tickets using it, too.

WHAT TO WEAR Dress small children in bathing suits for a day at Universal Studios because Kidzone will get them soaked. At Islands of Adventure, three of the best adult rides are water-based.

Universal Studios Florida

Universal Studios ★★★, which had 10.2 million visitors in 2017, within a half-million visitors of Disney's least popular park (Hollywood Studios), usually opens at 9am, and in winter months hours end at around dinnertime. In summer, it's open as late as 10pm. After you get your car parked ($20 and up in a mostly covered structure) and submit to security checks, take the covered sidewalks to CityWalk and head to the right. Pause now at the giant, rotating globe for the requisite photo op, because the sun is in your favor for photographs in the morning, but not later.

They pair your fingerprint to your ticket. The plaza after the turnstiles is where you take care of business. **Strollers and wheelchairs** are obtained to the left, and **lockers** are rented to the right. (You may bring your stroller to the other park within 2 hr. of closing; if you're taking the Hogwarts Express, there's a place to drop it off before boarding and another kiosk for getting a new one at Islands of Adventure.) Make sure to grab a free park **map** here; if you forget, the stores also stock them.

Although there are technically themed areas within the park, few are strictly defined. They fall into two general zones. Everyone enters along the main avenue of the simulated backlot (including **Production Central, Hollywood,** and **New York**), which contains many of the behind-the-scenes attractions, while the elongated lagoon stretches off to the right, encircled by many of the

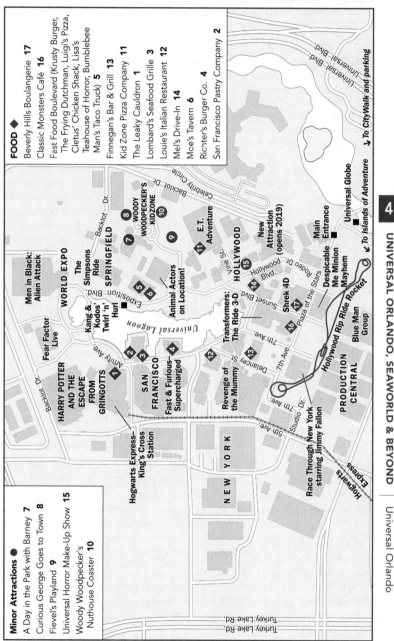

Minor Attractions ●

A Day in the Park with Barney **7**
Curious George Goes to Town **8**
Fievel's Playland **9**
Universal Horror Make-Up Show **15**
Woody Woodpecker's
Nuthouse Coaster **10**

FOOD ◆

Beverly Hills Boulangerie **17**
Classic Monsters Café **16**
Fast Food Boulevard (Krusty Burger,
The Frying Dutchman, Luigi's Pizza,
Cletus' Chicken Shack, Lisa's
Teahouse of Horror, Bumblebee
Man's Taco Truck) **5**
Finnegan's Bar & Grill **13**
Kid Zone Pizza Company **11**
The Leaky Cauldron **1**
Lombard's Seafood Grille **3**
Louie's Italian Restaurant **12**
Mel's Drive-In **14**
Moe's Tavern **6**
Richter's Burger Co. **4**
San Francisco Pastry Company **2**

↳ To CityWalk and parking
← To Islands of Adventure

4

UNIVERSAL ORLANDO, SEAWORLD & BEYOND | Universal Orlando

thrill-based rides in **San Francisco, Springfield, World Expo,** and **Woody Woodpecker's Kidzone. The Wizarding World of Harry Potter—Diagon Alley** is on the far side of the lagoon.

Some days (confirm times about a month ahead on its website, on its app, or when you grab your map at the front gate), Universal sends out its **Superstar Parade** (the map prints the times), packed with children's characters such as SpongeBob SquarePants, Dora, Diego, Gru, and the Minions. It stops by Mel's Drive-In and Battery Park so kids can meet them. After dark, if the park's open then, the water sometimes hosts the 18-minute **Cinematic Celebration,** a spectacle spotlighting the popular franchises from the parks with water screens, 120 Bellagio-style power fountains, projection mapping, and a few pyrotechnics. The park opposite Mel's Diner is the best vantage point for it.

> ### Empty Those Pockets!
>
> Lawyers have had their way with the fun: The fast rides now forbid loose articles of any kind. That includes phones, keys, lipstick—even coins. Everything but paper! And you may not leave your stuff on the platform while you ride, either. Metal detectors have been set up to make sure you comply. Leave your stuff at the hotel, use the free lockers by attraction entrances (very crowded, a real pain), or rent a locker at the front of either park.

PRODUCTION CENTRAL

The area along the entry avenue (called both Plaza of the Stars and 57th St.) and to its left is collectively marked on maps as Production Central, but who are they kidding? Nowadays, those soundstages are used mostly for the odd local commercial and for haunted houses at Universal's fiendishly popular Halloween event.

The initial dream was much bigger. When the park was built, it was intended to be more like the original Hollywood location, where an amusement area grew up around a working studio. Newspapers at the time trumpeted Orlando as "Hollywood of the East" because year-round production could be accomplished here and at Disney–MGM Studios, and millions of tourists could be a part of the process. One of Universal's soundstages housed a working TV studio for Nickelodeon, the kids' cable channel, and the game show *Double Dare* plucked families out of the park to compete on air. In front of the studio, a geyser of "green slime" (actually green water) gurgled in tribute to the Canadian show *You Can't Do That on Television* that helped make the channel's fortunes. (Today, that stage houses the equally messy Blue Man Group.) But the plan never took. It wasn't cost-effective to move productions here, celebrities didn't relish working in a theme park, and state tax credits were often spotty.

The first block of Production Central is mostly shops, including the largest gift shop in the park, **Universal Studios Store,** on the left. Across from that are the tempting Art Deco buildings of Rodeo Drive, the spine of the Hollywood area and for my money the prettiest part of the park.

Hollywood Rip Ride Rockit ★★★ RIDE
This is one advanced train: The 17-story height, vertical climb, hill-like loop, and near misses are just the

start of it. Most advanced are its cars, outfitted with LEDs and in-seat speakers. Riders personalize their trip on screens embedded in the beltlike safety restraint, choosing the song that will play during the trip. Pick from a broad menu including country, rap, rock, and disco, but if you don't pick a song, it'll choose one for you. When the ride's over, you can buy a movie of it, along with your soundtrack. Lockers are required for loose items, but they're free for the wait time plus 20 minutes. Single riders get their own line, and it moves quickly. (This is the coaster where Lisa Kudrow and Ellie Kemper had their climactic mother-daughter reunion scene in the second-season finale of *Unbreakable Kimmy Schmidt*; but since Kemper was pregnant, they actually shot it on a soundstage with a green screen. Good thing; it's getting bumpy as it ages!) Rockin'. *Strategy:* Don't close the safety bar too tightly! You'll have trouble breathing. And if you ride around noon, the lift hill will beam the sun straight into your eyes. *Tip:* There are "secret" songs not listed in the consoles. Google them ahead of time to get the code numbers, then while you're still in the train station, hold down the coaster logo for 10 seconds to unlock the number pad for them.

Despicable Me Minion Mayhem ★★ RIDE   The movies, if you don't know them, star a crotchety mad genius, Gru (voiced by Steve Carell), and his horde of nearly identical yellow henchmen (the Minions); their ride gives the little guys ample opportunity for some cartoon violence and giggly gags. The kid-friendly show/move-in-place ride takes place in a theater full of individual open-air ride platforms that have all the characteristics of motion simulators except claustrophobia. *Strategy:* Those prone to motion sickness can request a car that doesn't move at all—there's often a separate marked entrance for those cars.

Shrek 4-D ★★ SHOW   The high-priced voices of the movie characters (Mike Myers, Cameron Diaz, Eddie Murphy) star in a snarky 12-minute, 3-D movie-cum-spectacle—filmed in "OgreVision." John Lithgow plays the ghost of the evil Lord Farquaad, who crashes Shrek and Fiona's honeymoon at Fairytale Falls with a few dastardly deeds. The chairs look like standard theater seats but they're tricked-up to goose sensations—don't worry; it won't make you ill. Well, unless fart jokes gross you out. It's a good one to do when feet start aching, although the line can build in the afternoon. *Strategy:* Because the entertaining preshow is just as long as the movie, the Express Pass doesn't seem to buy you very much time. After the exit, visit **Donkey's Photo Finish,** featuring an interactive, robotic version of the movie's smart ass in his own stall; he chats with kids and poses.

Transformers: The Ride—3D ★★ RIDE   This East Coast version of a ride that first appeared at Universal Studios Hollywood repeats the technology and basic vehicle design of the gentler Adventures of Spider-Man next door at Islands of Adventure—that is, motion-simulator cars travel among sense-tricking rooms with 3-D projections. The difference is that here, the show is pumped up with crisper animation, clearer sounds, and a whole lot of

Don't miss if you're 6: Curious George Goes to Town

Don't miss if you're 16: Springfield

Requisite photo op: The rotating Universal globe out front

Food you can only get here: Butterbeer ice cream and Fishy Green Ale, Diagon Alley; Flaming Moe's and Duff Beer, Springfield

The most crowded, so go early: The Wizarding World of Harry Potter—Diagon Alley

Skippable: Fear Factor Live

Biggest thrill: Harry Potter and the Escape from Gringotts

Best show: Animal Actors on Location!

Where to find peace: On the lagoon

machine-on-machine violence and military-grade weaponry. But at heart, no matter how impressive the tech is, Transformers is still a version of Spider-Man, down to key plot points. The mayhem is so frenetic you can't always tell which Transformer is which, but then again, you can't in the movies, either, so it hardly matters. You'll emerge feeling like you survived a pretty, 4-minute car crash. *Strategy:* The clearest view is in the front row, and there's a fast-moving single-rider line.

NEW YORK

When there's a park on your right, you've entered the New York area. In a display of geographic acrobatics, the park is an imitation of San Francisco's Union Square while straight ahead, at the end of 57th Street (the main entry avenue) is a little cul-de-sac that looks, through a camera lens, like Manhattan—except for the roller coaster that keeps roaring through.

The rest of the New York section is gussied up to look like the tenements of the Lower East Side or Greenwich Village and is worth a few photos. A few street performances crop up all day here: actors jamming like **The Blues Brothers; Marilyn Monroe** with (weirdly) her backup girls the **Diamond Bellas;** and the powerhouse belters **Sing It!.**

Race Through New York Starring Jimmy Fallon ★ RIDE This grandma-appropriate theater-based attraction was borne of synergy—*The Tonight Show* airs on NBC, Universal Orlando's corporate cousin. The four-minute adventure, which hammers you with the show's running characters and jiggles your bench in motion simulation, starts in a pitch-perfect simulation of Rockefeller Center before devolving into a rollicking and geographically-challenged high-speed trip through the streets of Manhattan and the imagination of Jimmy Fallon, who spouts puns as you go. The motion won't make you throw up, but Fallon's smarm might. Named "Most Likely to Feel Outdated Soon" by Frommer's. You can use the Universal app or the kiosk out front to reserve a time to ride, although it's rarely crowded enough to need to. The waiting area is confusing—instead of a queue, you get a colored card and you must wait for the sconce lights to change to that color—use the time to look at old Tonight Show memorabilia such as Johnny Carson's Carnac the Magnificent turban.

Revenge of the Mummy ★★★ RIDE This brilliant attraction has an easy start but a exuberant finish: Part dark ride, part coaster, it goes backward and forward, twists on a turntable, and even spends a harrowing moment stalled in a room as the ceiling crawls with fire. (It doesn't go upside-down.) To say much more would give away some clever shocks. I've told you what you need to know, except that it's one of the best rides in this park, and it's miles better than the cheaper version at Universal in Los Angeles. *Strategy:* You must put loose articles in the lockers to the right of the entrance—they're free for the posted ride time plus 20 minutes, but after that they cost $3 every half-hour. There are three lines: express, standby, and single; there's no way to see if the single line is faster until you're deep in the building.

SAN FRANCISCO

The restaurants in this section are higher-toned than elsewhere in the park. Several times a day, the drumming construction studs known as **The Beat Builders** jam out on the scaffolding opposite Fast & Furious.

Fast & Furious—Supercharged ★ RIDE You'll be able to feel the simulated thrill of a freeway car chase without moving so much as a foot on this overly macho import from Universal Studios Hollywood. The setup is that you're VIPs trying to get to a party on time . . . exactly like a certain rockin' roller coaster at Disney's Hollywood Studios (hmmm). Once you leave the loading area on the tramlike "party bus," motion simulator technology and crisp lateral projections collide—so that you don't have to. It offers timed "virtual line" ride reservations via the Universal app and a kiosk out front. It's also one of the rides where you can pass time in the queue by whipping out the Universal app and playing a *The Fast and Furious* trivia game. *Verdict:* Underwhelming. Despite the testosteroned name, it's so tame that there's not even a seat belt. *Strategy:* Try to sit near the sides, where the view will be unobstructed.

THE WIZARDING WORLD OF HARRY POTTER— DIAGON ALLEY

From the outside, it appears to simply be a re-creation of some London landmarks, including a perfectly replicated King's Cross Station and some townhouses that would fool a lifetime resident of Bloomsbury (keep an eye on the curtains in the second balcony window of 12 Grimmauld Place, the shabby townhouse). You have the re-creation of the "Eros" fountain from Piccadilly Circus (unlike the original, this one is actually flowing), cab shelters selling Britannia souvenirs and jumbo hot dogs, and a three-level-tall **Knight Bus.** If its conductor is there, have a chat with him, but don't be alarmed if the shrunken Jamaican head hanging above his steering wheel butts into the conversation.

Hidden behind the London facade, through some sidelong brick portals, is the world's hottest theme park of the moment, essentially a wholesale construction of three city blocks around Diagon Alley, where wizards go for their provisions. It's not so much a single attraction as it is a cluttered streetscape of shops, beverage and dessert stores, and painstaking design work that seals you off from the outside world. There are few right angles, but plenty of opportunities to spend lots and lots of cash. You could pass hours simply exploring details, from animated window displays (the skeleton that imitates your movements from the window of Dystyl Phaelanges is a standout) to clever signage larded with inside jokes ("These Premises to Let: Reptiles/Arachnids Allowed").

The main thoroughfare is **Diagon Alley,** lined with the Leaky Cauldron restaurant, plus shops for wands, toys, and clothing. It leads dramatically to Gringotts Bank, which is crested by a petrified dragon that belches fire every few minutes. Gringotts is on **Horizont Alley,** a 2-block lane noted for its pet store, beer hall, and ice cream shop. On the left, it leads into **Knockturn Alley,** a fascinating indoor area that simulates a shady ghetto at night, right down to shifting clouds in a simulated sky and a tattoo parlor, Marcus Scarr's, where the animated sample designs writhe on the wall (do peek in). Branching off from Diagon Alley on the right, you find **Carkitt Market,** a covered area recalling London's Leadenhall Market, where the principal show stage for the land is located. Performances include **The Singing Sorceress: Celestina Warbeck and the Banshees** (a talented but somewhat out-of-theme singer—J. K. Rowling's favorite "offstage" character mentioned but not seen in the book series—rendering such classics as "A Cauldron Full of Hot, Strong Love") and **The Tales of Beedle the Bard** (a street performance with puppets of two tales from the Potter spin-off book).

Harry Potter and the Escape from Gringotts ★★★ RIDE

Another genre-busting creation, this indoor ride is among the most advanced anywhere: part roller coaster, part motion simulator amid dominating 3-D high-def screens. At times your respect for its razor's-edge complexity will overshadow the purity of the thrills, but it's still unmissable. The queue lingers in the sumptuous, echoing lobby of Gringotts Bank, where 10 robotic goblins pause long enough from their clerical duties to sneer at you, and you're taken by "lift" deep underground to begin the mine cart–like race through the vaults. Almost immediately, nasty lightning bolts from Bellatrix Lestrange (Helena Bonham Carter) put your course awry, sending you careening into the slithering presence of Voldemort (Ralph Fiennes). Can Bill Weasley and friends save you in time? (What do *you* think?) There are some mild spins and drops in the dark, but you wear 3-D glasses the whole time and they don't fall off, so it's not that rough, and it's less scary and height-restrictive than the Forbidden Journey ride at Hogsmeade. *Strategy:* Take the test seat out front seriously; if you don't fit, you shouldn't ride. Locker use for small items is mandatory; they're free and to the right of the front door. Express doesn't help you jump much of the line, but there's a single-rider queue that moves quickly and shortcuts past the pre-show. Front row is best for seeing the screens, the view from the left side of the fourth row can be obscured, and the middle two seats are the best overall.

reducio! WAYS TO LIGHTEN YOUR WALLET AT DIAGON ALLEY

Diagon Alley has the best theme-park merchandising you've ever seen. Nearly everything there is to do and taste comes with a price tag, and you can't get these experiences outside Universal's gates. It's extraordinarily easy to get swept along in the merchandising mesmerization. Some of the best bespoke purchasing potential includes these Potterized twists:

o **Gringotts Money Exchange, Carkitt Market.** Trade in "muggle money" (U.S. $10s and $20s only) for Gringotts Bank Rune Credit, a currency that you can use in both parks or, Universal hopes, take home as a souvenir for pure profit.

o **Ollivanders, Diagon Alley.** In addition to the same wand-selecting mini-show available at Hogsmeade (p. 138), you may purchase a $50 interactive wand (they have gold labels; non-interactive wands are $44) used to activate more than a dozen tricks wherever you see a medallion embedded in the ground here or in Hogsmeade. Stand on it, emulate the wand motion depicted on it, and you'll make toilets flush, suits of armor animate, fountains squirt, and so on.

o **The Hopping Pot, Carkitt Market, and the Fountain of Fair Fortune, Horizont Alley.** Sip sweet concoctions for $5 each: Otter's Fizzy Orange Juice, Tongue Tying Lemon Squash, Peachtree Fizzing Tea, and Fishy Green Ale with "fish eggs" (actually blueberry boba) on the bottom. They also sell the classic Potter potable, Butterbeer (in a mug made for Diagon Alley, $14; $8 in a plain cup), and two beers unique to the park, Wizards Brew (a light lager) and Dragon Scale (a chocolatey stout), both $10.

o **Florean Fortescue's Ice Cream Parlour, Diagon Alley.** Try a range of only-here flavors including Chocolate Chili, Clotted Cream, Earl Grey and Lavender, and a dangerously addictive soft-serve version of Butterbeer ($7, $8 in a souvenir plastic cup). Too busy? You can get Butterbeer ice cream next door at the **Fountain of Fair Fortune,** too.

o **Eternelle's Elixir of Refreshment, Carkitt Market.** Mix your choice of $4.25 "elixirs" (Draught of Peace, Fire Protection Potion, and so forth) with $4.50 "Gillywater" (water) and something magical happens: Universal makes $8.75 on sugar water. The water outside Diagon Alley is lower priced.

o **Weasleys' Wizard Wheezes, Diagon Alley.** The toy shop sells $11–$35 Pygmy Puff stuffed animals. When a purchase is made, the staff gongs a huge bell and announces a new adoption. At the connecting **Sugarplum's,** buy the candies Ron would eat to get out of school: Puking Pastilles, Fainting Fancies, Fever Fudge, and Nosebleed Nougat ($7 each).

o **Magical Menagerie, Horizont Alley.** Where windows are filled with animated pets such as pythons and giant snails, procure specialty animal souvenirs such as plush versions of Fluffy, griffins, huge purple toads, and Hermione's half-Kneazle cat Crookshanks ($25–$35).

o **Shutterbutton's, Diagon Alley.** Via a green screen, put your family in the middle of a 3- to 4-minute, 12-scene DVD/download ($70), like a moving postcard exploring the Potter universe.

Hogwarts Express ★★★ RIDE   Separate from Diagon Alley, through the vaulted brick interior of a cunningly accurate King's Cross Station, you board the hissing, steaming, and, to all appearances, vintage steam train to Hogsmeade. You are assigned a six-person, upholstered compartment, the door shuts, and off you go. Out the window, England and Scotland scroll by while in the train corridor, you overhear conversations and see ominous shadows through frosted glass. In reality, you're traveling through Universal's backstage area, but you never see it. The technical prowess is nearly totally convincing, and even where it isn't, it's still dazzling. Within 4 minutes, you disembark at Islands of Adventure outside the gate to the other Wizarding World (if you require an upgrade to a park-to-park ticket, which costs around $55, there are kiosks for the purpose). In the station, there's also a spot, done with mirrors and clever lighting, for you to re-create the moment when Harry and his fellow students walk through a brick wall to reach Platform 9¾. That photo op gets thronged, but there's a bypass if you don't want to wait for it.

Ollivanders ★★ SHOW   You enter this ancient boutique in small groups, and the kindly shopkeeper selects one child from the group for a personalized wand selection—it selects *them*—accompanied by music cues and light tricks. The brief spell thus cast, an attendant then ushers your child directly toward the cash registers in the wand department, where they demand you purchase them perfect replicas from nearly every major character of the Harry Potter universe (mostly $45–$50 each), from Harry to Hermione to Snape to Voldemort to Bellatrix Lestrange. They don't have price tags, but they do have stickers reading, preposterously, "This is not a toy." Treat them with care. Some are sturdy, but some, such as Professor McGonagall's, can break.

WORLD EXPO

There's not much to this area except a ride and a dated show.

Men in Black: Alien Attack ★★ RIDE   After a superlative queue area that does a pitch-perfect, "Jetsons"-style imitation of New York's 1964 World's Fair (ironically, the one Walt Disney created so many wonders for), you discover the "real" tenant of the futuristic building: a training course for the Men in Black alien patrol corps. You board six-person cars equipped with individual laser guns. As you pass from room to room—expect lots of herky-jerky motions, but nothing sickening—your task is to fire upon any alien that pops out from around doorways, behind trash cans, and so on. If they peg you first, it sends your buggy spinning. Each car's point score is displayed on the dashboard, and the number accumulated by the end determines the climactic video you're shown—Will Smith will either praise you as "Galaxy Defender" or mock you as "Bug Bait." *Strategy:* The single riders' queue moves quickly thanks to the odd number of seats in each row. Locker use for small items is mandatory, but free for the posted wait time plus 20 minutes. *Tip:* Look for "Steven Spielberg" sitting on a bench with a newspaper. After the ride, ask a staffer if you can tour the "Immigration Room," an area most guests don't visit. Trust us.

Fear Factor Live ★ SHOW   Like the meat-headed NBC-now-MTV show, ordinary people do stunts (usually involving being dangled on wires, maybe eating food-grade mealworms) for the twisted pleasure of a whooping audience while an inane master of ceremonies eggs everyone on. If you're over 18 and want to volunteer as a contestant (first prize: polite applause), be there 70 minutes before your selected showtime and you'll go through a tryout including jumping jacks and a game of Simon Says. Contestants can't wear jewelry, and if your hands sweat when you're nervous, you will stink at the gripping challenges. This show goes dark in September and October. Persistent rumors say this will be subsumed by a Harry Potter expansion. Soon, please?

SPRINGFIELD

After Diagon Alley, Springfield is the cleverest land in the Studios. The area is jammed with inside jokes from the longest-running comedy on TV that only fans catch—for example, **Lard Lad Donuts** sells "Ice Cream Conans." **Kwik-E-Mart** sells an array of bespoke souvenirs you can only get here (pick up the payphone there, by the way), **Moe's Tavern** pours **Duff Brewery's** signature quaff—the cause of, and solution to, all life's problems—and the statue of frontiersman Jebediah Springfield embiggens us all. Near the Hollywood end on the lagoon, check out the original locomotive from *Back to the Future III*.

The Simpsons Ride ★★★ RIDE   It's easy to love this highly amusing, top-quality, motion-simulator "Thrilltacular Upsy-Downsy Spins-Aroundsy Teen-Operated Thrill Ride" that takes place in front of an 80-foot-tall screen. The premise, dense and ironic enough to please devotees of the FOX series, punctures Orlando itself: You join Homer's clan at Krustyland, a greedy theme park, on a roller coaster that's sabotaged by the evil Sideshow Bob (voiced by Kelsey Grammer). During the dizzyingly fast-paced 6 minutes, you zoom through predicaments that mock the theme-park world, including skewers of Shamu, Pirates of the Caribbean, and "it's a small world." Add to that a giant killer panda bear and an extra layer of heightened sensory (like the whiff of baby powder—well, it makes sense when you ride). It's not too rough, but dehydrated people find it vaguely nauseating, and your brain may hurt from absorbing all the jokes. The queue area is so tongue-in-cheek and gag-packed that waiting is half the fun: Itchy and Scratchy furnish the gory

---

The Studios' Junk Shop

A delicious addition to the Studios, on Hollywood Blvd. near Mel's Diner, is **Williams of Hollywood,** where you can buy signs, costumes, and set pieces from Universal Orlando attractions and productions—plus some genuine vintage finds thrown in. If the item has a brown tag, it came from Universal. On a recent visit, I passed up the opportunity to drop $3,000 on the cow prop that flew across the stage for 17 years in the Twister attraction. I shall bemoan the decision forevermore.

safety warning and Krusty dispenses safety instructions such as "Wait here until someone comes and tells you to do something." *Strategy:* Seats are four across, so families can ride together.

Kang & Kodos' Twirl 'n' Hurl ★ RIDE Universal finally got its Dumbo ride. Here, silly slobbering aliens trick you into boarding a day-glow flying saucer (fitting two adults or one adult and two kids): "Please remain seated until the very end of the ride. You will know the ride has ended when your vehicle comes to a complete stop, or you have been eaten . . . I didn't just say that." As you rotate gently around, Dumbo-style, you use a joystick to pass in front of tentacle-shaped poles, triggering sounds of exclamation from the citizens of Springfield. *Spoiler alert:* You don't get eaten. *Strategy:* Keep an eye on park schedules, it closes early when there's a lagoon show.

HOLLYWOOD

This Art Deco stretch is a good place to buy Hello Kitty and Betty Boop merchandise (they have dedicated stores) and meet characters—Gru, SpongeBob SquarePants, Dora the Explorer, Scooby-Doo and Shaggy—at odd times listed on the map under **Character Party Zone** and **Hollywood Character Zone.** The Superstar Parade begins and ends at the Estoric Pictures gate, so it's the best place to catch it.

Universal Horror Make-Up Show ★★ SHOW It's the park's only homage to the B-movie origins of the Universal name and a rare survivor from the 1990 opening (though much revised). Inside a facade that honors Hollywood's Pantages Theatre, learn a few light facts about how horror-movie makeup effects are accomplished in this snarky, 25-minute, tongue-in-cheek exposé conducted by a nerdy type in his workshop and his straight-man (or -woman) emcee. On paper, that seems like the kind of thing you might otherwise skip, but in truth park regulars love its wit and playful edge. For ribald ad-libbing and gross-out humor, the park suggests parental guidance, but I find most kids have heard it all before, and it's certainly true that seeing terrifying movie gore exposed as the make-believe it is can be a good reality check. You can't get in once the show starts. Even if you skip it, there's something to see in the lobby: Real props from horror films.

> ### And One More Thing...
>
> In 2017, Universal finally retired the long-running *Terminator*-themed movie/show in Hollywood. Its replacement opens in 2019, but at press time, the only official detail was that it would be "high-energy." That space will probably fit another show (the fanboy money was on a Jason Bourne attraction); check to see if it's on yet.

WOODY WOODPECKER'S KIDZONE

Scuttlebutt has it that this area is endangered—Universal needs somewhere to build a new Nintendo-themed land, coming in a few years. For now, there's a ton to do, not least of which is **SpongeBob StorePants,** dedicated to merchandise and appearances by the absorbent doofus.

Animal Actors on Location! ★★★ SHOW A troupe of trained dogs, cats, birds, and a horse anchor this charming 20-minute show (times noted on the sign). Placing it here was inspired, because small children get a thrill out of seeing common animals do tricks, and as a consequence, it's popular and has been running in some form for nearly 30 years. Because it's in an amphitheater, you can sneak out in the middle if you need to. (If you see only one emphatically punctuated household-pets-doing-cute-tricks-to-jaunty-music theme park show, make it SeaWorld's superior Pets Ahoy!)

E.T. Adventure ★★ RIDE Based on the 1982 Steven Spielberg movie, this endearingly weird indoor ride is rightfully in the kiddie area because it's not intense and the plot cannot tolerate scrutiny by a fully developed brain. Upon entering, guests supply their name to an attendant, who encodes the info on a pass you hand over when you board the ride. The indoor queue area is a fabulous reproduction of a thick, cool California forest at night. Vehicles are suspended from rails to approximate the sensation of cruising in a flock of bikes, and they sweep and scoop across the moonrise and then through gardens on E.T.'s home planet (remember, he was a botanist), where a menagerie of goofy-looking aliens and creepy E.T. babies swing on vines. They miraculously speak English, throw a party, and greet us from the sidelines. At the climax, a grateful E.T. is supposed to call out your name as you fly home—hence those boarding passes—but E.T. either runs out of time to name everyone or he spouts gibberish, so don't get your hopes up unless your name is Pfmkmpftur. *Strategy:* If the queue looks dense from the outside, return later—before closing seems to be a charmed time for quick waits—since there are still more lineups indoors.

> ### Make Back Some Admission Expenses
>
> The **NBC Media Center** is marked on maps in Hollywood, but you can only get in by invitation (someone will approach you). Inside, Comcast-affiliated entities screen pilots and solicit audience opinions. On a quiet January day, I once earned $30 for enduring a pilot called *Psych*. I broke it to them gently, telling them that it was clichéd and strained. It then became an eight-season smash on USA Network.

Fievel's Playland ★★★ ACTIVITY Named for the hero of *An American Tail* (let's be honest—the kids who grew up with that are turning 40), it's the best of several playgrounds in Kidzone. The concept is that your kids have been shrunk down to a mouse's size, and they're playing among giant everyday items like sardine cans and eyeglasses. They'll discover slides, nets, and tubes, but my favorite element is the easy waterslide on a raft—so yes, make sure your kids have their swimsuits on. The ground is covered with that newfangled soft foam that all the modern playgrounds have. When I was a boy, we got concussions instead.

A Day in the Park with Barney ★ SHOW The small indoor area that can be accessed through its own gift shop is technically the postshow area for a singalong show for the Purple One. The doors close at the start and stay closed until the ordeal is over. Frankly, being locked in a room with that sappy purple dinosaur constitutes a chamber of horrors for me, but your littlest ones may find it enthralling. The play area mimics Barney's backyard with a waist-high counter for sifting through sand (so it won't get into shoes), a tree equipped with little slides, and a chance to have your picture taken with (and then buy it from) Barney the Capitalist Dinosaur.

Woody Woodpecker's Nuthouse Coaster ★★ RIDE   Kids can plainly see every drop before they commit to this straightforward thriller. It has no unpleasant surprises, unless you count hearing Woody's pecking as you go, and a run time of less than a minute.

Curious George Goes to Town ★★★ ACTIVITY   Welcome to the water playground that stole your child. This frenetic splash area is teeming with squealing children and soaked with streams of water from every direction—from squirt cannons, fountains, geysers, and, most importantly, from two 500-gallon buckets that, every 7 minutes, sound a warning bell and then drench anyone beneath. The wet and wild scene is ringed by a perimeter of dry parents keeping an eye on their suddenly wild offspring. Watching the children cheer and scamper when they hear the bucket's warning bell, and then watching them momentarily vanish in the deluge, is endlessly heartwarming. Through the wet area (there's a dry bypass corridor to it on the left) is the dry Ball Factory, where kids suck up plastic balls with light vacuums, pack them into bags, and then fire them at each other with weak cannons. It's not on the maps.

WHERE TO EAT AT UNIVERSAL STUDIOS

In addition to the random snack carts, there are counter-service and table-service restaurants. None require reservations the way Disney's do. *Tip:* Meals do not *have* to come with side dishes. The potato chip bags served hold a mere 1⅛ ounces. Lunch meals clock in at about $12, but ask to subtract chips or fries from your meal deals and you'll save about $2. All outlets are counter-service except Finnegan's and Lombard's. *Remember:* Restaurants at City-Walk (p. 205) are only a 5-minute walk from the park, so they're also options.

Classic Monsters Café ★★ AMERICAN   Indoor counter service on a non-scary B-movie set with some healthy options, such as rotisserie chicken, salad, cheeseburgers, and ribs. **Production Central.** Combo meal $12 to $21.

Finnegan's Bar & Grill ★★★ IRISH/BRITISH   A sit-down, Irish-style pub with loft ceilings good for a beer break, particularly after 3pm when a guitar singer performs. Scotch eggs ($10), split pea–and-ham soup ($7), Irish Cobb salad (it has corned beef), seafood pie, and bangers and mash are the kind of solid choices available, plus cocktails and good strong ales. Park workers pick this place when they're off-duty. **New York.** Mains $13 to $23.

Louie's Italian Restaurant ★ ITALIAN   Straightforward counter service near The Mummy. There's a **fruit stand** ($2/piece) outside. **New York.** Slices $14–$15 with side salad, meatball or chicken parm subs $13–$15.

San Francisco Pastry Company ★★ SANDWICHES This lightly trafficked counter-service bakery does sandwiches and loaded croissants in addition to cakes and pastries, and healthier fruit plates and salads. **San Francisco.** Meals $13 with potato salad, fruit, and chips.

Lombard's Seafood Grille ★★★ SEAFOOD/AMERICAN An excellent, relaxing table-service choice that is surprisingly affordable: Fish tacos are $16, just three bucks more than a Quick Service meal, and other fish dishes, including the fish of the day, such as mahi-mahi sandwiches, lemon garlic shrimp penne, and fried fish, are in the mid-teens. Splashing fountains serenade, fish tanks adorn the dining room, and you can sit outside on the water if you like. Special diet options, such as quinoa with Portobello mushrooms, are well marked, and you can even get gluten-free table rolls. **San Francisco.** Main courses $15 to $26.

Richter's Burger Co. ★★ AMERICAN A warehouse-like dockside option that slings stacked burgers, marinated grilled chicken sandwiches, and for those weary of greasy fare, salads with grilled chicken. Periodically, the dining area rumbles (but doesn't move) to simulate quakes. **Chez Alcatraz,** outside on the water, is a cocktail bar that also sells quick sandwiches and flatbreads. **San Francisco.** Main courses $12 to $17 with fries.

The Leaky Cauldron ★★★ BRITISH The fare at Diagon Alley's counter-service location is not mystical at all. It's plentiful and true to an English pub, serving British staples such as beef, lamb, and Guinness stew; cottage or fisherman's pie; and banger (sausage) sandwiches. The ploughman's lunch for two ($22) has three types of cheese and Branston pickle. There's a "secret" menu that offers pea soup, Scotch eggs, and a ploughman's lunch for one for $10. Also get Butterbeer, Fishy Green Ale, and other Potter potables here. Unlike at most Universal restaurants, they don't let you subtract fries to save money. **Diagon Alley.** Mains $11 to $16.

Fast Food Boulevard ★★★ AMERICAN This mouthy indoor food court in Springfield serves mostly standard food renamed with inside jokes and witticisms that puncture American culture. You could spend half your lunchtime just laughing at the dishes. **Krusty Burger** serves "meat sandwiches" such as the high-stacked double-bacon Clogger Burger with "cheez sauce" and curly fries and 6-inch Heat Lamp Dogs. **The Frying Dutchman** does Basket O' Bait fried fish and Clam Chowd-arr ($5). At the **Luigi's Pizza** area, get slices of Meat Liker's Pizza, and at **Cletus' Chicken Shack,** dig into the not-very-appetizing-but-accurate Chicken Arms (wings), Chicken Thumbs (tenders), and chicken-and-waffle sandwiches. Lastly, **Lisa's Teahouse of Horror** balances out the junk food with a cooler full of straight-up salads and wraps. You can also buy only-at-Universal treats such as **Lard Lad Donuts** (the platter-size Big Pink, coated with frosting, is $6—a life-size Chief Wiggum figure enjoys one nearby) and Buzz Cola (no-calorie cherry cola).

In both its parks, Universal offers a simple meal plan. Dubbed the **Universal Dining Plan—Quick Service,** it entitles you to one main plate, one nonalcoholic beverage, and one snack, which can be used for ice cream, frozen beverages, and more. Adults pay $23 and kids $15; it only pays off if you go for the most expensive choices and were going to get that dessert anyway. If you buy one at a kiosk in the park, you must activate it at Guest Services or at any restaurant (most won't open until 11am or so). Resort guests may avail themselves of a Full-Service **Dining Plan,** good for one table-service meal, one quick-service meal, and a snack for $52 adults, $18 kids each day (buy at your resort). The value is borderline, especially if you don't want table-service meals, and can only be redeemed inside the parks or a few CityWalk restaurants. Everyone can buy special cups good for free refills ($15).

Springfield. Outside and across the way, there's the **Bumblebee Man's Taco Truck,** which closes by dinner. Entrees $15 to $19.

Moe's Tavern ★★★ BAR   A spot-on re-creation of Moe's, down to team pennants for the Isotopes and the purple TV on the wall, only without sleazy service by Moe. There is, however, a life-size Barney by the bar, ruefully contemplating his empty mug. Duff Beer is specially brewed for the park (in generous servings of regular, Lite, or Dry ($10, $14 with souvenir cup; there's also an amber and a lager on draft), but the kid-friendly potent potable is a Flaming Moe's ($10), a nonalcoholic orange-flavored soda in a cup rigged with pellets that make it bubble and smoke (it's hard to breathe when you're sipping it). **Springfield.** Beverages $7 to $10, light bites $4 to $12.

Mel's Drive-In ★★ AMERICAN   A 1950s-style counter-service diner where fare leans toward chicken, burgers, and shakes. Air-conditioned seating has a view of the lagoon. **Hollywood.** Main courses $12 to $17.

Beverly Hills Boulangerie ★ SANDWICHES   A reasonably healthy fast meal: sandwiches (turkey, roast beef, tuna) with potato salad and fruit, plus pastries like eclairs. **Hollywood.** Sandwiches with sides $13.

Islands of Adventure

Probably the best choice in Orlando in pound-for-pound thrills and the original theme park home of Harry Potter, **Islands of Adventure (IOA) ★★★** has doubled in attendance between 2009 and 2017—the number is now 9.5 million, nipping at Disney's heels. The park usually opens at 9am. In winter months, operating hours will end around 6pm but in summer, they're often open as late as 10pm. After you park (from $20), go through security, take the moving sidewalks to CityWalk, and veer to the left, toward the 130-foot Pharos Lighthouse. If you doubt whether your kids are tall enough to ride everything, there's a gauge listing requirements before the ticket booths.

Islands of Adventure

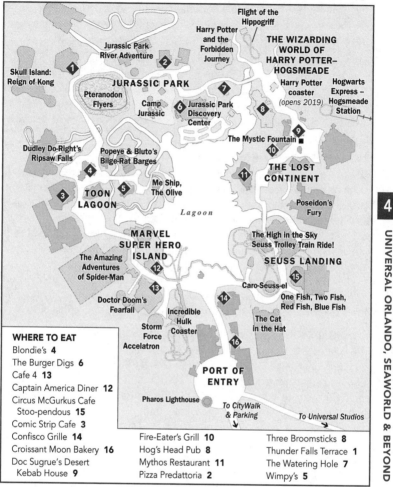

THE WIZARDING WORLD OF HARRY POTTER–HOGSMEADE

Flight of the Hippogriff

Harry Potter and the Forbidden Journey

Harry Potter coaster *(opens 2019)*

Hogwarts Express – Hogsmeade Station

JURASSIC PARK

Jurassic Park River Adventure

Skull Island: Reign of Kong

Pteranodon Flyers

Camp Jurassic

Jurassic Park Discovery Center

The Mystic Fountain

Dudley Do-Right's Ripsaw Falls

Popeye & Bluto's Bilge-Rat Barges

TOON LAGOON

Me Ship, The Olive

Lagoon

THE LOST CONTINENT

Poseidon's Fury

MARVEL SUPER HERO ISLAND

The Amazing Adventures of Spider-Man

The High in the Sky Seuss Trolley Train Ride!

SEUSS LANDING

Caro-Seuss-el

One Fish, Two Fish, Red Fish, Blue Fish

The Cat in the Hat

Doctor Doom's Fearfall

Incredible Hulk Coaster

Storm Force Accelatron

PORT OF ENTRY

Pharos Lighthouse

To CityWalk & Parking

To Universal Studios

WHERE TO EAT

Blondie's **4**
The Burger Digs **6**
Cafe 4 **13**
Captain America Diner **12**
Circus McGurkus Cafe Stoo-pendous **15**
Comic Strip Cafe **3**
Confisco Grille **14**
Croissant Moon Bakery **16**
Doc Sugrue's Desert Kebab House **9**

Fire-Eater's Grill **10**
Hog's Head Pub **8**
Mythos Restaurant **11**
Pizza Predattoria **2**

Three Broomsticks **8**
Thunder Falls Terrace **1**
The Watering Hole **7**
Wimpy's **5**

ORIENTATION IOA's 101 acres are laid out much like Epcot's World Showcase: individually themed areas (here, called "islands," although they're not) arranged around a lagoon (obscurely called the Great Inland Sea). To see everything, you simply follow a great circle. The only corridor into the park, **Port of Entry,** borrows from the Magic Kingdom's Main Street, U.S.A., in that it's a narrow, introductory area where guests are submerged into a theme. In this case, you're gathering munitions for a "great odyssey," so, in theme-park logic, it's where you do things like rent strollers and lockers and grab free maps. Most guests beeline through Port of Entry. Because attraction lines are shortest after opening, explore this area later.

STRATEGY Once you reach the end of Port of Entry, which way should you go? Right. That's the way to Harry Potter. Lines peak in late morning. If the typical Florida forecast calls for afternoon storms and you have a 2-park pass, do IOA in the morning because it has more rides that close in the rain.

SHOPPING The park will send your souvenirs to the Islands of Adventure Trading Company, at the Port of Entry, for collection as you leave the park at the end of the day. The deadline for purchases changes, but it's usually about 2 hours before closing. To the right as you exit the park, there's a **small stand** selling marked-down items (the inventory changes, but I've seen $8 Marvel action figures, two-for-ones on plush Curious George dolls, and $40 sweat-shirts for $22). It opens later in the day.

MARVEL SUPER HERO ISLAND

If Disney owns Marvel, how come Universal is allowed to have this island? The park licensed the brand in the 1990s, which grandfathered permission. Designs use the comic books of that period, which predates the film franchises of Spider-Man, the X-Men, Iron Man, and Fantastic Four, which is why char-acters don't look exactly the way you may be used to them. **Spider-Man** is sometimes one of them, but if you don't see him, head into the back of the Marvel Alterniverse Store, opposite the Captain America Diner. There, the hero has his own appearance zone where you can take your own photos (or buy one). The **Comic Book Shop** is worth a stop. Surprisingly legit, the store carries the latest Marvel issues, compilation books, and collectible busts.

Incredible Hulk Coaster ★★★ RIDE Every minute or so, a new train blasts out of the 150-foot tunnel, over the avenue, and across the lakefront. The ride is quick—a little over 2 minutes—but it's invigorating, and it's super-smooth again thanks to a 2016 extreme makeover that tore down the track and replaced it with an exact replica. First, trains cruise into the inclined tunnel. Then, synchronized rock music playing through in-car speakers, they're launched from a standstill to 40mph in 2 seconds and twist into a zero G-force barrel-roll 110 feet in the air, which means passengers are already upside down even though they're still going up the first hill. What follows is unbri-dled mayhem as you boomerang in a cobra roll and hit a top speed of 67mph through a tangle of corkscrews, loops, and misty tunnels. For many guests it's the first ride of the day, and its seven inversions are certain to work better than morning coffee. Loose items aren't allowed, so use the nearby lockers, good for the posted wait time plus 20 minutes. *Strategy:* The single-rider line here is fruitful.

Storm Force Accelatron ★ RIDE I can translate: Storm is the weather-controlling X-Man, so an Accelatron must be a 90-second spinning-tub ride, like Disney's teacups. Open, round cars spin on platters that themselves are on a giant rotating disk, and just to ensure maximum vomit velocity, each pod can be spun using a plate in the middle. *Strategy:* Skip it unless you have insistent kids.

Dr. Doom's Fearfall ★★ RIDE   Those twin 200-foot towers are fitted with rows of chairs that slide up and down them. The brave are rocketed 150 feet up at a force of 4Gs, where they feel an intense tickling in their stomachs, soak up a terrific view of the park, and bounce (safely) back down to Earth. The ride capacity is pretty low—you can see for yourself that each tower only shoots about 16 people up on each trip, with a reload period of several minutes in between—so either do this one early or very late so that waiting for it doesn't eat up too much time. You may hear the towers hiss like a snarling beast—it sounds like a Doctor Doom sound effect, but, in fact, it's part of the mechanism. A computer weighs each car before launch, and any excess compressed air is noisily expelled in the seconds before flight. *Strategy:* The seating configuration lends itself to lots of empty spaces, so the single-rider line moves much quicker than most.

The Amazing Adventures of Spider-Man ★★★ RIDE   The cliché "don't miss it" rightfully applies here. It fires on all cylinders, and the whole family can do it without fear. After passing through a simulation of the "Daily Bugle" newsroom (take special notice of the hilarious pre-ride safety video, done as a pitch-perfect "Superfriends"-era cartoon), riders don polarized 3-D glasses, board moving cars, and whisk through a 1.5-acre experience. Mild open-air motion simulation, computer-generated 3-D animation, and cunning sense trickery (bursts of flame, water droplets, blasts of hot air) collaborate to impart the mind-blowing illusion of being drafted into Spidey's battles against a "Sinister Syndicate" of supervillains including Doctor Octopus and the Green Goblin, who have disassembled the Statue of Liberty with an anti-gravity gun. Although the vehicles barely move as they make their way through the sets, you'll come off feeling as if you've survived a 400-foot plunge off a city skyscraper. Comics fans should keep a lookout for Spider-Man creator Stan Lee. He appears four times during the ride, and you'll hear him once. *Strategy:* Go early or late in the day to minimize waits. There's sometimes a single-rider line and it shoots past the slower standby queue. The middle of the front row is debatably the best place to sit.

> ### The Best of Islands of Adventure
>
> **Don't miss if you're 6:** The Cat in the Hat
> **Don't miss if you're 16:** The Amazing Adventures of Spider-Man
> **Requisite photo op:** Hogwarts Castle
> **Food you can only get here:** Butterbeer, Hogsmeade
> **The most crowded, so go early:** Harry Potter and the Forbidden Journey, Skull Island: Reign of Kong
> **Skippable:** Pteranodon Flyers
> **Biggest thrill:** Incredible Hulk Coaster
> **Best show:** Poseidon's Fury
> **Where to find peace:** On the lagoon in Jurassic Park

TOON LAGOON

The next zone clockwise after Marvel Super Hero Island, Toon Lagoon, harbors two water rides that are—both literally and figuratively—among the splashiest at any theme park. Both will drench you. If you're smart, you'll come just *before* it swelters, so that you'll be soaked and cool when the going gets rough.

Slow your pace when you reach the introductory section of Toon Lagoon, encountered after a brief zone of **midway games** (most: three tries for $5). Crawling with details, color, and fountains, it's the kind of place that reveals more the longer you look. Some 150 cartoon characters—some you'll recognize (Nancy, Annie, the Family Circus, Beetle Bailey) and some strictly for connoisseurs (Little Nemo in Slumberland, Zippy)—make two-dimensional appearances on the island, including inside the restaurants and on a soundtrack popping in and out of the action. Where you see a button or a possible trigger, press it or plunge it, because the environment has been rigged with sonic treats. Whimsical snapshot spots are worked in, too, such as the trick photo setup by the Comic Strip Cafe where you can pretend Marmaduke is dragging you by his leash. The deluge from the waterfall under Hagar's Viking ship provides cooling relief from the sunlight. Amid all this, the **Boop Oop A Doop** Betty Boop store sells rare specimens. My sister-in-law found a 75th-anniversary cookie jar here that no other real-world store carried. Personally, I worry about the mental health of the clerks, who are subjected to a brain-melting loop of Boop's oops.

Dudley Do-Right's Ripsaw Falls ★★★ RIDE Within this Technicolor snow-capped mountain, you'll find a wonderful perils-of-Pauline log-flume caper featuring Jay Ward's feckless Canadian Mountie bungling his rescue of Nell Fenwick from Snidely Whiplash. The winding 5-minute journey—ups, downs, indoor, outdoor, surprise backsplashes, chunky robotic characters—climaxes in a stomach-juggling double-dip drop that hurtles, unexpectedly, through a humped underground gully. Although the 75-foot drop starts out at 45 degrees, it steepens to 50 degrees, creating a weightless sensation. Front- and back-seat riders get soaked, and anyone who didn't get soaked probably will when they double back to the disembarking zone, because that's when they'll face the firing squad of sadistic bystanders who shoot water cannons at passing boats. Ripsaw Falls is terrific fun. No one gets off it grumpy—the mark of amusement success. The ride often closes for a few weeks in off-season for a scrub. *Strategies:* Seats are tight, but it helps if you straighten your legs as you get in and out. There are optional lockers in the nook to the left of the entrance gate—use them, because there's no boat storage. It's $4 for 90 minutes, which may allow you to also use it for Popeye & Bluto's Barges. The **Gasoline Alley** shop, across the main path, sells $10 ponchos, but on Ripsaw Falls, you straddle the seat so your feet won't be easy to cover. Best to wear sandals.

Popeye & Bluto's Bilge-Rat Barges ★★★ RIDE For my money, it's the best round-boat flume in the world. You board 12-passenger, circular bumper boats that float freely and unpredictably down an outlandish white-water obstacle course—beneath waterfalls, through tunnels, over angry rapids, and past features designed to mercilessly saturate you. It's like playing Russian roulette with water, except everyone loses. This journey is considerably wilder and unquestionably wetter than other rides like this one. And more elaborate: Even the river's walls have been sculpted and painted in hues to resemble a cartoon wooden chute. It's diabolical and one of Universal's best. On hot days, the wet effects are fully juiced, but when it's cold, they're turned down slightly. *Strategy:* There's a semi-waterproof cubby on board for personal belongings, but you'd be wise to slip your things into plastic bags, too, just in case. You may not be barefoot off the boat but once on, you may remove shoes for the ride. Watching your loved ones get humiliated brings a lifetime of satisfaction, but for onlooker schadenfreude, there are 25¢ water blasters on overlooking walkways, but there are free ones on Me Ship, the Olive. Near the lockers ($4 for 90 min., which may be long enough use to use for Ripsaw Falls, too), you'll find step-in People Dryers that, for $5, bake and blow the water off you after your journey. (That works well, except on jeans.)

Me Ship, the Olive ★ ACTIVITY   An interactive ship-shaped playground for children just beyond the Barges' entrance, there's also a slide and some fun to be had with a piano in the cabin (play the notes on the sheet music for an orchestral surprise). One of my favorite things to do in Orlando is to spend awhile on the bridge beside the Olive, which overlooks Barge boats as they drift helplessly under a leaky boiler's funnel. Watching the gleeful alarm on people's faces, hearing the peals of laughter—the sublime delight of amusement park togetherness is repeated, again and again, from the vantage point of that bridge. I could stand there all day. I also love the shore of the sea nearby, which is private almost all the time.

JURASSIC PARK

Steven Spielberg was a creative consultant to Universal, the studio that nourished him, and this "island," the largest and greenest in the park, is presented practically verbatim from his 1993 movie. Once you pass through a proud wooden gate, John Williams's bombastic score takes over, and there it burrows until you move on to another area of IOA. If you stand quietly, you may hear rustling—a witty, Spielbergian touch. With the success of *Jurassic World* and another Kong movie, this island is again a focus of Universal's developmental attention.

Skull Island: Reign of Kong ★★ RIDE   A fantastically terrifying stone facade warns wimps away, but despite gargantuan appearances, it's really mostly a screen-based motion-simulator ride, albeit one that uses a tram-like vehicle and requires 3-D goggles. This 2016 addition is a bigger version of the Kong segment of the Universal Studios Hollywood tram tour—the animation is superb, if arrestingly graphic, and there is one luscious post-movie moment when you encounter a splendidly executed Kong, live and in the fur. The height requirement, just 34 inches, is proof that despite all that, it's family-friendly mayhem. In bad weather, ride vehicles don't drive through the front gate, but instead use a less thrilling indoor route. *Strategy:* Seats on the right see more of the action. Get a drink before getting in line; the queue can be hot and tedious. It can also be scary—toward the end, characters may be hidden in the dark.

Camp Jurassic ★ ACTIVITY   The only dedicated kids' zone of this part of the park is a self-guided tangle of rope bridges, slides, bubbling pools in caves, surprise geysers, water guns, spitting dinosaur heads, and thick greenery. It's easy to get lost here, and easier to get wet.

Pteranodon Flyers ★ RIDE   The hanging carts gently gliding on the nifty-looking track over Camp Jurassic constitute a very short (about 75 seconds) clacking route through the trees. Cool as it looks, it was poorly designed, fitting only two at a time, and huge lines were inevitable. Facing irate crowds, Universal instituted a rule: No adult could ride without a child. That both prepared guests for the ride's tame deportment and cut down on the wait. Attendants may be willing to load child-free adults when the park is dead. *Strategy:* Skip this underwhelmer if the wait's more than 15 minutes.

Jurassic Park River Adventure ★★ RIDE   In that family-friendly Orlando tradition, the worst drop is clearly warned; gauge the 85-foot descent from behind the Thunder Falls Terrace restaurant, where river boats kick up quite a spray when they hit the water at 30mph. Before reaching that messy climax, boats embark on what's meant to be a benign tour of the mythical dinosaur park from the movie, only to be bumped off course and run afoul of spitting raptors and an eye-poppingly realistic T. rex that lunges for the kill. The dino attack is shrewdly stage-managed; note how, in true Spielberg fashion, you see disquieting evidence of the hungry lizards (rustling bushes, gashes in sheet metal) before actually catching sight of one. In all honesty, you're more likely to get soaked standing on the terrace of the restaurant than in the boat, but the trip down is enough to blow your hat off and sprinkle you above the waist. There's usually at least one delirious 12-year-old boy who stands in the splash zone for hours, giving himself a nigh-amphibious drenching. *Tip:* Front seats get wettest and back seats are better for taking in the story.

Jurassic Park Discovery Center ★ ACTIVITY   Enter a convincing reproduction of the luxury lodge from the film, down to full-size skeletons in the atrium (actual props from the first movie)—downstairs, line up your camera just so, and you can snap a witty shot of a T. rex chomping a loved one's cranium. Seek out the scientist carrying a baby triceratops that hatched on the grounds; it flinches and reacts to your touch. You can also handle the ostrich-sized dinosaur eggs and slide them into nifty "scanners." *Tip:* If you request a lab tour, the "scientists" may take you behind the glass. Behind the center, there's a network of pleasant garden paths where you can take a break from the bustle of the park. Out front, don't miss the regularly scheduled appearances of **Raptor Encounter,** which gives you a chance to take selfies with a chillingly lifelike, mobile, responsive, and strangely comical 9-foot velociraptor from the "safe" side of a fence. What could go wrong?

THE WIZARDING WORLD OF HARRY POTTER—HOGSMEADE

When it opened in June of 2010, the 10-acre **Hogsmeade** ★★★ was rightfully hailed as the most significant achievement in American theme park design, detailed down to the souvenirs, and with a new ride taking the place of the late Dragon Challenge coasters this year, it's only going to get better. It's as if the film set for Hogsmeade Village (the only British village for non-Muggles) and Hogwarts Castle have been transported to Florida, and indeed, it was designed by the same team. You don't have to know the books or the movies to enjoy the astounding level of attention: Stonework looks ancient, plaster was painted to appear moldy, rooftops and chimneys slouch in a jumble of snow-covered gables, and nearly every souvenir is a bespoke creation expressly for the Harry Potter universe—in fact, J. K. Rowling had final approval on everything, including on what's sold in the intentionally-too-small shops. Even the restrooms aren't spared Moaning Myrtle's whine. Spend time going from window to window to take in the tricks. In Spintwitches Sporting Needs, a Quidditch set strains to free itself from its carrying case. At Gladrags, the gown levitates. At Tomes and Scrolls, Gilderoy Lockhart (Kenneth Branagh) vainly preens himself among his best-selling travel books.

Those stores are brilliant facades, but there are real shops that are just as unmissable (and invariably thronged). **Devish and Banges** is where you find Hogwarts school supplies in the colors of all four Houses, from capes to scarves to diaries to parchment, wax seals, and quills. (The seething "Monster Book of Monsters" is kept in a cage here.) In the window of **Honeydukes,** there's a macabre contraption in which a mechanical crow pecks out the gumball eye of a skeleton, which rolls through various chutes to be dispensed below, presumably for consumption. That signifies the wondrous candy store within, where colorful Edwardian-style packages contain Chocolate Frogs, Fizzing Whizzbees, Bertie Bott's Every Flavour Beans (beware the vomit-flavored ones mixed in), Exploding Bon Bons, Peppermint Toads, and other confections that would disturb even Willy Wonka.

The park's signature concoction, **Butterbeer,** is pulled from two keg-shaped carts in the walkways. The only place in the world you can buy it is in Wizarding World parks or at the Harry Potter Studio Tour outside of London. Served frozen or unfrozen (I like it cold) with a creamy foam head on top, it tastes like a butterscotch Life Saver, and it's addictive. I once did laboratory analysis on it and found out that, surprisingly, it contains no more sugar than a Coke. It's $8 a cup, but for $13, you get a dishwasher-safe Butterbeer mug. **The Magic Neep** cart, between the Butterbeer stalls, sells **Pumpkin Juice** (really a Christmasy apple juice mix) in its unique pumpkin-top bottles for $8, along with actual fruit for $2 a piece.

Types of Butterbeer, Ranked

1. **Soft-serve ice cream:** Must have more!
2. **Frozen:** Deservedly most popular. Get it with foam.
3. **Regular:** Pretty good, too, but not as refreshing.
4. **Hot:** Like Regular, but only sold in the winter.
5. **Clotted Cream:** Not very butterbeery, only sold at The Leaky Cauldron.
6. **Fudge:** Waxy, like old white chocolate or plumber's putty. Gross.

After dark, you may want to check out the **Nighttime Lights at Hogwarts Castle,** a well-done, 4-minute projection mapping spectacle projected onto the school. It's tight in Hogsmeade, but it runs continuously, so you might have to wait briefly in a holding area before seeing the next showing. Before the holidays, it morphs into a Christmas version.

Ollivanders ★★ SHOW   It's not on the maps because it can't handle big crowds, but the queue to the left of Dervish and Banges is another Ollivanders Wand Shop (p. 125). If the line is too long—it usually is—there are three more showrooms with an identical experience on Diagon Alley at Universal Studios.

Harry Potter and the Forbidden Journey ★★★ RIDE   You will be drawn inexorably to the stunning re-creation of Hogwarts Castle, and within, you'll find a most technologically complex ride. I won't give away how it's done, but I will say it's an epic combination of motion-simulator movie segments and awe-inducing physical encounters as you travel on a jolting, four-person bench that has been enchanted by Hermione to transport you. This being Orlando, things quickly go wrong; and you encounter a dragon, Aragog the spider, the Whomping Willow, a Quidditch match, and Dementors, all in the space of 4 minutes. The mostly indoor queue is perhaps even more magical, taking you through Dumbledore's study and through the dim halls of Hogwarts, where real-looking oil paintings come to life and bicker with each other. At one point, fake snow falls on you, and a lifelike Sorting Hat supervises your arrival at the loading dock. It's a tour-de-force that takes the pain out of a long wait, and sometimes there's a tour-only route that lets you enjoy it without having to ride (ask). Once you're done, you go through Filch's Emporium of Confiscated Goods, a general-interest shop for Potteria. *Strategy:* No loose articles are permitted. Lockers are free for the posted wait time plus 20 minutes, but using them is confusing. The single-rider line lets you leapfrog much of the wait, but you will miss most of the queue's excitement. Some people feel queasy after riding, but if you sense that happening, just close your eyes during the three movie portions and you should be fine. Try the test seat out front if you're a larger guest—many people are not able to ride.

Flight of the Hippogriff ★ RIDE   For little kids, you'll find a standard training roller coaster (a re-themed holdover from pre-Potter years) that offers a glimpse of Hagrid's Hut from the queue. Don't expect more than a 1-minute figure eight with slight banking—adults, you can skip it. *Strategy:* The line is exposed to the sun and the back seats feel the fastest. The long-legged should cross their ankles to fit more comfortably.

Hogwarts Express ★★★ RIDE   The journey from Hogsmeade to London in Universal Studios works just like the one coming here, but you'll see different scenery and eavesdrop on different goings-on in the carriage. Notice the subtle rhythmic vibration of the seats. Hogsmeade Station is not as nice as King's Cross at Diagon Alley—there's no air-conditioning and no fun tricks like the Platform 9¾ photo op—but trains carry 168 people at a time and new ones load 5 minutes after the previous one departs. *Strategy:* To board, you

Harry Potter & the Helluva Ride

In mid-2019, the next blockbuster at Hogsmeade opens: a technologically advanced, thoroughly surprising, and lavishly themed roller coaster that repeatedly launches you around the grounds outside Hogwarts. Its name was still under wraps at press time, but I promise you that it does all kinds of amazing and unexpected tricks I won't dare spoil here—but let's just say you won't be going from Point A to Point B in a straight line, the way other coasters do. And unlike the more traditional Dueling Dragons/Dragon Challenge coasters that it replaced, this ride has a story and is family-friendly. Do not miss it.

must have a park-to-park ticket; if you don't, there's a ticket upgrade booth out front—it costs $55.

THE LOST CONTINENT

The gist of the next island, the Lost Continent, is amorphous. Think of it as part Africa, part Asia, part Rome—anything exotic wrapped up in stony vagueness. The **localARTicles Boutique** beside the Mystic Fountain is really something special for a theme park and worth a stop, selling cool stuff by local artisans like paintings, clothes, and accessories.

Mystic Fountain ★★ ACTIVITY   Stop by briefly. If it's merely gurgling with recorded sound effects, all is quiet. But when least expected, it comes to life with wisecracks and sprays. Someone in an unseen booth interacts with anyone foolish enough to wander near—usually naïve children. As *Time* magazine put it when the park opened in 1999, the fountain exasperates with "the droll sarcasm of a bachelor uncle roped into caring for some itchy 10-year-olds." If you don't want to get doused, check the ground for slick spots to determine the fountain's spitting reach.

Poseidon's Fury ★★★ SHOW   Despite its lowly status as a walk-through attraction, it has a stunning exterior, carved within a millimeter of reason to look like a crumbling temple. Young folk might be freaked out by the dark and the fireballs. Mature folk might disdain the vapid storyline involving a row between Poseidon and Lord Darkenon (who?). But it bemuses with an interesting (if fleeting) "water vortex" tunnel and some of its other special effects, such as walls that seem to vanish, are diverting. Like Sindbad, it's boisterous and pyrotechnic. *Strategy:* For the best views, head for the front of every room, especially the third one.

SEUSS LANDING

Nowhere other than Harry Potter is IOA's extravagance on finer display than this 10-acre section, which replicates the good Doctor's two-dimensional bluster with three-dimensional exactitude. Just try to find a straight line. From the lakefront, you can get a good look at what the designers accomplished. Notice how even the palm trees twist. They were knocked sideways near Miami in 1992's Hurricane Andrew, and because palm trees always grow upward, by the time they were scouted for IOA, they had acquired a perfectly loopy angle. Scout for hidden gags. Sprinkled around are Horton's Egg and, by the sea, the two Zaxes, which appropriate to their own book (a commentary on political rivalry in which they stubbornly face off while a city grows up around them), were the very first things placed in the park, and everything else was built around them. The area around the Mulberry Street Store hosts regular appearances by the Cat in the Hat and the Grinch, who looks as annoyed to be there as you might imagine.

By the Port of Entry, look for the **Green Eggs & Ham Café,** the house-size slab of emerald ham with a giant fork stuck into it. This beauty is one of the best pieces of mimetic architecture in America. It's also never open, but at least you should notice it.

High in the Sky Seuss Trolley Train Ride! ★★★ RIDE   Everything on this island is appropriate for kids. The railway threading overhead is a cheerful family-friendly glide, narrated in verse. Like Dueling Dragons, there are two paths. The purple line surveys more of the area than the green line, which dawdles above the Circus McGurkus Cafe. The ride takes about 3 minutes and because there's so much to take in, time flies fast. You have to line up all over again if you want to do the other track.

Caro-Seuss-el ★★★ RIDE   Its bobbing menagerie of otherworldly critters actually reacts to being ridden—ears wiggle, heads turn, snouts rise—making it delightfully over-the-top and appealing to kids who sniff at kiddie carousels. Beside the Caro-Seuss-el, seek out the quick but trenchant walk-through grove of Truffula Trees retelling Dr. Seuss's environmental warning tale, the **Street of the Lifted Lorax.**

One Fish, Two Fish, Red Fish, Blue Fish ★★★ RIDE   Here we have another iteration (albeit a good one) of Disney's enduring tot bait, Dumbo. Riders (two passengers per car normally, three if one of them loves the Wiggles) go around, up, and down by their own controls while a gauntlet of spitting fish pegs them from the sides—listen to the song for the secret of how to avoid getting wet, although the advice isn't foolproof. There are benches good for watching kids giggle malevolently when parents get spritzed.

If I Ran the Zoo ★★★ ACTIVITY   Getting wet is part of the bargain, so there's a rack to keep shoes dry. The interactive playground for young children contains some 20 tricksy elements. Let your brood slide, splash in a stream, turn cranks, and play Tic Tac Toe on characters' bellies. Beware the cheeky fountain—it pays to follow all posted instructions in Seuss Landing. Thanks, Universal, for the hand-sanitizer dispensers by the exit.

The Cat in the Hat ★★★ RIDE   Take a nonthreatening excursion through the plot of the famous storybook as viewed from slow-moving mobile "couches" (really a typical flat-ride car). The design racks up points for replicating the look of the beloved children's book with precision, even in three dimensions. The story is just as faithfully retold; it's clear from this sweet, 3½-minute ride that the family of Dr. Seuss (Theodor Geisel) had a strong influence in steering the execution of this section of the park. Parents will probably emerge feeling glad they tagged along. *Tip:* The vehicles spin a few too many times for some adults (kids don't seem to mind), but you can ask to have rotation turned off when you board.

WHERE TO EAT IN ISLANDS OF ADVENTURE

In addition to the random snack carts there's no use in listing here, there are many counter-service spots and one sit-down restaurant (Mythos) in the park. None require advance reservations the way Disney's do. *Tip:* Menu items do not *have* to be served with sides. The potato chip bags served with posted meals hold a mere 1⅞ ounces. Subtract them, or fries, from your meal combos to save about $2. Clockwise through the park from Port of Entry:

Croissant Moon Bakery ★ SANDWICHES   Lighter bites such as sandwiches and panini (breakfast sandwiches until 11am; combos served with a muffin), plus pastries such as cream horns and vanilla éclairs, can be snagged without much of a line. Nearby is the **Last Chance Fruit Stand** cart, which sells fruit cups ($4.30) and giant turkey legs ($15). **Port of Entry.** Sandwiches $13; soup and salad $10.

Confisco Grille ★ INTERNATIONAL   The menu of this rare (one of only two in the park) table-service location has an identity crisis—beef fajitas, salmon, pad Thai, French dip—but that also means there's probably something for everyone in your group. The attached **Backwater Bar,** overlooked by most and therefore ideal for sundowners. **Port of Entry.** Main courses $14 to $23.

Captain America Diner ★ AMERICAN   This indoor counter-service location serves the usual burgers and chicken, plus shakes (just like the Captain never drinks!). Outside you'll find a **fruit stand** where pieces of whole fruit cost $2. **Marvel Super Hero Island.** Main courses $15 to $19 with fries.

Cafe 4 ★ PIZZA   Counter service with indoor seating for grabbing sandwiches as well as individual pizzas. **Marvel Super Hero Island.** Pizza and simple pasta $13 to $15 with side salad; whole pies $35–$38.

Comic Strip Cafe ★★ INTERNATIONAL   Toon Lagoon's largest counter-service location offers four schools of food: burgers and dogs, pizza and salad, Chinese, and fish and chicken. There's more indoor seating with air-conditioning here than anywhere else in this island. **Toon Lagoon.** Main courses $13 to $14.

Blondie's ★★ SANDWICHES   If you know that Dagwood is another name for a hero, you'll know who Blondie is, too. This indoor counter location does subs served with pickles and potato salad. It usually closes after lunch. **Toon Lagoon.** Mains $11.

Wimpy's ★ AMERICAN   It's the stand that furnishes its namesake's obsession (hamburgers), although the staff will not permit you to pay next

Tuesday for a hamburger today, mostly because it's almost never open. **Toon Lagoon.** Main courses $12 to $15.

The Burger Digs ★ AMERICAN   The Discovery Center's indoor counter-service spot is upstairs, across from the dinosaur-theme toy store. Guess what it makes? There's a toppings bar, so load up. **Jurassic Park Discovery Center.** Combo meal $14 to $19.

Pizza Predattoria ★ AMERICAN   The menu is small but big on calories: pizzas, meatball subs, and chicken Caesar salad. It's counter service with outdoor seating. **Jurassic Park.** Nearby is the **Natural Selections** fruit cart ($2/piece). Mains $13 to $16 with side salad.

Thunder Falls Terrace ★★★ BARBECUE   Watch the Jurassic Park boats splash down in the comfort of air-conditioning while noshing on food that's a cut above the rest: chargrilled ribs served with whole unhusked ears of corn, rotisserie chicken, those giant turkey legs, and bacon cheeseburgers. Soups are just $3.50. **Jurassic Park.** Meals $12 to $17.

Three Broomsticks ★★★ BARBECUE/BRITISH   The film tavern was gorgeously re-created, up to its wonky cathedral ceiling and down to the graffiti scratched in the timbers, as the only restaurant in this island, and the filmmakers reportedly liked the design so much they featured the set more prominently in later movies. Get chicken, ribs, fish and chips, beef pasties, shepherd's pie, or The Great Feast, which feeds four for $60 (add $15 for each additional person) with salad, rotisserie chicken, spareribs, corn on the cob, and roast potatoes. **Hog's Head** pub ★★★ is attached. Under the squinty gaze of a grunting mounted boar's head (it responds to tips), a selection of truly British quaffs (Boddingtons, Tennant's, Strongbow cider) is pulled. There are two more beers of note: One is Hog's Head ale, a hoppy, only-here beer made by the Florida Brewing Company, and the other is Butterbeer, so if the line is long at the keg carts outside, grab a faster fix in here, where it's cool in more ways than one. (They won't spike it with rum. I've asked.) There's no happy hour here. **Wizarding World of Harry Potter.** Meals $10 to $17.

Mythos Restaurant ★★★ INTERNATIONAL   The cavelike interior, carved from that ubiquitous orange-hued fake rock that scientists should term Orlando Schist, commands a marvelous view of the lagoon (go around to the water, where you'll be alone, to see the god holding the place up with his bare hands). You could sit and watch the Incredible Hulk Coaster fire all day from this subdued environment. Food many rungs higher than most theme park stuff is served, with pad Thai, fish tacos, a seasonal risotto cranberry/blue cheese–crusted pork, crab-cake sandwiches, plus a healthy slate of sandwiches and salads. **The Lost Continent.** Reservations recommended; ✆ **407/224-4534.** Main courses $15 to $26.

Doc Sugrue's Desert Kebab House ★ MEDITERRANEAN   This outdoor-only counter-service spot serves its namesake in beef, chicken, and vegetables, or Greek salad, plus hummus with veggies ($5). **The Lost Continent.** Main courses $12 to $14.

Fire-Eater's Grill ★ INTERNATIONAL   Another outdoor-only counter-service spot with the usual suspects: chicken fingers, chicken stingers (Buffalo chicken fingers), hot dogs, and gyros. **The Lost Continent.** Meals with fries $13 to $15.

Circus McGurkus Cafe Stoo-pendous ★★★ AMERICAN   Looking like a circus tent coated in cake frosting, it serves the usual burgers and pizzas, leavened with spaghetti and meatballs, chicken Caesar salad, and a fried chicken platter with mashed potatoes and corn on the cob so there's something for everyone. For dessert, the **Moose Juice Goose Juice** stand by the bridge to the Lost Continent sells Moose Juice (a tart orange mix) and Goose Juice (watermelon or grape) for $4.50. **Seuss Landing.** Meals $12 to $18; whole pizzas $35 to $38.

Universal's Volcano Bay

Universal Orlando's first custom-built water park, the tiki-tastic, 28-acre **Volcano Bay** ★, opened in the summer of 2017, and even with only a half-year of business, became number six in the world's most-attended water parks. It's a beaut: The centerpiece, a 200-foot volcano gushing with waterfalls and steaming with mist, is now a landmark beside I-4. Its systems are just as audacious. Guests borrow a sensor wristband, called TapuTapu, that they use to make purchases (if they've linked their credit card to the Universal app first), trigger fun tricks and photos at stations around the park, and reserve a place in a virtual line for most the flumes. When it's time to ride, the wristband screen notifies the guest to head to the attraction for a very short wait. And what rides, none of which require you to tote a raft around: Highlights of the 11 or so choices, which truly run the gamut from mild to wild, include **Krakatau,** an aqua coaster that pushes riders up and down slopes in a toboggan; **Ko'okiri Body Plunge,** a 70-degree, 125-foot body slide that begins with a trap door and rockets you along a clear tube through the wave pool; four **Punga Racers** slides; **Waturi Beach** wave lagoon (the gong mean's it's time to surf); toddler and kids' areas; **Ohyah** and **Ohno** slides that drop you into a pool from 4–6 feet; the six-person **Maku Puihi** round raft rides that spit you into a massive bowl; the **Kopiko Wai** winding river that passes through the illuminated "Stargazer's Cavern"; and many twisted flumes besides those. (Yeah, those names get confusing fast, so get a guide map as you enter or better yet, bone up before you arrive.) Walkways are kept wet and cool, and you'll find many pockets with free loungers and powdery sand—they're emptier at the back of the mountain.

It all sounds wonderful, but it's not a park where you can expect to ride every single thing in a day, though arriving right at opening will help squeeze in more. TapuTapu only permits one reservation at a time on the flumes (the two lazy rivers, kiddie zone, and pools don't require reservations; neither does anything with a sign reading RIDE NOW), and you're free to replace any current reservation with a new one. While you wait, you're expected to do the non-reservation stuff—nosh at the six distinct food locations (quite good), drink cocktails (nice and strong), and sunbathe. You can ease the logjam somewhat by paying more for Express ($21–$53 depending on how busy), which allows you to cut the lines once per ride, but to be honest, riding everything would be exhausting here: You will have to climb the equivalent of 13 floors each time you want to do the most extreme slides, and there's not much shade, neither of which is unusual for a water park. Most visitors, especially older ones and those with young children, are satisfied with the amount of stuff they wind up getting to do, but completists and obsessive thrill-seekers may come away frustrated. Renting a cabana, if you can afford it, also helps since you'll be able to join virtual queues from a tablet there; you also get bottled water, snacks, a butler, and a home base kids can always return to (from $199). More affordably, "Premium Seating" consists of a pair of padded loungers with canopy, lockbox, and wait service. (Book those and cabanas at ✆ **877/489-8068.**) There's no drop-off at the front gate; Universal hotel guests take buses, and outsiders park in the Universal structure ($22) and take the free shuttle from there. Guests of Cabana Bay (p. 249) can just walk next door.

6000 Universal Blvd, Orlando. www.universalorlando.com. ✆ **407/363-8000.** $85 adult, $80 kids 3–9; towel rental $5; locker rental $12–$15; private cabanas $199–$550; parking $22, then free shuttle bus. Typically opens around 9am and closes around dusk.

SEAWORLD ORLANDO

The second theme park chain to set up shop in town, after Disney, was **Sea-World Orlando** ★★★ (Central Florida Pkwy., at International Dr., or exit 71 and 72 east of I-4; www.seaworldorlando.com; ✆ **407/545-5500;** $99 for everyone, discounts of $20 and $10 meal plans available online for some days; parking $22 ($20.65 via its app), up to $30 on peak days; open 9am–7pm with extended hours in peak season). The park began in San Diego in 1964 and staked a claim in Orlando in 1973, predating Universal by 17 years, but the last few years have been the hardest. The *Blackfish* flap hit hard, and although the park has always touted its legitimate rescue and conservation efforts, now such boasts can feel awkwardly defensive even though they were always part of the spiel. In 2009, before its troubles began, it was the 12th most popular theme park in the entire world. Now it has tumbled. It received 4 million visits in 2017 (10% less than 2016, enough to bump it out of the top 10 in the U.S.). Although SeaWorld operates three American parks (the third is in San Antonio), its Orlando location is the company's most important. Across the road you'll find its luxury animal park, **Discovery Cove** ★★★ (p. 157), and a fine water slide park, **Aquatica** (p. 157), and if you buy ahead online, you can often get free admission to either Aquatica or Busch Gardens Tampa Bay (p. 159), too.

Although SeaWorld is amid a multi-year investment strategy to remake itself as an amusement park and sidestep away from animal entertainment, it's not happening fast enough to turn around attendance woes. The focus is still aquatic animals and conservation. It's not hard to enjoy a fish tank, but if

SeaWorld

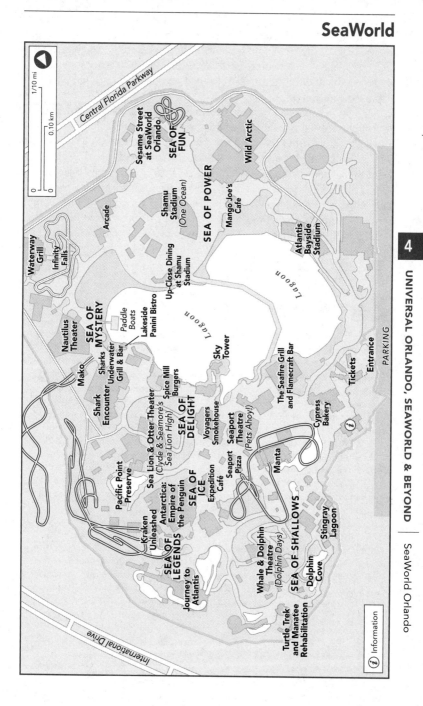

watching larger animals such as dolphins obey commands for food makes you uncomfortable, you'll hate it. As more alternative attractions are built, it's increasingly easy to avoid those shows, but they haven't gone away entirely. Otherwise, there's a lot going for SeaWorld: 200 acres of space for gardens, a compound that absorbs crowds well—and you don't have to pre-plan every move the way you do at Disney.

For now, the optimal SeaWorld experience is mostly **show-based.** Your day here will revolve around the scheduling of a half-dozen regular performances in which animals (mostly mammals, but some birds, too) do tricks—except here, they're called "behaviors"—with their human trainers. To some, Sea-World's banner attraction will always be that controversial Shamu show (named for a killer whale that died in 1971—and also savagely bit a trainer), and when you're not watching killer whales do backflips, you're ambling through **Animal Connections** habitats stocked with other beautiful creatures. Thoughtfully, **schedules are posted online** a few weeks ahead of time so that if you're really detail obsessed, you can map out your day in advance; the show schedule calendar is under "Plan Your Day."

Ethical Entertainment? The *Blackfish* Controversy

Some conservationists say SeaWorld's animals endure misery in captivity. Other conservationists laud SeaWorld for being an advocate for marine life. Each side presents statistics that seem convincing but are then shot down by rivals. And therein lies the ongoing tug-of-war over this profit-generating amusement park. SeaWorld is hostile to accusations of mistreatment and exploitation—in 2013, the low-budget documentary *Blackfish* asserted that the 2010 death of senior trainer Dawn Brancheau, which was witnessed by an audience at Shamu Stadium, was the result of inadequate care. (For its part, the Brancheau family distanced itself from the documentary, saying in a statement: "Dawn would not have remained a trainer at SeaWorld for 15 years if she felt that the whales were not well cared for.") An anti-SeaWorld social media campaign has raged ever since. Although SeaWorld has been fined about $26,000 by OSHA in California for improperly protecting its human employees, it sharply rebuts some of the film's points, objecting to one-sided reporting and complaining that the editing deceives viewers into believing the park collects its performing animals from the wild, something it hasn't done for decades. Excepting a few aged animals that were born in the seas and rehabilitated from accidents in the wild, SeaWorld insists, most of its animals were born in captivity and raised by hand and so they would not know how to survive in the wild. The orcas that live there, SeaWorld promises, will be the last generation to do so and not be bred. The park says it has rescued more than 30,000 animals to date, and reminds the media that when marine animals are threatened in the oceans, it regularly steps in to help. But *Blackfish* also alleges that the tanks at SeaWorld could never be large enough to contain animals biologically programmed to roam wide territory—a charge that's harder to deny, and one the company has promised to address in coming years. Defenders say that opens up a new can of worms—why single out Sea-World, they say, for things that zoos and animal parks across the country do every day?

The Best of SeaWorld

Don't miss if you're 6: Pets Ahoy!
Don't miss if you're 16: Mako, Manta
Requisite photo op: Orcas in flight, One Ocean, Shamu Stadium
Food you can only get here: Shamu ice-cream bar at carts parkwide

The most crowded, so go early: One Ocean, Shamu Stadium
Skippable: The movie at TurtleTrek
Biggest thrill: Mako, Kraken Unleashed
Best show: One Ocean, Shamu Stadium
Where to find peace: Anywhere around the lagoon

The free **SeaWorld Discovery Guide app** (there's free Wi-Fi in major park areas) orients you, supplies showtimes and wait times, allows you to buy shorter wait times for the rides, reserve show seating, and helps you remember where you parked. It drains your battery, though, so come with backup juice. SeaWorld sells **Quick Queue Unlimited** ($19–$38 depending how busy it is), which allows you to cut lines on the adult rides by entering through the exit, but lines are rarely long enough to warrant it. (There's a version for the kiddie rides, too, and one for good seating for the shows; both are priced $15–$29 and it's rarely busy enough to need them.) You can often buy single-use Quick Queue to jump the line at the most popular rides ($10) via electronic kiosks labeled Upgrade Your Day!, but check the regular wait first. The 6-hour **Expedition SeaWorld VIP Tour** (starting at $79 adults plus entry fee, $59 kids 3–9 in low season) includes reserved seating to three shows, food, and Quick Queue.

TIMING YOUR VISIT You will spend time waiting for shows to begin. People show up early for seats, so it's smart to arrive at least 30 minutes ahead of showtimes. Crowds are lightest Tuesday and Wednesday. *Important:* If the weather forecast shows prolonged rain (as opposed to Florida's typical spot showers), reschedule your visit. Not only will you spend lots of time outside, but it's also harder to see marine animals when the surface of the water is pelted by raindrops—not to mention the fact that if there's so much as a twinkle of lightning anywhere in the county, these water-based attractions and tall coasters close faster than a shark's mouth on dinner.

GETTING ORIENTED Once you park or get off the I-Ride (the stop is near the front gates), head for the lighthouse that marks the entrance. Inside, grab a placemat-size park map. On the back, printed fresh daily, is the **show schedule.** Performances usually begin an hour after park opening, and the signature Shamu show, One Ocean, has the fewest presentations. I always prefer the last one because it's less crowded. The map also lists "Animal Connections"—a manatee keeper talk here, a stingray feeding there. If you're interested in thrill rides, the best time is when the Shamu show is scheduled, because it soaks up hundreds of people at once. The Cape Cod–style entrance plaza is where you do the necessaries such as rent strollers and lockers. The area is really just a warm-up for the rest of the park.

On the map, the park is broken up into vague areas called "Seas," but you can't tell a difference between them as you walk.

The Best Shows

Be choosy about shows, because if you plan too many, you'll miss some habitats—yet spreading SeaWorld over 2 days would be excessive.

One Ocean ★★ SHOW   While orcas still live at SeaWorld they'll be given something to do in the "Shamu" show. When the orcas start to fly, the crowd comes alive. Closed-circuit TV cameras capture and display the spectacle on four huge, aging rotating screens as the animals thunder dauntingly through the water's surface, pointedly deluging seating sections in 52-degree water. The 25-minute plotless show occurs on such a scale as to make it required viewing. Now that trainers are no longer permitted to swim in the tank, they narrate from the sides, and they have to vamp for long periods if the orcas aren't in the mood to exercise on cue. Trainers fill the gaps with weak Temptations-style choreography, quasi-inspirational scripted gibberish ("Pass the word from generation to generation: A bright and beautiful future is in our hands…"), and some defensive patter about how scientists can better observe orcas in captivity. But you instantly forget about the flaws when the animals reappear to leap skyward and belly flop back into their tank. The stadium, which fits 5,000 and can still fill early, is covered, but the sides may catch sun, so arrive at least 30 minutes early. *Strategy:* Soak zone seats offer excellent views of the animals hurtling through the 2.5-million-gallon, 36-feet-deep tank, and in case the splashes miss you, the dozens of fountain jets will finish the job. Seats near the shelf-like front platform will also have a close-up view of a killer whale out of the water. Seats at the back of the stadium, higher than the central aisle, must rely on the TV cameras to make out what's going on underwater. Using the SeaWorld Discover Guide app, you can book reserved seating until 15 minutes ahead, but that's not usually necessary. *Shamu Stadium, Sea of Power.*

Clyde & Seamore's Sea Lion High ★★ SHOW   SeaWorld's long-running Pirate Island show was retired in 2014, but Clyde and Seamore, a pair

---

Smart Seating

Try to be at shows at least a **half-hour early,** and for Shamu, add another 10 minutes to walk around the lagoon to the stadium. SeaWorld is not obsessive about where you're permitted to sit, so if you're near the front of the line, you can claim the best seats. Several shows ("Pets Ahoy!" especially) don't permit latecomers.

Three of the shows—"One Ocean," "Dolphin Days," and "Clyde and Seamore"—have a clearly marked **"soak zone"** in the front rows of the seating section. Don't take this warning lightly; you have no concept of how much water a 10,000-pound orca can displace. Of course, sitting with your kids in the soak zone on a hot day is one of the great pleasures of SeaWorld, and most soak zone seating has the added advantage of affording side views through the tank glass. For those with expensive hairdos, ponchos are sold throughout the parks, including at stalls beneath Shamu Stadium, for $10. Keep electronics somewhere dry, because salt water fries circuits.

of sea lions, returned in 2015, with otters and sometimes a walrus, in a similar spectacle. Expect a prototypical sea lion act: cheesy, anthropomorphic (animals doing double takes, sliding, waving, and pretending to attend school with human companions), and slapstick. Their cute 25-minute presentation remains one of SeaWorld's most cherished franchises. *Strategy:* The worst seats are to the left as you face the stage (they have partial views and get hot). *Sea Lion & Otter Stadium, Sea of Delight.*

Dolphin Days ★★ SHOW   It's the kind of dolphin show that has been standard for decades—trainers chat about the animals, which leap and flip and otherwise frolic for your applause—and that's what makes it so good. You don't need fancy frippery to appreciate the strength and agility of these dolphins (which were all born in parks), although in this presentation, there is also a brief appearance by a flock of parrots. If you don't see the Shamu show, this is the best alternative. Sit in front and you may get drenched, but don't blame the dolphins—they're only doing it for the fish. *Dolphin Theater, Sea of Shallows.*

Pets Ahoy! ★★★ SHOW   Under-5s lose their minds at this indoor show at Seaport Theater, and you may, too—it's the show most worth watching repeatedly. Although the furry cast is a deviation from SeaWorld's usual finny ones, the tricks are no less entrancing. A menagerie of common animals (cats, dogs, pigs, ducks, a skunk), most rescued from animal shelters, do simple tricks and trigger tickling surprises on a rigged wharfside set. As the supercute gags multiply and compound in rapid succession (dachshunds pour out of a hot dog cart, a cat chases a white mouse in and out of hatches), and as more creatures are added into the mix precisely on cue, the amusement escalates. There's nearly no dialogue for its 20-minute run time. Afterward, trainers allow kids to pet some of the performers. *Strategy:* It's fun to sit under the catwalk (literally—cats walk on it) over the aisle between the first and second sections. This 850-seat theater fills well in advance, so show up 30–45 minutes ahead. *Seaport Theater, Sea of Delight.*

Sea of Shallows

This themed area is along the left as you first enter the park.

Manta ★★★ RIDE   Rising above the park is SeaWorld's thrill-ride pride, a "flying coaster" ridden face-down and head-first, in a horizontal position. You board sitting upright, and after your shoulders and ankles are secured, you're tipped forward and the train is dispatched over curious pedestrians for the 2½-minute ride. The queue meanders through 10 aquaria containing cow-nose rays, spotted eagle rays, and weedy sea dragons behind floor-to-ceiling windows, so you get a dose of sea life while you wait. Even nonriders can see rays through a separate entrance to the left of the ride's line, labeled **Aquarium: The Beautiful Ocean.** Speeds approach 60mph with four inversions, in a fanciful approximation of what it feels like for a manta ray to swim. Manta is a pretty unique coaster experience, and it's solid fun. *Strategy:* Lockers are $1/hr., credit cards or cash. There's an (unattended) basket on the platform for loose items if you don't use the lockers. Because you're in "flying" position, no seat has an obstructed view. The line can be long, so do it early if you can.

Dolphin Nursery ★★★ ACTIVITY   Between the entrance plaza and the Waterfront, the young mammals are kept with their mothers for the first few years of their lives before graduating to the larger Dolphin Cove elsewhere in the park. Much of the day, human trainers can be found here, feeding the adolescent animals and getting them acclimated to human interaction. A newly added glass siding allows you to look into the water.

Stingray Lagoon & Feeding ★ ACTIVITY   A not-quite-reproduction of Front Street in Key West, Florida, features the **Stingray Lagoon,** where you can lean over and feel the slimy, spongy fish. You can buy food to feed the rays for $5 per tray, $10 for three trays, of about four fish.

Dolphin Cove ★★ ACTIVITY   Next door, make appointments for the **Dolphin Encounter** ($20, and no cameras allowed), in which your 3–5 minutes of face time—from land, you may pet them, not feed them—are doled out as part of 15-minute blocks (times later in the day are less crowded). Kids under 13 must be with an adult. If you want to get into the water with dolphins, you'll need to pay for Discovery Cove (p. 157). Around feeding times, dolphins congregate at the trainers' dock, which can make seeing them difficult, so come between meals for a better look. Walk around the far side of the tank, and you'll find a little-used underwater viewing area with air-conditioning.

TurtleTrek ★★ ACTIVITY/FILM   A circuitous entrance ramp brings you to a popular air-conditioned underwater viewing area for 1,500 Caribbean fish and sea turtles the size of coffee tables—that's what earns our two-star rating. If you look closely, you can tell which turtles are rescues—one lost her lower jaw from a fishing net, another gave a flipper to a shark near Bermuda. In the **Manatee Rehabilitation** freshwater tank, much attention is paid to the manatee's status as one of America's most endangered animals, and, in fact, the sluggish creatures on display here were all rescued from the wild, where hot-dogging boaters are decimating their numbers. You'll be herded into a domed room where a (rather poorly) computer-animated 3-D film traces the life cycle of a sea turtle from its point of view. It's hard not to notice that 7-minute story hits the same beats as *Finding Nemo* (jellyfish fields, marauding birds, sharks prowling a shipwreck). After that, you might be better off staying longer in front of the tank, where the view is more authentic. *Tip:* If you skip this, at least see the rescued manatees in their rehab center, located out the attraction's exit.

Hook the Trainers

To get the most out of a visit, try to be in the same place as the animal trainers. Ask questions. Get involved. They may even allow you to feed or stroke the animals (set aside another $25 or so for fish food). These zoologists love sharing information about the animals they have devoted their lives to. Feeding times are usually posted outside each pavilion's entrance.

Sea of Legends, Sea of Ice

In the back left of the park, these two zones are for thrills and chills.

Journey to Atlantis ★★ RIDE   On this 6-minute flume-cum-coaster ride (you can't see the brief coaster section from the front), getting drenched is unavoidable, as the 60-foot drop should warn. Atlantis is incoherent but fun enough. First you pass through a few rooms as if you're on a family-friendly dark ride (the effects aren't great), and then you rocket down the hill you saw outside, and finally the water gives way and your boat becomes, briefly, a roller-coaster car with no upside-down moments but yet another splashdown. It feels cheap, but it's different enough to amuse. *Strategy:* Front seats get wettest. Try to balance the weight; otherwise you'll list disconcertingly. Keep stuff dry in a nearby locker ($1/hr., bills or credit cards), and leave it there when you ride Kraken next door. Ponchos are sold nearby for $10; $9 for kids.

Kraken Unleashed ★★ RIDE   Take a 2-minute dose of testosterone. After you settle into your pedestal-like seat, the floor is retracted, dangling your legs while you undergo seven upside-down "inversions" of one sort or another. You have the option of donning an attached helmet to watch a synchronized animated video of a wild undersea submarine trip involving volcanoes and giant squid—you can even look around in that virtual world. If you do, some riders report feeling queasy afterward, and you're warned incessantly to keep your head against the headrest because once you can't see upcoming track maneuvers, you're unable to brace yourself. The coaster, which hits 65mph and drops 144 feet on its first breath-stealing hill, is plenty terrifying on its own; you can do without the gimmick (most riders do). *Strategy:* Tighten the headset more than you think you need because when you get going, it may feel insecure (it's not). Because the train is floorless, you can't ride with flip-flops, but you may leave shoes on the loading dock and go barefoot (if you do that in the front row, which I recommend, you'll feel like you're about to lose a foot in the rails). Lockers cost $1/hr. (bills or credit cards). To save, use one locker for both this and Journey to Atlantis next door.

Antarctica: Empire of the Penguin ★★ ACTIVITY/RIDE   SeaWorld's tribute to penguins is this 4-acre, iceberg-styled, fishy-smelling pavilion. As your teeth chatter in the frigidity, view a colony of 245 Gentoo, Rockhopper, Adélie, and King birds with a fascinating underwater viewing of the little birds zipping around underwater and from a 30-degree area where they waddle helplessly on dry land. The ride is pointless, with sub-par animation, but you don't have to take it (no matter what, there's a line): It's based on some cool trackless technology that allows cars, which will remind you of air hockey pucks, to aimlessly roam the same room, even cross paths. Choose "Wild" or "Mild," although the wild version isn't much more intense than a few light pirouettes. Don't confuse this exhibition with Wild Arctic, which contains the beluga whales. *Tip:* Do this early because the line tends to stack up the fastest.

WHAT THE BASICS cost AT SEAWORLD

Parking: $22 (closer "Preferred" spaces are $30 and not worth it); $30 peak days
Single strollers: $15 per day
Double strollers: $25 per day
Wheelchair: $12 per day

ECV (electric convenience vehicle): $60 per day, $65 with a canopy + $10 deposit
Lockers: $10 (small) or $15 (large) per day
Coke: $3.30
Bottle of water: $3
Cup of beer: $9

Sea of Delight, Sea of Mystery

In the heart of the park, find classic shows and newly built adrenaline-pumpers.

Infinity Falls ★★★ FLUME On this new (2018) 5-minute round raft ride, groups of eight ride along 1,500 curling feet of flume through jungle and are sent flying through rapids bouncing between waterfalls and soaking fountains operated by sadistic fellow guests. That's just the beginning. By the end, the floats are raised on a vertical elevator in 5 seconds and dropped 40 feet along a steep ramp to a messy splashdown. You will not come off dry. SeaWorld is backing away from fishy exhibits, but that doesn't mean it can't immerse guests in water instead. Nearby, **Whitewater Supply** is a notch more interesting that the park's other souvenir stores, offering driftwood art, candles, sun dresses, and waterproof protection for your electronics.

Mako ★★★ ROLLER COASTER Wholly independent of animals, Mako ("*MAY*-ko") takes the crown as Orlando's longest (nearly a mile of track), fastest (73mph), and tallest (200 ft.) coaster. It's billed as a "hypercoaster" with "relentless air time," which means there are lots of humps and drops, including several over water, that combined with its deceptively loose restraint system make you feel weightless. That first brutal sideways drop is called "the hammerhead." On an industry level, it's a sign SeaWorld is serious about moving away from animal shows. On a thrills level, this is one helluva ride—Orlando's best coaster. The nearby lockers ($1/hr., bills and credit cards) are necessary unless your item is small because you can leave little items unattended in a bin on the platform. If someone in your party doesn't want to make a foray on this nerve-tangler, send them to the **flamingo paddle-boats** on the lake across the walkway ($7 per person for 20 minutes).

Pacific Point Preserve ★★★ ACTIVITY Like Dolphin Cove, Pacific Point is an open-air, rocky habitat that encourages feedings, but here the residents are incessantly barking California sea lions and a few demure seals. There's a narrow moat between the tank and the walkway, but you're encouraged to lean over and toss the doglike animals fresh fish, which are sold for $5 per tray, $20 for five. More often than not, marauding birds snatch what you toss. The area gets busy around Clyde and Seamore showtimes at the neighboring Sea Lion & Otter Theater.

Shark Encounter ★★★ ACTIVITY   The onetime Terrors of the Deep was given a more responsible name to rehabilitate the public image of the much-maligned creatures within. It's one of the better exhibitions, with 60-foot acrylic tubes passing through 300,000 gallons of water stocked with sharks—you're ushered along quickly via moving sidewalks. Don't ignore the shallow tank in front of the building, because that's where the smaller species are kept. There, you can feed rays and tarpon shrimp for $5 a tray.

Sky Tower ★★★ OBSERVATION RIDE   Jutting above the lagoon—and topped to still-greater heights by a colossal American flag—is the 400-foot, old-fashioned "Wheel-o-vater" ($2 when the park is busy, otherwise free) that rotates as it climbs 300 feet for a panorama. At the top, it slowly spins for two or three revolutions, giving you a good look around, before lowering you back to the Waterfront at the end of 6 minutes. You can spot Orlando landmarks, including Spaceship Earth and the skyscrapers of downtown.

Sea of Power, Sea of Fun

Shamu lives on the far side of the lake (which you may remember as the setting for the hilarious *Jaws IV*), along with a brand new kiddie section and walruses.

Shamu Stadium ★ ACTIVITY   The home to One Ocean has something to offer outside of showtime. A few of the killer whales are visible in the viewing area (accessed from the lakefront) that surveys one of their holding pods. Above the surface of that pen, the **Dine with Shamu** ★★ supper (p. 156) is held, separated by netting from the water (reserve several weeks ahead).

Sesame Street at SeaWorld Orlando ★★ ACTIVITY   Behind Shamu Stadium, kids have their own amusement area. Early 2019 (rushed 3 years ahead of schedule to shore up attendance bleed) sees the opening of the product of SeaWorld's partnership with Sesame Workshop. Children can romp among re-created sets of Mr. Hooper's store, Abby Cadabby's garden, and the 123 stoop, but there are some mild carnival-style wet and dry rides, too. The park promises roaming characters such as Big Bird, Bert, Ernie, Grover, and Cookie Monster, plus a new parade—a first for SeaWorld Orlando—starring Elmo (check the map for the times). Some of the rides from Shamu's Happy Harbor, the whale-themed kiddie enclave that stood here before, will remain and be re-themed to *Sesame Street*, including a carousel, an 800-foot kiddie coaster, and a bench that lifts kids 20 feet off the ground before gently bringing them back down in a series of short drops. It makes for adorable photos.

Wild Arctic ★★ ACTIVITY/RIDE   One of SeaWorld's most interesting exhibitions deserves more attention than it gets marooned here, at the Nowheresville end of the park, and the only time it seems crowded is a half-hour after every Shamu showtime. There are two ways to get in. Either you opt for the motion-simulator ride that re-creates a turbulent 5-minute helicopter ride (an old ride, and its bumpiness makes me ill), or you much more quickly make straight for the swimmers after a short movie. After that, you can walk through at your own pace, enjoying first a surface view and then an underwater look at the Pacific walruses, and the parks' utterly beautiful white beluga whales, which look like swimming porcelain. There are not currently any polar bears; the last elderly one died in 2014 and has not been replaced. There's probably more than a half-hour's worth of investigation here, including mock-ups of a polar research station and a fake "bear den" for young kids to explore. You'll also find it *very* cooling, which makes it a must on hot days.

Where to Eat at SeaWorld

In case you were wondering, SeaWorld only serves sustainable seafood. Prices are in line with everyone else's: $12–$14 a meal, before a drink. **All-Day Dining Deals** (one entree, one side or dessert, one nonalcoholic drink each time through line) cost $35 for adults and $20 for kids; rare is the person who will stay (or eat) long enough to make it pay off.

Disney World has its Mouse-ear ice-cream bar, but at SeaWorld, you'll be served a variety shaped like Shamu ($5). Plastic drinking straws choke animals, so you don't get one. SeaWorld often has a happy hour good for 2-for-1 drinks, usually at Flamecraft Bar and Sharks Underwater Bar; ask if it's available.

The headline meal event is **Up-Close Dining at Shamu Stadium ★★**, served from noon to 2pm in peak summer and from 4:30 to 6:30pm in other seasons alongside the orca pools with the narration of trainers. Prices fluctuate by the day, but expect $30 to $36 for adults and $15 to $25 for kids. On weekends and in high season, look for **Breakfast with Elmo and Friends (© 407/545-5500;** $30 adults, $15 kids; 9:15am).

Expedition Café ★★★, with exposed seating outside Antarctica, serves ($11–$15) teriyaki chicken, beef and pepper steak, and chef's salad.

The Seafire Grill ★★★, at the Waterfront, does fajitas, rice bowls, and salads, and the newly installed **Flamecraft Bar** has some appealing terrace seating overlooking the lagoon and a changing selection of Florida craft beers (Funky Buddha, Bold City, 3 Daughters, and Dead Lizard, which is made in Orlando). It's becoming a hangout; there's even occasional live acoustic music.

Farther up the Waterfront, the **Spice Mill Burgers ★★** offers steak or chickpea burgers, Buffalo chicken sandwiches, and chicken Caesar salad, and it also has pretty water views. **Voyagers Smokehouse ★**, facing the Seaport Theater's entrance, offers baby back ribs, spare ribs, and barbecue chicken.

Like Epcot's The Seas, the park devotes a section of an underwater viewing area to **Sharks Underwater Grill & Bar ★**, one of the park's premier tables (open 11:30am). It doesn't particularly specialize in seafood. Despite some cute touches, such as a bar that's also an aquarium and chairs that look like sharks' teeth, prices such as $29 for tempura shrimp and $29 for chicken piccata strike me as too high (salads are $12; kids' meals are $13). Some tables are right against the glass, but I prefer the ones farther back, which have a wider view.

New this year is **Waterway Grill,** indoors behind Infinity Falls. In addition to casual South American–style food, it has a good selection of a dozen beers on tap, some of them craft brews from around the state, such as Florida Avenue from Tampa and Swamp Head from Gainesville.

Captain Pete's Island Hot Dogs in the Key West area has foot-longs such as one with sauerkraut ($9–$12). At the Shamu end of the boardwalk, **Mango Joe's Cafe ★★** does a short menu of burgers, Italian subs, and pizza.

Backstage Tours

As a place that prides itself on sharing conservation information—in fact, as a place that keeps animals on display, its reputation depends on it—**SeaWorld** (www.seaworldorlando.com; ℂ **800/327-2424**) offers **Exclusive Park Experiences** that are less about touting its vaunted design team, as Disney's are, and more for learning about animal care.

SeaWorld's Other Parks

Aquatica ★ WATER PARK   SeaWorld's water slide park is across International Drive from its parent park (a free, 3-min. van ride links it), and you can pay for admission as an add-on to your SeaWorld visit. On hot days, it can be busier than SeaWorld itself. It's a perfectly nice park, favored somewhat by locals because it's less gimmicky than the others in town. Newly added for 2018 was **Ray Rush,** a family raft slide through a few elements like an enclosed sphere and a manta-shaped parabola. The **Dolphin Plunge** slide is a tube that curls off a tower and then turns clear acrylic as it passes through a habitat for Commerson's dolphins. It looks exciting on paper, but in truth you're going too fast to see anything, even if the dolphins could be reliably near the tubes (they aren't) and there wasn't water splashing in your eyes (there is, but don't fret because there's a viewing cave opposite Kiwi Traders). There are nearly two dozen slides, many of them similar to each other, the most intense of which is **Ihu's Breakaway Falls,** three curling slides that you begin by standing eight stories up in a shower-sized chamber on a floor that gives way, dropping you onto the ride. The pleasantly aggressive lazy river of **Loggerhead Lane** passes you by a big window into an aquarium. **Roa's Rapids** is novel in that it's a river with a very fast current meant to sweep your body along, without a tube (floaters, grab a life vest—they're free). You can pay $35 adults, $20 kids for unlimited fare. Otherwise, **Banana Beach** does not-so-great chicken, pizza, and hot dogs at typical prices; **Mango Market** sells chicken tenders, burgers, and sandwiches; and **Waterstone Grill** slings the usual grub, all $11 to $15. If you're bringing a picnic, stick to snack-sized bags; large ones will be confiscated and so will straws of any kind, which choke animals. For free wristbands that allow you to go cashless, sign up at the ticket booth or Info desks as you enter. *Tip:* Bring pool footwear because the sidewalks get hot. There are unattended shoe cubbies by each ride. If you pay $25 for Quick Queue, you can jump the lines.

5800 Water Play Way, Orlando. https://aquatica.com/orlando/. ℂ **888/800-5447.** $65 adults, $60 kids 3–9; online tickets $10 less, online discounts for combination SeaWorld tickets; lockers $15–$20; reserved lounger $20; private cabanas $50–$300; parking $22 (free if you visited SeaWorld earlier that day), $16 online.

Discovery Cove ★★★ THEME PARK   The most expensive park in town (prices shift by the season) is an all-inclusive experience. Only around 1,000 people a day are admitted, guaranteeing this faux tropical idyll is not marred by a single queue. Admission lanyards include breakfast, equipment rental, sunscreen, beer if you're of age, and unlimited lunch—a good one, too, with options such as fresh grilled tilapia (a fish that drew the short straw at Sea-World, I guess). Discovery Cove, in fact, is essentially a free-range playground. When you arrive, first thing in the morning, you're greeted under a vaulted atrium more redolent of a five-star island resort than a theme park. Coffee is poured, and once you're checked in you're set loose to do as you wish. Wade from perfect white sand into **Serenity Bay,** feed fresh fruit to the houseguests at the **Explorer's Aviary** for tropical birds, snorkel with barbless rays over the trenches of **The Grand Reef,** swim to habitats for marmoset monkeys and otters in the **Freshwater Oasis,** or float with a pool noodle down the slow-floating **Wind-Away River,** which passes through waterfalls into the aviary, preventing the birds from escaping. Many guests elect to simply kick back on a lounger (there are plenty) on incredibly silky sand (imported, of course) at the natural-looking pool. Since everyone wears free wetsuits or vests, there isn't much call for body shame or sunburned shoulders. When it's your turn— if you've paid extra—guests older than 5 can head to the **Dolphin Lagoon,** where in small groups of about eight you wade into the chilly water and meet one of the pod. Like children, dolphins have distinct personalities and must be paired to people the trainers think they'll enjoy being with—but many of these dolphins are docile and friendly, having dwelled at SeaWorld for decades. Here, the mostly hand-reared animals peer at you with a logician's eye while your trainer shows you basic hand signals. The climax of the 30-minute inter-action is the moment when you grasp two of the creature's fins and it swims, you in tow, for about 30 feet. Naturally, a photographer is on hand so if you want images or video, you'll pay for that, too, pushing a day over $400. Other add-on experiences: a shallow-water **Shark Swim** ($100); **Ray Feeding** ($60); and **SeaVenture** (from $49, minimum age 10), which places an air helmet on your head and brings you underwater to walk along the floor of the Grand Reef. Really, though, even a quiet day here is divine.

6000 Discovery Cove Way, Orlando. www.discoverycove.com. © **407/513-4600.** Price changes with the seasons, but ranges are $149–$240, including free admission to Sea-World and Aquatica for 2 weeks, plus $50–$190 for 30-min. dolphin interaction. Parking included in admission. Daily 8am–5:30pm.

LEGOLAND FLORIDA

Legoland Florida ★★★ is not just the youngest Central Florida theme park. It's also the oldest. That's because it took over the historic property of Cypress Gardens, a park on the cypress tree–lined shores of pretty Lake Eloise that helped put Orlando on the tourist map. Today, this extremely kid-friendly, soothingly mellow 150-acre park 45 minutes south of Disney World is a god-send for parents who crave a breather from the mechanical and authoritarian environment of Disney World. No other Florida park feels so spacious and caters so directly to kids aged 2 to 12. Everything is designed for little ones, from easy-to-tackle versions of adult rides to a large selection of things to do—somehow, its energy is not stressful, and there are two good hotels (p. 264).

Highlights include **Lost Kingdom Adventure,** an indoor target practice game in the style of a Lego-bright Indiana Jones tomb; easygoing boat tour **The Quest for Chi; Coastersaurus,** a mild out-and-back wooden roller coaster suitable for grammar school lightweights; **DUPLO Valley** for toddler rides; **Driving School,** the Ford-sponsored, free-driving mini-auto course that teaches kids how to obey traffic rules (or, in truth, ignore their first ones); **The Great Lego Race,** a wild mouse coaster where you can wear virtual reality goggles for an out-of-body experience (it's also perfectly situated for nonriders to take embarrassing shots of loved ones' faces as they hurtle downhill); **Flying School,** a tiny hanging coaster for a kid's first grown-up coaster thrills; **Safari Trek,** a wholly adorable car ride past wild African animals made of Legos; and **Royal Joust,** a mini steeplechase-style plastic horse race for wee ones that just may be the cutest ride in the world. For a break from the excitement, a healthy portion of the carefully tended **Cypress Gardens Historic Botanical Garden** (closes 30 min. before the park) was preserved, complete with Spanish moss, cypress knees jutting from tannic water, old-growth banyans (protected in the winter by hidden gas heaters), and signs warning of alligators, which live in the lake. Only now do you remember you're in Florida, which is sad, considering Florida made its tourist name by selling its natural wonders. Along its lakefront, search for a **Florida-shaped swimming pool.** It was built for Esther Williams's *Easy to Love* (1953), a jaw-dropping heli-water-ski MGM picture. For all that, and lots more like it, nothing competes with the fascination of **Miniland,** the tour de force display of Lego construction. The longer you linger, the more touches you see: a Space Shuttle misting during takeoff, dueling pirate ships, a mini *Star Wars* cantina, and marching bands in front of the Capitol. If you like those gags, stick around for the signature **Pirates' Cove Live Water Ski Show,** which replaces Cypress Gardens' pyramids of maidens with ski-jumping socket-headed Minifigure toy people. On top of all that, there's a modest **Water Park** (add $20, summers and warm-season weekends) attached, and the option to buy an unlimited pizza and pasta buffet, with fountain drinks ($10, in advance). Legoland offers $5 round-trip shuttles from ICON Orlando 360 (✆ **877/350-5346**). Because it usually closes by evening, arrive near opening time to get the most out of a day.

1 Legoland Way, Winter Haven. http://florida.legoland.com. ✆ **877/350-5346.** Admission $100 adults, $95 ages 3–12 and 60+ (advance purchase $20/$15 cheaper). Open daily 10am to 5pm–8pm, depending on the day, closed Tues–Wed outside of high season.

BUSCH GARDENS TAMPA BAY

Seventy miles southwest of Disney, and just 8 miles northwest of Tampa, **Busch Gardens Tampa Bay** ★★★ (3000 E. Busch Blvd., at 40th St.; www.buschgardens.com/tampa; ✆ **813/884-4386**), dating to 1959, is a world-class theme park combining thrill rides with top-notch animal enclosures for

PAST THAT turnstile IN THE SKY

Not all of Orlando's attractions have thrived. Tupperware Museum, we miss you. Kindly remove your Mouse ears to honor the forgotten fun—if not for an accident of time, you'd be vacationing here instead:

o **Circus World (1974–86):** Started by Mattel as a walk-through museum dedicated to circus history (after all, most of the big-top crews wintered in Florida), it collapsed under its own weight after competition with Disney tempted it into building too many rides. Also, clowns are terrifying.

o **Boardwalk Baseball (1987–90):** Textbook publisher Harcourt, Brace and Jovanovich recycled Circus World in the image of Florida's other winter tradition, baseball, and the Kansas City Royals were enticed to train there. Few cared. On January 17, 1990, 1,000 guests were asked to leave.

o **Xanadu (1983–96):** This walk-through "home of the future" was made by coating giant balloons with polyurethane—an early exercise in ergonomics. Sister homes in Gatlinburg and Wisconsin Dells were also built, but all outlived their curiosity value quickly. You'll find the site near Mile Marker 12 of U.S. 192.

o **JungleLand Zoo (1995–2002):** The demise of this low-rent Gatorland rip-off was hastened in 1997 when a lioness went missing among Kissimmee's motels for 3 days. A few trainers got nipped by the gators, too. Bad news.

o **Splendid China (1993–2003):** On 73 acres 3 miles west of Disney's main gate, China's wonders (the Forbidden City, a Great Wall segment containing 6.5 million bricks, and so on) were rebuilt in miniature. Who would blow $100 million on such a bad idea? The Chinese government, which pulled the strings.

o **River Country (1976–2005):** Disney's first water park, incorporated into Bay Lake beside Fort Wilderness Resort, simply wasn't good enough anymore.

gorillas, rhino, and other rare creatures—more than 300 species in all. Coasters are its jam. The newest ones are the most terrifying: 335-foot-tall (102 m) **Falcon's Fury,** America's tallest drop tower sends riders plummeting face-down, and **Cobra's Curse,** a novel steel coaster that begins with an elevator instead of a hill on which the cars gently spin as they race along. Other detour-worthy roller coasters include the vertical drop of **SheiKra** and the deliriously sidewinding launch coaster **Cheetah Hunt.** If the coaster wars were an arms race, Busch Gardens easily annihilates Orlando's efforts, yet relatively few tourists make the 75-minute trip here—and it's a shame that such a high-quality theme park winds up being the eighth-best choice for most Orlando visitors. The park knows coaxing visitors from Orlando is a problem, so it grants **free round-trip coach transportation** from many Orlando hotels with a ticket (© **800/221-1339**).

Admission to the park is $105 for everyone, with decent discounts often available online for pre-purchase. Or for $150 ($100 online), buy a ticket that gets you SeaWorld, too. Parking is $22 ($1 less if bought online).

MORE ORLANDO ATTRACTIONS

There's so much more to see and do in Orlando. When you're sick of parking trams and cattle queues, divert yourself with something new. Actually, something old—some of these places are among the original attractions that sparked the fertile vacationland that Central Florida is today.

INTERNATIONAL DRIVE AREA

The attractions around International Drive aren't plush—they're convention-goer diversions and rainy-day amusements, mostly—but they are the stuff of a quintessential family holiday and they won't break the bank. I-Drive is the only touristy area in Orlando where a car isn't necessary, not least because the I-Ride Trolley (p. 271) will tote you along, if you're tired of strolling.

Andretti Indoor Karting & Games ★★ AMUSEMENT CENTER   This booming, hectic, $30 million pleasuredome (with auto racer Mario Andretti as a partner) makes Dave & Busters look like a tea party: 100,800 square feet of climbing walls, ropes courses, laser tag, a full arcade with prizes (in the "Victory Lane"), bowling lanes, a restaurant, and a bar that overlooks it all. The booze flows, the music pumps, and the birthday parties for yelling grade-school boys roll non-stop. The centerpieces are its three multi-level indoor go-kart tracks using SODI RTX electric carts and designed by Andretti, with plenty of banked curves (closed-toed shoes required). From 4pm–7pm, bowling is just $5 per person/hour with free shoe rental.

9299 Universal Blvd, Orlando. www.andrettikarting.com.✆ **407/374-0085.** One race $22 adult and $15 riders shorter than 48 inches, other amusements charged separately (generally $10–$13 each, with packages available). Sun–Thurs 10am–midnight, Fri–Sat 10am–1am.

Chocolate Kingdom ★ TOUR   Yes, they make and sell chocolate, but they also roast, skin, and grind the beans before your eyes using clunky antique equipment so heavy the floor had to be reinforced. All in all, the third-generation chocolatier who owns it and the national Schakolad franchise have put together a surprisingly educational guided tour, good for kids and with free samples along the way, based on the rich history of the cocoa bean. (Did you know the Aztecs wouldn't let women eat them because they thought abstaining would keep them dull-witted and compliant?) Call ahead if you can so they'll have a guide ready for you. There's a second location at 2858 Florida Plaza Blvd., Kissimmee.

9901 Hawaiian Court, Orlando. www.chocolatekingdom.com. © **407/705-3475.** Adults $17, kids 4–12 $13. Tours daily 11am–5pm, closes at 6pm.

Crayola Experience ★★ ACTIVITY   When we were kids, the most fun we could have with a crayon was to peel the wrapper off—maybe eat one, too. Your kids, though, can scamper around a department-store-size fantabulous multi-station sensory playhouse where they may, among other things, print wrappers they write themselves, animate their drawings on giant screens, melt crayons into art, animate homemade puppets in a magic theater, frolic in a two-story playground shaped like crayons, color a printout of their own face, mess around on a giant Lite-Brite, and pitch an epic fit the moment you suggest it's time to leave. Adults will first feel bitter jealousy and then nostalgia pangs of their receding childhood—Lemon Yellow, we hardly knew ye—but will prob-ably then indulge in the adjoining shop (no admission required), which sells every Crayola product known to the world of little Picassos, including a wall filled with some 120 current colors, which they can bulk-buy in buckets.

Florida Mall, 8001 S. Orange Blossom Trail, Orlando. www.crayolaexperience.com. © **407/757-1706.** Admission $25, $3 discount online. Daily 10am–8pm (closes earlier in winter).

Fun Spot America—Orlando ★ AMUSEMENT PARK   A recent recipient of immense investment and careful improvements, Fun Spot in Orlando, at the top of I-Drive, is Orlando's largest (15 acres), cleanest, best-lit midway-style diversion. Although it became famous for its four **Go-Kart tracks** (concrete, multilevel; the Quad Helix's stacked figure-eight turns make it a favorite, but the Conquest's peaked ramp is a pip), the spacious grounds are also stocked with a two-level arcade, a scrambler and other carnival rides, plenty of snack bars, a Ferris wheel called **Revolver** (Charlize Theron rode it in *Monster*), and a section of kiddie rides. There's also **White Lightning,** a smooth-as-silk wood-frame coaster (the only one in town); **Freedom Flyer,** a wee version of a hanging, foot-dangling train; and a few alligators on loan from Gatorland. The 250-foot-tall SkyCoaster is the second-tallest anywhere (the first is at Fun Spot's location in Kissimmee, p. 174).

5700 Fun Spot Way, Orlando. www.fun-spot.com. © **407/363-3867.** Free entry. Pay-per-ride $5–$10, SkyCoaster $40, unlimited rides $50 ($45 online). Generally daily 10am–midnight, winter weekdays noon or 2pm–midnight.

I-Drive NASCAR ★ THRILL RIDE   A kids' birthday party diversion with a go-kart track (a half-mile, 12 turns, three of them hairpin), snack bar, and arcade. It was Orlando's first indoor track before Andretti (p. 161) stormed on

Orlando Area Attractions

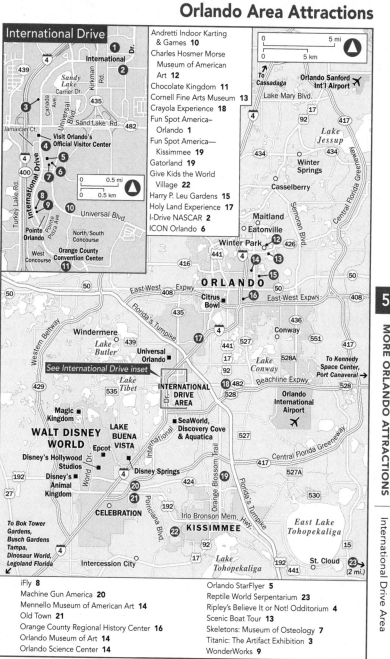

International Drive

Andretti Indoor Karting & Games **10**
Charles Hosmer Morse Museum of American Art **12**
Chocolate Kingdom **11**
Cornell Fine Arts Museum **13**
Crayola Experience **18**
Fun Spot America–Orlando **1**
Fun Spot America—Kissimmee **19**
Gatorland **19**
Give Kids the World Village **22**
Harry P. Leu Gardens **15**
Holy Land Experience **17**
I-Drive NASCAR **2**
ICON Orlando **6**

iFly **8**
Machine Gun America **20**
Mennello Museum of American Art **14**
Old Town **21**
Orange County Regional History Center **16**
Orlando Museum of Art **14**
Orlando Science Center **14**

Orlando StarFlyer **5**
Reptile World Serpentarium **23**
Ripley's Believe It or Not! Odditorium **4**
Scenic Boat Tour **13**
Skeletons: Museum of Osteology **7**
Titanic: The Artifact Exhibition **3**
WonderWorks **9**

the scene, but the vehicles are the thing here: Silent electric carts that go 45mph with state-of-the-art shock absorption and adjustable steering and seats.

5228 Vanguard St., Orlando. www.idrivenascar.com. © **407/581-9644.** $19 adult, $17 kids under age 16 for 16 times around; frequent discounts. No open-toed shoes. Minimum height 55 inches. Sun–Thurs noon–10pm; Fri–Sat 11am–midnight.

iFly ★ ACTIVITY   In 2017, this long-running vertical wind tunnel opened a glassy new 14,000-square-foot facility. Visitors are strapped into jumpsuits and given a short training session on how to walk over the netting into the 125mph airflow. Mastering the necessary arched-back, splay-legged posture can be tricky, but should you fail, there's a master diver with you to grab you by the sleeve and guide you into a series of adrenaline-fueled climbs and plunges. Or not—you can just hover there, if that's what floats your butt.

8969 International Dr., Orlando. www.iflyworld.com/orlando. © **407/337-4359.** $70 for 2 1-minute flights, $112 for 4. Daily 8:30am–10:30pm.

Madame Tussauds ★★ TOURIST MUSEUM   The world-famous wax museum opened and Orlando outpost in **ICON Orlando 360** (formerly I-Drive 360), a complex of shops and restaurants. It's so silly and pleasantly touristy that it's astounding it took so long. First, they try to get you to pose for a tourist photo, but skip that, because Tussauds is already essentially one extended photo op. As you go from room to room, you get right beside the few dozen full-size figures of current and historical celebrities, many of which are so lifelike that you'll be astounded (Obama, Taylor Swift, Selena Gomez), and some so off the mark you have to check the signage to tell who it is (Madonna, Katy Perry). If the sign says they were "sculpted from a sitting" rather than merely "portrayed," you know it's more accurate. Midway through, you can pay $10 to create a wax cast of your own hand—protect it from the Florida heat thereafter if you do.

ICON Orlando 360, 8387 International Dr., Orlando. www.madametussauds.com/orlando. © **866/630-8315.** $28 adult, $23 child 4–12; discount packages available to add ICON Orlando and SeaLife Aquarium; frequent discounts online. Free parking. Daily 10am–10pm or midnight, depending on the season.

Magical Midway Thrill Park ★ AMUSEMENT PARK   This small concrete area is built on adrenaline and rash decisions, blaring with rock music and heaving with idle youth. The most obvious generator of regret is the world's tallest **Slingshot** ride ($25, not included on passes), a colossal fork strung with a pod. Two at a time sit inside and are catapulted more than 200 feet into the sky, wailing to wake the dead. Meanwhile, the skyscraping circular swing carousel **StarFlyer** is a pipsqueak compared to the new one a few blocks south (it may even be removed in 2019). The rest is dominated by two thunderous, wooden Go-Kart tracks (the Avalanche track has slightly steeper ramps than the Alpine), a few minor rides (cheerless bumper boats), and a dirty arcade. Its unsophisticated virtues are something 11-year-old boys idolize.

7001 International Dr., Orlando. www.magicalmidway.com. © **407/370-5353.** $8 Go-Kart rides, $3 midway rides, 3-hr. unlimited rides $25, all-day unlimited $32. Park, daily noon–midnight; arcade, daily 10am–midnight.

ICON Orlando ★★ AMUSEMENT PARK You probably know it by its previous name, the Orlando Eye. After enduring a regrettable, stand-up "4-D Experience" (a mindless green-screen 3-D film of aerial footage of Orlando— Disney's noticeably absent—that peppers you with mist), you board 15-passenger pods for your slightly quivering ride on the East Coast's tallest (400 feet) observation wheel, which is constantly spinning at 1 mph for a 30-minute rotation. You're too far to see into the Disney parks, but you do see the spires of Hogwarts at Universal Orlando, 2 miles north. It's pretty enough, but any city would be at that height. Fun ride, odd spot.

ICON Orlando 360, 8401 International Dr., Orlando. www.officialorlandoeye.com. ✆ **407/370-5353.** $28 adult, $23 child 3–12; discounts available to add Madame Tussauds, SeaLife Aquarium, Skeletons: Museum of Osteology, and the StarFlyer; frequent discounts online. Free parking. Sun–Thurs 10am–10pm; Fri–Sat 10am–midnight. Generally closed in early Feb for maintenance.

Orlando SeaLife Aquarium ★ AQUARIUM The McDonald's of aquaria has some four dozen locations worldwide, and it's such a success because it's fairly well-stocked, theatrically lit, and charmingly designed: There are clear walkway tubes passing through huge tanks, for example, and kids can crawl under the moray eel habitat and see from "inside" the tank through bubble-like head spaces popping through its floor. SeaLife angles for kids in particular, what with the annoying voices of anthropomorphic fish delivering factual tidbits on the loudspeakers and the chipper docents sticking religiously to a corporate-approved script ("Here's your Discovery Fact of the day!") that pummels you with boasts about its good deeds of conservation. Concluding the self-guided tour of the 5,000-plus creatures (including jellyfish, small sharks, and clownfish) there's a shallow touch tank where kids can pet live starfish. Adults will be satisfied in 30 minutes, but kids might prefer an hour.

ICON Orlando 360, 8387 International Dr., Orlando. www.visitsealife.com/orlando. ✆ **407/370-5353.** $28 adult, $23 child 3–12; discounts available to add Madame Tussauds and ICON Orlando; frequent discounts online. Free parking. Daily 10am–10pm, last admission 1 hr. before closing.

Rainy-Day Mayhem

The massive **Outer Limitz** (6725 South Kirkman Rd., www.outerlimitzorlando. com; ✆ **407/704-6723**), near Fun Spot America, and **AirHeads** (33 West Pineloch Ave., http://orlando.airheads usa.com; ✆ **407/270-4611**), south of downtown Orlando, are indoor trampoline-filled arenas where netting keeps your offspring from cracking their heads open as they bounce off walls and fling themselves into pits filled with foam blocks. At Outer Limitz, there's basketball and dodgeball, too. That's pretty cool, but high-octane teens might prefer slaughtering the undead at the walk-through shoot-'em-up **Zombie Outbreak,** next to the *Titanic* attraction (7364 International Dr., www.zombie outbreak.co; ✆ **407/745-4068,** $25 for 15 minutes).

Ripley's Believe It or Not! Odditorium ★ TOURIST MUSEUM   The ticketed equivalent of a meme, Ripley's is well-maintained and clean, but it's too expensive for the thin diversion it delivers. Mostly it consists of optical illusions, vaguely ominous specimens from foreign cultures, panels from the old Ripley's comic (does anyone under 60 even remember those?), and the odd coin-operated device. There are too many signs and fewer artifacts than you'll be expecting, unless you count a portrait of Beyoncé made out of candy. Don't set foot in it without harvesting coupons from any tourist brochure.

8201 International Dr., Orlando. www.ripleys.com/orlando. ⓒ **407/345-0501.** $22 adults, $15 kids 3–11. Free parking. Daily 9am–midnight, last entry 11pm.

Skeletons: Museum of Osteology ★★ TOURIST MUSEUM   The macabre, tchotchke-crammed gift shop entry beside ICON Orlando doesn't do much to disabuse you of dread, but hidden within is a thoughtful and diverse museum of more than 500 animal skeletons huge and small, many mounted in detailed habitats with the right touch of whimsy. All of them were collected and painstakingly prepared by an osteological outfit in Oklahoma City, where an earlier version proved popular enough to warrant export here. It's a particular fascination for kids into science or anatomy. What a lucky break—an Orlando attraction that actually nourishes young minds!

ICON Orlando 360, 8441 International Dr., Orlando. www.skeletonmuseum.com. ⓒ **407/203-6999.** $20 adult, $13 child 3–12, $4 discount online. Free parking. Daily 10am–10pm.

Orlando StarFlyer ★ RIDE   As everyone knows, there are three necessary components to carnival thrills: height, speed, and flimsy-feeling restraints. The StarFlyer nails the trifecta. At 450 feet (your altitude will be about 350 feet), this 2018 erection is the tallest of the 35 such spinning swing towers around the world. The four-minute ride is able to go 60 mph but after many experiments in which customers fled traumatized, the proprietors settled on a top speed of 45 mph. It starts fast but slows down once your pants are good and wet, so there's time to look around at that incredible view, the best in town. Never once does it seem possible that the chains are enough to support the weight of your two-person bench, yet they are, by several factors. And that's what gives it a kick. No items, including sunglasses, are permitted on board (lockers are free), so if it's very bright out, come back at night. There's a bar at the base where you can toast whatever god you worship for bringing you back to the ground safely.

ICON Orlando 360, 8265 International Dr., Orlando. www.starflyer.com. ⓒ **407/640-7009.** $13 ride, $8 re-ride. Minimum height 44 inches/112 cm. Free parking. Daily 10am–2am.

Titanic: The Artifact Exhibition ★★ TOURIST MUSEUM   More than 100 genuine artifacts from the *Titanic* itself—a teak deck chair to cookware to tile fragments to a boarding card—give this permanent exhibition salt. For those interested in the topic, this theatrically presented museum, which walks guests chronologically from boarding to the abbreviated voyage to rediscovery, provides a balanced dossier of the sorry tale. There's a little conflation of Hollywood storytelling with history (at the replica of the First Class Grand

Staircase, a piano rendition of "My Heart Will Go On" repeats *ad nauseam*), but there's still plenty of meat on this hambone. Join a regular tour, because guides are knowledgeable; after the tour, you can backtrack for closer looks. The 2-ton slab from the hull, cast in an eerie light, is a moving epilogue.

7324 International Dr., Orlando. www.premierexhibitions.com. 📞 **407/248-1166.** $22 adults, $16 kids 5–11, senior $19.75. Daily 11am–10pm, last admission 8pm.

WonderWorks ★ TOURIST MUSEUM   You know it's touristy because the facade looks like someone ripped a mansion out of the ground and turned it upside down. But the inverted motif doesn't continue beyond its doors. Instead, you get about 100 hands-on curiosity exhibits not unlike what you'd find at a science museum or an arcade—cubicles simulating earthquakes and hurricanes, a bubble-making area, a kiosk where you can use Google Earth to find your house, lots of posters of optical illusions—all decently maintained and cheerful. Bring Purell because exhibits get smeary, your patience to

SPRING training daze

Baseball is inextricable from Florida's calendar. Way back in 1923, the Cincinnati Reds began spring training in Orlando at Tinker Field (which was only torn down in 2015), in the 1930s the Brooklyn Dodgers hit here, and the Washington Senators then arrived and stayed for the better part of half a century. A few teams in the so-called Grapefruit League (the Arizona teams are the Cactus League) still call Orlando or its environs their temporary home, and in the preseason you can watch them practice or play exhibition games. Unlike at season games, players often mingle with fans—in fact, some facilities were built to cozy proportions (leave the binoculars at home), with interaction areas where you can collect autographs from athletes before or after practice. Sometimes it feels like the spirit of old-time baseball, the one supplanted by high-priced players and colossal arenas.

Tickets (usually $15–$25) go on sale in January. Pitchers and catchers report first, in mid-February, and by the end of the month, the whole team is on hand. They play against other teams through March before heading to their home parks by April.

o **Atlanta Braves** (Disney's Wide World of Sports, 700 S. Victory Lane, Lake Buena Vista; http://atlanta.braves.mlb.com; 📞 **407/939-4263**). Since they took up residence in 1997 at Walt Disney World, the Braves can brag about having one of the nicest and largest (9,500 seats) training stadiums under the sun, where they play 18-odd games.

o **Houston Astros** (Osceola County Stadium, 1000 Bill Beck Rd., Kissimmee; http://houston.astros.mlb.com; 📞 **321/697-3200**). The smallest training park in the Grapefruit League (5,200 seats—still hardly tiny) has hosted the Astros since 1985. Team members make themselves available for fan greetings in their Autograph Alley.

o **Detroit Tigers** (Joker Marchant Stadium, Al Kaline Dr., 2301 Lake Hills Rd., Lakeland; http://detroit.tigers.mlb.com; 📞 **866/668-4437**). Lakeland, between Orlando and Tampa on I-4, has hosted the Tigers since 1934, the longest relations for any major league team, and the team is such a local institution that their so-called "Tiger Town" training complex, built on the site of a World War II flight academy, has grown up with them.

combat field trip swarms, and lots of cash, because there's a slate of add-ons like a ropes course, a "4-D" simulator chair, and an arcade that aren't included in admission. Adults may find it cheesy but young kids love it, especially if they have a nascent interest in science—then again, they have no concept of the value of your hard-earned dollar. It's mostly for rainy days.

9067 International Dr., Orlando. www.wonderworksonline.com. © **407/351-8800.** $34 adults, $25 seniors over 54 and kids 4–12, Extra charges for laser tag, ropes course, motion-simulator ride, games. Daily 9am–midnight.

North of Universal & Orlando

Holy Land Experience ★ THEME PARK   The Trinity Broadcasting Network owns this peculiarly American park, a lightly patronized, heavily sanitized version of Jerusalem that has received a few refreshes in recent years but is still more popular with the devout than with casual tourists. The small property (that charges admission yet is exempt from property taxes) has no rides so must rely on presentations to fill the hours. Performance times are spread across the clock to force completists to purchase a second day, which isn't necessary to do. For oddity, there will never be its equal. Will there ever again be a theme park where major attractions are an existential drama featuring the resurrection of Lazarus, a putt-putt course weaving through Bible stories, and a model of Jerusalem in the year A.D. 66? Biblical characters stroll around greeting visitors, while the nearby Scriptorium provides an automated 55-minute tour of a truly precious collection of rare specimens of Bible publishing history. It seems wholesomely innocuous until late afternoon, when it turns into a gory snuff show: An actor playing Christ endures a lingering beating and blood-spattered "crucifixion" by villainous Romans for an audience that holds up their palms in testimony. Entertaining people with execution is more Roman than most guests perceive. There's no political context unless you can decode it: Recorded narration is all-male, Catholics are depicted as getting God wrong, and Christians always God's chosen heroes persecuted by savages. If you have been to the real Holy Land, you will quickly grasp that this version of Israel is Hollywoodized and suburban, a costume-party catechism marrying the tone of Charlton Heston movies and the tenor of contemporary Christian music.

4655 Vineland Rd., Orlando. www.holylandexperience.com. © **800/447-7235** or 407/872-2272. $50 adults, $35 children 5–17, kids 4 and under free. Free parking. Tues–Sat 10am–6pm.

Mennello Museum of American Art ★★ MUSEUM   The Mennello is a repository for the luridly vivid paintings of Earl Cunningham, a chicken farmer and folk artist whose conceptions sometimes seem refreshingly naive, and then a moment later become brazenly modernist. Cunningham, who died in 1977 while running a curio shop in St. Augustine, is now considered so important that the Smithsonian devoted an exhibition to him. The museum also hosts exhibitions of fine American folk art.

900 E. Princeton St., Orlando. www.mennellomuseum.com. © **407/246-4278.** $5 adults, $4 seniors over 59, $1 students, 18 and under free. Tues–Sat 10:30am–4:30pm; Sun noon–4:30pm.

You're locked in a room that looks like the set to a play—an office, a ship's hold—and given the clues hidden there, you must solve puzzles, crack codes, and find the key to get back out within an hour. Don't worry: There are no scary gotchas, and because of fire codes, the door's not *really* locked. If you're struggling with the mental challenge, staff is monitoring you via camera (don't pick your nose) and can nudge you in the right direction. It's much easier, and a lot more fun, to play with a group. Escaping has flooded the Orlando market, and while some locations put on games that look as if they were decorated using a gift card at Home Depot, real gamer love goes into creating these puzzles, so each one is unique. There may be an age minimum of about 12 and you're allowed to fail (many do), but always make a reservation first. Alphabetically:

o **America's Escape Game:** 8723 International Drive, Suite 115, Orlando; www.americasescapegame. com; ✆ **407/412-5585.** Rooms: White House, asylum, Egyptian tomb, hermit cabin (nearly impossible to solve), pandemic. $29–$39.

o **Breakout Escape Rooms:** 8155 Vineland Ave., Orlando; www.room breakout.com/orlando; ✆ **407/778-4562.** Fairly near Disney. Rooms:

Zombies (the hardest), spy, evil circus. $32.

o **Doldrick's Escape Room:** 2943 Vineland Rd., Kissimmee; www.doldricks escaperoom.com; ✆ **407/507-0506.** This one near Disney isn't a chain but a privately owned labor of love with high production values. Room: Bomb squad. $33.

o **The Escape Game:** 8145 International Dr., Suite 511, Orlando; www.orlandoescapegame.com; ✆ **407/501-7222.** Rooms: Mars, Western, art heist, terrorist threat, prison break. $32–$38.

o **Escapology:** 11951 International Dr., Orlando; www.escapology.com; ✆ **407/278-1515.** Rooms: Western, pandemic, Cuban missile crisis, drug lord, submarine, train murder, hackers. $30–$60.

o **The Great Escape Room:** 23½ S. Magnolia Ave., Orlando; www. thegreatescaperoom.com/orlando; ✆ **386/385-8860.** Rooms: Sherlock Holmes, nuclear crisis (most difficult), surgical emergency. $21–$28.

o **Lockbusters:** 8326 International Dr., Orlando; www.lockbustersgame. com; ✆ **407/930-0822.** One of the best-detailed choices in town, near ICON Orlando. Rooms: Serial killer, pirates, chopper crash, haunted manor (the hardest). $32.

Orange County Regional History Center ★★★ MUSEUM People who think Central Florida history began with Walt will have their eyes opened in this underrated museum in a handsome 1927 Greek Revival former courthouse. Head first to the **fourth floor,** where the timeline starts 12,000 years in the past and work your way down. In 1981, a high school student rooting through lake muck found a Timacuan dugout canoe from around A.D. 1000, and now it is proudly displayed, as are mastodon teeth, pots from 500 B.C., and a 12-foot-tall oyster midden. As you advance through time, artifacts keep coming: saddles used by the forgotten Florida cowmen (the swampy ground made meat chewy, which Cuban customers liked); recipes for Florida Cracker delicacies (Squirrel Soup, Baked Possum); artifacts from the steamship tourist trade (in the 1870s, the St. John's River system was America's busiest one south of the Hudson); and a wall of gorgeous vintage labels from the many citrus companies that once dominated the area. The exhibitions are noticeably conflicted about the growth explosion wrought by the theme parks—the "Building a Kingdom" exhibition was created without Disney funding so it would have the freedom to be frank. An interesting sidelight is the retired Courtroom B, a handsome, wooden chamber out of *Inherit the Wind* silenced by cork floors and emblazoned with the slogan "Equal and Exact Justice to All Men." That was painted over the bench at a time when people were still being lynched here (there's a KKK robe in a nearby gallery), and until as late as 1951 in Orlando, black mothers had to give birth in the boiler room of the hospital. Some justice *was* served here: In 1987, Courtroom B tried the first case in America in which DNA evidence obtained a conviction.

65 E. Central Blvd., Orlando. www.thehistorycenter.org. ℂ **407/836-8500.** $8 adults, $6 kids 5–12, $7 seniors over 54, including audio tour. Mon–Sat 10am–5pm; Sun noon–5pm.

Orlando Museum of Art ★ MUSEUM   Although this fixture of local pride is touted as *de rigueur* in much tourist literature, OMA takes less than an hour to see. Most of it is not particularly important, just high atmosphere, but of note are Robert Rauschenberg's "Florida Psalm," a collage paean to the state's fading tourism emblems; Chuck Close's 1982 portrait of his wife done in fingerprints, and John James Audubon's Great Blue Heron. Temporary exhibitions up the par. Expect a pleasant outing, especially if you pair a visit with an amble around the surrounding Loch Haven Park, but not a milestone.

2416 N. Mills Ave., Orlando. www.omart.org. ℂ **407/896-4231.** $15 adults, $5 college students, $8 seniors over 64, $5 kids 4–17. Tues–Fri 10am–4pm; Sat–Sun noon–4pm.

Orlando Science Center ★ MUSEUM   The center is an excellent (if expensive) example of its type, and recent investment has bestowed it with some fun, large-scale set pieces that make it feel more like a hands-on play complex than an educational facility, including a giant network of tubes kids blow kerchiefs through; a three-level indoor playhouse; play troughs pumping with water; a toddler version of a citrus farm; and an outdoorsy-looking NatureWorks with baby gators, turtles, and snakes. However, in a town so crowded with amazing things for kids, if you have a good science museum back home, you could probably skip it.

777 E. Princeton St., Orlando. www.osc.org. ℂ **407/514-2000.** Admission including exhibition $20.95 adults, $18.95 seniors age 55 and over and students with ID, $14.95 kids 3–11, including movies. Parking $5. Sun–Thurs 10am–5pm; Fri–Sat 10am–9pm.

Winter Park & North Orlando

Winter Park has long been a bastion of wealth, particularly from New Money families who failed to find favor among the Old Money of the North. Its expensive tastes are represented by its lakefront mansions, red-brick streets, and a few wrongly overlooked gems for true masterpieces.

Charles Hosmer Morse Museum of American Art ★★★ MUSEUM   The best museum in the Orlando area, and perhaps the finest in the state,

A TOWN OF psychics

George P. Colby was reared in the Midwest by Baptist parents, but incessant visions (and poor health) compelled him south, where in 1875, he came across land that, he said, appeared exactly as it had been shown to him by his spirit guide, Seneca. Soon after that, Colby enticed a group of refugees from chilly Lily Dale, New York—a town populated by spiritualists that still exists on the **Cassadaga** lakes outside of Buffalo—to join him in the then-rural wilds of Florida. The winter "camp" of **Cassadaga ★★★** (exit 114 from I-4; www.cassadaga.org) was born. Nowadays, its residents offer a daily slate of services, laying-on of hands, and readings. The anachronistic village 40 miles northeast of Universal is untouched by development, and only accredited mediums may live among the ramshackle 1920s homes and Spanish moss. Tree-shaded, whitewashed, and more than slightly creepy, Cassadaga, on the National Register of Historic Places, is a bastion of metaphysicality in a region otherwise devoted to Christian fundamentalism.

Before setting out, check the town's website for the full list of events and psychics. When you arrive, consult the bulletin board in **Cassadaga Camp Bookstore** (1112 Stevens St., Cassadaga; ✆ **386/228-2880**; Mon–Sat 10am–6pm, Sun 11:30am–5pm) to see which mediums are available to take walk-in clients for readings or healings. Everything in town, including gift shops for gemstones and talismans, is within a few blocks, so park and explore. Because the rent's so cheap (the land is owned by the Southern

Cassadaga Spiritualist Camp Meeting Association, which subscribes to a form of Biblical Spiritualism—Jesus is real, Satan isn't), services go for a fraction of what they cost in the outside world.

Wednesdays from 7:30–9pm at Colby Memorial Temple, mediums deliver messages from deceased loved ones ($5), and Fridays (except the first Friday of the month) from 7pm to 9pm, there's a workshop on how to be a medium yourself. Historic walking tours leave from the bookstore (Thurs–Sat at 2pm; $15), but the coolest ticket is the **Spirit Encounters Night Photography Tour,** Saturdays at 7:30pm ($25) where you bring your digital camera and go hunting for energy orbs. The next morning at 9:30, you can attend Lyceum—that's Sunday School for spiritualists—before Healing Service and church at the Colby Memorial Temple.

Residents shoo away outsiders at 10pm, so the only way to linger at night is to stay at the town's old-fashioned inn: the 1928 **Cassadaga Hotel** (355 Cassadaga Rd., Cassadaga; www.cassadaga hotel.net; ✆ **386/228-2323**; $65–$75 Sun–Thurs, $80–$90 Fri–Sat, including continental breakfast; no guests under age 21), run by the New Age sect of the town and widely said to be haunted. Rooms (the cheapest ones don't have TVs or phone) are guaranteed to keep you anxiously listening for bump-in-the-night creaks. I asked the owner if I could take photos of the time-warp lobby. "Sure, you're welcome to," she said, "but most people get a kind of orb or white light instead." I haven't found those, but my shots *did* come out blurry. I'm just saying.

presents an unparalleled cache of works by genius designer Louis Comfort Tiffany, from stained glass to vases to lamps, and even the lavishly decorated Daffodil Terrace and Reception Hall of his lost Long Island mansion, Laurelton Hall, and the bespoke fountains that ran through it. The Morse displays the best collection of Tiffany glass on the planet, including an entire room reconstructing the master's tour de force chapel, made for the World's

Columbian Exposition in 1893. Once face-to-face with the uncanny luminescence of Tiffany's best work, even those who previously knew nothing about him can't help but come away dazzled. The museum's founders also collected hundreds of other top-quality pieces from the Arts and Crafts movement, including sculpture, but the focus here is definitely Tiffany and his impeccable taste. Set aside an hour or more, though it's easy to combine a visit with a stroll through Winter Park's boutiques, because it sits among them.

445 N. Park Ave., Winter Park. www.morsemuseum.org. © **407/645-5311.** $6 adults, $5 seniors over 59, $1 students, free for kids 11 and under. Tues–Sat 9:30am–4pm; Sun 1–4pm; open until 8pm on Fri Nov–April. Free Fri 4–8pm Nov–Apr.

Cornell Fine Arts Museum ★ MUSEUM   Rollins College, whose graduates include none other than Mister Fred Rogers, has long been a university of choice for parents with social aspirations for their children, and so it makes sense that its star exhibition hall would be bequeathed with such a fine collection in such a country-club setting. It's too small to showcase its impressive holdings, so even remarkable pieces (such as Vanessa Bell's portrait of Mary St. John Hutchinson) tend to rotate in and out of storage to make way for changing exhibitions, which spotlight a wide range of arresting works, from Matisse prints to 18th-century European portraits. Small but top-notch.

100 Holt Ave., Winter Park. www.rollins.edu/cfam. © **407/646-2526.** $5 adults, free for students, sometimes free thanks to grants. Tues–Fri 10am–4pm (Tues to 7pm); Sat–Sun noon–5pm.

South & East of Disney

Diversions get populist as you go south, and their character says more about eccentric Florida than imported wealth; two of Central Florida's most authentic reptile parks are roughly between Disney and the airport.

Bok Tower Gardens ★★★ GARDENS/HISTORIC SITE   About an hour south of Disney, the elegant, 250-acre gardens—designed by Frederick Law Olmsted, Jr., who worked on the National Mall and the Jefferson Memorial—are not often visited, which is too bad, because it's a big reason you're in Orlando at all: It was one of Central Florida's first world-famous attractions. They're genuinely tranquil and among the best surviving remnants of early-20th-century philanthropic privilege. The gardens (don't miss the water lilies, big enough to support a child) and their 205-foot, neo-Gothic Singing Tower, safely behind a fence, were commissioned as a thank-you to the American people by a Dutch-born editor, Edward William Bok, publisher of *The Ladies' Home Journal* and a pioneer in public sex education. Bok was buried at the tower's base in 1930, the year after its completion and dedication by President Calvin Coolidge. The 57-bell carillon on the tower's sixth level sounds concerts at 1 and 3pm daily, and although you can't enter the tower, the 1930s Mediterranean-style Pinewood estate ($6 more; shorter seasonal hours) is open for tours. The sanctuary was enshrined in 1993 as a National Historic Landmark.

1151 Tower Blvd., Lake Wales. www.boktowergardens.org. © **863/676-1408.** $14 adults, $5 kids 5–12. Daily 8am–6pm, last admission at 5pm.

The standard tourist literature won't point them out, but pop history happened here:

o **1418½ Clouser Ave., in the College Park area.** In July 1957, 9 months before the publication of *On the Road,* writer Jack Kerouac moved in with his mother, and he inhabited a 10×10-foot room with just a cot, a desk, and a bare bulb. Here, he wrote *The Dharma Bums,* an exploration of personal spiritual renewal through a connection with nature. By the time he moved out in the spring of 1958, he was a literary superstar. The Kerouac Project (www.kerouac project.org) now owns the home and invites writers to live rent-free for 3-month working tenures.

o **Post Parkside, 425 E. Central Blvd., Orlando.** This apartment building was once the Cherry Plaza Hotel. Here in 1964, LBJ was the first sitting president to spend the night in Orlando. And on November 15, 1965, while the hotel was still segregated, Walt Disney made his only public appearance in Orlando in its Egyptian Room, where he and Roy Disney announced their plans for "the equivalent of Disneyland" in Florida.

o **1910 Hotel Plaza Blvd., Lake Buena Vista.** The very first building to be completed on Walt Disney World property was this low-slung glass-and-steel creation, considered painfully modern in January 1970. It was the Walt Disney World Preview Center, on what was then Preview Boulevard. Here, pretty young hostesses guided some one million visitors past artists' renderings, models, and films promoting Phase One of the resort that was being constructed.

o **Ballroom of the Americas B, Disney's Contemporary Resort, Walt Disney World.** On November 17, 1973, President Richard Nixon gave his "I'm not a crook" speech to a convention of Associated Press editors here, throwing gasoline on the fire of Watergate and bestowing him with his catchphrase of infamy.

o **Disney's Polynesian Resort, Walt Disney World.** While on vacation on December 29, 1974, John Lennon signed the document that officially dissolved the Beatles forever. Disney isn't positive which room he was staying in, but it's thought it was a ground-floor corner room in what's now the Samoa longhouse.

o **839 N. Orlando Ave., Winter Park.** In March 1986, the Canadian rock group The Band was in the middle of a disappointing reunion tour. After playing the Cheek to Cheek Lounge at the Villa Nova Restaurant, which stood here, pianist Richard Manuel, 42, returned to his hotel room at the Quality Inn and when his wife briefly left the room, hanged himself. The lounge site is now a CVS drugstore and the motel site is now a Wawa.

5

MORE ORLANDO ATTRACTIONS

International Drive Area

Dinosaur World ★ TOURIST MUSEUM   An only-in-America roadside attraction, this is not someplace to pass hours—one will do, but it'll be a endearingly weird one. Kids like to wander the jungle-y plot, happening upon more than 100 life-size versions of various dinosaurs, some 80 feet long. A labor of love by a Swedish-born man and his family, it's well kept, even if the foam-and-fiberglass models sometimes look more like aliens than reptiles. It's easy to catch on the drive to Busch Gardens.

5145 Harvey Tew Rd., at I-4's exit 17, Plant City. www.dinosaurworld.com. ✆ **813/717-9865.** $17 adults, $15 seniors over 59, $12 kids 3–12. Daily 9am–5pm.

Fun Spot America—Kissimmee ★ AMUSEMENT PARK   Fun Spot's flagship property is near Universal (p. 162), but this southern outpost delivers the same well-kept carnival-ride playground experience. There's a selection of basic rides that wouldn't be out of place beside a circus (the **Hot Seat** swings riders on the end of a big stick), bumper cars, a wild mouse-style coaster **Rockstar** with spinning cars, and a few outdoor Go-Kart tracks (the 4-story Vortex has 32-degree banking, the world's steepest, owners say). That 300-foot-tall skyline-scarring contraption is **SkyCoaster** ($40 a ride), which harnesses up to three would-be pants-wetters so that they're face-down, hoists them backward, and swings them forward at 80mph like wingless hang gliders. It's the world's tallest. Don't miss **Mine Blower,** a compact wooden coaster that makes a brief inversion. It only takes a minute, but it's an epic minute. It's the meanest jackrabbit of a coaster in Orlando. The downmarket Old Town complex (p. 176) is next door and is usually seen on the same visit.

2850 Florida Plaza Blvd., Kissimmee. www.fun-spot.com. ✆ **407/397-2509.** Pay-per-ride $6–$10 (except SkyCoaster), unlimited rides $50 ($5 cheaper online). Free rides for another day if its rains within 90 min. of pass purchase. Generally daily 10am–midnight.

Gatorland ★★★ ANIMAL PARK   Back in 1949, the reassuringly hokey Gatorland became Orlando's very first mass attraction, featuring Seminole Indians wrestling the animals for tourists; the house-sized jaw at its entrance was a state landmark. Back then, Florida was crawling with alligators—you would see them basking by the sides of the roads—but these days, the reptiles have been mostly evicted by development, so sanctuaries like these are the best places to see the beasts, such as the resident diva, the 15-ft.-long, 1,400-lb. Bonecrusher II, in their ornery glory. Gatorland is rustic in an Eisenhower-era, family-friendly way, and easy to love. There's a kids' splash area (suit them up), and in recent years, a **wading bird rookery,** a **petting zoo,** a miniature **train,** and a five-stage **zip line** over gator ponds ($70; it's a good time and guests who need accessible accommodations can also do it) were added. It also just created the (extraordinarily bumpy) **Stompin' Gator Off-Road Adventure** (another $10), a tongue-in-cheek narrated ride in custom vehicles that jostles you around the overgrown back acres and crawls through the middle of a roiling gator pond. The core of a visit are the showtimes, when good ol' boy gator rangers, buzzed on their own testosterone, wrassle, tickle, and otherwise pester seething gators, and for 10 bucks, they'll bring your children into the fray—safely, with a wad of duct tape around the critters' snouts—for snapshots. It's cornpone fun and they know it; signage is full of gags and every show is staged to contain a fake near disaster to titillate and thrill tourists. Most of the fun is trawling the 110-acre plot on walkways and docks as the critters teem ominously in murky waters underfoot. *Strategy:* It's easy to get the highlights in 2 or 3 hours, but don't miss the **Jumparoo,** when gators leap out of the water for suspended chunks of chicken. Bring a fistful of extra cash if you'd like to partake of extras such as feeding gators, that photo op, and the train (or add a package to your entry for $7 more). And save a few bills for one of its 1960s-era vending machines which press a toy alligator out of injected hot wax right before your eyes—it's just one of many unmissable throwbacks here.

14501 S. Orange Blossom Trail, Orlando. www.gatorland.com. ☎ **407/855-5496** or 407/855-5496. $30 adults, $20 kids 3–12. Free parking. Daily 10am–5pm; summer: Daily 10am–6pm.

Give Kids the World Village ★★★ LANDMARK   Of the annual wishes granted by the Make-A-Wish Foundation and other wish-granting organizations for terminally ill children, *half* of them are to visit Central Florida. Make-A-Wish turns to this nonprofit to fulfill those dreams, which it does for 196 families at a time plus some 7,000 international families a year. No one is refused, and each family spends an all-expenses-paid week in their own villa, eating as much as they want (including ice cream for breakfast) and playing in a compound that looks like a second Magic Kingdom.

It's the most magical place you never knew existed. The 79-acre, gated operation is its own fantasy world with a 6-foot rabbit mascot, Mayor Clayton, who provides nightly tuck-ins. Perkins Restaurants and Boston Market discreetly support the dining pavilion, which looks like a gingerbread house, and there's an Ice Cream Palace where no child is ever refused a scoop. Christmas falls every Thursday, when there's a parade, holiday lighting, and an appearance by Santa, who gives everyone a toy provided by Hasbro. The carousel is the only one in the world that a wheelchair can drive right onto, plus there's horseback riding, a small-gauge train route, miniature golf, and more.

As you can imagine, it depends on volunteers—to the tune of 1,200 slots a week. You don't have to commit to anything longer than a few hours and if you're there for dinner, you'll eat; just apply online about 2 weeks ahead and be at least 12 years old, although exceptions can be made for families who want to volunteer together. Universal Orlando offers a "Volunteer Vacation Package" (☎ **855/275-4955**) of discounted 3-night hotel and park tickets for you and your family in exchange for 4 hours at Give Kids the World. Mornings or evenings are best because the kids want to spend their days at the theme parks, too. The workload is easy. That could mean turning person-size cards at the World's Largest Candy Land game, held Sunday nights on a board measuring 14,400 square feet. You could help at Mayor Clayton's surprise birthday party, thrown every Saturday, or at the "dive-in" movies screened weekly. You can spoon hash browns at breakfast (until about 11am), run the train, or serve dinner with a smile—the opportunities are virtually boundless and the staff matches talents with the right post.

Your mission is not to lavish pity or love, but to simply run the resort where families escape from hard times. You'll be a host, not a nurse. Not every child is sick—their brothers and sisters come, too, and many of them are starved for attention after their siblings' often long illnesses. You'll find that the village is quite a joyous place as families are, perhaps briefly, liberated from the burden of their lives. A favorite part of Give Kids the World is the Castle of Miracles, where the rafters are covered with thousands of golden stars. Each star is affixed by a child on the last night of his or her stay. Years later, moms and dads sometimes return and ask to see, one last time, the star their child left behind.

210 S. Bass Rd., Kissimmee. www.gktw.org. ℭ**407/396-1114.**

Machine Gun America ★ AMUSEMENT PARK You may find it in sick, poor taste that this pricey tourist attraction could exist just a few miles from the place where 49 people were gunned down on June 12, 2016. Yet here it is: A playground to spray bullets from weapons of all types and eras, many of which are not available to purchase anymore. It's true that the staff, many of whom are ex-military, is assiduously responsible, knows its stuff, and puts you on a simulator before ushering you behind reinforced glass for your simulated slaughter. But you may find it disconcerting to see people firing not at a target symbol but at a figure of a human. You may bristle to see men who buy a cheaper gun package forced to wear a tiara and a sash by way of being ridiculed for not being manly enough for bigger weapons. And it's hard to charitably interpret that the most expensive package ($800) concludes with customers being presented with their "Man Card." International tourists are particularly transfixed by this violent American fetish, and many guests report leaving with kickback bruises—these are some powerful massacre weapons being used as playthings for thrills rather than in the context for which they were made.

5825 W. Irlo Bronson Memorial Hwy./U.S. 192, Kissimmee. www.machinegunamerica. com. ℭ**407/278-1800.** Packages $100–$800. Sun–Fri 10am–8pm; Sat 10am–9pm.

Old Town ★ AMUSEMENT PARK Built to look like 4 blocks of a Main Street–style town, expect working-class Americana to the extreme: saloon-style bars, Old Glory T-shirts, and a gantlet of no-name stores peddling impulse buys from ice cream to fried food to gag portraits. Refined it ain't, loud it is, but after years of decline it's enjoying some investment and the Fun Spot, next door, has stocked it with a few carnival staples like a Ferris wheel and a haunted house. The real time to be here is after 4pm on weekends for its vintage car shows: muscle cars on Fridays, pre-1975 cars on Saturdays.

5770 W. Irlo Bronson Memorial Hwy./U.S. 192, Kissimmee. www.myoldtownusa.com. ℭ**407/396-4888.** Daily 10am–11pm.

Reptile World Serpentarium ★★ ANIMAL ATTRACTION Snake milking! What other enticement do you need? Truthfully, it's more of an unassuming biotoxin supply facility—and venom-collection wonderland—than a zoo. Begun in 1972 to collect poison for medical research and to save the lives of bite victims, its location 20 miles east of Disney tempted its operators into joining the ranks of tourist attractions 4 years later, and daily at noon and 3pm, you can thrill (safely behind glass) as George Van Horn grabs deadly serpents, plants their yawning fangs over the venom-collection glass, and gets the creatures spitting mad. There are about 80 snakes on display (including a 13-ft.

PUTTERING around

Orlando is a world capital for miniature golf. Here, you play crazy golf under waterfalls, through caves, over motorized ramps, and even into volcanoes that "erupt" if you hit your shot. The coupon booklets print discounts for all but Disney's courses; also check individual course websites for coupons.

- **Congo River Adventure Golf** (www.congoriver.com): One of the best options, the challenging courses wind through man-made mountains speared with airplane wreckage—and there are live alligators in the pools! Play 18 holes for $13 adults, $11 kids. Two locations: 5901 International Dr., Orlando (© **407/248-9181**); and 4777 W. Hwy. 192, Kissimmee (© **407/396-6900**). Both open daily (Sun–Thurs 10am–11pm; Fri–Sat 10am–midnight). Discounts online.

- **Disney's Winter Summerland** (outside Blizzard Beach, Walt Disney World; © **407/939-7529**; $14 adults, $12 kids; daily 10am–11pm; 50% discount on the second round): Two cute 18-hole courses themed around Christmas. The Winter side, piled with fake snow, has more bells and whistles (love that steaming campfire and that squirting snowman). Combine it with Blizzard Beach without moving your car. Summerland beats the other Disney course, **Disney's Fantasia Gardens** (same rates), themed to the movie *Fantasia*, with its two courses: Fairways and Gardens. The Fairways course has challenging shots; Gardens is sillier. Find it by the Swan and Dolphin hotel duo.

- **Hollywood Drive-In Golf** (CityWalk Orlando, 6000 Universal Blvd., Orlando; www.hollywooddriveingolf.com; © **407/802-4848**; $16 adults, $14 kids 3–9; daily 9am–2am): The coolest 36 holes in town, CityWalk's "haunted & sci-fi double feature" is kitted out, hilarious, and always surprising. Spinning vortices! Corkscrew ball elevators! At night, the lighting effects are impeccable. You can even download its own scorecard app and putt an eyeball.

- **Pirate's Cove** (www.piratescove.net): Navigate wooden ships—a newly installed one is life-size—and falls of blue-ish water. Choose Captain's Adventure or Blackbeard's Challenge. Two locations: 8501 International Dr., Orlando (© **407/352-7378**), and 12545 S.R. 535, behind the Crossroads shopping center, Lake Buena Vista (© **407/827-1242**). $12 adults, $11 kids 4–12; open daily 9am to 11pm; that second location may close soon, so check ahead.

- **Topgolf Orlando** (9295 Universal Blvd., Orlando; www.topgolf.com; © **407/218-7714**; $30/hr until noon, $40/hour noon–5pm, $50/hr 5pm–close; Mon-Thurs 9am–midnight, Fri 9am–2am, Sat 8am–2am, Sun 8am–midnight). More than 100 bays on a multi-level driving range, gussied up with colored targets, food, and a bar. Balls contain microchips for instant scoring. Classier and exponentially more expensive than putt-putt, it's one of dozens of worldwide locations.

cobra and 11 types of rattlers) at any time, plus some baby gators and parrots, but obviously, this one's about venom spewing. Gotta admit—that's cool.

5705 E. Irlo Bronson Memorial Hwy./U.S. 192, St. Cloud. www.reptileworldserpentarium.com. © **407/892-6905**. $11.50 adults, $9.50 kids 6–17, $8.50 kids 3–5. Tues–Sun 10am–5pm.

KENNEDY SPACE CENTER

In the late 1960s, Central Florida was the most exciting place on Earth, thanks to the moon. **Kennedy Space Center ★★★**, which was established on Cape Canaveral in 1958 and ruled the tourist circuit with Disney in the 1970s, was eventually eclipsed by attractions based on fantasy. These days, it's out of this world again.

KSC is on the Space Coast about an hour east of Orlando, and it's worth the trip. Gray Line bus (graylineorlando.com; ✆ **407/522-5911**) does a $109 day tour from Orlando, but for optimal touring, you really should drive yourself and start at opening time. At the main Visitor Complex, many are waylaid by the retired rockets, IMAX films, and simulators, but that's not the best stuff—do them at the end of the day if you have time. Unless there's an **Astronaut Encounter** going on—that's an hour-long presentation in which an actual astronaut talks about their experience and answers questions—proceed instantly to the can't-miss the **Behind the Gates** bus tour, which leaves every 15 minutes until about 2:15pm, and takes most people around 3 hours. Be warned that the last buses don't leave you enough time to browse. Coaches, which are narrated by a live person, zip you around NASA's tightly secured compound. Combined with the nature reserve around it, the area (which guides tell visitors is one-fifth the size of Rhode Island and is home to 16 bald eagle nests) is huge but you'll be making one stop not too far away. You'll see the launch sites used by the shuttle and by the Apollo moon shots, and you'll receive an intelligent explanation of the preparation that went into each shuttle launch. You'll buzz by eagles' nests, alligator-rich canals, pads now leased by private space-mission contractors SpaceX and Boeing, and the confoundingly titanic **Vehicle Assembly Building,** or VAB, where the shuttle—which NASA folk call "the orbiter"—was readied. It's just one story tall, but it's a doozy: The Statue of Liberty could fit through those doors with 200 feet left over. The main bus stop, the **Apollo/Saturn V Center,** is themed "Race to the Moon" and begins with a mandatory 5-minute film and then a full-scale mock-up of the "firing room" in the throes of commanding Apollo 8's launch, in all its window-rattling, fire-lit drama—to skip that 30-minute show and get to the good stuff, pass through. The adjoining hangar contains a Saturn V rocket, which is larger than you can imagine (363 ft. long, or the equivalent of 30 stories)—but the new SLS rockets are even bigger. Don't overlook the chance to reach into a case to touch a small moon rock, which looks like polished metal. The presentation in the **Lunar Theatre,** which recounts the big touchdown, is well produced and even includes a video appearance by the late, reclusive Neil Armstrong. There's a cafeteria here, and look around for retired engineers and astronauts who are often on hand to answer questions.

After that, hasten back via the bus to the Visitor Complex for the grand finale: The $100-million home of the **space shuttle** *Atlantis.* Without giving too much away, the way in which it's revealed to you is probably the most spine-tingling moment in all of Orlando. Hanging 26 feet off the ground at an angle of 43.21° (like the numbers in a launch countdown), it's still covered with space dust, and it now tips a wing at everyone who comes to learn about

The end of the space shuttle program has enabled previously off-limits areas to be opened for visits. Availability shifts, but on a variety of additional "Explore" tours (generally $25 adults, $19 kids 3–11, plus admission), there's always something that's not on the standard KSC bus tour. You can visit the shuttle's launch pad, the Launch Control Center used in the shuttle's last liftoffs, the core of the Mercury and Gemini missions, and find out what NASA's up to now, including the new SLS (Space Launch System) that will carry the new Orion module into space for longer trips than ever before.

it on the many interactive displays that surround it. Don't miss the commemorative **Forever Remembered.** Alongside favorite mementos provided by 11 of the 14 families of their crews, you'll find respectful displays of a section of the hull of the *Challenger,* lost in 1986, and a slab of cockpit windows of the *Columbia* (lost in 2003), still encrusted with grass and mud from where it fell to Earth. You can also try the $60-million **Shuttle Launch Experience,** in which 44-person motion-simulator pods mimic a 5-minute launch with surprising (but not nauseating) clarity, and **Heroes & Legends** that tributes the 100-odd explorers in the Astronaut Hall of Fame. The entire state-of-the-art, hyper-engaging space shuttle section can easily consume 2 hours.

Once you've completed the bus tour and *Atlantis,* it's up to you whether you want to plumb the sillier, kid-geared business at the Visitor's Complex. By this point, much of it will be redundant, and some of it is pure malarkey, but take the time to check the 42-foot-high black granite slab of the **Astronaut Memorial,** commemorating those lost; **Early Space Exploration,** where you'll see the impossibly low-tech Mission Control for the Mercury missions (they used rotary telephones!), plus some authentic spacesuits from the Gemini, Mercury, and Apollo series. Astoundingly, the actual Mercury command building was torn down in 2010.

Daunted? You can prepare by downloading its free app, which helps you prioritize with maps and attraction descriptions. For lunch, though, you're marooned. There is nowhere else to eat within a 15-minute drive, and food is horrendous ($8–$10 a plate)—hamburgers taste like they were surplus from the Apollo program. Come on, NASA. Hospitality isn't rocket science.

Route 405, east of Titusville. www.kennedyspacecenter.com. ✆ **866/737-5235.** Admission $57 adults, $47 kids. Handheld multimedia guide $9. Parking $10. Daily 9am to btw. 5 and 7pm, depending on the season. Bus tours every 15 min., last one usually 3:30pm.

Kennedy Space Center Special Tours

Astronaut Training Experience ★★ ACTIVITY   KSC dubs the program ATX, but you could call it Space Daycamp. You'll test simulators of planet rovers, spacewalks, and Mars explorations and try a mock-up of a launch. Nothing is as intense as what astronauts experience, but it's still plenty rigorous for most terrestrials, and the facilitators can answer nearly any question

Although the Space Shuttle has flown into history, Cape Canaveral still launches unmanned rockets—SpaceX conducts spectacular liftoffs from pad 39A, where the Apollo missions launched. Because launches are often postponed, it would be dangerous to plan a trip to Orlando just to catch one, but then again, if there's one when you're in town, it would a shame to miss it, even if it means waking up at 5am. Kennedy Space Center maintains an updated schedule online at **www.kennedyspacecenter.com/events** and sometimes it arranges VIP seating at a safe distance. The general public is not permitted to flood NASA turf during the actual events, but Titusville, a town at the eastern end of S.R. 50, is a good place to get a clear, free view, because you'll be across the wide Indian River from the pad. Even if you can't leave Orlando for a launch, you can still see the fire of the rockets ascend the eastern sky from any east-facing window in town. Night launches are even more spectacular.

you can launch at them. You can also book one-off time slots on the simulators for $30–$40. For something brainier, the **Mars Base 1** program ($150; 7 hrs. including lunch) casts your kids as true scientists running a research center on the Red Planet, from collecting plants to programming drones.

Astronaut Hall of Fame, 6225 Vectorspace Blvd., Titusville. www.kennedyspacecenter. com/atx. ✆ **866/737-5235.** $175 age 14 and older, $169 age 7–11, includes admission to KSC, minimum age 7. 5 hr.

Lunch with an Astronaut ★★★

One of the coolest benefits of visiting the Space Coast is the chance to meet a real astronaut, many of whom have retired to the same area where they once worked. At times, you'll have seen headliners such as Jim Lovell and Story Musgrave making the rounds. Typically, these guys (and a very few women) love basking in fandom and in reliving old tales of glory—and unlike out-to-pasture sportsmen, these old-timers really did risk their lives the way heroes are supposed to—so these small-group sessions are geared toward questions. Every month or so, KSC also mounts **Fly with an Astronaut** ($200 adults, $174 kids), during which an astronaut actually conducts your tour of the complex where they once worked.

www.kennedyspacecenter.com. ✆ **855/433-4210.** $30 adults, $16 kids 3–11, not including required admission. Daily at noon.

NIGHTLIFE IN ORLANDO

After nightfall, the exertion of visiting theme parks has turned most visitors into exhausted puddles, and the resorts mop up the remaining energy at their on-premises nightspots. Touring shows and concerts pop up at the gorgeous new **Dr. Phillips Center for the Performing Arts** downtown (www.drphillips center.org). But this is Orlando. Diversions get a lot more creative than that. These novel nighttime pursuits are worth the rally:

Enzian ★★★ CINEMA   This thoughtfully programmed cinema would be the envy of any city in America. Before the movie, kick back at the Brazilian walnut patio bar, watching the sunset paint the Spanish moss red. Some of the drinks come from the private cellars of the Enzian's founder, the granddaughter of an Austrian princess. The relaxation continues inside at a large single-screen cinema, where a selection of art films and documentaries is shown, plus Hollywood biggies. Unlike multiplexes, there aren't rows of seats, but lollipop-colored levels of tables with cushy seating. Servers take your order (if you have one—eating's not required) before the movie; after the lights dim, your meal arrives surreptitiously and the air fills with the aroma of popcorn and truffled fries. After the show, a 20-minute drive has you back at Disney World. 1300 S. Orlando Ave., Maitland. www.enzian.org. ✆ **407/629-0054.**

Howl at the Moon Saloon ★★ BAR   The 17-strong chain is good fun: a saloon delivered as a theme park experience, where bands and dueling pianists whip up fun and the patrons, mostly over 35 and white, clap earnestly to the beat. 8815 International Dr., Orlando. www.howlatthemoon.com. ✆ **407/354-5999.** Sat–Thurs 7pm–2am; Fri 6pm–2am; piano show starts 1 hr. after opening; cover $5–$10.

Icebar ★ BAR   The gimmick: a bar made of 50 tons of ice, from the chairs to the frozen goblets. You're loaned gloves and a cape for warmth. The Arctic cocktailerie is only the size of a hotel room, dotted with ice sculptures, and aglow with cobalt lighting; when you've had enough, there's a larger, room-temperature lounge where you can continue the party. 8967 International Dr., Orlando. www.icebarorlando.com. ✆ **407/351-0361.** $32–$42 including 2 drinks, $20 without drinks, discounts on packages online. Sun–Wed 5pm–midnight; Thurs 5pm–1am; Fri–Sat 5pm–2am. Kids 8 and older permitted 5pm–9pm, 21+ thereafter.

Kings Bowl Orlando ★★ BOWLING ALLEY   Like Splitsville at Disney Springs, this new-brew nightspot in the shadow of the Eye turns a bowling alley into an all-evening party, with 22 ten-pin lanes, servers delivering surprisingly decent food (from pizza to ginger soy glazed salmon), serve-yourself beer, shuffleboard, bocce balls, billiards, ping pong, and dancing. Some nights it's for over-21s only, so if it's your family night, check first. 8255 International Dr., Orlando. www.kingsorlando.com. ✆ **407/363-0200.** Bowling $7–$10, shoe rental $5. Mon–Sat noon–2am; Sun noon–midnight.

Minus5° Icebar ★ BAR   Put on your parkas, because it's another frigid icebar. Orlando's second ice bar, part of a chain with locations in Vegas and Manhattan, gradually changes color thanks to a flashy lighting system and ultimately, it depends not on local revelers but on convention crowds. Before 9pm, you can bring kids. Pointe Orlando, 9101 International Dr., Orlando. www.minus5experience.com. ✆ **407/704-6956.** $42 including 2 drinks, $22 without drinks, kids' version from $10, discounts online. Mon–Thurs 5pm–midnight; Fri–Sun 4pm–midnight.

Mango's Tropical Cafe ★★ NIGHTCLUB   Mango's is what it is. This Caribbean-inflected nightclub, a cavernous copy of the Miami original, is colorful, boisterous, calculated with every flourish for maximal are-you-having-fun-yet mass appeal, and surprisingly expensive but still full of frolic for those who'd rather be wearing a Carmen Miranda fruit headdress than a thinking cap. The multi-level party machine—humdrum food, overburdened staff, but effortful non-stop entertainment and flowing booze—is lousy for singles but popular among corporate groups, birthday parties, and bachelorettes who can't get enough of the Michael Jackson impersonators and Celia Cruz tribute singers. For all that, it's a new mainstay among the I-Drive nightspots, and it's appropriate for children. You don't have to eat to enjoy the show and you can stay as long as you like. 8126 International Dr., Orlando. www.mangos. com. © **407/673-4422.** Mains $28–$36, cover $5–$20 depending on capacity, valet parking $15. Daily 6pm–2am.

Orlando Brewing and Taproom ★★★ BREWERY   Because it's buried in an industrial area, you have to know about it to find it. There's no food served, either, but that doesn't mean there isn't some delicious cooking happening. At least 35 organic beers (ales, IPAs, stouts—it changes according to how the brewers experiment) are on tap at 42°F (6°C) and served at a copper-top bar. Mon–Sat at 6pm, the owners grant a free 30-minute tour of the beerworks, where quaffs are made without pasteurization (like the Old World) for sale within 2 weeks. The bar area is simple but convivial, like a rec room your dad might have slapped up in the basement, uncluttered by TVs or pool tables. 1301 Atlanta Ave., Orlando (just east of the Kaley St. exit off I-4, exit 81). www.orlandobrewing.com. © **407/872-1117.** No food; beer only. Mon–Thurs 3–10pm; Fri–Sat 1pm–midnight; Sun 1–9pm.

Parliament House Orlando ★★★ BAR/THEATER/DISCO   There are few American institutions quite like it. In 1975, a dying Johnson-era, 130-room motel was revitalized as an amusement megacenter for gay folks. Its rambling size—10 acres, including a beach on a small lake out back—justifies it as a hangout not only for gay guys, but also for the friends who love them, women who want to dance with them without being accosted, and open-minded straight guys. Think of it as a fabulous entertainment mini-mall: There's the Footlight Theater for cabaret and drag hosted by longtime resident mistress Darcel Stevens; a diner; a pool; a disco, which gears up around 9pm; a video bar; and a scuzzy cubby called Western Bar, for leather-and-jeans-wearing guys who play pool. The scene is especially remarkable when you consider that its operators are a straight couple from Canada. It's considered a nucleus of Florida gay life and increasingly one of the most vital and longest-lived landmarks of gay history—no matter how endearingly run-down it is. 410 N. Orange Blossom Trail, Orlando. www.parliamenthouse.com. © **407/425-7571.** Cover and hours vary.

Player 1 Orlando ★ BAR   Right outside the Disney Springs–area of WDW is this spot where you can play video games all night long. Reasonable drink prices, a dignified beer selection (craft beer, even meads), and a huge inventory of totally free games for superfans and nostalgics alike (consoles to cabinet) make it a fun secret of the Orlando leisure scene—theme-park workers hang out here. All ages are permitted before 5pm, but kids under 18 must always have an adult with them. 8562 Palm Parkway, Lake Buena Vista. www.player1 orlando.com. © **407/504-7521.** Cover $5, higher for those under 22 depending on the night. Daily 4pm–2am.

SAK Comedy Lab ★★ COMEDY CLUB   Too often, people describe improv comedy clubs as like "Whose Line Is it Anyway?"—only here, it's true, because this is where Wayne Brady got his start, as well as his *Let's Make a Deal* announcer Jonathan Mangum, *SNL*'s Paula Pell, and *MADtv*'s Paul Vogt. There's improv and sketch comedy every day but Sunday, and earlier shows are more kid-friendly. The big improv battle is Saturday night's "Duel of Fools." 29 S. Orange Ave, Orlando. www.sakcomedylab.com. © **407/648-0001.** Cover $5–$18. Shows Mon–Sat btw. 7:30pm and 9:30pm.

OUTDOOR ORLANDO

Picture an old-fashioned steamship, not unlike the *African Queen,* puttering along a narrow river of clear spring-fed water beneath a cool canopy of Spanish moss. Alongside, a few docile manatees nibble contentedly on river grass.

It's hard to believe, but that's what Central Florida really is. Well, was. When you tire of artificial rocks that conceal loudspeakers, remember that Orlando was adored first for natural beauty. Developers cleared everything but the lakes, ripping out natural vegetation. (And people wonder why they feel so hot.)

Central Florida's building explosion only kicked in a generation ago, and some people were smart enough to rope off land from destruction. Look around, and you'll find examples of the land's primacy—natural springs that Ponce de Leon once toured, swamps where alligators lurk beneath bladderwort and spatterdock, and marshy preserves thronged with migrating birds. And should all of that scenery bore, you can speed by it on bracing boat tours or observe it from above in a balloon or hang glider.

Blue Spring State Park ★★ NATURE RESERVE   You stand a fair chance of seeing manatees here, especially in the morning on a cold day. The creatures venture up the St. Johns River from the Atlantic Ocean to seek out the warmth of the springs of this 2,600-acre park, which maintain a constant 72°F (22°C) temperature even in winter. From mid-November through March 15, all boating, swimming, and snorkeling are suspended while the big guys (more than 75 in some years) are in residence. An exception is made daily at 10am and 1pm, when a **2-hour guided boat tour** (www.sjrivercruises.com; © **407/330-1612;** $25 adults, $23 seniors, $18 kids 3–12) is given, and the park also coughs up a few nature trails and canoe rental. Find it 60 miles north of Disney from exit 114 off I-4; go south on U.S. Rte. 17/92 to Orange City, and then make a right onto West French Avenue (there are signs).

2100 W. French Ave., Orange City. www.floridastateparks.org/bluespring. © **386/775-3663.** $6 per car. Daily 8am–sundown; arrive early to avoid full parking lot.

De Leon Springs State Park ★★★ NATURE RESERVE   Florida has some 300 springs, and 27 of them discharge more than 60 million gallons of pure water a day. In fact, Florida has more springs than any other American state, so it's easy to conclude that natural springs are more authentically Floridian than pretty much anything else you might see in Orlando, and there's no more enjoyable place to experience them than here. The Spanish,

Seminoles, and pre-presidential Zachary Taylor all fought over this spot of land, and Audubon saw his first limpkin here. (Remember *your* first time?) It's impossible to overstate the importance of the St. Johns River on the development of Florida—before rail, everybody used it—and, like the Nile, it's one of the few world rivers to flow north, not south. On this segment of the river, there are 18,000 acres of lakes and marshes to canoe (boats can be rented by the hour), a concrete-lined area to swim in, and 6 miles of trails to forge as you try to spot black bears, white-tail deer, swamp rabbits, and, of course, gators. It gets cooler: At its general store–style **Old Spanish Sugar Mill** (www.oldspanishsugarmill.com; ℂ **386/985-5644;** Mon–Fri 9am–3:45pm, Sat–Sun and holidays 8am–3:45pm), you make your own all-you-can-eat pancakes on griddles built into every table, but they can cook you other things, too). Niftier still, the designated swimming area beside the Griddle House is in a spring-fed boil—30 feet deep in spots—that remains at a constant 72°F (22°C), year-round. To reach it, take I-4 north, exit for Deland, and 6 miles north of Deland on U.S. 17 turn left onto Ponce DeLeon Boulevard for 1 mile. Get there early, because when the weather sizzles, it gets busy.

601 Ponce de Leon Blvd., Deland. www.floridastateparks.org/deleonsprings. ℂ **386/985-4212.** $6 per carload. Daily 8am–sundown.

Harry P. Leu Gardens ★ GARDENS Botanical gardens seem dull on paper, yet once you find yourself within one, inhaling perfume and being warmed by the sun, you're in no hurry to leave. So it is with this 50-acre lakeside escape just north of downtown that gives visitors an inkling of why so many Gilded Age Americans wanted to flee to Florida, where the fresh air and gently rustling trees were a tonic to the maladies inflicted by the industrial North. Here you'll find Florida's largest formal rose garden (peaking in Apr); a patch planted with nectar-rich blooms favored by migrating butterflies; a large collection of camellias that bloom in late fall; and the lush Tropical Stream garden, crawling with native lizards and opening onto a dock where freshwater turtles swim and ducks bob.

1920 N. Forest Ave. www.leugardens.org. ℂ **407/246-2620.** $10 adults, $3 kids, free the first Mon of the month. Daily 9am–5pm.

Tibet–Butler Preserve ★ NATURE RESERVE Located more or less between Disney and SeaWorld (it's incredible it hasn't been turned into a golf course yet), it's the closest to the parks: about 5 miles north of the Lake Buena Vista hotel area. The 438-acre spread is combed by 4 miles of well-maintained boardwalks and trails (which close when flooded) that will give you respite among the cypress swamps and palmetto groves that once dominated this area.

8777 C.R. 535, Windermere. ℂ **407/254-1940.** Free. Sat–Sun 8am–6pm.

Wekiwa Springs State Park ★★★ NATURE RESERVE The closest major spring to Orlando (just 20 min. north, off I-4's exit 94) is, despite encroachment by suburbs and malls, one of the prettiest preserves in the area. When you think of Florida, you don't normally picture rambling rivers, but the

42-mile Wekiva (yes, spelled differently than the park's name and pronounced "Wek-*eye*-va") is federally designated as "Wild and Scenic," meaning it hasn't been dammed or otherwise despoiled by development, despite the fact it's just northwest of Orlando's sprawl near Apopka. The springhead, fed by two sources, flows briskly over rock and sand, and some people come to fish, but most agree that its canoeing is among the most spectacular in the state. **Wekiwa Springs State Park Nature Adventures** (www.canoewekiva.com; ✆ **407/884-4311**) rents canoes and kayaks ($25 for 2 hr.). Developers would love to sink their bulldozers' claws into this paradise; in fact, so much water is being siphoned from it that its flow is expected to diminish by 10% by 2025. 1800 Wekiwa Circle, Apopka. www.floridastateparks.org/wekiwasprings. ✆ **407/884-2009**. $6 per car. Daily 8am–sundown; arrive early to avoid full parking lot.

Boat Tours

The real Florida Everglades don't begin until south of Lake Okeechobee, which is why you'll hear Central Florida referred to as the *headwaters* of the Florida Everglades. The waterlogged land is still home to a wide diversity of life forms.

BK Adventure ★ TOUR   An hour's drive from Orlando, you'll find a mesmerizing natural phenomenon: dinoflagellate plankton that literally light up salty water in a glowing blue hue. In peak season, June to October, easy kayak tours bring visitors into the mystical spectacle (best with no moon) 3–4 times nightly. www.bkadventure.com. ✆ **407/519-8711**. Guided tours $55 adults, equipment provided. 90 min. Reservations required.

Central Florida Nature Adventures ★ TOUR   Kayak tours take a little more elbow grease than your typical Orlando diversion, but the company has a menu of seven tours (most 2–3 hours) of varying difficulty, and they're staged at prime waterways all around the area. Those include the Wekiva River, Rock Spring (45 min. from Disney), and Blue Spring (p. 183), where between April and November you can kayak in crystal clear waters right above fish and turtles; in winter, you share the spring with manatees. www.kayakcentralflorida.com. ✆ **352/589-7899**. Guided tours $64–$95 adults, equipment provided. Reservations required.

Boggy Creek Airboat Rides ★ TOUR   Airboats use powerful, backward-facing propellers to skip through shallow bogs, and they're a common form of eco-entertainment in Florida, particularly farther south in the Everglades. Though much wildlife is spooked by the din (you'll get ear mufflers), water snakes and alligators appear too thick-headed to care, so you should see a few on one of the continuously running 30-minute tours—boat skippers will cut the engine and float near the critters. The boats don't operate in the rain. The wildlife spotting is better in South Florida, but this still is a long-running crowd-pleaser. Coupons are commonly distributed. One-hour night tours ($54 adults, $50 kids 3–12) are also available, but require reservations; check the website for times. 2001 E. Southport Rd., Kissimmee. www.bcairboats.com. ✆ **407/344-9550**. 30-min. tours $28 adults, $24 kids 3–12. Daily 9am–5:30pm.

Scenic Boat Tour ★★★ TOUR This Winter Park institution has been showing visitors glorious lakeside mansions since 1938, when they were in their heyday of attracting wealthy snowbirds from the North. Three of Winter Park's seven smooth cypress-lined lakes, which are connected by thrillingly narrow, hand-dug canals, are explored in a 1-hour, 12-mile tour narrated by neighborhood old timers. The lakes are flat and relaxing, with plenty of bird life, and your guide will pay particular attention to the works of James Gamble Rogers II, a virtuosic architect responsible for many of the area's finest homes. Among the high points is a glimpse of the modest condominium where Mamie Eisenhower spent her waning years and 250-year-old live oaks. You'll find this charmer 3 blocks east of the shops on Park Avenue. Bring sunscreen: the pontoons are exposed.

312 E. Morse Blvd., Winter Park. www.scenicboattours.com. ⓒ **407/644-4056.** $14 adults, $7 kids 2–11. No credit cards. Hourly departures 10am–4pm daily.

> ### Christmas Greetings
>
> **Christmas, Florida,** a blip on S.R. 50 between Orlando and Titusville, usually isn't much to write home about: farm supplies, roadkill. Unless, of course, it's the holiday season, when people come from far and wide to give their cards a Christmas postmark from the local post office. You'll find the P.O. at 23580 E. Colonial Dr./S.R. 50 (ⓒ **407/568-2941;** Mon–Fri 9am–5pm, Sat 9:30am–noon).

Golf

Orlando is a golf town. This is truth despite the great damage courses do to an ecosystem as precarious as Central Florida's. Some of the brightest names in the sport, including Tiger Woods, Annika Sorenstam, Ernie Els, and Nick Faldo, have called Orlando home, as does cable's Golf Channel (which isn't open to visitors). In January, the Convention Center is home to the annual PGA Merchandise Show (www.pgashow.com).

Every self-respecting resort has a course or three, as do luxe condo developments. There are some 170 courses around town, and the competition has caused rates to plummet in recent years, although some still command around $150. The booking websites **TeeOff.com** and **GolfNow.com** both sell discounted tee times, driving rates down further. Some courses give priority to players who stay in their hotels through advantageous tee times, early reservations privileges, or cheaper fees. Prices can be steeper in high season (Jan–Apr), and they may be lowest in the fall and early winter. They usually sink to about half the day's rate for "twilight" tee times, which start around midafternoon. Club rentals cost $40 to $60. Reservations are all but required and most courses have a dress code and even an age minimum, so always ask.

DESTINATION COURSES

From pedigrees by well-known designers to clubhouses that operate more like spas, these fashionable courses are the theme parks of the fairway set. Tee time at these pricey greens fill quickly because the courses have national reputations. Count on paying about $10 per hole. Most of the big courses will now arrange to ship your personal clubs to the course in time for your visit, if you like.

Arnold Palmer's Bay Hill Club & Lodge ★★★ Designer: Arnold Palmer, who owned it and built the golf school. This guests-only resort course rambles for 270 acres over lakelands and regularly receives the most accolades from experts. Palmer renovated the main course just before his 2016 death.

9000 Bay Hill Blvd., Orlando. www.bayhill.com. ⓒ **888/422-9445.** 27 holes.

ChampionsGate Golf Resort ★★ Designer: Greg Norman. Headquarters of the 37-unit **David Leadbetter Golf Academy** (ⓒ **407/787-3330;** www.davidleadbetter.com), this resort and handsome high-rise hotel is 10 minutes south of Disney.

1400 Masters Blvd., ChampionsGate. www.championsgategolf.com. ⓒ **407/787-4653.** 36 holes.

Mystic Dunes Golf Club ★★ Designer: Gary Koch. Located 2 miles south of Disney, it has steadily won *Golf Digest* praise for its distinct character. Elevation changes up to 80 feet over the course of play and the grounds retain their mature oaks and wetlands.

7600 Mystic Dunes Lane, Celebration. www.mysticdunesgolf.com. ⓒ **407/787-5678.** 18 holes.

Reunion Resort & Club ★★ Designers: Jack Nicklaus, Arnold Palmer, Tom Watson—three world-class designers' courses, all a 10-minute drive south of Disney. There's also on-site golf instruction with a staff of 11 teachers.

7593 Gathering Dr., Kissimmee. www.reunionresort.com/golf. ⓒ **866/380-8563.** 54 holes.

The Ritz-Carlton Golf Club Orlando, Grande Lakes ★★ Designer: Greg Norman. Golf instruction at this very well-maintained facility is overseen by former PGA Tour player Larry Rinker. Family packages are available.

4040 Central Florida Pkwy., Orlando. www.grandelakes.com. ⓒ **407/393-4900.** 18 holes.

Shingle Creek Golf Club ★ Designer: Thad Layton, Arnold Palmer Design Company. A proud, Orlando-centered resort, Shingle Creek is home to a school overseen by Brad Brewer (www.bradbrewer.com).

9939 Universal Blvd., Orlando. www.shinglecreekgolf.com. ⓒ **866/996-9933** or 407/996-9933. 18 holes.

Tranquilo Golf Club at Four Seasons Resort Orlando ★★★ Disney's former Osprey Ridge course, an Audubon sanctuary 2 miles east of the Magic Kingdom, was redesigned by its creator Tom Fazio in late 2014. Each hole has four sets of tees to appeal to all skill levels, and there's a fancy new 16-acre practice facility for drives, chipping, and putting training.

3451 Golf View Dr., Lake Buena Vista. www.tranquilogolf.com. ⓒ **407/313-6880.** 18 holes.

Villas of Grand Cypress ★ Designer: Jack Nicklaus. This club, right next to Disney in Lake Buena Vista, was noted one of Orlando's best golf resorts by the readers of *Condé Nast Traveler,* who know about such things. Its New Course is Nicklaus' salute to the Old Course of St. Andrews, Scotland.

One North Jacaranda, Orlando. www.grandcypress.com/golf. ⓒ **407/239-1909.** 45 holes.

Walt Disney World Golf Courses ★ Disney has been closing courses or parceling them to other resorts, but there are currently four left, including the Lake Buena Vista (once a PGA tour host), the recently refurbished Palm, and the Magnolia (the one with the sand bunker shaped like Mickey). Oak Trail (9 holes) is the better choice for family outings. They're all run by Arnold Palmer's company. Greens fees include golf cart, when available, and kids under 18 get half-off full tee time rates at the 18-hole courses. All courses opened with the resort in 1971, when golf was more important to the resort, and if truth be told, their maintenance is spotty. At Oak Trail, there's a 9-hole course dedicated to **FootGolf,** which is scored just like golf except you kick soccer balls instead of swinging clubs ($22, about 2 hours).

Walt Disney World. www.golfwdw.com. ℭ **407/938-4653.** 63 holes.

MORE AFFORDABLE COURSES

Unlike the aforementioned courses, these don't have big marketing budgets and they don't always come attached to celebrity names, but they nevertheless are high-quality courses you can enjoy at sensible prices.

Celebration Golf Course ★★ In the Disney-built town next door to the Disney-built world, English master designer Robert Trent Jones, Sr., and his son pocked their well-groomed course with water hazards on 17 of its 18 holes.

701 Golf Park Dr., Celebration. www.celebrationgolf.com. ℭ **407/566-4653.** 18 holes.

Falcon's Fire Golf Club ★ Designer: Rees Jones. Decently maintained and fairly priced (in the mid-$40s for prime tee times), this public course a few minutes east of Disney can be crowded, but holes are straightforward and a beverage cart makes the rounds.

3200 Seralago Blvd., Kissimmee. www.falconsfire.com. ℭ **407/239-5445.** 18 holes.

Hawk's Landing Golf Club ★ Because it's part of the Orlando World Center Marriott resort on World Center Drive near Disney, it crawls with convention-goers who keep prices high. Water is in play on 15 of the 18 holes, and the par-71 course carries a slope rating of 131.

8701 World Center Dr., Orlando. www.golfhawkslanding.com. ℭ **800/567-2623.** 18 holes.

Highlands Reserve Golf Club ★★ This highly praised public course, with a fair mix of challenges and cakewalks, is a strong value, charging a top rate of $39, and its twilight rates kick in as early as noon. It's about 10 minutes southwest of Disney.

500 Highlands Reserve Blvd., Davenport. www.highlandsreserve-golf.com. ℭ **863/420-1724.** 18 holes.

MetroWest Golf Club ★★ This Marriott Golf–managed course is the work of Robert Trent Jones, Sr., famous for tight greens protected on both sides by sand traps, trees, or water. It's one of the city's most popular courses, found less than 3 miles north of Universal Orlando.

2100 S. Hiawassee Rd., Orlando. www.metrowestgolf.com. ℭ **407/299-1099.** 18 holes.

Orange County National Golf Center and Lodge ★ At this wide-open complex (922 acres, unspoiled by houses—atypical around here), holes have five sets of tees, allowing you to choose a game that ranges between 7,300 yards and a little over 5,000. Golf Channel's Matt Ginella put it on top of his list of must-do Orlando courses. It's just north of Walt Disney World and it's cheapest early in the week.

16301 Phil Ritson Way, Winter Garden. www.ocngolf.com. ✆ **407/656-2626.** 45 holes.

Royal St. Cloud Golf Links ★★ Aiming to recall Scotland's great links—there's even a stone bridge that looks like it was built during the days of William Wallace, not in 2001—this affordable club, 25 miles east of Disney, has fairways that are noted for being wide, well groomed, and firm, and planners promise you'll use "every club in the bag."

5310 Michigan Ave., St. Cloud. www.royalstcloudgolflinks.com. ✆ **877/891-7010** or 407/891-7010. 27 holes.

Timacuan Golf and Country Club ★★ There are five sets of tees, adapting this exceptionally well-groomed course from 7,000 to 5,000 yards, and unusually, designers were careful to leave its handsome Old Florida features (undulating fairways, Spanish moss, wetlands) mostly intact. Only 3 holes are riddled with water, which might make it easier for kids. The greens were renovated in 2013. Lake Mary is 10 miles north of downtown.

550 Timacuan Blvd., Lake Mary. www.golftimacuan.com. ✆ **407/321-0010.** 18 holes.

Up in the Air

Florida is well suited to hot-air ballooning for many of the same reasons that it's ideal for golf: flat, even topography and often placid morning weather. A trip involves a very early start—6am is common. You'll be finished with your hour-long ride by the time the theme parks get cranking. If balloons don't float your boat, there are other ways to see Orlando from up high as well.

Magic Sunrise Ballooning ★★ More intimate than its supersized competition, with just two to four people in the basket with the pilot, this company, flying since 1987, greets landings with a champagne toast.

603 N. Garfield Ave., Deland. www.magicsunriseballooning.com. ✆ **866/606-7433.** $215 per person for 2–4 people, $135 kids under 90 lb., no kids 5 or under.

Orlando Balloon Rides ★★ In business since 1983, its flagship balloon, launched as the world's largest in 2011, is 11 stories tall and its basket fits an incredible 24 people. Weekday mornings are cheapest.

2900 Parkway Blvd., Kissimmee. www.orlandoballoonrides.com. ✆ **407/894-5040.** $195–$225 adults, $99–$109 kids 4–12, frequent discounts online.

Orlando Tree Trek Adventure Park ★★★ In some woods 3 miles south of Disney, nine elevated obstacle courses, from 10 to 40 feet off the ground and ranging from simple to tricky, challenge families to conquer their fear of heights while they puzzle how to navigate suspended obstacles. Sometimes you're stepping on boards, sometimes wires, sometimes nets, but you're always hooked into a safety line, and guides are always cheering you on. Budget two to three hours.

7625 Sinclair Rd., Kissimmee. www.orlandotreetrek.com. ℂ **407/390-9999.** $55 adults, $33–$40 kids 7–11, based on height. Daily 8am–dusk.

Wallaby Ranch ★★   In flat Central Florida, where there are no mountains that don't contain roller coasters, hang gliders can't soar from cliffs. Instead, they're launched by ultralight "aerotugs," to an altitude of 2,000 feet—with a GoPro capturing every squeal (another $40).

1805 Deen Still Rd., Davenport. www.wallaby.com. ℂ **863/424-0070.** Tandem flights $175.

SHOPPING

Orlando is a hotbed for outlet activity, partly because international visitors, with their often-stronger currencies, are prone to buying frenzies. Like most modern outlet malls, not all of the items you find for sale here will have come from higher-priced "regular" stores; much of the stock has been specially manufactured for the outlet market (although *Consumer Reports* doesn't think the quality is substantially different from retail). You'll usually find prices between 30% and 50% off sales at retail stores, and after the holiday rush, discounts go deeper.

Florida Mall ★★★ MALL   Judging by this mercenary sprawl a few miles southeast of Universal, the decline of the American shopping mall is a dirty lie. This rainy-day citadel is massive: 270 stores, everything recently renovated, with plenty of the usual suspects but also some unusual touristy perks like an M&Ms World shop, American Girl, and the Crayola Experience (p. 162). International tourists flock here to blow fortunes. 8001 S. Orange Blossom Trail, Orlando. www.simon.com/mall/the-florida-mall. ℂ **407/851-7234.** Mon–Fri 10am–9pm; Sat 10am–10pm; Sun noon–8pm.

The Mall at Millenia ★ MALL   Classier and more expensive than Florida Mall, the 150-unit center's anchor stores include Bloomingdale's and Neiman Marcus, but Disney Springs has pilfered a bit of its retail thunder. It's a few minutes up I-4 from Universal. 4200 Conroy Rd., Orlando. www.mallat millenia.com. ℂ **407/363-3555.** Mon–Sat 10am–9pm; Sun 11am–7pm.

Outlet Malls

Orlando International Premium Outlets ★ OUTLET MALL   At this stupendous 180-store (give or take) open-air village, you're very unlikely to come away empty-handed or with a full wallet. Proprietors charge $10 for the best parking spaces, leaving the rest of the lot so jammed that it's a misery to come. Still, nearly every conceivable brand has a presence here; the chief threats include Neiman Marcus Last Call—a clearance center that sells genuine department store castoffs from its namesake stores, Bergdorf Goodman, and the Horchow catalog—Saks Fifth Avenue Off Fifth, Victoria's Secret, and Adidas. Hours are Monday to Saturday 10am to 11pm, Sunday 10am to 9pm. Weekdays are quietest. The website lists sales by store. 4951 International Dr., Orlando. www.premiumoutlets.com. ℂ **407/352-9600.**

Orlando Vineland Premium Outlets ★ OUTLET MALL   The owners of this open-air mall tout it as the most productive outlet center in America, with sales exceeding $1,000 per square foot among 160 stores. And it has made them greedy: They charge $10 for the best parking spaces and force families to fight it out for the scraps. Among the stores: Banana Republic Factory Store, Tory Burch, and Burberry. One popular shop, because it's so close to the Mouse House, is Disney's Character Warehouse, for cast-off official theme park souvenirs. Open Monday to Saturday 10am to 11pm and Sunday 10am to 9pm. It's 10 minutes from Disney Springs; the turnoff is just south of I-4's exit 68 on S.R. 535/Apopka Vineland, by Bahama Breeze. The I-Ride Trolley (p. 271) touches down here ostensibly every 20 minutes, or you can book the mall's three-times-daily free shuttle (© **407/238-0703**) at least an hour ahead at maingatetaxi.com. 8200 Vineland Ave., Orlando. www.premium outlets.com. © **407/238-7787.**

Lake Buena Vista Factory Stores ★ OUTLET MALL   The third-best outlet shopping in town is a strip mall–style collection of about 50 stores. The offerings here, about 2 miles south of the Disney Springs gate, are not as shimmering as those at its two rival outlet malls, but they're decent for kids. There are enough names you know (including Tommy Hilfiger, Carter's for Kids, Old Navy Outlet, OshKosh B'Gosh, and Aéropostale) to warrant a quick trip. Theme Park Outlet has some bargains (half-price mugs, shirts, toys, and some souvenirs dated from a few years ago), and there's a Travelex office for currency exchange. The mall provides a free daily shuttle to and from major hotels around Disney and I-Drive. 15657 S. Apopka Vineland Rd. (S.R. 535), Orlando. www.lbvfs.com. © **407/238-9301.**

Disney Springs

Disney Springs ★★ (www.disneysprings.com), until recently called Downtown Disney, is Walt Disney World's outdoor center for shopping and restaurants—alas, just as expensive as elsewhere in the World. Its unwieldy layout ambles along the southern shore of Village Lake a few miles east of Epcot, connected to no theme park. A recent top-to-bottom renovation and expansion made it a new star, adding dozens of brand-name stores. The food is great but from a shopping perspective, despite the improvements, it's still just a snazzy and overpriced mall. When lined up beside the four theme parks, I can't say it must be integral to your Disney experience, but it without question has the best casual food choices in Disney World.

The district has four zones; because of the size, it's helpful to know which one you're heading for because the walk between them can be up to 15 minutes. The easternmost area is called the Marketplace, and it's for Disney-themed shops of every type. The middle two zones are Town Center (the outdoor shopping mall, and where the bus stops are) and The Landing (waterfront dining and bars). The westernmost zone is the West Side, which leans toward nightlife and entertainment, with **Splitsville Luxury Lanes** bowling, and a 24-screen **AMC cinema,** as if you came to Disney World to go to the movies.

Parking is free in two state-of-the-lot structures (a third opens in 2019) with cool overhead lights indicating at a distance if the space below them is free. The "Orange" structure is most convenient to evening entertainment of the West Side, and "Lime" is closer to the restaurants of The Landing and the shopping of the Town Center and the Marketplace.

When it comes to shopping, the major shops at **Town Center** are not likely to tickle you much if you've ever been to a mall: Zara, UNIQLO, Lilly Pulitzer, Tommy Bahama, Under Armour, and UGG are among the additions—nice shops, but nothing you couldn't find elsewhere. But shops at the **Marketplace** (☎ **407/939-3463**) are the best place for Pure Mouse. Stores are themed for maximum souvenir sales, including one for toys and games **(Once Upon a Toy),** one for Christmas and holiday decorations **(Disney's Days of Christmas),** one for high-end collectibles **(The Art of Disney),** one for kitchen tools **(Mickey's Pantry),** one for urban wear **(Tren-D),** one for stationery and albums **(Disney's Wonderful World of Memories),** and **Disney's Pin Traders,** a hub for collectors of the park's badges where you can also buy MagicBands. The most interesting is the **Marketplace Co-Op,** which contains some great mini-stores such as funky contemporary art versions of Disney characters at **WonderGround, D-Tech on Demand** for you-design-it smartphone cases and MagicBands (they cost twice as much as standard MagicBands, but for fans, the wide selection of more obscure characters is worth it), **Centerpiece** for Disney-retro homewares, **Cherry Tree Lane** for handbags, **Twenty-Eight & Main** for casual clothes with arcane Disney references, and **TAG** for travel gear. For the Disney fan, there's a lot to discover.

The Marketplace's tent-pole is the big kahuna of Disney merch: **World of Disney,** the largest souvenir department store in the resort. It's a rambling cathedral-roofed barn stocked from rug to rafter with every conceivable Disney-branded item. You'll find stuff here you won't find at other Disney stores here or at home, especially if it's a "park exclusive." World of Disney may not carry items that might fit better at another store at the Marketplace (tree ornaments, for example, would be at Days of Christmas), so hunt around the area.

Very few Marketplace stores sell non-Disney plunder. Kids can't be separated from **The LEGO Store** (still here despite the fact the toymaker now brands a competing park, p. 158), where children can play with kits for free, or **Build-A-Dino** which does for reptiles what Build-A-Bear does for teddies. **Basin** sells bath products for those teeny hotel room tubs.

Bibbidi Bobbidi Boutique ★★★ SALON   Little girls bask in the star treatment as they are lavished with glittery, pink makeovers as princesses from $60 (Crown Package with hair and a sash) to several hundred (the Castle Package adds gown, wand), overseen by a kindly "Fairy Godmother-in-Training" who sprinkles fairy dust. *Warning:* The dresses are hot and scratchy, so bring a change of clothes if the sun is strong. Boys are steered to the Knight Package ($16), where similar gender beauty roles are ascribed. There's also a salon in the Magic Kingdom in the Castle, but you'll need a park ticket for that and slots are scarcer. Try to get a morning appointment so your child has time to prance around the parks in all her fabulousness. Open daily 8:45am to

Disney Springs

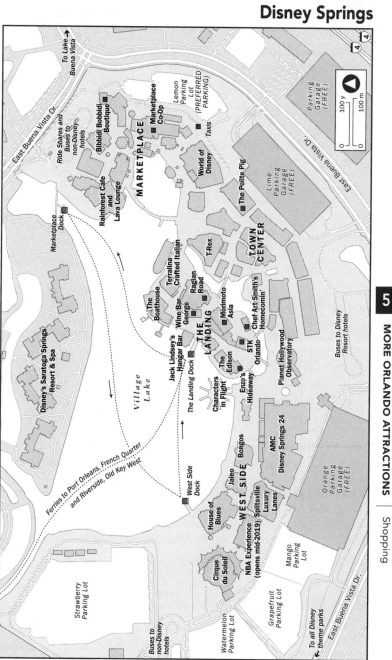

Map labels:

To Lake Buena Vista

East Buena Vista Dr.

Ride Shares and Buses to non-Disney hotels

Bibbidi Bobbidi Boutique

Marketplace Co-Op

Lemon Parking Lot (PREFERRED PARKING)

MARKETPLACE

Taxis

Rainforest Cafe and Lava Lounge

World of Disney

The Polite Pig

Parking Garage (FREE)

Lime Parking Garage (FREE)

East Buena Vista Dr.

Marketplace Dock

T-Rex

TOWN CENTER

The Boathouse

Terralina Crafted Italian

Raglan Road

Morimoto Asia

Wine Bar George

Chef Art Smith's Homecomin'

THE LANDING

Jack Lindsey's Hangar Bar

The Landing Dock

The Edison

STK Orlando

Enzo's Hideaway

Planet Hollywood Observatory

Buses to Disney Resort hotels

Characters in Flight

Disney's Saratoga Springs Resort & Spa

Village Lake

West Side Dock

Ferries to Port Orleans, French Quarter and Riverside, Old Key West

Bongos

Jaleo

AMC Disney Springs 24

WEST SIDE

House of Blues

Splitsville Luxury Lanes

Orange Parking Garage (FREE)

NBA Experience (opens mid-2019)

Cirque du Soleil

Mango Parking Lot

Buses to non-Disney hotels

Strawberry Parking Lot

Grapefruit Parking Lot

Watermelon Parking Lot

To all Disney theme parks

East Buena Vista Dr.

100 y
100 m

5

MORE ORLANDO ATTRACTIONS | Shopping

One of the most special souvenir traditions on Disney turf is the collection of little enamel and cloisonné pins featuring every known character, ride, movie, and promotional event. Sometimes it seems it's easier to get your hands on a pin than it is to find a bottle of water—there's even a pavilion that sells nothing but pins at Disney Springs' Marketplace. They are usually worn on lanyards, and when cast members clock in for their shifts, they replenish their pin supply at a special window in the backstage area—a dozen to a lanyard at all times. The rule is that if a cast member is wearing almost any pin you want (barring ones commemorating employment milestones), you're allowed to ask them to trade it for one of your own and they're not allowed to refuse if the pin is legit. Universal sells a fair supply, too, but the craze is fiercest at Disney, where the backings are shaped, of course, like a mouse head.

7:30pm. Once Upon a Toy, Marketplace. www.disneyworld.com. ✆ **407/939-7895.** Ages 3–12, enforced. $60–$200. Reservations required.

Other Interesting Stores

If you feel moved to learn more about Florida history, the bookstore at the **Regional History Center ★★★** (✆ **407/836-8594;** p. 169) is a good start. You'll find a well-stocked **Barnes & Noble ★★★** (Venezia Plaza, 7900 W. Sand Lake Rd., Orlando; ✆ **407/345-0900;** daily 9am–10pm) among the terrific restaurants of Sand Lake Road west of I-4 and by the Florida Mall (8358 S. Orange Blossom Trail, Orlando; ✆ **407/856-7200;** Mon–Sat 10am–10pm, Sun 10am–9pm).

Orange World ★★ SHOP   Agra has the Taj Mahal. Sydney has its opera house. Orlando has a 60-foot-tall orange. Back when most of this land was citrus groves, Hwy. 192 was the main drag into Disney, and this fruity folly was erected to induce dads to pull the station wagon over and buy a bag of citrus in a red mesh bag. Fruit changes by the season: Fall is for navel and ambersweet oranges, January sees honeybell tangelos, and February through May sees a procession of oranges, honey tangerines, and Valencia oranges; Indian River grapefruit is available year-round. A timeshare hawker tries to pitch, and shelves teeter with the sort of roadside souvenirs that time forgot, including shellacked alligator heads and local jellies. There are *lots* of schlocky, fluorescent-lit barns selling junky souvenirs around here—but this is *landmark* schlock. Open daily 8am to 9:40pm. 5395 W. U.S. Hwy. 192, Kissimmee. www.orangeworld192.com. ✆ **800/531-3182** or 407/239-6031. Daily 8am–10pm.

CRUISES FROM PORT CANAVERAL

Only four family-targeted lines sail from Port Canaveral (www.portcanaveral.com), an hour east of Orlando, and focus on short Bahamas and general-interest Caribbean itineraries—the upscale lines and routes leave from South Florida instead. Parking costs $17 per day—and there's nothing to do around the port.

As usual, you won't find many discounts from Disney, although MouseSavers. com tells which departures are going cheap. Quotes from specialty agents are often hundreds lower than those the lines themselves offer, and prices of $100 a night or less can be had if you book through a specialist. Check **Cruise Brothers** (www.cruisebrothers.com; ✆ **800/827-7779**), and **Cruises Only** (www.cruisesonly.com; ✆ **800/278-4737**). Don't quit before you consult a terrific site called **Cruise Compete** (www.cruisecompete.com), on which multiple cruise sellers jockey for your business by offering low bids.

Carnival Cruise Lines ★ CRUISE   Considered a bargain line, it's noisy and atwitter with neon, like the inside of a pinball machine. Think "Real Housewives of the Atlantic Ocean." Carnival is popular with families and there are few pretensions. Each ship has a twisting water slide that has also become a line signature. Carnival sails the *Liberty* on short Bahamas runs. The *Elation* does 3-night Bahamas or 4-night Eastern Caribbeans, the *Breeze* goes to the Caribbean for a week, and the *Sunshine* generally does Eastern Caribbean runs that take a week or more. www.carnival.com. ✆ **800/764-7419.**

Disney Cruise Line ★★★ CRUISE   These high-quality, casino-free ships include character appearances, fireworks at sea, and top-drawer entertainment. The hallmarks are the kids' program and a restaurant that changes from black and white to full color as you dine. Two of its four ships are here in 2019. The *Dream* makes 3-, 4-, and 5-night trips to the Bahamas, the *Fantasy* sails 3-day Bahamas runs and weeklong Eastern and Western Caribbean trips. Disney packages trips with theme park stays and provides seamless transitions between the two; although because it's a Disney package, it won't give you the best deal on the Walt Disney World portion. www.disneycruise.com. ✆ **800/393-2784.**

Norwegian Cruise Lines ★ CRUISE   The middle-priced Norwegian has the kitted-out *Epic* (2010) for a mix of weeklong Western and Eastern Caribbean cruises and 3- and 4-night Bahamas ones plus the occasional 11-night Western Caribbean one. The newly refurbished *Sun* does trips of less than a week that include the Bahamas or Key West with an overnight in Havana. On that ship, you get free beverages, including booze, the entire trip. September is a quiet month, but the schedule is otherwise busy. www.ncl.com. ✆ **866/234-7350.**

Royal Caribbean International ★ CRUISE   It's the line for young couples and teens, with active diversions such as rock-climbing walls. It hits the sweet spot between the gaudy tackiness of Carnival and the twee branding of a shopping mall. The principal ships here in 2019 are the Voyager-class *Mariner of the Seas* and *Navigator of the Seas* making 3-night and 4-night Bahamas jaunts, but the goliath *Harmony of the Seas* (2016), fitting between 5,500 and 6,600 passengers and kitted out with state-of-the-art amenities, arrives in May to sell weeklong routes to both the Eastern and Western Caribbean. www.royalcaribbean.com. ✆ **866/562-7625.**

6 DINING AROUND TOWN

You don't need a guidebook to decide if you want to eat at a chain restaurant—Orlando is crawling with those, and they all seem to serve the same menu of burgers, ribs, pizza, and salad topped with meat. But you could use help locating independent, unusual, and family-run small businesses. The restaurant options in this guide are the worthy discoveries you might not otherwise have noticed among the clamor.

That's not to say corporate food can't have local provenance. In Orlando, even supersized brands have a pedigree: Darden, which owns Olive Garden and LongHorn Steakhouse, is based here, and so is Hard Rock Cafe. But for those, you know what you're going to get. We want to show you more flavors.

Pretty much every restaurant we list is open for lunch and dinner. Don't expect places to accept checks—credit cards are Orlando's cash. Also, this is a town where it bears asking for discounts.

In addition to our recommendations, check out Scott Joseph's Orlando Restaurant Guide (**www.scottjosephorlando.com**) by longtime food critic Scott Joseph, who reviews places to eat in the "real" Orlando north of the tourist zone. In late August and September, dozens of area restaurants band together for **Orlando Magical Dining Month** (www.orlandomagicaldining.com), when three-course (appetizer, entree, dessert) prix-fixe dinners cost $35.

Prices are classified based on the price range for a main course at dinner:

o **Inexpensive:** $12 or less
o **Moderate:** $13 to $18
o **Expensive:** $19 or over

OUTSIDE THE DISNEY PARKS

These are the restaurants on resort property or publicly accessible hotels but not inside a ticketed park. For places inside the theme parks, plus info on the Disney Dining Plan, see chapter 3.

Reservations are a necessity for all of Disney's table-service restaurants. Walk-ins are accepted, but tables are often full.

Bookings open 180 days in advance, and families throw themselves into it early as if they're Panzer units invading Poland. Obnoxiously, Disney slaps you with a $10–$25 per person fee if you fail to show up for your reservation, which is unfriendly, but the side benefit is that restaurants that seemed impossible suddenly have space 24 hours ahead, when people dump bookings to avoid penalty. All Disney-run restaurants (https://disneyworld.disney.go.com/dining; ✆ **407/939-3463** [DINE]) can be booked by phone, online, or using the My Disney Experience app. Tenant-run places (like the ones at Disney Springs) can be booked directly or, usually, on OpenTable.

Parking and hotel gate access is free with a reservation. Reservationists have schedules of other resort events (such as fireworks times) and will help you plan around them, but Disney's website withholds prices.

Within Disney's hotels, the nicest restaurants generally serve from 5 to 9:30 or 10pm, as it's assumed patrons will eat lunch in parks. Some are more special than others, and many are just there to feed the masses, so focus your attentions on these recommendations (all unfortunately in the Expensive category).

EXPENSIVE

Boma—Flavors of Africa ★★ AFRICAN   Make a reservation here and you get a bonus: a fine excuse to visit Disney's Animal Kingdom Lodge and pay a visit to the animals in its backyard paddocks, floodlit after dark—think of the high price as an admission fee for that. Dinner is a good time, too: A 60-item buffet menu, served in a dramatically vaulted dining room of thatching and bamboo, is not all African. It runs the gamut from roast chicken and beef to a very few African-themed delights such as watermelon rind salad and *bobotie* (a *moussaka*-like pie of ground beef from South Africa).

Disney's Animal Kingdom Lodge, 2901 Osceola Pkwy., Bay Lake. www.disneyworld.com. ✆ **407/939-3463.** Adults $30–$48, kids $18–$26. Daily 7:30–11am and 4:30–9:30pm.

California Grill ★★★ AMERICAN   For a blowout night with a view, the best choice is this beloved space on the 15th floor of the Contemporary Resort. The wine list is elaborate (300 selections), and the California fusion-style menu is bright and seasonal but hearty—swordfish, braised lamb shank, flounder—and sushi and flatbreads are popular sidelines. Book as soon as you can—the maximum is 180 days before—and get a window seat for the fireworks. If you have a reservation that doesn't coincide with the show, you can still come that night to watch. The music for the show is even piped into the outdoor viewing platforms, which are practically on top of Tomorrowland. A dinner here is a fantastic excuse to stroll through the atrium of this iconic hotel.

Disney's Contemporary Resort, 4600 N. World Dr., Lake Buena Vista. www.disneyworld.com. ✆ **407/939-3463.** Mains $35–$60, Sunday brunch $80 adults, $48 kids.

Deep Blu Seafood Grille ★★ SEAFOOD   The higher-end Deep Blu marks itself a niche in seafood creations such as crab mac and cheese, calamari "fries," and some divinely soft crab cakes that are plated as savory fall-apart patties, bucking most kitchens' tendency to over-fry. This being appeal-to-everyone Orlando, there's plenty of steak and chicken, too. You'll find Deep Blu in the

The Boathouse **9**
Boma—Flavors of Africa **5**
California Grill **3**
Chef Art Smith's Homecomin' **9**
Deep Blu Seafood Grille **8**
Disney's Spirit of Aloha Show **2**
Flying Fish **7**
Garden View Tea Room **1**
Gospel Brunch at House of Blues **9**
Havana's Cuban Cuisine **12**
Hoop-Dee-Doo Musical Revue **4**
Jiko—The Cooking Place **5**
Mickey's Backyard BBQ **4**
Miller's Lake Buena Vista Ale House **11**
Morimoto Asia **9**
Polite Pig **9**
Punjab Kitchen **13**
Raglan Road **9**
Rainforest Cafe **10**
STK Orlando **9**
T-Rex **10**
Todd English's bluezoo **6**
Trattoria al Forno **7**
Victoria & Albert's **1**
Wine Bar George **9**

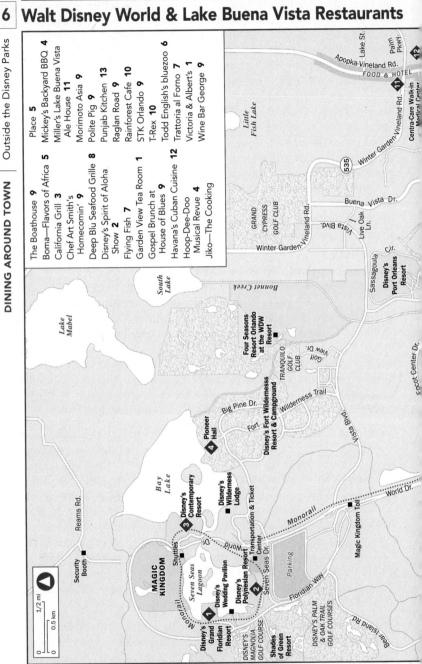

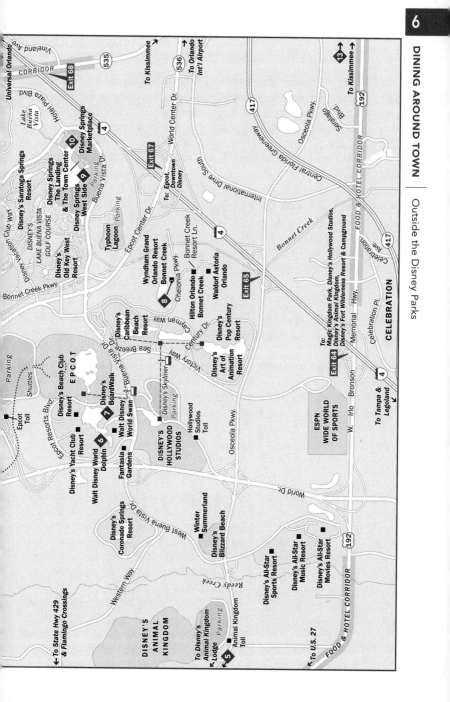

massive Wyndham development close to Disney Springs on the south side of Disney property; turn left at the second Wyndham-marked entrance.

Wyndham Grand Orlando Bonnet Creek, 14651 Chelonia Parkway, Orlando. www. deepbluorlando.com. ✆ **407/390-2420.** Mains $29–$49. Daily 5:30–10pm.

Jiko—The Cooking Place ★★ AFRICAN

The a la carte fine dining room across the hall from Boma is considered by many to be one of the resort's most romantic spots. It serves entrees that are good, too, but they often cost what the entire banquet does at Boma. The food coming from the open kitchen is pan-African, but waiters are eager to pander to American palates (note the flatbreads on the menu). That said, there are some delicious twists such as sweet tamarind butter for the bread, wild boar tenderloin as a starter, peri-peri (spicy) chicken as a main. Animal Kingdom Lodge claims a large list of South African wines. When you're on premises, you can also see the animals in the game viewing area at the Lodge, though they're not visible from the restaurant. **Sanaa,** in the Kidani Village building nearby, has a similar culinary vibe, but it's cozier, more casual, a touch less expensive, and also does lunch. It's just as good of a choice.

Disney's Animal Kingdom Lodge, 2901 Osceola Pkwy., Bay Lake. www.disneyworld. com. ✆ **407/939-3463.** Mains $30–$55. Daily 5:30–9:30pm.

Todd English's bluezoo ★ SEAFOOD

Although it's not the showplace it once was, it's still quite good compared to the other resort restaurants. The menu is mainly fish with few detours. Eaten among Jeffrey Beers' decor of colored-glass baubles that suggest being underwater, the menu changes but the focus is fresh fish. The nightly herb-rubbed "dancing fish" is grilled on a spinning skewer (watch them spin alongside the raw bar); the light clam chowder comes infused with bacon; and the 2-pound "Cantonese" lobster is painted in a sticky soy glaze that must be shared. The Lounge (open at 3:30pm) serves a bar menu.

Walt Disney World Dolphin Hotel, 1500 Epcot Resorts Blvd., Lake Buena Vista. www. swananddolphin.com/bluezoo. ✆ **407/934-1111.** Mains $22–$60. Daily 5–11pm.

Victoria & Albert's ★★★ FRENCH

Disney's flagship restaurant is the ultimate destination for anniversaries, proposals, and gourmands—and it may be the only place in the resort where you don't find kids. The company puts much stock in Chef Scott Hunnel, a multiple James Beard nominee, who oversees the kitchen. Praised as the only AAA five-diamond restaurant in Central Florida, a citation V&A's has earned since 2000, the adults-only, 65-seater lays on its indulgent seven-course menu (think amuse-bouches, Osetra caviar, Iwate Japanese beef with oxtail jus, elk tenderloin) revealed to you from under cloches like a parade of debutantes. It's like the Very Fancy Restaurant where a character might take a date on a sitcom, which adds to the theater. The resort's most exclusive reservation is here: the four-table Queen Victoria's room, where a private 10-course meal is served behind closed doors for $235 per person before wine. It sells out. Reserve 180 days ahead.

Disney's Grand Floridian Resort & Spa, 4401 Floridian Way. Lake Buena Vista. www. victoria-alberts.com. ✆ **407/939-3463.** 7-course prix-fixe from $185, wine pairings from $65. 10-course Chef's Table prix-fixe from $235, wine pairings from $105. 2 nightly seatings, 1 for Chef's Table and Queen Victoria's room. Jacket required for men (loaners available), no children under 10 permitted.

Disney Springs

Disney Springs (formerly known as Downtown Disney), a shopping-and-entertainment district at the southeastern edge of the property, is now the best place inside Disney to find food you'll like. There are dozens of restaurants and quick-service choices to appeal to every taste. The huge, free-to-enter outdoor mall still charges extreme prices ($30+ for sit-down dinner entrées, $17 a burger, $5 a cupcake—welcome to Disney!) but a few places, reviewed below, actually return that money in the form of skilled cuisine. Self parking is free. Most places serve food from 11am to 11pm.

Yet some choices still serve regrettably lackluster food, so be careful. You can count these joints out unless you just don't care: **Paddlefish** does so-so seafood in a fake boat cemented to its dock; **D-Luxe Burger** (just fine, enough said); **Bongoes Cuban Café** (merely passable food but the bands and patio can be pleasing); **Paradiso 37** (international tapas); **Planet Hollywood Observatory** is packed with unbelievable movie memorabilia (Judy Garland's *The Wizard of Oz* dress! The floating *Titanic* door Rose wouldn't let Jack on!), while its deep-fried menu teeters with elaborate concoctions (a Ferris wheel of fried apps, towering sundaes) that will weigh you down.

Some standouts: the new **Jaleo** (a chain by humanitarian celeb chef José Andrés; www.jaleo.com) for Spanish tapas; and the fast-casual chain **Blaze Fast-Fire'd Pizza** for cheap build-your-own 11-inch pies (a chain, but more affordable than most other choices in the Springs). **Frontera Cocina** (www.fronteracocina.com) is celeb chef Rick Bayless' homemade Mexican offering (a little expensive for tacos, and no views). There's also a waterfront Italian spot, **Terralina Crafted Italian** (www.terralinacrafteditalian.com), near The Boathouse (see below) by *Top Chef* Tony Mantuano; the pasta there is handmade, the marinara flecked with lots of fresh garlic, and tables are set with an entire bottle of olive oil and bowls of fresh *giardiniera* (house-pickled vegetables). The other strong Italian place, the more romantic **Enzo's Hideaway and Tunnel Bar** (www.patinagroup.com), slices from carefully selected meats like salumi and aged prosciutto that hang by the kitchen, and pours a wide selection of classic cocktails. The best deal there is the family-style Sunday Supper ($45 adults, $19 kids). Those are all excellent choices, but these are my favorites:

EXPENSIVE

The Boathouse ★★★ AMERICAN   This convivial loft-like complex with three bars is elbow-to-elbow with people making a boozy evening out of its cocktails, craft beers, steaks, seafood, chops, and raw bar. Towering slices of baked Alaska are more daunting than the peak of Mt. Denali, and the nautical theme (there are rare boats affixed overhead) isn't superficial: After dinner, you can take a surf-and-turf ride ($125 per 25 minutes) from the boat ramp in an original 1961 Amphicar, a versatile vessel that transports passengers from the sidewalk to a 20-minute tour out on the lake. It is one of the top places to eat at Disney Springs.

The Landing, Disney Springs. www.theboathouseorlando.com. ℂ **407/939-2628.** Mains $14–$65. Bookable on OpenTable.com. Sun–Thurs 11am–midnight; Fri–Sat 11am–1:30am. Reservations recommended.

Chef Art Smith's Homecomin' ★★★ AMERICAN

Oprah's onetime personal chef, Art Smith, oversees a casual choice for tip-top Southern American comfort food: Fried chicken in several forms, "Church Lady" deviled eggs, plus slaw, pimento cheese, and biscuits galore. Just to prove their barbecue is cooked perfectly, they won't give you a steak knife. The bar specializes in infused moonshine cocktails that will kick your butt all the way to Georgia, and a pineapple-banana Hummingbird Cake that will fly you back. This menu plucks the heartstrings of Disney World's core crowd (and is irresistible to curious Europeans), so book ahead.

Town Center, Disney Springs. www.homecominkitchen.com. ℂ **407/560-0100.** Mains $16–$32. Sun–Thurs 10am–11pm; Fri–Sat 11am–midnight.

Morimoto Asia ★★★ ASIAN

Iron Chef Masaharu Morimoto, known for innovative feats of kitchen derring-do, oversees this sweeping loft-like space (one of the grandest on Disney property), and if you're wondering if an Iron Chef had to dumb down delicate inventions to pander to the Disney crowd, the answer is he struck an admirable balance between populism and panache. Yes, you can get approachable dishes like dim sum, pad Thai, and sushi, but dare to delve into specialties like whole house-roasted Peking duck, the "buri-bop" twist on hot-pot *bibimbap* with seared yellowtail, the unbelievably flavorful sweet-and-sour deboned sea bass (don't neglect the flaky cheeks), and rock shrimp tempura coated in a spicy Korean *gochujang* aioli. Outside, its Street Food window serves dumbed-down, mass-appeal Chinese grub—call it Pander Express—but after 10pm indoors, a funkier bar menu is rolled out for the Forbidden Lounge, where chefs from around Disney show up after work to unwind. At this standout, multiple visits would be rewarded.

Town Center, Disney Springs. www.patinagroup.com/morimoto-asia. ℂ **407/939-6686.** Mains $13–$54. Bookable on OpenTable.com. Mon–Thurs 11:30am–midnight; Fri–Sat 11:30am–1am; Sun 11:30am–midnight.

Raglan Road ★★ IRISH

The pub looks historic, but not in the way you think. Raglan Road was the first to bring well-reviewed independent cuisine to Disney Springs in 2005, so it was permitted to survive the post–Downtown Disney purge. Irish staples are turned into sprightly new visions, including glazed loin of bacon with cabbage, beef stew infused with Guinness, and good old fish and chips. Although the massive dining area is styled after an Irish pub, it's 20 times noisier. There's free live music most evenings. If you only want fish and chips, get it (plus beer) for less on the south side of the building at the counter-service hole-in-the-wall **Cookes of Dublin ★**, run by the same people.

Town Center, Disney Springs. www.raglanroad.com. ℂ **407/938-0300.** Mains $17–$29. Bookable on OpenTable.com. Daily 11am–11pm, Cookes until midnight.

Rainforest Cafe ★ AMERICAN   Another over-the-top themed doozy. Families dine in a faux jungle with lions, pythons, elephants, and other robotic animals that periodically spring to life, stoking similarly wild behavior in small children. Like so much in Orlando, it opts to be all things to all eaters: burgers, salads, pizza. The roof is capped by a volcano that steams and growls every half-hour. The reason I like it is the **Lava Lounge,** out on the water, an ideal perch for frozen drinks; it serves the same menu but rarely has the same line.

Disney Springs Marketplace. www.rainforestcafe.com. ✆ **407/827-8500.** Mains $18–$34. Daily 11am–10:30pm.

STK Orlando ★★ STEAKS   Like all STKs (it's an upscale chain), this always-busy, never-cheap newcomer is an urban-chic version of a steakhouse—there's a DJ after 6pm, and he's loud, which kills any romance—where every known preparation of beef is served alongside cocktails. The ground-level dining area is the main event, but head upstairs, where a (usually less crowded) smaller second bar overlooks the only rooftop dining area in the Springs. Strangely, free sourdough bread isn't served up there like it is downstairs.

Town Center, Disney Springs. http://togrp.com/venue/stk-orlando. ✆ **407/917-7440.** Mains $28–$65. Bookable on OpenTable.com. Daily 11:30am–3:30pm; Sun–Thurs 5pm–11pm; Fri–Sat 5pm–midnight.

T-Rex ★ AMERICAN   If *The Simpsons* were to spoof Orlando theme dining, this would be the creation. Nothing is a more surefire theme park–style diversion than life-size robotic dinosaurs braying above your table. Every so often, the ceiling (at least, the one outside the simulated ice cave) is lit with a projected meteor shower and, for your amusement, the destruction of all prehistoric life forms is delightfully simulated. You can predict the fare: Bronto Burgers, Tar Pit fried shrimp, and to end it all, the Chocolate Extinction, a fudge cake sundae for two or more people.

Disney Springs Town Center. www.trexcafe.com. ✆ **407/828-8739.** Mains $16–$34. Sun–Thurs 11am–11pm; Fri–Sat 11am–midnight.

Wine Bar George ★★ WINE BAR   A welcome escape into adulthood in stroller-clogged Disneydom, WBG is run by a master sommelier who chooses the huge slate of wine and makes more than 100 choices available by the ounce, glass, or bottle. The wine is obviously the point, and so the liquor and beer selections are standard. You can also order what the menu calls small bites that will satisfy most average people as a light meal. Don't sit downstairs. Go upstairs, away from the din, where there's more space, more comfortable seats, and another bar. This concept and setup are unlike most places around here, which for many visitors will make for a refreshing change.

The Landing, Disney Springs, 1610 E. Buena Vista Dr., Lake Buena Vista. www.winebar george.com. ✆ **407/490-1800.** Small plates $7–$16. Bookable on OpenTable.com. Sun–Wed 11am–midnight; Thurs–Sat 11am–2am.

INEXPENSIVE
Polite Pig ★★★ BARBECUE   If you can't get up to Winter Park to eat at the long-running The Ravenous Pig (p. 215), the people behind it opened this

smashing counter-service 'cue joint in 2017. Find excellent sandwiches (brisket with cheese fondue, smoked chicken salad, fried chicken with hot honey and pickles) plus plates of meat from the smoker and fun twists on side dishes such as charred broccoli and smoked corn with lime butter.

Disney Springs Marketplace. www.politepig.com. ℂ **407/938-1762.** Sandwiches $11–$15, smoker meat plates $14–$19. Daily 11am–11pm.

Disney's BoardWalk

BoardWalk, a lakefront promenade that's notionally themed to an old-time pier, has been left in the dust by the radical improvement of Disney Springs, and now the only people who bother with it are those too lazy to leave the area or who are stuck here for a convention. You'll find a few midway games, Surrey bike rentals, occasional buskers, and hair wrap stands—not much except a pretty lake. Most of the meals are pricey; the only truly cheap food is pizza from a kiosk and good ice cream from **Ample Hills Creamery.** The **ESPN Club** serves food as an excuse to bask in the blare of countless TVs airing live sports while **Big River Grille & Brewing Works** serves mundane burgers, pastas, and salads (mains $13–$26). It's a rare Disney joint that doesn't accept reservations, so if all other places are full, try there. You can park at the BoardWalk Inn and get your parking validated or you can walk there via Epcot's World Showcase, 10 minutes away, where the dining is much more fun. The prime dining hours at BoardWalk are 5pm to 10pm.

Rent-a-Poppins

Parents: I know you came to Orlando to spend some time with your family, but I also understand that you might need to get away from some of them for a few hours. If you're staying in a luxury resort hotel, the management may offer some kind of paid babysitting or supervised kids' club service. If not, there is always **Kid's Nite Out** (www.kidsniteout.com; ℂ **800/696-8105;** from 6 weeks to 12 years old, $18/hr. for the first child, $3 for each additional child, 4 hr. minimum, plus $10 transportation fee; $2/hour surcharge after 9pm). As the official Disney contractor, it is insured, bonded, and licensed, and it would appreciate a few days' warning for reservations for in-room sitting. Expect $10 to $12 in transportation fees. Four resorts (the Polynesian, Dolphin, Yacht/Beach Club, and Animal Kingdom Lodge) operate supervised "Activity Center" clubs (ℂ **407/824-5337;** call at least 2 days ahead) for potty-trained kids ages 3 to 12 starting at 4:30pm and ending at midnight. These cost between $15 per hour per child, 2 hours minimum, and $55 as a flat rate, which includes a simple meal during dinnertime and a 10pm snack, and are sometimes open to people who aren't staying in a Disney hotel. From 6pm to 10:30pm, the Contemporary Resort mounts a nightly Pixar Play Zone (ℂ **407/824-5337;** reservations strongly recommended), including activities and characters, for $65 for each kid aged 4–12. The Four Seasons resort offers free babysitting as part of its nightly tariff. Although your kids would love it, I do *not* recommend depositing your offspring at the curb of the Magic Kingdom and speeding away, as actress Tracy Pollan's father did to her.

EXPENSIVE

Flying Fish ★★ SEAFOOD   To say this recently renovated spot is one of the most underrated restaurants on Disney property is true, but it's also not to say it's a knockout. Its open kitchen is careful to source truly fresh food and deliver a good time in a theme-parky environment. Sustainable seafood is its principal domain, but it also does plenty of land-based meats. The entree of note has long been the potato-wrapped red snapper, which should tell you about the carbohydrated concessions a fresh-ingredient kitchen must make to keep the booths packed in Orlando. The tiny **AbracadaBar** cocktail lounge, with a loose old-timey magic theme and properly strong drinks, is attached.

Disney's BoardWalk. www.disneyworld.com. ✆ **407/939-5100.** Mains $30–$48. Reservations recommended (available on OpenTable.com). Daily 5–9:30pm.

Trattoria al Forno ★ ITALIAN   This open-kitchen affair serving $20–$37 pastas, hand-made mozzarella, and Neapolitan-style pizzas is really nothing special. It wouldn't give your Italian *nonna* a moment of competition in her kitchen, although the pasta is made here, it cures its own meat, the ingredients are fresh, and the service is good. Many people only come here because it's where the Bon Voyage character breakfast (p. 222) is held.

Disney's BoardWalk. www.disneyworld.com. ✆ **407/939-5100.** Mains $20–$37. Reservations recommended. Daily 7:30–noon and 5–10pm.

Universal Orlando

There are worthwhile dining options in Universal Orlando that are outside the parks—ones for which you don't need a park ticket. Universal's hotels have upscale restaurants (**Bice Ristorante** at Portofino Bay, **The Palm** steakhouse at the Hard Rock), while the CityWalk (www.universalorlando.com) outdoor entertainment mall, located between the resort's parking garages and the entrances to the parks, attracts locals who have no intention of proceeding to any rides.

Most restaurants are closed until dinner since guests tend to eat lunch in the parks. Exceptions include spots closest to the park entrances, **Red Oven Pizza Bakery, Burger King, Panda Express, Moe's,** and **Bread Box Handcrafted Sandwiches.** The Hard Rock Café is open, too. Universal coaxed Oregon institution **Voodoo Doughnut** to bring its extravagant creations here, but those don't really qualify for meals unless you've fallen off the carb wagon.

After dark (parking is free after 6pm), CityWalk has kiosks serving stuff like **Fat Tuesday** boozy slushies. Arrive before 9pm, because some of these places charge covers after then. Everything closes by 2am, some stuff earlier than that. (For CityWalk's nightlife, see p. 225.) If you intend to linger at CityWalk for the nightlife, there are a few package deals that combine a set meal, including a beverage, with a movie ($22) or entry to the clubs ($21), tip included. The **Meal & Blue Man Group** deal ($75) pairs dinner at one of four restaurants with a performance of the show (p. 225) and can be purchased at the CityWalk Guest Services window.

Entrees cost more than they would in the real world; they're mostly priced in the teens, with burgers sliding in around $15. Not everything is worth chewing: **Bubba Gump Shrimp Company** (yawn!), the counter-service **Hot Dog Hall of Fame** (shrug!), and woe, **NBC Sports Grill & Brew** (which feels like an airport bar). You may (but don't have to) make reservations online for the more compelling restaurants, named here. For each place, ℂ **407/224-3663** for more information unless there's a different number listed.

MODERATE

Antojitos Authentic Mexican Food ★★★ MEXICAN   Beneath the Day-Glo pink bell tower, banish thoughts of beany burritos and trashy Tex-Mex at this peppy place that conjures up the flair of easy Mexican street food. Options range from casual (nachos, queso with chorizo, *elotes*) to a little more refined (grilled guajillo orange salmon, slow-roasted achiote pork loin).

CityWalk. www.universalorlando.com. ℂ **407/224-2779.** Downstairs mains $13–$28. Sun–Thurs 3pm–midnight; Fri–Sat 3pm–1am.

Bob Marley—A Tribute to Freedom ★ CARIBBEAN   Jamaican food (spicy jerk chicken, fried plantains, even oxtail) done passably, but stick around for when it turns into a reggae nightclub with a dance floor.

CityWalk. www.universalorlando.com. ℂ **407/224-3613.** Mains $11–$21. $7 cover after 9pm. Sun–Thurs 3–10pm; Fri–Sat 3–11pm; bar open to 2am.

The Cowfish Sushi Burger Bar ★★ BURGERS/SUSHI   You'll find burgers. You'll find sushi. And you'll find sushi made with burger components (called Burgushi—it's a good time on rice). This offbeat concept is rendered with a cocktail bar and some interactive screens to pass the time. If there's a wait, head to the second floor for about 30 first-come, first-served bar seats; there are eight more on the third floor. People agree that it's a refreshing idea, so it gets busy.

CityWalk. www.thecowfish.com. ℂ **407/224-2690.** Mains $8–$30. Daily 10:30am–1am.

Hard Rock Cafe ★★ AMERICAN   Hey, look! It's . . . well . . . a Hard Rock Cafe. Granted, the world's largest (600 seats) and possibly the loudest. You've probably already sampled the Hard Rock shtick on offer at more than 180 of them: A loud tavern tarted up with music memorabilia (and a Cadillac spinning above the rotunda bar) but here, there's a slab from the Berlin Wall out back. *Fun fact:* The company's headquarters is 3½ miles north of here. *Funner fact:* Between 2pm and 9pm, ask for a free "VIBE" tour of the memorabilia in areas not open to diners—there's incredible stuff here, including John Lennon's writing loveseat.

CityWalk. www.hardrock.com. ℂ **407/351-7625.** Mains $16–$30. Daily 11am–midnight.

Jimmy Buffett's Margaritaville ★★ AMERICAN   Because it's nearest to Islands of Adventure at the park's closing time, it gets jammed with park-goers clamoring for margaritas and grub like Cheeseburgers in Paradise. In late afternoon, there may be a strummer on the "Porch of Indecision" (not inside, not out), and after 10pm, the indoor area morphs into a three-bar club with a band and that $7 CityWalk cover. Across the way, under a 60-foot Albatross plane, the *Hemisphere Dancer,* is the **Lone Palm Airport** for margaritas and appetizers on the go. It usually opens at 11:30am but if it's closed, get your margaritas inside.

CityWalk. www.margaritavilleorlando.com. ℗ **407/224-2155.** Mains $15–$25. $7 cover after 9pm. Daily 10:30am–2am.

Pat O'Brien's ★★ SOUTHERN   Like its bawdy Nawlins namesake, it does Cajun-style dishes such as shrimp gumbo, étouffée, and jambalaya, optionally served with a fat rum Hurricane cocktail in the hand. The potent drinks account for a clientele with fewer kids, but there is a kids' menu.

CityWalk. www.patobriens.com. ℗ **407/224-3663.** Mains $10–$21. $7 cover after 9pm. Daily 4pm–2am.

Toothsome Chocolate Emporium & Savory Feast Kitchen ★★★ AMERICAN   The wild-looking, Steampunk-style faux chocolate factory and restaurant is the new star at CityWalk, promising the Orlando usual (so-so steak, pasta, burgers, salads, plus all-day brunch, all average), but done as over-the-top, towering and teetering constructions, and with themed characters walking around and interacting with diners. What it really does best is its major desserts—there's almost always a separate line out the door for a milkshake counter cranking out elaborate and expensive mixes in Mason jars. No reservations, so the wait to eat can be up to 2 hours; try for off-hours.

CityWalk. www.universalorlando.com. ℗ **407/224-7223.** Mains $12–$25. Daily 11am–late.

Vivo Italian Kitchen ★★ ITALIAN   In a contemporary open-kitchen setting, dine on house-made pasta (from the classics to modern inventions such as fiochetti stuffed with Gorgonzola and pear), fresh mozzarella, braised short ribs, and cured meats. A good choice if everywhere else is full.

CityWalk. www.universalorlando.com. ℗ **407/224-7223.** Dinner mains $11–$32. Daily 3–11pm.

U.S. 192 & Lake Buena Vista

Around Disney, you can find every chain known to familydom, especially in **Lake Buena Vista,** a mile east of Disney Springs. The Disney South zone, on **U.S. 192,** goes both east and west from Disney's southern gate—here, lower rents mean you'll find a lot of garbage food. The two zones are linked by a few miles of Interstate 4, making it easy to shift from one to the other.

EXPENSIVE

Columbia Restaurant ★★★ CUBAN   Not everything in Celebration, the Disney-built town just east of Walt Disney World, is fake. The original location of this palatial restaurant opened in Tampa in 1905, and this outpost bustles as boldly as its daddy. The hot, fresh Cuban bread is so delicious you'll want to fill up on it, but don't, because portions are giant. Tampa was a major arrival city for Cubans, and their tradition holds sway with flavorful grilled steaks and chicken, sangria, paella, mojitos and sangrias. My favorite, the 1905 Salad, is mixed tableside with ham, cheese, lettuce, olives, greens, and a garlicky wine vinegar dressing that won't help you consummate any courtships, but is deservedly on sale by the bottle in the gift shop. Men must wear sleeves.

649 Front St., Celebration. www.columbiarestaurant.com. ℂ **407/566-1505.** Tapas plates $8–$15; mains $13–$33. Daily 11:30am–10:00pm. Reservations recommended.

MODERATE

Bruno's Italian Restaurant ★★★ ITALIAN Your temptation would normally be to drive past this place since it shares a building with a dog-ugly gift shop that's garishly painted with killer whales, but inside, it's the food that's killer. There's a lot of junky pasta in the tourist zone, but it's the rare Italian table where the owner is not only cooking with pride, but is also actually Italian. In this one modest room, Bruno, gruff but generous, loads plates with garlicky goodness, from his puttanesca to his buttery rolls, and he also does New York–style pizzas, calzones, and fresh cannoli. Ask about the daily specials, which might include a concoction called "eggplant Pavarotti," a rich piling of eggplant, ricotta, spinach, crabmeat, shrimp, and vodka sauce. Cash-only delivery is available to the vacation homes of Disney South.

8556 W. Irlo Bronson Memorial Hwy./U.S. 192, Kissimmee. www.brunos192.com. ℂ **407/397-7577.** Mains $11–$23. Daily 11:30am–10pm.

Havana's Cuban Cuisine ★★ CUBAN It would be a shame to come to Florida without tasting authentic Cuban food. Disney only does touristy Cuban, but this modest family-run place nearby is hosting the real thing—tender *bistec palomilla* (thin-pounded steak with sautéed onion), aromatic *congri* (red beans and rice), and specials such as red snapper in garlic sauce. For dessert, the milk-soaked *tres leches* cake makes you wish you could start again for another round. It also does pressed sandwiches, a Cuban standard. Beware the green hot sauce—it'll knock you back. The decor is plain (cream walls, reproduction travel posters), but there's heartiness is in the food.

8544 Palm Pkwy., Orlando. www.havanascubancuisine.com. ℂ **407/238-5333.** Mains $14–$30. Mon–Sat 11:30am–10pm; closed Sun.

Punjab Kitchen ★★ INDIAN Punjab isn't just for tourists—you'll see local expats picking up a taste of home, too. That's a good sign for authenticity. The dining room isn't much to look at, but then again, after a few days of noisy theme park fakery, you may find acoustic tiles and blank diner tables to be soothingly authentic, too. This is a great place to try things you haven't before: The menu is plainspeaking for those who don't know their Indian food, and the staff, strong on service, knows the difference between mild and spicy. Delivery is free. This is *not* Punjab Indian, an inferior buffet joint nearby; you want the Kitchen.

5479 W. Irlo Bronson Memorial Hwy./U.S. 192, Kissimmee. www.punjabkitchenorlando. net. ℂ **407/507-2764.** Mains $11–$16. Daily 11:30am–11pm.

INEXPENSIVE

El Tenampa ★★★ MEXICAN From the outside, you'd swear it was just a grungy mini-mart best avoided, but inside, you discover a family-friendly hideaway of slotted-pot lanterns, hand-carved thrones, and big plastic cups in orange, magenta, and lime. Because Hispanic families show up in droves, you

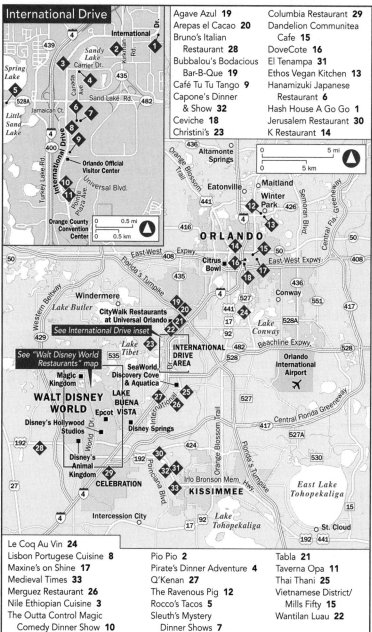

Agave Azul **19**
Arepas el Cacao **20**
Bruno's Italian Restaurant **28**
Bubbalou's Bodacious Bar-B-Que **19**
Café Tu Tu Tango **9**
Capone's Dinner & Show **32**
Ceviche **18**
Christini's **23**

Columbia Restaurant **29**
Dandelion Communitea Cafe **15**
DoveCote **16**
El Tenampa **31**
Ethos Vegan Kitchen **13**
Hanamizuki Japanese Restaurant **6**
Hash House A Go Go **1**
Jerusalem Restaurant **30**
K Restaurant **14**

Le Coq Au Vin **24**
Lisbon Portugese Cuisine **8**
Maxine's on Shine **17**
Medieval Times **33**
Merguez Restaurant **26**
Nile Ethiopian Cuisine **3**
The Outta Control Magic Comedy Dinner Show **10**

Pio Pio **2**
Pirate's Dinner Adventure **4**
Q'Kenan **27**
The Ravenous Pig **12**
Rocco's Tacos **5**
Sleuth's Mystery Dinner Shows **7**

Tabla **21**
Taverna Opa **11**
Thai Thani **25**
Vietnamese District/ Mills Fifty **15**
Wantilan Luau **22**

209

also know the food is authentic and good. The fresh *aguas frescas* (rejuvenating fruit-infused water drinks, eight flavors ranging from tamarind to lime) flow freely, and portions are big and reliable. Start with free salsa and delicate corn chips that are still shiny and hot from the fryer, but don't fill up, because mains are huge and cheap. On weekends, when it's busiest, you might find a live mariachi duo; at its market next door, get Mexican popsicles at its *paleteria*.

4565 W. Irlo Bronson Memorial Hwy./U.S. 192, Kissimmee. ⓒ **407/397-1981.** Mains $8–$14. Sun–Thurs 10am–9pm; Fri–Sat 10am–10pm.

Jerusalem Restaurant ★★ MIDDLE EASTERN   Unknown to tourists, a growing Middle Eastern immigrant community happily calls Kissimmee home (you'll see a few halal grocery stores around this area), and this family restaurant is one of the benefits: A super-friendly choice hidden in an elbow of a quiet strip mall, embellished with bougainvillea, stone walls, and a gurgling fountain. Lunch specials (11am–3pm) get you kebabs for around $10, and wraps (falafel, *shawarma*, gyros) start below that. I love the garlicky hummus, couscous dishes, and *kibbeh* fritters made of beef, cracked wheat, pine nuts, and seasonings.

2920 Vineland Rd., Kissimmee. www.jerusalemorlando.com. ⓒ **407/397-2230.** Mains $8–$17. Daily 11am–11pm.

Merguez Restaurant ★ MOROCCAN   Real halal Moroccan cooking—stuffed savory pastry, kebabs, dry-and-spicy beef Merguez sausage, tagine, piles of couscous, and mint tea—all freshly made and quite good. This isn't very common in these parts, but the straight-ahead protein-and-flavor infusion is welcome. Service can be aloof but the flavors aren't; the strip mall location is spacious but downright kooky—its covered patio is beside a grand staircase festooned with full-size Roman-style figure sculptures—which adds to the uniqueness. Ask for sauce if you want it; they figure you're a meat lover and don't automatically include it. During Ramadan (in 2019, May 5 to June 4), the kitchen omits couscous and pastry and focuses on the meats and salads. If your kid's a picky eater, there are always nuggets and burgers.

11951 International Dr., Orlando. www.merguezrestaurant.com. ⓒ **407/778-4343.** Mains $9–$15. Daily 10am–10pm.

Miller's Lake Buena Vista Ale House ★ AMERICAN   The Ale House has 86 locations and counting, so it's a rare restaurant chain in this book, but I recommend it because this location has a unique clientele: It attracts Disney cast members after their shifts are finished. *That's* what makes it authentic. Drink with them! This is the kind of publike sports bar Florida does well—lots of TVs, beers on special by the bucket, and a menu of finger foods like burgers, wings, and sandwiches.

12371 Winter Garden Vineland Rd., Lake Buena Vista. www.millersalehouse.com. ⓒ **407/239-1800.** Mains $9–$20. Daily 11am–2am.

Q'Kenan ★★ VENEZUELAN   This family-run prize is worth a celebration! The strip mall location about 10 minutes east of Disney may daunt, the room may not contain even a dozen tables plus counter seating, the lighting may be harsh—but the food is made with unbound generosity. A row of stews and meats lines the bar, from which meals are piled so high on plates that customers, largely local Venezuelans, gasp when they're set down in front of them. The owners opened their doors expressly to share their authentic cuisine with the area, and you should witness the joy on their faces when a tourist asks what to try. Suggestions: empanadas, overstuffed *arepa* (griddled corn flatbread) and *cachapas* (corn pancakes) filled with creamy aged cheese and sauces of every kind, or mixed plates like the *parrilla tepui*, with several kinds of meats, salad, yucca, and an *arepa*, and fresh juices, all of which will barely crack a $10 bill, and much of which won't even use up a $5.

8117 Vineland Ave., Orlando. ✆ **407/238-0014.** Mains $5–$13. Tues–Sun 10am–9:30pm.

International Drive & Convention Center

This is a major hotel and entertainment center. The stretch of **Sand Lake Road** west of Interstate 4 is known, somewhat jokingly, as "Restaurant Row," and it's true that some popular date-night chain restaurants (**Eddie V's** and **Bonefish Grill** for seafood, **Roy's** for Pacific Rim) are scattered along a couple of blocks. If you don't feel like hunting around, head to the bottom of the ICON Orlando (p. 165, free parking), where you'll find a selection of decent (but not gourmet) mainstream choices including **Shake Shack,** an **Outback Steakhouse,** wine-focused **Cooper's Hawk,** upscale beer hall **Yard House,** and the all-American **Tin Roof,** which has live music after dark.

EXPENSIVE

Christini's ★ ITALIAN   Christini's, a fixture since 1984, is much more expensive than most Italian places, and it doesn't permit young children. Those facts qualify it as a special-occasion restaurant and not one at which to suck down a bowl of spaghetti. Picture a prototypical high-end Italian splurge and you've got it: wandering accordion player, sommelier, lifetime waiters alert to your every twitch. It does pasta well, but guests tend to most praise its meats, particularly the tender *osso buco*. Reservations are recommended, and the dress code is business casual at the least.

7600 Dr. Phillips Blvd., Orlando. www.christinis.com. ✆ **407/583-4472.** Reservations recommended. Mains $23–$57. Daily 6–11pm.

Lisbon Portuguese Cuisine ★ PORTUGUESE   The ICON Orlando 360 complex beneath the wheel has precious few places to eat that aren't chains. This spacious and modern-feeling exception, where Bruno, the son of the owner, may even be your server, is a quality but too-often-overlooked exception. Supple gravy, buttery codfish, grilled octopus that's the talk of the town, sirloin steak in brandy sauce, wine from Portugal, all wrapped up with warm custard tarts. It's unusual to say this in Orlando, but you'll be hard pressed to find a more authentic meal anywhere, and it's pleasant indeed to wind down with a stroll beneath the great illuminated observational wheel.

8441 International Dr., Unit 291, Orlando. www.lisbonorlando.com. ✆ **407/757-0500.** Mains $14–$27. Tues–Thurs noon–10pm; Fri–Sat noon–11pm; Sun noon–9pm.

MODERATE

Agave Azul ★★ MEXICAN   Hidden in a strip mall, as so many of Orlando's most delicious places to eat are, Agave Azul cultivates a following with classic Latin dishes, from gourmet to Tex-Mex (ceviches, tacos, a few types of guacamole including one with shrimp and goat cheese) in a soothing, modernist environment with lots of space, huge booths, and a gentle indoor fountain. The margaritas pack a wallop—the drinks here come stronger than the attentively measured pours around the corner at Universal.

4750 S. Kirkman Rd., Orlando. www.agaveazulorlando.com. ☏ **407/704-6930.** Mains $9–$20. Mon–Thurs 11am–11pm; Fri–Sat 11am–midnight.

Café Tu Tu Tango ★★★ INTERNATIONAL   Fun, festive, and noisy in a good way, this casual tapas-style hangout flies high with an artist theme. Actual artists somehow concentrate on painting at easels amid the frolic of tables, cocktails, and nightly entertainment of belly dancing, salsa, or flamenco dancing. Their works fill the walls up to the rafters while boisterous diners and drinkers spill out into the front patio. Despite the fun gimmick, the locally sourced food comes from sustainable ingredients and packs flavor. I love the guava BBQ ribs; the shrimp and grits, and brick-oven pizzas, other people like the Cajun chicken egg rolls. Sometimes there are even alligator bites with Key lime mustard—cliché aside, it tastes like chicken.

8625 International Dr., Orlando. www.cafetututango.com. ☏ **407/248-2222.** Small plates $6–$12. Mon–Thurs 11am–midnight; Fri–Sat 11am–1am; Sun 10am–11pm.

Hash House A Go Go ★ AMERICAN   There's something demented about Hash House: its shocking immoderation. Dishes are laughably immense, piled as high as Jenga games. Even Guy Fieri would think it's in bad taste. Everything on the down-home menu, which the restaurant calls "Twisted Farm Food," sounds like a good idea mostly in anticipation: one-pound burgers (stuffed with the likes of bacon and cheese), skyscrapers of fried green tomatoes, a platter of fried chicken and waffles deserving of its own area code, non-stop brunch. The HH is an import from Vegas, which makes sense: This is a meal with a high risk-reward ratio, and it's a sure bet there'll be leftovers.

5350 International Dr., Orlando. www.hashhouseagogo.com. ☏ **407/370-4646.** Mains $11–$18. Sun–Thurs 8am–10pm; Fri–Sat 8am–11pm.

Pio Pio ★★ PERUVIAN/COLOMBIAN   You want a restaurant in the tourist zone to be kid-friendly, affordable, delicious, and most of all, patronized by locals. Pio Pio, a modest and easygoing family-run group of seven locations, tags all those bases with expertly made and generous portions (a glass of sangria could fill a fishbowl). The rotisserie chicken is the star dish, but you'll find a caravan of other robust South American delights including ceviche, heaps of Peruvian *chaufa* fried rice, a rich *lomo saltado* (sliced beef sautéed with potatoes and vegetables in a soy sauce reduction), plus lots of steaks and fish. They know how to please children, too.

5800 Precision Dr., Orlando. ☏ **407/248-6424.** www.mypiopio.com. Mains $11–$18. Tues–Sat 11am–10pm; Sun–Mon 11am–9pm.

Rocco's Tacos ★★ MEXICAN   Every night's a party at Rocco's, a loud, popular, tequila-drenched upscale hangout (the brand is based in Florida) where friends meet to kick back with margaritas and dig into guacamole mixed tableside. After sunset, flaming torches illuminate its lakeside terrace, and deeper into the night, a DJ spins and the bar gushes with tequila—of which there are a lot of choices. It serves all kinds of Mexican entrees, but its specialty is the fajita-like *molcajetes,* marinated and slow-cooked for hours and served in a lava rock bowl to keep them hot longer.

7468 W. Sand Lake Rd., Orlando. www.roccostacos.com. ✆ **407/226-0550.** Mains $12–$25. Mon–Fri 11:30am–2am; Sat–Sun 11am–2am.

Taverna Opa ★★ GREEK   It would be hard not to find something to eat, from tapas-like *meze* (hummus with garlic chunks and hot pita bread, *taramosalata, keftedes* meatballs), salads, hearty wood-fired and long-marinated meats and grilled fish, and *moussaka* (an eggplant lasagna with béchamel). But this is Orlando, where nothing goes unamplified. After 7pm or so, waiters and customers alike toss napkins and dance on the tables as belly dancers and "Zorba" dancers (their term) swirl. Kids really get into it. Lunches are more subdued, and mains are $10 cheaper.

9101 International Dr. at Pointe Orlando, Orlando. www.opaorlando.com. ✆ **407/351-8660.** Meze $6–$16, mains $15–$39. Sun–Thurs noon–11pm; Fri–Sat noon–2am.

Thai Thani ★★ THAI   A strip-mall anchor store by SeaWorld channels Chiang Mai with surprisingly ornate wood carvings, brass, and powerfully romantic private booths. The lemongrass soup is tame, with few chilies, indicating the chef holds back for newbies—but more advanced eaters should choose from the "spicy dishes" section to get the full flair of the cuisine—I like the Thai chili jam stir-fried with veggies and your choice of protein. It interconnects to (and shares a kitchen with) **Best Shabu Shabu and Pho,** where you can cook your own soups and meats in (toddler warning) a boiling pot in the center of your table—the Thai side is better.

11025 S. International Dr. www.thaithani.net. ✆ **407/239-9733.** Mains $11–$16. Daily 11:30am–11pm.

INEXPENSIVE

Arepas el Cacao ★★ VENEZUELAN   This local success story started as a family-run food truck that rapidly cultivated a following that funded the launch of several brick-and-mortar locations. The specialty is simple: handmade corn flatbread (*arepas*) or pancakes (*cachapas*) overstuffed with slow-cooked meats, veggies, and your choice of sauce, from creamy to spicy. It's simple and filling, if greasy, and it's made even more satisfying when you pair it with tropical juices such as blackberry or mango. You'll find it just east of the Universal complex, and it's open late for midnight binges.

5389 S. Kirkman Rd., Orlando. www.arepaselcacao.com. ✆ **321/252-2226.** $7–$9.50. Daily 9am–3am.

Bubbalou's Bodacious Bar-B-Que ★★ BARBECUE   Real barbecue done the way devotees like it, from cornbread to fall-off-the-bone ribs proven to stain shirts. There's no pretense at this tidied-up dive: Order at the counter and eat at picnic-style tables stocked with paper towel rolls and squirt bottles of sauce going from "sweet" to "killer." Get the standards: Texas brisket, pulled pork, ½ chicken, fried catfish, even gizzards. Sandwiches come with two sides (like baked beans, black-eye peas, Brunswick stew, or collard greens), or order them by the pint, quart, or gallon. Or opt for meat by the pound and take it back to the gang.

5818 Conroy Rd., Orlando. www.kirkman.bubbalous.com. © **407/295-1212.** Mains $8–$17. Mon–Thurs, Sat 10am–9:30pm; Fri 10am–10:30pm; Sun 11am–9pm.

Hanamizuki Japanese Restaurant ★ JAPANESE   The theme parks never saw a fish they didn't want to batter-fry. So here, the fresh sushi, chicken and salmon teriyaki, and udon or soba noodle soups make for a refreshing palate-cleanser. The blond wood and fabric decor conforms neatly to expectations of a soothing Japanese restaurant (it's the favorite of the *Orlando Sentinel*'s critic)—but if you know Japanese food, you'll find it's of a higher caliber, and as a result it draws a steady trade of Asian visitors hungry for a taste of home. Best of all, because of a tucked-away location in a strip mall near the Kings Bowl Orlando, it's rarely crowded. On Mondays, the menu goes ramen crazy—it's a flavorsome highlight here.

8255 International Dr., Ste. 136, Orlando. www.hanamizuki.us. © **407/363-7200.** Mains $8–$14. Tues–Sat 11:30am–2pm and 5–10:30pm; Sun 5–10:30pm.

Nile Ethiopian Cuisine ★★★ ETHIOPIAN   Nile's owners are so eager to share their cuisine they have made themselves a devoted fixture on I-Drive. They even offer a few hutlike booths in which you can sit on the ground to eat, East Africa–style. It's a positive experience for families. Everyone tears off a piece of spongy *injera* bread to scoop up various stews and meats (beef, lamb, chicken, vegetarian) collected on a platter. You can even request gluten-free or a traditional coffee ceremony, in which beans are brewed in a *jabena* pot at your table and the eldest in your party is served first. Ethiopian cuisine is made with infused oil, not butter, so there are true vegan options; with advance notice, the *injera* can be made gluten-free. It's memorable and not daunting.

7048 International Dr., Orlando. www.nile07.com. © **407/354-0026.** Mains $10–$14. Mon–Fri 5–10pm; Sat–Sun 4–10pm.

Downtown Orlando

Although the historic heart of Orlando has a healthy culinary scene, people who travel for the theme parks are unfairly unlikely to seek out meals in the "real" part of town 25 minutes north. But a few places are special and long-running enough to warrant a visit despite the gravitational pull of the parks.

EXPENSIVE

K Restaurant & Wine Bar ★★★ AMERICAN   The mastery of rich flavors using Southern bistro classics and local ingredients made this neighborhoody place a star of Orlando cuisine, and the departure of chef-owner Kevin Fonzo hasn't fazed it a bit. The menu changes but almost always includes a steak tartare (sometimes served with Brussels sprout kimchi), fried green tomatoes, and the K Filet dusted with wild mushrooms and accompanied by a wildly scrumptious wine sauce. Ask to be served by the long-running, much-loved Rocky Mazza, who's famous in these parts. This uproariously flamboyant merry-maker carries a leather wallet full of photos from his colorful past, and he's got a hundred funny stories for each one. There's a big wine list, too.

1710 Edgewater Dr., Orlando. www.krestaurant.net. ℂ **407/872-2332.** Mains $19–$48. Mon–Thurs 5–9pm; Fri–Sat 5–10pm; Sun 10am–2pm.

Le Coq Au Vin ★★★ FRENCH   Longtime Chef Louis Perrotte hand-picked his protégé Reimund Pitz to take the reins at this classic French romantic restaurant, an Orlando institution since 1976. Diners, many of whom are here celebrating a special occasion, feel more like they're guests in a home than paying patrons, an illusion that's extended by its mostly residential neighborhood. Pitz is a classically trained French chef, so you get the complicated flavors (well-marinated coq au vin, daily selection of game meat, Grand Marnier soufflé) that the prices demand, plus Gallic staples such as steak tartare and Gruyère cheese soufflé. Some dishes come in ample half portions that can cost two-thirds what larger servings do.

4800 S. Orange Ave., Orlando. www.lecoqauvinrestaurant.com. ℂ **407/851-6980.** Mains $21–$42. Tues–Sat 5:30–9pm; Sun 5–8:30pm.

The Ravenous Pig ★★★ SOUTHERN   James and Julie Petrakis have given Orlando some culinary renown (and published a cookbook) for knowing just when to deploy bacon and in what amount, a talent dear to me, and they have been rewarded by operating one of the city's most influential dining choices. Expect a beer-friendly yet sophisticated evening where the food is gourmet without pretentiousness. The menu changes seasonally but always features traditional farmhouse meats—in the form of frites, say—and some Southern comfort dishes with an upscale spin, like shrimp and grits with Gruyère biscuits. Get the Old Fashioned: bacon-infused Old Forester bourbon with vanilla and maple, garnished with candied bacon.

565 W. Fairbanks Ave., Winter Park. www.theravenouspig.com. ℂ **407/628-2333.** Mains $17–$33. Wed–Sat 11:30am–3pm and Mon–Thurs 5–10pm, Fri–Sat 5–11pm; Sun 10:30am–3pm and 5–9pm. Reservations recommended.

MODERATE

Cevíche ★ TAPAS   For a lively night out, head to Church Street Station, a revitalized pedestrian district of red-brick warehouses, gas-lit lamps, and late-night lounges. This rococo dining hall feels like it was plucked off Las Ramblas in Barcelona. The menu, also true to Spain, is piled with more than 100 tapas dishes, including daring-for-Orlando meats (quail, crispy chicken livers, oxtail), standard ones (chorizo, veal, lamb chops), and plenty of vegetable and fish choices. And, of course, there's ceviche (I like the tuna, with garlic, lime, onion, and a touch of jalapeño). Because everything's meant to be shared, the energy is social and vibrant. Things get loud when the flamenco band clacks and strums, so enjoy the evening on the front patio. Then club-crawl on

Church Street late into the night. Go for Tapas Tuesday (they only cost $3–$10 then).

125 W. Church St., Orlando. www.ceviche.com. ℂ **321/281-8140.** Tapas $7–$14. Sun–Thurs 4–11pm; Fri–Sat 4pm–midnight.

DoveCote ★★★ FRENCH   How did a richly authentic yet distinctly modern and youthful French brasserie wind up in the lobby of a generic banking skyscraper in a vacation town like Orlando? Never mind. The country pâté, dense and cool, comes in a little tub under a protective layer of fat. The croque madame is indulgently slathered in Mornay sauce and Gruyere cheese. Mashed potatoes are sculpted into a nest for a dollop of creamy horseradish. The cocktails are intriguing, the beef tartare accompanied by Worcestershire sorbet. (*Worcestershire sorbet*, people.) Brunch, it should be no surprise to learn, is divine, and coffee is from a kiosk in the corner run by Foxtail Coffee Co., a Winter Park–based roaster that attracts a devoted walk-in clientele of its own.

390 N. Orange Ave., Orlando. www.dovecoteorlando.com. ℂ **407/674-6841.** Mains $8–$19 lunch, $16–$38 dinner. Free valet parking at dinner. Mon–Fri 11:30am–2:30pm and 5:30–10pm; Sat 5–10pm; Sun 10:30am–2:30pm.

Maxine's on Shine ★★ INTERNATIONAL   Hidden in a residential neighborhood (blink and you've passed it), it's a labor of love by its owners, who frequently emerge from the kitchen to party with guests. There's a good wine list plus a tiny stage hosting a roster of entertainment (1970s karaoke one night, classical piano the next). Chicken Maxine's blends pan-seared diced chicken with shallots, mushrooms, a Marsala wine cream sauce, and penne pasta. On weekends, it brings in live, chill music, which is popular with locals from the neighborhood, so reservations are recommended for then. As you depart, a sign thanks you for helping "this little restaurant's dreams come true."

337 N. Shine Ave., Orlando. www.maxinesonshine.com. ℂ **407/674-6841.** Mains $14–$27. Tues–Fri 5–10pm; Sat 10am–10pm; Sun 10am–4pm.

INEXPENSIVE

Dandelion Communitea Cafe ★★★ VEGETARIAN/VEGAN   When you hang out at Dandelion, you feel like you're a part of something. That's because it's as much a neighborhood hangout as it is a cafe. Once a private home, hardwood floors and cabinets were left intact, and now diners of all ages (including kids) roam. A huge selection of tea is served with menu items (bowls, wraps, burritos) made with local ingredients. There's no meat, and nearly everything is gluten-free. The signature dish is the Giddyup (usually $10, but only $6 on Monday), a filling nacho bowl of tempeh chili piled with blue corn chips, diced tomatoes, scallions, and cheese. My favorite is the Homemade Hearty Chili, the most flavorful veggie chili I've ever had ($4–$7).

618 N. Thornton Ave., Orlando. www.dandelioncommunitea.com. ℂ **407/362-1864.** Mains $8–$10. Mon–Sat 11am–10pm; Sun 11am–5pm.

Ethos Vegan Kitchen ★★ VEGAN   As one of the only fully vegan restaurants in Central Florida, Ethos garners a loyal following. That's because when vegan cuisine is all that you do (even the cheese qualifies), you have to

A GASTRONOMIC TOUR OF little vietnam

Just north of Orlando's downtown, along a stretch of 1950s storefronts around Colonial Avenue and Mills Avenue, a thriving Vietnamese area (variously called Little Vietnam, ViMi, and **Mills Fifty**) is flourishing. Many people fled here upon the fall of Saigon, and now diners can find cheap meals here, true to Vietnam's reputation for nuanced flavors. Park anywhere (most buildings hide secret lots behind them).

The quickest meal is *bánh mi*, addictive baguette-style sandwiches stuffed with thinly sliced veggies (cucumbers, daikon, carrots), cilantro, hot peppers, a buttery secret sauce, and meats such as roast pork, pâté, or meatball (or tofu). They're shockingly cheap: $4, hot, and made to order. The best are at **Bánh Mì Nha Trang,** hidden in an ancient strip mall (1237 E. Colonial Dr.; ✆ **407/346-4549;** Mon–Wed and Fri 10am–7pm, Sat–Sun 10am–6pm), where they barely speak English but are improbably friendly—every transaction ends with a chipper "See you tomorrow!" Also get them at the counter beside checkout at **Tiên-Hung Market** (1108 E. Colonial Dr.; ✆ **407/422-0067;** daily 9am–6pm), a catch-all for Asian groceries.

At most of the area's Vietnamese restaurants, where entrees range $8 to $12, menus drone on like a Russian novel, but each place has its specialty. **Phó 88** (730 N. Mills Ave.; www.pho88orlando.com; ✆ **407/897-3488;** daily 10am–10pm) excels with *pho* beef noodle soup; bowls seem as large as hot tubs, with many flavors vying for dominance. Its two enormous spring rolls could fill an average stomach for $3.25. The specialty at **Ánh Hông** (1124 E. Colonial Dr.; www.anhhong orlando.com; ✆ **407/999-2656;** daily 9am–10pm), on the corner of Mills, is tofu (especially fried), while **Viet Garden** (1237 E. Colonial Dr.; www.vietgardenorlando. com; ✆ **407/896-4154;** Sun–Thurs 10am–9pm, Fri–Sat 10am–10pm) wows with its crispy noodle dishes. **Mamak** (1231 E. Colonial Dr.; www.mamakasianorlando. com; ✆ **407/270-4688;** Mon–Thurs 11am–10pm, Fri–Sat 11am–11pm, Sun noon–10pm) does pan-Asian street food. Neophytes prefer the mass appeal of **Little Saigon** (1106 E. Colonial Dr.; www.little saigonrestaurant.com; ✆ **407/423-8539;** daily 10am–9pm), which has dining areas with orange walls and green tablecloths that place it as slightly more upscale than its utilitarian one-room neighbors.

be skilled. Among the favorites are pecan-encrusted eggplant, "Yo Mama's Lasagna," gyros, and 10-inch pizzas. Kelly and Laina Shockley, who run it, are assiduous about ingredient sourcing and proudly pay their servers a living wage (not minimum wage). Specials change according to seasonal crops, and there's always a soup of the day. About a third of the menu is gluten-free.

601-B New York Ave., Winter Park. www.ethosvegankitchen.com. ✆ **407/228-3898** or 407/228-3898. Mains $10–$14. Mon–Fri 11am–11pm; Sat–Sun 9am–11pm.

Dinnertainment

Besides TV talent competitions, there may be no purer form of vaudeville left in America than the Orlando dinner show. Part banquet and part spectacle, most of these guilty pleasures involve stunts, audience participation, and plenty of noise. While the show grinds on, waiters scurry, distributing plates of banquet food the way Las Vegas dealers deal blackjack cards. Nowhere else on Earth—at least not since Caligula's Rome—will you find so many places in which to stuff your face while fleets of horses, swordsmen, and crooners labor to amuse you. Dinnertainments represent the delight of Orlando's shtick.

Most times of the year, most of them kick off daily around 6 or 7pm, but during peak season, there may be two shows scheduled around 6 and 8:30pm. Upon arrival, crowds are corralled into a preshow area where they can buy cocktails and souvenirs—feel free to be slightly tardy, and feel free not to buy anything, because non-alcoholic drinks come with dinner. Most shows will be mopping up two hours later. Kids will find chicken fingers, hot dogs, and so on, while drinks, draft beer, and wine (the cheap stuff, watered down) are unlimited. Bring enough cash to tip your server because gratuities aren't included. *Money-saving tip:* The free coupon books and discount ticket suppliers always have deals. The ones thrown by the theme parks, though, tend to sell out.

IN ORLANDO & KISSIMMEE

Capone's Dinner & Show ★ ITALIAN   High schoolers in wigs pretend to be 1920s flappers and warble to recorded music in this affordable dinnertainment effort. Dinner's a bog-standard steam table buffet of lasagna, gluey pasta, pizza, nuggets, and a few token non-pasta choices, such as a hot-meat carving station of iffy quality. Unusually for these shows, it's all-you-can-eat, and unlimited Bud Light or a few other alcoholic drinks are included. This troupe's own brochures and website promise half-off discounts, which grant the price I name here, but I've never seen the so-called full price charged.

4740 W. Irlo Bronson Memorial Hwy./U.S. 192, Kissimmee. www.alcapones.com. ✆ **407/397-2378.** $38 adults, $25 kids 4–12. Nightly, some 1pm shows.

Medieval Times ★ AMERICAN   The long-running coach-tour favorite is also an attraction in nine other North American cities, qualifying it as the McDonald's of dinnertainment: "Knights" do horse tricks in an arena to please the Crown. Waitresses were once called "wenches," but it finally got the #MeToo refurbishment: The Queen, not the King, now runs this show. You eat spareribs and chicken with your hands (or the veggie stew with a spoon) while the jousters compete in an arena. For $12 more, the Royalty Package gets you front-row seating, a banner to cheer on your randomly assigned knight, and a souvenir towel. Its "castle" is located a few miles east of Disney on U.S. 192, in a downtrodden area of Kissimmee. It's also always greatly discounted by brochures, to the tune of 30%–50% less.

4510 W. Irlo Bronson Memorial Hwy./U.S. 192, Kissimmee. www.medievaltimes.com. ✆ **866/543-9637** or 407/396-2900. $63 adults, $37 kids 12 and under, kids under 3 free if they sit on parent's lap. Nightly, plus mornings or afternoons in high season.

The Outta Control Magic Comedy Dinner Show ★★ PIZZA   More affordable and easygoing than its dinnertainment competition, the show mounted by the WonderWorks science/video playground targets kids—and parents weary of overproduced, overpriced glitz. Unlimited pizza, salad, beer, wine, and soda are distributed while buddy-buddy magicians engage in family-friendly jokes, tricks, mindreading, and improv. Discount coupons get $2 off.

WonderWorks, 9067 International Dr., Orlando. www.wonderworksonline.com. © **407/351-8800.** $30 adults, $20 kids 4–12 and seniors. Daily 6 and 8pm.

Pirates Dinner Adventure ★★ AMERICAN

For kids who just can't get enough Jack Sparrow–like misbehavior, there's this high-energy eye-popper, set on an 18th-century galleon with 40-foot masts amid a 300,000-gallon lagoon—the arena is the most spectacular of the Orlando dinnertainments. In September 2017, Hurricane Irma ravaged its show building, putting it out of commission for 10 months, but it rebuilt to continue a run that started more than 2 decades ago. Expect a circus of rope swinging (lots of it), trampolining, singing, and arrrghing, winding up with the Pirates Bash Dance Party, where little ones boogie with the buccaneers. Buying online yields discounts; free brochures dispensed around town are good for even more off.

Pirate's Town, 6400 Carrier Dr., Orlando. www.piratesdinneradventure.com. © **407/206-5102.** $62 adults, $36 kids 3–10. Parking $5. Nightly (times range 5:30–8:30pm).

Sleuth's Mystery Dinner Shows ★★ AMERICAN

After mingling with a few zany characters and watching this long-running show, which takes about an hour and contains at least one murder, you confer over dinner with your tablemates, grill the suspects, and, if you feel confident, accuse a killer. The 12 cases change nightly, so you can attend several times without duplicating the riddle. Actors seem to be having fun, and they'll tone down the grown-up jokes if they see kids in the crowd, although these entertainments are clearly more suited to adults. Audiences appear to be grateful for a rare chance to employ their brains in this town. Lots of brochures offer discount rates.

8267 International Dr., Orlando. www.sleuths.com. © **800/393-1985.** $65 adults including beer and wine, $27 kids 3–11; $3–$7 less if booked online. Daily 7:30pm.

AT THE THEME PARK RESORTS

Disney's Grand Floridian resort does afternoon tea for little princesses (© **407/939-1947**), but these are the parks' dinner shows for the whole family.

Disney's Spirit of Aloha Show ★ POLYNESIAN

The chicken-and-ribs luau presided over by fire twirlers, hula dancers, and the like has been going strong for years in an open-air theater on Seven Seas Lagoon. Bookings begin 6 months ahead, and usually the last people to reserve are shunted to the rear tables, which can feel as remote as the Cook Islands; the tables that are farthest away are the least expensive. It bores some kids, but it has its adult adherents (although most of them cite not its educational qualities but its food—pineapple bread pudding being at the top of their lists). It's on the monorail line from the Magic Kingdom, so it's easy to catch the fireworks after early shows.

Luau Cove, Disney's Polynesian Resort. www.disneyworld.com. © **407/939-1947.** $66–$78 adults, $39–$46 kids 3–9. Tues–Sat 5:15 and 8pm.

Gospel Brunch ★ AMERICAN There is no plot, and it's not sanctified, but the live music featuring weekly guests artists is jumping and the all-you-can-eat carving station combines Southern and breakfast foods. The morning show fills first, and they do sell out weeks ahead.

House of Blues, Disney Springs West Side, 1490 E. Buena Vista Dr., Lake Buena Vista. www.houseofblues.com/orlando/gospelbrunch. © **407/934-2583.** $43 adults, $24 kids 3–9. Sun 10:30am and 1pm.

Hoop-Dee-Doo Musical Revue ★★ AMERICAN Book 6 months out, not necessarily because it's the best, but because it's Disney's most kid-friendly dinnertainment. Six-performer shows put on a hectic and helter-skelter music-hall carnival of olios and gags, which elementary-school age children usually find riveting, and much quarter is given to trumpeting birthdays and special events. The headlining menu item is ribs served in pails—enough said? I prefer seats in the balcony, overlooking the stage (the cheapest, anyway).

The Campsites at Disney's Fort Wilderness Resort. www.disneyworld.com. © **407/939-1947.** $64–$72 adults, $34–$43 kids 3–9. Shows scheduled from late afternoon to evening, typically 4, 6:15, and 8:30pm.

Mickey's Backyard BBQ ★ AMERICAN The dinner show of choice for very young children features rope tricksters and taxi-dancing costumed characters wearing Western-style gear. More informal than the Hoop-Dee-Doo in that it takes place under an open-air pavilion (come dressed for humidity), it serves passable buffet-style picnic food, but the toddler factor makes it chaotic. You might be less disappointed if you see this as a photo op with Mickey and not as a proper show.

Fort Wilderness Resort. www.disneyworld.com/dining. © **407/939-1947.** $62–$72 adults, $37–$47 kids 3–9. Thurs and Sat (also Tues, Fri in peak season) at 6:30pm.

Wantilan Luau ★★★ POLYNESIAN Universal's weekly 2-hour luau is held in a covered pavilion. It, like Disney's Spirit of Aloha Show, has fire dancers and hula girls aplenty, but it beats the rest for authenticity: Food includes pit-roasted suckling pig with spiced rum–infused pineapple puree, and a catch of the day; Mai Tais are included. Should kids be grossed out by carving flesh off the pig, there's a tamer children's menu. The show is more culturally documentary than Disney's, too, as it's attentive to the differences between the various Pacific islanders it represents. You can walk from the Universal parks.

Royal Pacific Resort. www.universalorlando.com. © **407/503-3463.** $71 adults, $36 kids 3–9, under 3 free. Free parking. Sat 6pm.

CHARACTER MEALS

A character meal is a rite of passage. Usually all-you-can-eat and mostly buffet, it guarantees face-to-fur time with beloved costumed characters. Always, *always book ahead*—as soon as you can. If you can't find a slot, check 24 hours before, when people whose plans change cancel before the no-show penalty.

At Disney, meals are themed by location; at Chef Mickey's, they emerge in chef's aprons and do a towel-twirling dance. (Reading that, it sounds like a Chippendales show, not a Chip 'n' Dale show, but it's all preschool-friendly.) The characters (six to eight headliners make appearances) circulate, working the room the way a good host does, and signing autographs. This, as you binge on a smorgasbord that would give Jillian Michaels apoplexy—Mickey-shaped waffles topped with M&Ms start your day's first sugar rush.

They're cheaper at hotels than inside theme parks. When a meal is held inside a park, you'll still have to buy an admission ticket., For breakfast, try to book the earliest seating available (they'll let you in if it's before opening time) so that by the time you're done, you'll be among the first in line for the rides; you'll also have first crack at the stroller rentals. Tips are not usually included.

Cinderella's Royal Table, inside Magic Kingdom's Cinderella Castle, is the big "get"— that place always sells out 180 days early. Also try Chef Mickey's, which is next door to the Magic Kingdom, and the Tusker House, a good start for the early day at Animal Kingdom. Less prestigious addresses, such as the Beach Club near Epcot, can be smart choices— they tend not to be as crowded and you're likely to have more one-on-one time with the stars.

At SeaWorld Orlando on weekends and in high season, look for **Breakfast with Elmo and Friends** (𝓒 **407/545-5500;** $30 adults, $15 kids; 9:15am).

Inside Disney Parks

These are the regular meals, but during special events, there may be temporary events that cost more. There is a dessert-only option, **Tiana's Riverboat Party & Ice Cream Social** (Magic Kingdom) that costs a chilling $49 adults/$30 kids 3–9 for a 45-minute parade-viewing event.

Cinderella's Royal Table The most difficult reservation (reserve 180 days ahead at 7am Orlando time) features Cinderella, with possible appearances by her Fairy Godmother and other Princesses. The price includes a wand for girls or a sword for boys (ages 3–9). See p. 63. Cinderella Castle, Fantasyland, The Magic Kingdom. www.disneyworld.com/dining. 𝓒 **407/939-1947.** Meals $45–$80 adults, $35–$65 kids, according to season, plus park admission. All three meals.

Crystal Palace Winnie the Pooh and his friends, and a visible kitchen. See p. 62. Crystal Palace, Main Street, U.S.A., The Magic Kingdom. www.disneyworld.com/dining. 𝓒 **407/939-1947.** Buffet $34–$47 adults, $20–$28 kids, plus park admission. All three meals.

Dining with an Imagineer When your kids have outgrown furry friends, there's still this occasionally scheduled exceptional mealtime meet-and-greet. Over a four-course meal, groups no larger than 10 or 11 hang out with a long-time Disney Imagineer—an art director, designer, or engineer—and have the chance to ask them anything about the mechanics of the resort. Once a month, there's a dinner at Citricos at the Grand Floridian. Both are incredibly hard to get into—start trying 180 days ahead. Hollywood Brown Derby, Disney's Hollywood

Studios. www.disneyworld.com/dining. © **407/939-1947.** $89 per person, plus park admission (lunch version); kids under 14 not recommended. Mon, Wed, Fri.

Disney Junior Play 'N Dine   Appearances by Handy Manny, Jake, Doc McStuffins, and Sofia the First. See p. 107. Hollywood & Vine, Echo Lake, Disney's Hollywood Studios. www.disneyworld.com/dining. © **407/939-1947.** Buffet $34–$50 adults, $20–$30 kids, plus park admission.

Donald's Dining Safari   Appearances by Donald, Daisy, Mickey, and Goofy. See p. 96. Tusker House Restaurant, Africa, Disney's Animal Kingdom. www.disneyworld.com/dining. © **407/939-1947.** Lunch and dinner $47 adults, $28 kids 3–9, plus park admission.

Garden Grill   Appearances by Mickey, Chip 'n' Dale, and Pluto. See p. 82. Garden Grill, The Land, Epcot. www.disneyworld.com/dining. © **407/939-1947.** Meals $32–$47 adults, $19–$28 kids 3–9, plus park admission. All three meals.

Princess Storybook Dining   Appearances by the Princesses in the Norway section of Epcot. The price includes photos of your party. See p. 83. Akershus Royal Banquet Hall, Norway, Epcot. www.disneyworld.com/dining. © **407/939-1947.** Meals $49–$59 adults, $29–$35 kids 3–9, plus park admission. All three meals.

In the Disney Area

You don't have to be a guest of any particular hotel, or pay park admission, for these meet-and-greet meals.

Bon Voyage   A slight twist: Romantic couples from *The Little Mermaid* and *Tangled* are your hosts. The Italian-inflected food is a cut above the others. Trattoria al Forno, Disney's BoardWalk. www.disneyworld.com. © **407/939-5277.** Breakfast only. $34 adults, $20 kids 3–9.

Cape May Café   Appearances by Goofy, Minnie, Donald, and Daisy Duck. Cape May Café, Disney's Beach Club Resort. www.disneyworld.com/dining. © **407/939-1947.** Breakfast $35–$41 adults, $20–$22 kids 3–9.

Chef Mickey's   The most popular breakfast outside park gates, next door to the Magic Kingdom, is served by Mickey, Goofy, Donald Duck, and Pluto. Chef Mickey's, Disney's Contemporary Resort. www.disneyworld.com/dining. © **407/939-1947.** Breakfast, brunch, dinner $41–$52 adults, $25–$31 kids 3–9.

Cinderella's Happily Ever After Dinner   Appearances by Cinderella, Prince Charming, and others. Prices surge in peak season. 1900 Park Fare, Disney's Grand Floridian Resort and Spa. www.disneyworld.com/dining. © **407/939-1947.** Dinner $45 adults, $27 kids 3–9.

Garden Grove   Appearances by Goofy, Pluto, and others. This is not the same as Garden *Grill* inside Epcot. Garden Grove, Walt Disney World Swan. www.disneyworld.com/dining. © **407/939-1947.** Breakfast on weekends, a la carte dinner nightly. Reservations accepted on OpenTable.com. $30–$37 adults, $14–$17 kids 3–9.

Good Morning Breakfast with Goofy & Pals Appearances by Goofy and friends, who (ssh!) usually include Mickey and Minnie. Strongly recommended for the high-quality buffet and lots of character face time that comes with being uncrowded. Ravello, Four Seasons Resort Orlando at Walt Disney World. 10100 Dream Tree Blvd. www.fourseasons.com/orlando. ✆ **407/313-7777.** Breakfast Thurs, Sat, and some Tues. $46 adults, $24 kids 3–12, including photos.

'Ohana Character Breakfast Family-style meal with appearances by Mickey, Pluto, Lilo, and Stitch. Disney's Polynesian Resort. www.disneyworld.com/dining. ✆ **407/939-1947.** Breakfast $34 adults, $20 kids 3–9.

Supercalifragilistic Breakfast Appearances by a variety of characters, including Mary Poppins. 1900 Park Fare, Disney's Grand Floridian Resort and Spa. www.disneyworld.com/dining. ✆ **407/939-1947.** Breakfast $32 adults, $20 kids 3–9.

Universal Orlando

In addition to these, Universal does Grinch meal meets around Christmas and ghoulish "scareactor" meals around Halloween. Sept–Oct; $50 one and all.

Despicable Me Character Breakfast Start the day with Gru, Margo, Edith, Agnes, and the Minions, if you like mayhem. Cayman Court, Loews Sapphire Falls Resort. www.universalorlando.com. ✆ **407/224-2690.** Breakfast $35 adults, $21 kids 3–9, including one photo. Sat at 7:30, 9, and 10:30am.

Marvel Character Dinner Hard to imagine crusty Wolverine gladly taking snapshots with the kiddos over supper, yet there he is along with Captain America, Spider-Man, Cyclops, Storm, and Rogue. Cafe 4, Islands of Adventure. www.universalorlando.com. ✆ **407/224-2690.** Dinner $50 adults, $25 kids 3–9, including one photo, plus park admission. Thurs–Sun at 5pm.

NIGHTLIFE AT THE RESORTS

After a long day trooping through the parks, your wish list for nightlife may begin and end with a hot bath. But if, once the fireworks fizzle, you're still ready to party, the amusement giants are happy to serve to 1 or 2am daily, and it's set up so you can move from dinner table to bar without breaking stride. In fact, the resorts' nightlife zones are the same as their dining zones. The tenor of the amusements is never too ribald or cynical—these are corporate-run family playgrounds, after all.

For nightlife outside the resort bubble in real-world Orlando, see p. 180.

Disney Springs

Disney Springs offers tons of shopping and food (no admission required; the best places to eat are on p. 201), but not really nightclubs. Still, there's lots of fun to be found wandering its rambling lakeside alleys between open-air musical acts, so it's the best destination for after-dark diversions on resort property. There are plenty of places to drink, including bars in pretty much every restaurant; highlights (there are dozens of options) include **Jock**

Lindsey's Hangar Bar (strong drinks loosely themed after Indiana Jones's plane pilot, and a few specialty souvenir glasses, if you're a collector); **Dockside Margaritas** at the Marketplace; the waterfront **Lava Lounge** at Rainforest Cafe (p. 215); and an outdoor slushie bar at **Splitsville Luxury Lanes.** Nearly all the restaurants have their own bars—**STK Orlando**'s upstairs bar has one of the best views. The top deck of Paddlefish seafood restaurant (shaped like a steamboat) is the little-known **Paddlefish Lounge,** a terrific spot for lakeview cocktails. Most bars at Disney Springs close around 11pm, but **Raglan Road** (p. 202) goes later, with great acoustic music, and Jock Lindsey's serves to midnight (but does not serve food the final hour).

The Edison ★★   A fuzzy exception to the Springs' non-club rule is this multi-level riff on the 1920s and 1930s. It adapts a concept that originated in an abandoned electrical substation in downtown Los Angeles, where dance floors and multiple cocktail bars (which don't use pre-made mixes) share space with rusty, century-old equipment. The Disney version, cleaned up but still free-spirited with roving flapper girls, shoos away the kids at 10pm and brings in the musicians and a dance floor. The fare, mostly comfort food and meats, sometimes does some stunts of its own (your candied bacon hangs in strings from a little rack). The Landing, Disney Springs, 1570 E. Buena Vista Dr, www.theedisonfla.com. ✆ **407/560-9288.** No cover, minimum age 21 after 10pm. Sun–Wed 11:30am–1am, Thurs–Sat 11:30am–2am.

> ### Don't Stop the Party
>
> For more nighttime fun with the whole family, see "Disney After Dark with Kids" on p. 112, but if you're craving a night out without the tikes, check out the box on babysitting (p. 204) for childcare options.

Disney's BoardWalk

Disney's BoardWalk (no admission required; its few food options are on p. 204) is no match for the popularity of Disney Springs. It can be reached from Epcot's International Gateway side entrance, and if you park at Epcot, they'll usually let you walk back to the parking lot even if the park has closed. At the very least, expect a scrubbed-down idealization of 1930s Atlantic City that makes for a pleasant backdrop for an evening stroll on the water. **Atlantic Dance Hall** (✆ **407/939-2444;** no cover; minimum age 21; Tues–Sat 9pm–2am), a video dance club for Top 40 and '80s hits, is pretty but under-patronized unless the convention crowd fills it. At **Jellyrolls** (✆ **407/560-8770;** $15 cover; minimum age 21; daily 7pm–2am), dueling pianists enliven an otherwise mediocre and overpriced venue. Pianists start at 8pm. There is a single cozy spot, **AbracadaBar** (attached to Flying Fish) that does grown-up mixology cocktails, but even that closes around 10:30pm. Most BoardWalk visitors grab an ice cream and stick around for a half-hour or so.

In Disney Hotels

Disney's upper-level hotels all have a bar or two, but most of them aren't magnets for nightlife and many of them shut down earlier than you'd hope. **Rix** at Coronado Springs is only busy if there's a convention on property.

Trader Sam's Grog Grotto ★★★   At this terrifically fun but criminally unknown tiki bar at the Polynesian Village Resort, the rum drinks pack an un-Disney-like punch and the volcano in a painting erupts if you order a certain one of them. Fans come just to collect the ceramic souvenir tiki mugs. You have to buy the drink that goes with them to qualify for a purchase—the Nautilus, shaped like Captain Nemo's submarine, is exclusive to Florida. Kids are only allowed until 8pm. You might have to wait for one of the 51 seats inside, although the more spacious outdoor patio, while not nearly as fun and devoid of tricksy decor, is pleasant, too (and a great place for a long view of the Magic Kingdom fireworks—the soundtrack is piped in). Since it's on the monorail, it makes for a boozy park break, and there's a menu of decent bar bites. https://disneyworld.disney.go.com. ✆ **407/560-8770.** No cover. Daily 4pm–12:30am.

Universal Orlando & CityWalk

Blue Man Group ★★★   Three taciturn, bald, blue dudes get into hilarious mischief, play with bizarre homemade noisemaking toys, and trash their custom-made theater; the most expensive seats, in the first four rows, are in the so-called "poncho section" (you'll get a plastic cloak)—get one if you think it's a blast to get splattered with banana goo. (It is.) Guests can start drinking cocktails as soon as they arrive and even bring them into the theater; it's connected to both CityWalk and Universal Studios (it's practically beneath the Rockit coaster). 6000 Universal Blvd., www.blueman.com. ✆ **407/258-3626.** Sun–Thurs adults $70–$110, Fri–Sat $80–$120, students $36 if available. Dinner packages from $75. Free parking after 6pm. 1 hr. 45 min.

Bob Marley—A Tribute to Freedom ★★   You often get live music for the $7 cover, but mostly it's an easygoing place to kick back, eat, and listen to recorded reggae—an antidote to the high-energy clubs around it. www.universalorlando.com. ✆ **407/224-3663.**

CityWalk ★★   Universal Orlando's 30-acre entertainment mall is found in the front yard shared by Universal's two theme parks and is open daily from 11am to 2am. Drinks are strong and the liveliness is bolstered partly by regular concerts at its Hard Rock Live venue, but it's still pretty vanilla as party zones go. There is no charge to enter the common area, so tour around before deciding whether to pay to enter any clubs. The clubs usually open after 9pm and are $7 a pop after 10pm, but you can often buy a pass for multiple clubs (not usually worth it) for about twice as much. All Universal park tickets with multiday admission automatically come with a pass that waives cover fees. Some places open only in the evening. Many clubs only admit patrons 21 or older because drinking is permitted outdoors anywhere in CityWalk, and they prefer you don't wear super casual clothes like tank tops. Expect some offerings to be scaled back on off nights Sun–Tues. 6000 Universal Blvd., Orlando, exit 75A coming off I-4 from the west, or exit 74B coming from the east. www.citywalkorlando.com. ✆ **407/363-8000.** $12 admission to all clubs. Parking $22 before 6pm, free after 6pm, excluding event nights such as Halloween Horror Nights.

CityWalk's Rising Star ★   This karaoke joint has a spin: You get a band and backup singers (Sun–Mon, just the singers). Like all karaoke, the more you drink, the more ridiculously fun it gets. Cover is $7, usually charged after 9pm. www.universalorlando.com. ℂ **407/224-2189.**

the groove ★   Sleek and state-of-the-art, this multilevel DJ dance club is also middle-of-the-road; DJs hold court Wednesday to Saturday. The cover is $7, and it opens at 9pm. www.universalorlando.com. ℂ **407/224-2165.**

Hard Rock Live ★★   A 3,000-seat, top-of-the-line live-music arena attached to the famous burger joint is one of Orlando's primary concert and comedy venues. The second-floor seating is spacious and has good sightlines; for some concerts, the first floor is converted to a dance floor or to standing room. www.hardrock.com/live. ℂ **407/351-5483.** Ticket prices vary.

Jimmy Buffett's Margaritaville ★★   Live music nightly in a touristy environment that's first about the cheeseburgers in paradise, secondly about margaritas (there are three bars), and thirdly about island music. Get there before the live music starts at 10pm to avoid the $7 cover charge. www.universalorlando.com. ℂ **407/224-2155.**

Pat O'Brien's ★★   It's "an authentic reproduction of New Orleans's favorite watering hole," and although its Hurricane rum drinks could make you see double, there are truly two dueling pianists playing nightly. This spot is among the most popular here—the party starts at 4pm—and kids can join in. Cover is $7, usually after 9pm. www.patobriens.com. ℂ **407/224-3663.**

Red Coconut Club ★★   A vanilla version of an ultralounge, it mixes stylish cocktails but can't decide between Latin, dance, Top 40, and '80s. Still, it's the district's most upscale venture. www.universalorlando.com. ℂ **407/224-2425.**

ORLANDO'S HOTELS

Orlando has more than 123,000 hotel rooms—that's 45.6 million nights to sell each year—with an average nightly rate of $139. As you can imagine, competition can be fierce, yet at properties where heavy turnover is a given, quality can be lax. We'll show you the good ones.

A little too often, you find yourself in a hotel shrugging and saying, "Eh, it does the job." Most of Central Florida's monolithic architecture steals and inflates Europe's palatial traditions; often on such a scale that even a Texan would blush. But Orlando's resorts rarely achieve true opulence, and hotels that pass themselves off as "deluxe" are actually just three-star. You usually won't even find a minibar in your room. Often, when you pay for a fine Orlando hotel, you're just paying for mood.

Following are a few key questions to ask:

How much space do I want? If you have kids with you, will a single room supply the elbow room everyone needs? Disney's most affordable rooms, for example, have a maximum occupancy of four people in two double beds, so if your group exceeds that number, you'll have to rent two rooms or upgrade to something more expensive. For most families, renting a home or condo solves the space issue, and usually for less money.

Will I need a car? Unless you're a Disney-only type of person, you should have one. Cars enable you eat cheaper and see both Disney *and* Harry Potter as well as Orlando's many other appealing diversions. No car, no freedom.

How much time will I spend at my accommodations? If your schedule is full, you'll only use a room to hit the sack. Do you *really* need a fitness center after slogging miles around theme parks for 15 hours a day? No, you don't.

Then grill your potential hotel: **Is there a resort fee?** It's common, and it dramatically increases the cost. **Is there a parking fee?** It's another way to hide the true price of a stay. **Is breakfast included?** If it's "continental," it could be instant coffee and a mound of stale muffins. **What's the view?** Properties boast a fireworks view—but don't mention it's from 8 miles away.

FINDING THE BEST RATES

Ask any hotel what it charges, and you're unlikely to get a straight answer. They delight in changing rates according to how full they are. As a rule of thumb, prices are highest when kids are out of school (summers, spring break), and lowest in the light periods such as late January, September, October, and early December. Weekends see slightly higher prices, too, because Florida residents drop by. The prices in this guide represent an average rate.

The good news is that Orlando's average nightly rate is around $110, which is cheaper than the national average, so you're already working at an advantage. Primary websites that collect quotes from a variety of sources (whether they be hotel chains or other websites) include **HotelsCombined.com, Booking.com**, and **Mobissimo.com**. Always canvas multiple sites. The bidding areas on Hotwire.com and Priceline.com are more likely to get you the best rates in the month before you travel; hotels hold out for higher prices until then. Then call the local number of the hotel, not the toll-free one (that usually connects to a switchboard far away), to see if they'll do even better. Also check **Hotel coupons.com** for discounted rates for some of the cheapest motels in town (no promises about quality, and some hotels frequently refuse to honor the lowest rates if they hit 75%–80% occupancy).

Another reliable way to get a cheaper room is to use an **air/hotel package.** No domestic company operates charter flights to Orlando anymore, but several packagers buy cheap hotel rooms in bulk and sell them with scheduled airfare. Check **Funjet** (www.funjet.com; ✆ **888/558-6654**), **Lastminute.com** (✆ **866/999-8942**), as well as some of the vacation wings of major airlines such as **Southwest Vacations** (www.southwestvacations.com; ✆ **800/243-8372**), **JetBlue**

Theme Park Shuttles: Going Your Way?

Almost all of the hotels located off theme park property tout some kind of "free" shuttle service to the major parks (often covered by a resort fee). When they work, they're a dream, but you need to know that most are restrictive. Many run once or twice a day, on their schedule, and you must book ahead, sometimes by 24 hours or more. A typical hotel shuttle may leave for the Magic Kingdom twice a morning and return at, say, 5 and 10pm, a rigid schedule that may cost you a fireworks viewing. Also, many hotels provide shuttles to only one area (Disney or Universal/SeaWorld) but not the other. **Ask.**

Many hotels share shuttles. They can be dirty, worn, and crowded, and you might have to stop at up to a half-dozen other places on your way. Not great if you're hungry, thirsty, tired, or your kids are restless.

Before settling on a hotel based on its advertised rides, ask questions:

- What time do they leave and return?
- Which theme parks are *not* covered or incur a fee?
- How many other hotels share the same shuttle?
- If the shuttle fills up, do you send another one for me?
- Is there a fee? (That $30 for two could have been used to rent a car.)
- How far ahead do I have to reserve?

Getaways (www.jetblue.com/vacations; ✆ **800/538-2583**), **Delta Vacations** (www.deltavacations.com; ✆ **800/800-1504**), and **American Airlines Vacations** (www.aavacations.com; ✆ **800/321-2121**). Internationally, **Virgin Holidays** (www.virginholidays.co.uk) is a huge player, with lots of customer service reps available on the ground should things go wrong. Increasingly, these websites may sell hotel-only deals using their negotiated rates. Use properties highlighted on specials pages, though, because prices often come out higher in searches.

Few of these players will truly discount a Disney hotel (they may show up on the **Hotel Tonight** late booking app, though). If you want a Disney hotel, price be damned, book it separately from tickets or airfare—"room-only," on a separate phone call—because it gives you more scheduling flexibility with tickets and room-only cancellation rules are far kinder. Don't accept *any* package from a Disney receptionist, even if it's for harmless trinkets, because then it means you're subject to a $200 fee for cancellations made 30 to 2 days ahead; room-only bookings have no penalties for cancellations made more than 5 days ahead (6 days if you booked online). When it comes to non-Disney hotels, though, package away, because that's where great deals live.

If everything seems full, Visit Orlando's **Official Visitor Center** (8723 International Dr.; www.visitorlando.com; ✆ **407/363-5872;** daily 8:30am–6pm) will help you find something. You'll also always find a room (grotty though it may be) on U.S. 192 east of I-4.

INSIDE ORLANDO'S HOTELS

Every hotel in this book has a swimming pool (because of liability issues, few are much deeper than 5 ft.), Wi-Fi, and ample air-conditioning, and almost every hotel offers shuttles to at least some theme parks, although fares around $10 may apply and they may be slower than garden slugs. Every hotel is also kid-friendly. So friendly that you should expect even top-end places to crawl with scampering children hopped up on a perpetual vacation-permitted sugar buzz, and no minibars in your room to take the edge off. If you crave peace, steer toward a rental home or a splurgy resort that leans toward the convention trade, in which case the rugrats will be replaced by phone-wielding conference-goers in chinos. If you stay in a unit with a kitchen, you may be in a timeshare that was rented to you because it was empty—this is normal, and it can be a good deal, but you may have to fend off "welcome" calls that are overtures to purchasing one. *Warning:* Until it's declared illegal, many big hotels still engage in the sleazy American practice of **resort fees,** which vastly inflates what you pay—we warn you about those in bold letters. The highest in town is now $40/night. Isn't that awful?

Beware of believing overly positive online reviews for Orlando hotels! Timeshare owners overpraise properties to convince people to stay there, and Disney hotels are overpraised because they're Disney and you know how starstruck that makes some people.

How to Save on Lodging

- **Come when kids are in school.** Hotel prices are trimmed then.
- **Avoid holidays.** If the kids are out of school, you might pay double.
- **Make sure the room rules permit everyone in your party.** If you go over the guest maximum, you'll have to rent two rooms, doubling costs.
- **Always get a quote directly from the hotel.** It might be lower.
- **See what's on offer from a packager.** They have purchasing power.

- **Plug Kissimmee into Web searches.** It's cheaper than Orlando.
- **Good locations have food options.** Are there affordable restaurants nearby or are you stuck eating overpriced hotel food?
- **Ask if there's a discount.** Disney reservationists will tell only if asked. But when Disney does deal, it gives great stuff away, like free meal plans.

Following are the categories and price ranges for this chapter. These are almost unfair since so many hotels pretend to be cheaper by charging resort fees on top of posted rates:

- **Inexpensive:** Up to $105 a night
- **Moderate:** $106 to $175
- **Expensive:** $176 and up

Note: Prices in this book don't include taxes, which for hotels add as much as 14.5% to your bill depending on the municipality in which you're staying.

Inside Walt Disney World

Some people don't mind spending twice Orlando's going rate so they can be on Disney property near the resort's storied "magic," although they are usually hard-pressed to explain what that precisely means. And for them, Disney has some 30,000 hotel rooms to fill, which it does partly by punishing people who don't rent one. Disney has an active policy of making non-resort guests feel like second-class citizens by putting them at a planning disadvantage. It's also worth noting that Disney hotels tend to promote or hire from within, and over time, that has caused staff to become noticeably out of step with customer service standards in the outside world. But strictly from a non-pixie-dusted, consumer-advice standpoint, there are advantages and disadvantages to saying on property in one of Disney's extremely busy hotels.

DISNEY PRICING SEASONS

Unlike most hotels, which price dynamically, Walt Disney World's hotel rates are fixed by a calendar. The seasons you need to remember are, in descending order of expense: **Holiday, Peak, Summer, Regular, Fall,** and **Value.** The major price spikes are around spring break, Easter, and the late December holidays—put simply, when more people can travel to Disney World.

Likewise, there are three categories of Disney hotel: **Deluxe, Moderate,** and **Value** plus Disney Vacation Club apartments. Ergo, for the cheapest room, book a Value room in a Value period.

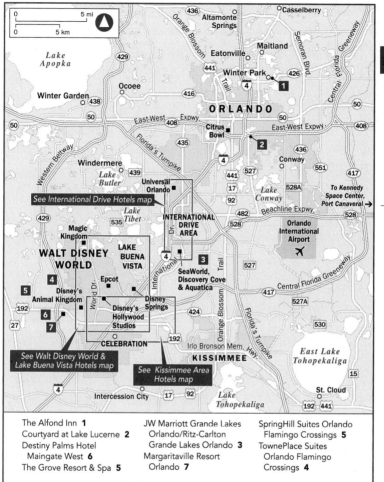

The Alfond Inn **1**	JW Marriott Grande Lakes	SpringHill Suites Orlando
Courtyard at Lake Lucerne **2**	Orlando/Ritz-Carlton	Flamingo Crossings **5**
Destiny Palms Hotel	Grande Lakes Orlando **3**	TownePlace Suites
Maingate West **6**	Margaritaville Resort	Orlando Flamingo
The Grove Resort & Spa **5**	Orlando **7**	Crossings **4**

SEASONS The dates for each season shift annually and are tweaked per property, but they follow the same pattern on the calendar. For 2017, the schedule for prices generally shook out like this for a Value hotel room in an All-Star resort. These are the bottom lines of the lowest-priced standard Disney room on a midweek night of each season, including tax (on weekends, prices go up as much as 25%):

- **Value season:** Jan to mid-Feb, mid-Aug to Sept. Value price: $112.
- **Fall season:** Mid-Sept to mid-Dec. Value price: $125.
- **Regular season:** Late Feb to early Mar, late Apr to May. Value price: $142.
- **Summer season:** June to July. Value price: $167.

Walt Disney World & Lake Buena Vista Hotels

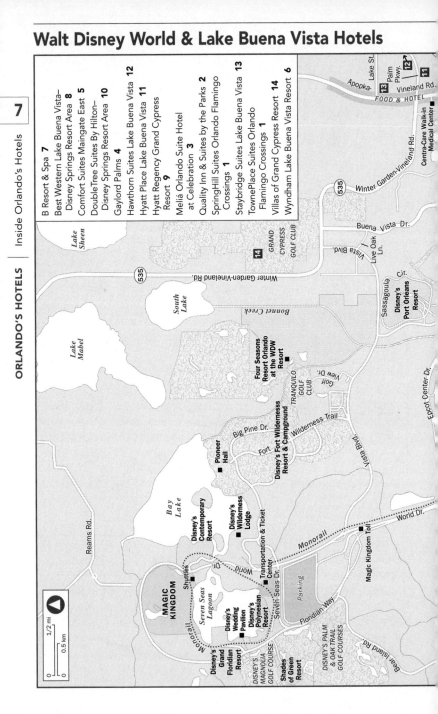

B Resort & Spa **7**
Best Western Lake Buena Vista–Disney Springs Resort Area **8**
Comfort Suites Maingate East **5**
DoubleTree Suites By Hilton–Disney Springs Resort Area **10**
Gaylord Palms **4**
Hawthorn Suites Lake Buena Vista **12**
Hyatt Place Lake Buena Vista **11**
Hyatt Regency Grand Cypress Resort **9**
Meliá Orlando Suite Hotel at Celebration **3**
Quality Inn & Suites by the Parks **2**
SpringHill Suites Orlando Flamingo Crossings **1**
Staybridge Suites Lake Buena Vista **13**
TownePlace Suites Orlando Flamingo Crossings **1**
Villas of Grand Cypress Resort **14**
Wyndham Lake Buena Vista Resort **6**

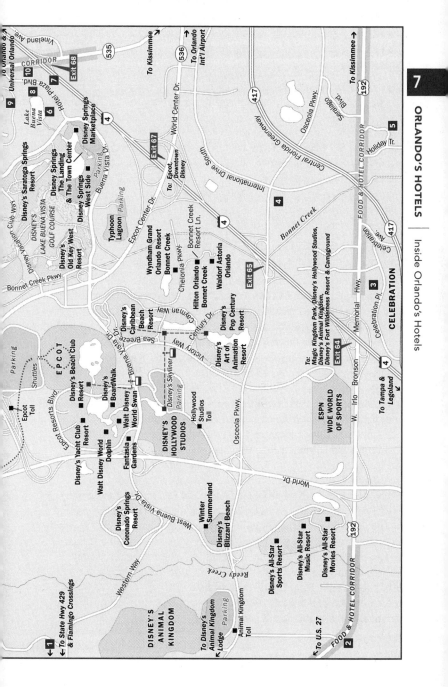

- **Peak season:** Mid-Feb, mid-Mar to mid-Apr, mid-Dec. Value price: $170.
- **Holiday season:** End of Dec, New Year's. Value price: $217. (Since this is only one week, we don't include this as the upper range in hotel listings.)

MouseSavers.com and **TheMouseForLess.com** post codes of all current known discounts. In general, AAA and military service may help cut costs.

STANDARD AMENITIES All Disney hotels, regardless of class, have touches that provide relief for families, including big pools and shallow kiddie pools, coin laundries, and playgrounds. Nearly all rooms have two double beds unless you pay for something more (like a bunk or a pullout), but no microwave. Wi-Fi is free. There will always be somewhere to eat, although at Value resorts it will be a food court. Disney shuttle buses (p. 271) serve all resorts for free, and every property is protected by gated security. And, of course, every resort has at least one souvenir store. Check-in time is usually 3pm (you can use the pool while you wait) and you must check out by 11am (and use the pool for the rest of the day).

YAY! THE BENEFITS OF STAYING ON DISNEY PROPERTY

- For those without cars, there's **free bus, monorail, new gondola, and ferry transportation** throughout the resort. This is the biggest consideration for most people. (Then again, it's free to *everyone* at Disney, guest or not.) Guests can use the MDX app to check transit wait times.
- Disney transit drops you at the Magic Kingdom gates. Other hotel shuttles deposit you on the other side of the lake, by the parking lot.
- The right to make **Fastpass+ reservations** 60 days ahead (instead of 30). Increasingly, Disney is denying non-resort guests Fastpasses for the best attractions, hoping it will force more people to book Disney hotels.
- Each day, during **Extra Magic Hours,** one or two parks open an hour early or up to 3 hours past closing for the express use of Disney hotel guests. The major attractions, but not all of them, will be open during this period, and lines tend to be shorter than when general admission is in effect.
- Free coach transfers to Orlando International Airport through **Disney's Magical Express** program. See p. 269 for its drawbacks.
- **Every room has a small balcony or patio** (except at Value resorts).
- The right to **charge purchases** on your room key card or MagicBand.
- The right to have in-park **shopping delivered to your room.** (The delivery lag time is such that you should be staying for at least 2 more nights.)
- Three or four timed **kids' activities** a day, albeit some at a charge.
- **Free theme-park parking** (but you still have to pay for it at the hotel).
- **Wake-up calls** featuring Disney characters.
- **Free wheelchair rental.**
- **Guaranteed admission** if parks are full.
- Option to purchase soft drink **mugs** ($19) that you refill endlessly while at the hotel (and not a minute more—they're embedded with computer chips).

BOO! THESE THINGS ABOUT STAYING WITH DISNEY STINK

- **"Free" resort transportation doesn't mean "fast."** Routes can be circuitous and require changing buses, waits can be aggravating, and you may have to stand.

- **Rates are 40%–70% higher** than off-property rooms of comparable quality. So is food.

- **Parking fees for overnight guests,** added in 2018, aren't cheap: $13/night at Value hotels, $19/night at Moderate hotels, $24/night at Deluxe ones.

- **Stingy occupancy limits.** Most rooms add $10 a night for each person past the limit of two up to the room's stated maximum capacity, so a $105 room will in fact be $125 if four people over 18 stay there. (One child under 3 can stay without being counted.) Value and Moderate resorts cap occupancy at four (not including a babe in a crib) and Deluxe cap at five. Families larger than four must rent two units, doubling the expense, but if you have seven or more people to accommodate, it gets ugly.

- **Haphazard room assignment.** In busy times, families with multiple rooms may get split apart. Requests for specific locations may not be honored.

- Disney resorts are so large (often 2,000 rooms) that **lines,** even for a cup of coffee, are an endless nuisance and **sprawling layouts are confusing** to small children, to say nothing of their weary parents. Disney has turned the failing into profit: It charges more for "Preferred" rooms nearer the lobby.

- The more affordable a room is, the more you could use a rental car. The most expensive resorts are beside the best parks, but Value rooms are about as **far from the action** as many off-property hotels. The Value resorts, in particular, are a good 15-minute drive from the Magic Kingdom (no farther than a decent vacation home).

- **Safes** are tiny (laptops won't fit). In-room cooking is made difficult in that the most affordable rooms lack **microwaves** or **coffeemakers.**

- At the cheaper properties, it's **hard to call the front desk;** you'll usually have to call the main Disney number. **Baggage service** may also be impossible.

- The most affordable Disney hotels **don't have restaurants.** They have food courts (burgers, sandwiches, pasta—all at theme-park prices of around $12) and the only room service item is pizza. This is less of a problem if you intend to save money by eating off property anyway.

DELUXE RESORTS

No one who has experienced a true luxury hotel can seriously attest that Disney's quality standards compare. They're three-star hotels in fancy dress, and only VIPs get true luxury treatment. Sure, they have sit-down restaurants, spas, lounges, and big pools. But rooms and service are nothing special unless you're in a top-tier room. What Disney's Deluxe hotels mostly have is uplifting theming—a prevailing mood—that makes a stay fun, and it's a genuine thrill to be so near a theme park, to get such fantastic views of the Magic Kingdom or African animals—there's just something special about it. And

Disney's announced *Star Wars*–themed hotel in which each guest is given a storyline to follow sounds like the coolest idea in hotels since pillows, but that's still a couple of years away. You can certainly pay less than the $300 to $1,100 you pay to sleep in only a standard room. But for many people, they're more than just a place to crash.

Most Deluxes (standard room maximum guests: four unless noted) enable you to dart to the parks easily. Three are by the Magic Kingdom on the monorail line encircling the Seven Seas Lagoon: the Contemporary (the most iconic), the Grand Floridian (the fanciest), and the Polynesian (the most private). A fourth, Wilderness Lodge, is linked to the Magic Kingdom by ferry, while the Beach Club, Yacht Club, and BoardWalk are walking distance from Epcot's side door. Only Animal Kingdom Lodge is marooned by roads, but it has other perks that counterbalance that.

For an extra $100 to $150, Disney sells "Club Level" concierge-style rooms with a private lounge stocked with free continental breakfast, snacks, and beverages including champagne. In some hotels, it entitles you to better views or to buy additional experiences, such as a sunset tour of the savannah at Animal Kingdom Lodge, and Club Level guests can also buy additional Fast-passes for $50 a day.

Disney's Animal Kingdom Lodge ★★★

No grander lodge ever existed on the African veldt, and the higher tariff returns to you in the form of a 24-hour safari and lots of themed activities. The hotel, which has a dark wooden look and hand-carved furniture, is built within a system of paddocks, so if you've got a Savannah view (they start around $500—careful that you don't accidentally book a Standard one overlooking the parking lot or pool), when you look out of your window, you'll hopefully see whatever genial African animal is loping by at that moment, be it a giraffe, an ostrich, a zebra, or a warthog. You'll find a game-viewing guide beside your room-service menu. Because animals tend to be active in the early morning, when families are gearing up for their days, the idea works well. Anyone can visit, even if they're not staying here; there's even a public animal viewing area straight out the back door of the awe-inspiring vaulted lobby. Its principal drawback is its distance from everything except for Animal Kingdom; all connections are by road. Standard room: 344 square feet.

2901 Osceola Pkwy., Bay Lake. www.disneyworld.com. ✆ **407/934-7639** or 407/938-3000. 1,293 units. $308–$801 non-club standard. 2-adult maximum, extra person $25. Children 17 and younger stay free in parent's room. **Amenities:** 2 restaurants; cafe; babysitting; supervised kids' program; Club Level rooms; health club & limited spa; heated outdoor pool; kids' pool; room service; self-parking $24/day, valet parking $33/day; free Wi-Fi.

Disney's Beach Club/Disney's Yacht Club ★★★

Both excellent choices with 381-square-foot rooms, these adjoining sisters are on a pond across from the BoardWalk entertainment area (you'll need it since the hotels are short on decent choices for cheap food) and a short stroll out the International Gateway exit of Epcot's World Showcase, which brings the fun close to your room, although you can't watch IllumiNations from it. Their shared 3-acre pool area, Stormalong Bay, has the crazy Flying Jib waterslide that forms a straightaway shooting off the mast of a pirate ship, plus sandy shores. (It's easily the best pool on Disney property, and it's restricted to guests.) The difference between the two is nearly negligible—they're connected and many guests think they're one giant hotel, but the Yacht Club has slightly nicer furnishings, bigger balconies, attracts slightly fewer families with kids, is a tad quieter, and is a 10-minute stroll from Epcot instead of 5 from the Beach Club. Other than that, it's a toss-up. Both of them have layouts that confuse kids.

1800 Epcot Resorts Blvd., Lake Buena Vista. www.disneyworld.com. ✆ **407/934-7639** or 407/934-8000. Beach: 583 units. Yacht: 630 units. $456–$775 non-club standard. Extra person $25. Children 17 and younger stay free in parent's room. **Amenities:** 2 restaurants; grill; 3 bars; Club Level rooms; babysitting; children's program; character meals; health club & small spa; 3-acre pool and play area; 2 outdoor heated pools; kids' pool; room service; 2 lighted tennis courts; boat rental; self-parking $24/day, valet parking $33/day; free Wi-Fi.

Disney's BoardWalk Inn ★★ The theme here, in a property split between DVC owners and nightly trade, is ostensibly turn-of-the-century Atlantic City (not tatty, present-day Atlantic City), which translates to touches such as a miniature carousel in the lobby, vintage flip movie viewers in common areas, and beachball-patterned carpets in the halls. Rooms are recently renovated and a fair 371 square feet. The Luna Pool's 200-foot slide evokes a wooden roller coaster, but I prefer the quieter, tucked-away pool near Building 1 on the east side of the property. You might hit the Belle Vue Lounge to buy bagels, muffins, and coffee in the morning and cocktails in the evening, but really, you stay here because the baked goods and ice cream of the BoardWalk is right outside and the side door to Epcot is a 10-minute lakefront stroll away.

1800 Epcot Resorts Blvd., Lake Buena Vista. www.disneyworld.com. ✆ **407/934-7639** or 407/934-8000. 379 units. $498–$868 non-club standard. Extra person $25. Children 17 and younger stay free in parent's room. **Amenities:** Restaurant; bar; lounge; Club Level rooms; babysitting; children's program; health club & small spa; 3-acre pool and play area; 3 outdoor heated pools; kids' pool; whirlpool; room service; boat rental; bike rental; self-parking $24/day, valet parking $33/day; free Wi-Fi.

Disney's Contemporary Resort ★★★ Nothing says, "I'm at Disney World" more than the awesome sight of that monorail sweeping dramatically through its glassy Grand Canyon Concourse, which it does every few minutes on its way to and from the Magic Kingdom. The hotel, one of the first two to open in 1971, is now a midcentury architectural treasure, and indicative of the revolutionary methods that Walt Disney World hoped to pioneer: The United States Steel Corporation helped design it; its modular rooms were prefabricated down the road and slotted into place by crane. The current look: soothing putty and slate business-class colors, and soft goods were renewed in 2016. Best rooms (422 sq. ft., among the largest standard rooms at Disney) are high up in the coveted A-framed Contemporary Tower, but there are stylish low-level Garden Rooms along Bay Lake, too, near the surprisingly blah pool, that are about $150 cheaper. Rooms on the west of the tower face the

Magic Kingdom itself (and, ahem, an intervening parking lot)— the ninth floor has the *ne plus ultra* of Disney views—and every water-view room takes in the nightly parade that floats after dark. Even if you can't stay here, this is the best hotel to tour. Drop by via monorail to see the 90-foot-tall mosaics of children by the visionary Imagineer Mary Blair, which encapsulate the late 1960s futurist optimism out of which the resort was born.

4600 N. World Dr., Lake Buena Vista. www.disneyworld.com. ℂ **407/939-6244** or 407/824-1000. 1,008 units. $465–$862 non-club standard. Extra person $25. Children 17 and younger stay free in parent's room. **Amenities:** 3 restaurants; grill; 4 lounges; babysitting; Club Level rooms; character meals; small health club and spa; 2 outdoor heated pools; kids' pool; watersports rental; self-parking $24/day, valet parking $33/day; free Wi-Fi.

Disney's Grand Floridian Resort & Spa ★★

It's strange to spend $700 a night on a hotel room and then have to walk outside in the rain to reach the building it's in, but from a value standpoint, that tells you a lot. This is the Disney hotel with snob appeal, since the whole point is to put on a costume of exclusivity and luxury (two things Walt despised, which is why *his* hotels had generic themes) and brag about it when you get home. So it's encrusted with upper-class affectation, from high tea to a pianist tinkling away in an outrageously pretty lobby (chandeliers, glass dome, wedding-cake balconies). It can't help but strum your imagination of what a true Victorian grande dame hotel might have felt like, but anyone can enjoy that on a day visit without paying insane rates for what amounts to a three-star room. There *are* vacation-making pluses I'd unreservedly celebrate here if money were no object, such as next-door access to the Magic Kingdom, gourmet restaurants, careful staff, and an atmosphere more romantic than at any other Disney hotel—in fact, you'll probably have to dodge a few wedding parties. Typical standard rooms are 440 square feet, although rooms with dormer windows are smaller.

4401 Floridian Way, Lake Buena Vista. www.disneyworld.com. ℂ **407/934-7639** or 407/824-3000. 867 units. $664–$1,135 non-club doubles. Extra person $25. Children 17 and younger stay free in parent's room. **Amenities:** 5 restaurants; grill; character meals; babysitting; kids' program; Club Level rooms; health club & spa; heated outdoor pool; kids' pool; room service; 2 lighted tennis courts; watersports rental; self-parking $24/day, valet parking $33/day; free Wi-Fi.

Disney's Polynesian Village Resort ★★★

The 25-acre hotel, thickly planted and torch-lit by night, was one of the first two hotels built here, back when the South Pacific tiki craze was still swinging, and the longhouse-style thatched-roof complex remains one of the most transporting of the Disney resorts. The most expensive rooms block the view of the Magic Kingdom across the Seven Seas Lagoon (swimming in it is not allowed, but the newly renovated pool area is huge and lush), but most have greenery views. The Polynesian is a notch above for families as there's an on-site child-care facility, the monorail is steps away, and rooms are on the big side, sleeping five. An easy favorite. The downside is availability: In 2015, Disney converted several buildings into Disney Vacation Club "Studio" units, reducing the standard room count by several hundred, so it's harder than ever to enjoy this hotel now. When available, those studios cost about $20 more than a standard room but include a minifridge and a microwave. Make a detour off the lobby for Trader Sam's Grog Grotto (p. 225), one of the coolest cocktail bars in town.

1600 Seven Seas Dr., Lake Buena Vista. www.disneyworld.com. © **407/939-6244** or 407/824-2000. 484 standard units, 360 Studios. $552–$1,008 non-club doubles. Extra person $25. Children 17 and younger stay free in parent's room. **Amenities:** 3 restaurants; cafe; tiki bar; on-site babysitting; kids' program; Club Level rooms; nearby health club & spa (at Grand Floridian); 2 heated outdoor pools; kids' pool; character meals; room service; watersports rental; gas grills; free 7:30pm marshmallow roast; free 9pm outdoor movie; self-parking $24/day; valet parking $33/day; free Wi-Fi.

Disney's Wilderness Lodge ★★ This effective riff on Yellowstone's woody Old Faithful Lodge, swaddled by oaks and pines, is picturesque but disconnected from the rest of the park—the Magic Kingdom, 10 minutes away by ferry, is the only thing easy to reach if you don't have your own car (the other parks involve a laborious bus trek). Most of its tricks are in its dramatic atrium lobby: giant stone hearth, springs that flow to a thronged pool area out back—a geyser nearby spouts water 120 feet high on the half-hour from 7am to 10pm. Because of surrounding woods, rooms (340 sq. ft.) are dark, but have adorable rustic touches such as headboards carved with woodland creatures.

901 W. Timberline Dr., Lake Buena Vista. www.disneyworld.com. © **407/934-7639** or 407/938-4300. 909 units. $378–$766 non-club standard. Children 17 and younger stay free in parent's room. **Amenities:** 3 restaurants; babysitting; Club Level rooms; health club & limited spa; 2 spa tubs; 2 heated outdoor pools; jogging trail; boat rental; kids' pool; room service; self-parking $24/day; valet parking $33/day; free Wi-Fi.

MODERATE RESORTS

The next category up from Value is Moderate. Compared to Value, what do you get for the extra dough? Put simply, the main pools have more elaborate themes with slides, and there are usually a few additional, simple pools; rooms measure 314 square feet instead of 260 square feet (so 2 ft. wider); most have two sinks instead of one (both outside the shower/toilet room); all rooms have a small balcony or patio with seating (though most have no view to speak of); and you can rent a bike or a boat on the premises. The upgrade doesn't win you the right to fit more people: Rooms mostly fit four (only two adults) plus one child under 3, same as the Value class.

The grounds of Moderate properties feel more resortlike when compared to the glorified motels of the Values, but at heart, they're still upgraded motels, with exterior corridors (close your drapes) and windowless bathrooms. You'll still be eating mostly in high-priced food courts located at a building that might be distant from your room. Although the bedrooms aren't much plusher than the Value properties, you will sense more breathing room and personality since Disney has been pouring money into glorifying its Moderate pool areas.

Disney's Caribbean Beach Resort ★ This resort sprawls around a central pond—1½ miles around!—with a loose island theme. Rooms (mostly full beds) are the Moderate category's largest (by a little); Disney spent a ton theming some rooms to *Pirates of the Caribbean* (beds like ships, carpet like decking) that can add about $70 to a regular room. The main Old Port Royale pool area emulates a waterfront Spanish fort and has a giant tippy bucket, so you can see why families favor this property. The resort's principal drawbacks are a lack of elevators, bland food, a risk of being placed very far from the lobby and pool, and the fact no other major resort areas connect to it. At least Port Orleans, for nearly the same money, has boats to Disney Springs; from Caribbean Beach, all connections are by road, so it's strongly recommended to have a car here.

900 Cayman Way, Lake Buena Vista. www.disneyworld.com. © **407/934-7639** or 407/934-3400. 2,112 units. $194–$363 standard doubles. Extra person $15. Children 17 and younger stay free in parent's room. **Amenities:** Restaurant; food court; arcade; heated pool; 6 smaller pools in the villages; kids' pool; parking $19/day; free Wi-Fi.

Disney's Coronado Springs Resort ★

Built to attract convention crowds with a vibe to match, it nonetheless has fans for its subdued tone. The well-planted grounds, done in a hacienda style around a pond, are far-flung (some rooms are a 15-minute hike from the lobby, which gets old), and rooms, with kings (for two) or queens (for four), have a single sink, as at the Values. The food court is above average, though, as is the pool area (with a 123-foot slide) themed after a Mayan pyramid, and there's a cocktail lounge, Rix, with a semblance of sophistication. The hotel is 10 minutes' drive from any parks. If you need a room accessible for those with disabilities and the cheaper hotels are out of such units, you can try here, where there is an inventory of 99 rooms. In 2019 it opens a new 15-story tower with 500 more rooms, which gives some guests a new option for fairly decent views quite near Hollywood Studios.

1000 Buena Vista Dr., Lake Buena Vista. www.disneyworld.com. © **407/934-7639** or 407/939-1000. 1,921 units. $208–$388 doubles. Extra person $15. Children 17 and younger stay free in parent's room. **Amenities:** Restaurant; grill/food court; arcade; health club & limited spa; 4 outdoor heated pools; kids' pool; parking $19/day; free Wi-Fi.

Disney's Fort Wilderness Resort & Campground ★★

Not to be confused with the Wilderness Lodge, an imitation of Yellowstone Lodge, this 780-acre wooded enclave near Magic Kingdom consists of campsites and mobile home–style cabins with decks and grills that sleep six on a mix of beds, pullouts, and bunks. Camping and RV parking under the thick pines are far and away the cheapest and most distinctive way to sleep on property, but it's twice the market rate, and without equipment (tents are $30, cots $4, if a group hasn't booked them first). The nightly marshmallow roast and outdoor Disney film screenings are perennial hits.

3520 N. Fort Wilderness Trail, Lake Buena Vista. www.disneyworld.com. © **407/934-7639** or 407/824-2900. 784 campsites, 408 wilderness cabins. $62–$190 campsite/RV doubles, $377–$655 wilderness cabin doubles. Children 17 and younger stay free in parent's room. **Amenities:** Restaurant; grill; babysitting; extensive outdoor activities (archery; fishing; horseback, pony, carriage, and hay rides; campfire programs; boat rental; and more); 2 outdoor heated pools; kids' pool; character dining; 2 lighted tennis courts; parking $19/day; free Wi-Fi.

Disney's Port Orleans and French Quarter ★★ An unwieldy name for an unwieldy property. It's actually two resorts, both built on a canal and awkwardly fused together. The French Quarter (1,000 rooms), built along right angles on simulated streets, purports to sorta imitate the real one in New Orleans. Riverside (2,048 rooms), where buildings are more successful pastiches on magnolia-lined Mississippi-style homes (Magnolia Bend, where princess-themed "Royal Rooms" have touches such as headboards with push-button light shows; about $50 surcharge) and rustic cabins (Alligator Bayou, where trundle beds sleep five—good for a Moderate resort), is the nicer of the two, because it has more water for rooms to face (though the privilege will cost you another $30 a night) and is the locale for most activities for the two resorts. The main pool at Riverside is less elaborate than French Quarter's, and room windows all face an exterior corridor there, although it has five pools to French Quarter's one. The properties are far enough apart (about 15 min. walking) that many people choose to use the free boat service linking them. The boats will also take you to Disney Springs—the trip is one of the most pleasant, least-known free rides at Disney World—but the parks are served only by buses.

2201 Orleans Dr., Lake Buena Vista. www.disneyworld.com. © **407/934-7639** or 407/934-5000. 3,048 units. $242–$357 doubles. Extra person $15. Children 17 and younger stay free in parent's room. **Amenities:** 2 restaurants; grill/food court; 6 heated outdoor pools; 2 kids' pools; arcade; parking $19/day; free Wi-Fi.

Shades of Green ★★★ Operated as a golf resort for 21 years before being handed to the military as the only Armed Forces Recreation Center (AFRC) in the continental U.S, it's the best deal on WDW soil if you or your spouse is an active or retired member of the U.S. military (a full list of eligibility requirements is posted online). Standard rooms are among the largest at Disney (just over 400 sq. ft.) and suites accommodate up to eight. All rooms have balconies or patios, and pool or golf-course views. *Bonus:* You can walk to the monorail and the Magic Kingdom.

1950 Magnolia Palm Dr. (across from the Polynesian Resort), Lake Buena Vista. www.shadesofgreen.org. © **888/593-2242** or 407/824-3400. 587 units. $98–$138 doubles (based on military rank); $289 6- to 8-person suites (regardless of rank). Extra person $15. Children 17 and younger stay free in parent's room. **Amenities:** 2 restaurants; cafe; health club; arcade; 2 heated outdoor pools; kids' pool; 2 lighted tennis courts; parking $19/day; free Wi-Fi.

VALUE RESORTS

Although the Mouse pushes you toward its most expensive hotels by making them so cool, Disney, in fact, has more "Value" rooms: 9,504 of them, more than many midsize cities have in total—available mostly for $100 to $200. The T-shaped building blocks with outdoor corridors can feel at times like thin-walled battery-hen hutches, gurgling with noisy plumbing and seething with kids who don't realize how sound carries (especially when school groups and cheerleader meets are in town). The walk to each hotel's lobby/food building can be a marathon. There are elevators.

FACILITIES   Value rooms are motel-style, often of standard cinder-block construction and exterior corridors. They come with two full beds, but a few have kings (request one when you reserve). Rooms fit four (there's a $10 daily charge for each third and fourth adult over 17), plus one child under 3—a full room would be a mighty tight squeeze. If your party is bigger, spring for a six-person Family Suite, which is usually just two rooms with a door banged through and a minikitchen (little fridge, microwave, coffeemaker) added. Those are at the All-Star Music resort and Art of Animation, where the design is more spacious, but at $240 (lowest price at Music) to $303 (lowest price at Animation), you can do *much* better outside the World. There's no room service, but you can have pizza delivery from late afternoon until midnight.

The food court, front desk, and sundries shop are all in the same building by the bus stops to the parks, and some rooms are a 15-minute walk away unless you shell out $15 to $20 more for a "Preferred" room.

TRANSPORTATION   No Value or Moderate resort is connected to a theme park by monorail. Roads are your only option, be it by bus or your car.

Disney's All-Star Movies/Disney's All-Star Music/Disney's All-Star Sports ★

Depending on your point of view, at the Value resorts, Disney treats you either like a second-class guest or like an average American family on vacation. The fun is in the outdoor areas, not in the rooms, which are only faintly themed. The setup of all three is identical—an expanse of concrete-block buildings at the edge of the property studded with enormous emblems, as if a giant had spilled the Legos in his toy box. But because they're older (they opened in the late 1990s) and there's no enlivening central pond, they are the last-choice Values. At the very least, sinks are outside of the toilet-and-shower room, which eases life for multitasking families. Of the three, I prefer Movies, not just because it's the youngest (opened 1999), but also because its exterior is laden with Disney-specific iconography while its sisters stick to dull musical and sports-equipment icons. Disney shuttle buses also tend to stop there last on their circuit of the three, which cuts transportation time. Then again, some choose Sports for the same reason, because it's the first stop and so it's easier to get a seat there. (That concern says a lot about the Value resorts.) The Music is the only one with suites fitting six people.

Buena Vista Dr., Lake Buena Vista. www.disneyworld.com. © **407/934-1936.** 1,920 units each. Standard rooms $112–$239, family suites $277–$497, 3rd and 4th adult $10. Children 17 and younger stay free in parent's room. **Amenities:** Food court; arcade; babysitting; 2 outdoor heated pools; kids' pool; parking $13/day; free Wi-Fi.

Disney's Art of Animation Resort ★★★

This attractive 2012 addition benefits from theming more lavish than at other Values, including a spot-on Radiator Springs pool area. Family Suites have two bathrooms, convertible couches, and demi-kitchens (no stove). Standard *Little Mermaid* rooms are gorgeously and whimsically themed, too—better than at other Values. Suites draw on *Finding Nemo* (where there's the Big Blue pool, WDW's largest) and

The Lion King. Unfortunately, six-person suites cost three times more than basic four-person Value rooms, which is hard to justify.

1850 Century Dr., Lake Buena Vista. www.disneyworld.com. ☎ **407/938-7000.** 1,120 suites, 864 standard units. Standard rooms $153–$253, 6-person family suites $366–$595. **Amenities:** 3 pools; food court; kids' pools; arcade; parking $13/day; free Wi-Fi.

Disney's Pop Century Resort ★★ The largest Value resort (opened 2002, many rooms recently renovated) is a fair choice, with smallish (260 sq. ft.) rooms—one king bed or two queens—with one sink and one mirror, and for dining, a heaving central food court with quality akin to the average mall's. As if to counteract such dormlike austerity, the boxy sprawl of T-shaped buildings, some of which face a pleasant lake across from the Art of Animation Resort, is festooned with outsized icons of the late-20th-century: gigantic bowling pins, yo-yos, and Rubik's Cubes—which kids think is pretty cool.

1050 Century Dr., Lake Buena Vista. www.disneyworld.com. ☎ **407/938-4000.** 2,880 units. Rooms $130–$251. **Amenities:** Food court; 3 pools; kids' pools; arcade; jogging trail; parking $13/day; free Wi-Fi.

DISNEY VACATION CLUB

Disney sells timeshares, too. Because this isn't a real estate guide, there's no need to explain the fact that after you crunch the numbers, **Disney Vacation Club (DVC)** is economical only for people who never want to vacation anywhere that isn't Disney. DVC really needs to slow its roll, because it's grafting properties onto all the major hotels and ruining their views. Plus there are stand-alone properties including **BoardWalk Villas, Saratoga Springs Resort & Spa** and its **Treehouse Villas** built on platforms above the ground, **Old Key West,** and the **Riviera Resort** (coming 2019), serving hundreds of thousands of DVC investors. These units are heavily promoted around the resort and even inside the theme parks themselves, which Walt surely would have detested as a fantasy-killer. The company rents empty villa units to walk-up customers who have no intention of signing on any dotted lines, but the best ones are usually claimed by the time you book. During value season, the

---

The "Good Neighbor" Policy

Scattered throughout town are properties that brag Disney has certified them as "Good Neighbor" (www.wdwgoodneighborhotels.com). The appellation is mostly meaningless. It means that hotel will have shuttles, can sell Magic Your Way tickets, and screens a mesmerizing 24-hour "Must Do Disney" channel featuring the insanity-inducing Stacey Aswad, the world's most nose-wrinklingly perky Disney fan (to her, everything is "amazing"), and her favorites at each park. To be brutally honest, most Good Neighbor hotels are mediocre. Only the Good Neighbor properties on the west side of Apopka Vineland Road (mostly on Hotel Plaza Boulevard) enjoy half-hourly shuttles; the rest don't. Legoland's version, with its own shuttles, are sometimes called **"Bed & Brick"** hotels (☎ **800/979-9983**). So don't select a hotel just because it's a Good Neighbor hotel. Choose it because it's the right hotel for you.

simplest studio with a kitchen starts at an insane $368 (at Old Key West, the cheapest) a night, a multiple of what a vacation home costs outside the resort. One-bedrooms at the Contemporary Resort's Bay Lake Tower range $655 to $1,056—*a night.* Those Polynesian Village bungalows are sumptuous, and you can see Cinderella Castle from the spa tub on your private deck—but they cost $2,400 to $3,300 a night. All this is, of course, crazypants, so I cannot in good conscience suggest the average family will find any value in renting a DVC room. I have, though, now informed you they're available.

Non-Disney On-Property Hotels

The best way to think of these choices is "location without immersion." These properties are permitted to run their own shows on Disney turf, supplying convenience and often, higher standards than Disney's busy hotels. Bonnet Creek–area hotels (technically not on Disney property but you can only reach them on Disney roads) are newer, more remote, and nicer than the more tired ones on Hotel Plaza Boulevard, which are decades old but run their own bus systems to the Disney parks and are often within walking distance to Disney Springs. (For nearby hotels that aren't on property, see Lake Buena Vista, p. 257.)

EXPENSIVE

Four Seasons Resort Orlando at Walt Disney World Resort ★★★

Orlando's most genuinely luxurious resort is deep inside the custom-built gated community of Golden Oak, within sight of the Magic Kingdom. Four Seasons' largest property in the world is a stunner in both looks and service: Quiet, 500-square-foot (46 sq. m) rooms come with furnished balconies, walk-in closets, concierge iPads, and marble bathrooms. The par-71 golf course, once Disney's Osprey Ridge but now renovated by Tom Fazio, is also a bird sanctuary, and the landscaped 5-acre pool complex (with free sunscreen and valets bearing refreshments) goes on and on—adults-only pool, zero-entry family pool, lazy river with waterfalls, two waterslides in a faux fort. To see the fireworks just 2 miles away from your balcony, you must spring for a "Park View Room," which are as much as $300 more than a "Lake View Room" on the lower floors, or opt for a meal at the rooftop Capa restaurant. The sky-high rate, which is comparable to a Disney Deluxe hotel, comes with no resort fee and gets you a lot more: daytime babysitting for kids 4 to 12 is free and kids 5 and under eat free. Its Goofy breakfast is one of the best character meals because it's less crowded and you get lots of photo time with him. If you can afford such pampering, it does it better than nearly any other property in town. The free shuttle is on a fixed schedule and doesn't go to Disney Springs, so if you want flexibility, have your own car or hail an Uber.

10100 Dream Tree Blvd., Golden Oak. www.fourseasons.com/orlando. © **407/313-6868** or 407/313-7777. 434 units. From $529 for a standard double. No resort fee. Valet parking $30 (no self-parking). **Amenities:** 3 restaurants; 3 bars; 3 pools; splash zone and waterslides; lazy river; spa; tennis courts; 24-hr. fitness center; sundries shop; character breakfast; free kids' club; kids under 6 eat free; free Disney parks shuttle; free Wi-Fi.

Hilton Orlando Bonnet Creek ★ Linked to the Waldorf Astoria by a convention hall and set in 482 mostly unbuilt acres, the hotel has rooms that lack balconies, which is a real bummer, but it's on Disney turf, which counts for a lot. Kids eat free for breakfast and dinner, which is fortunate considering how expensive the restaurants are. The 3-acre pool area is done in contemporary stonework—a bit like riding a lazy river in a hotel bathroom—and is abuzz with cocktails and activities. Overall, it's a fine place to disappear but it's too large and corporate to be romantic. And that resort fee! *Resort fee warning:* $40/night.

14100 Bonnet Creek Resort Lane, Orlando. www.hiltonbonnetcreek.com. © **407/597-3600.** 1,001 units. $134–$309 standard king. Parking $27/night (self), $35/night (valet). Resort fee $40/night. **Amenities:** 6 restaurants; coffee bar; pool bar; pool with activities; Disney shop; golf course; business center; fitness club; spa (at neighboring Waldorf Astoria); game room; free meals for kids under 12 at Harvest Bistro; free Disney shuttles; free golf club rental after 2pm; free local and toll-free calls; free Wi-Fi.

Waldorf Astoria Orlando ★★★ The first time the Waldorf expanded its brand outside of Manhattan it was in Orlando, and while the original's Upper East Side ethic was traded for Florida's tropical colors, the service standard is noticeably higher than at most other Orlando luxury hotels. Between the Rees Jones–designed par-72 golf course, the formally arranged adults-only swimming pool, the high-end Bull & Bear steakhouse, and the sink-deeper-into-slumber beds, this is the best choice of all the Bonnet Creek properties. If the price is similar to the Hilton, book here; for the same money you'll get perks such as bathrobes, better-aligned views of distant fireworks, and much more attentive service. You may use the lazy river of the Hilton next door. *Resort fee warning:* $40/night.

14200 Bonnet Creek Resort Lane, Orlando. www.waldorfastoriaorlando.com. © **407/597-5500.** 498 units. $209–$449 double queen. Parking (valet only) $35/night. Resort fee $40/night. **Amenities:** 5 restaurants; pool; kids' activities; free bike rental; free welcome cocktail; spa; fitness center; free practice at golf course; free golf club rental after 2pm; free local and toll-free calls; free Disney shuttles; free Wi-Fi.

Walt Disney World Swan and Dolphin ★ Rewards points are a main appeal to the Starwood-run Swan and Dolphin, which are linked by a footbridge over the lake they share. Former Disney CEO Michael Eisner controversially allowed outside corporations to intrude on resort property, and the result was these dated 1989 exteriors—let's regret the 56-foot-tall dolphin statues. No doubt: Staff is distracted, but the properties are stuffed with amenities and the location never quits—you can walk to Epcot's side door in 15 minutes and Hollywood Studios in 20, avoiding the bus. Both specialize in conferences, with lobby bars, steakhouses, and sushi counters to suit, although they strive to welcome families, too (rooms fit five and there are tons of poolside activities). Rooms and common spaces just enjoyed a modernizing renovation (blues, grays, chrome, more outlets). They're hospitality robots that lack the tonal fantasy at Disney-run hotels, but guests get the same perks as at a Disney-run hotel including 60-day advance Fastpass+ bookings—except no Magical

Express from the airport, no access to the Dining Plan, and no ability to make park purchases by room key or MagicBand. ***Resort fee warning:*** $28/night.

1500 Epcot Resorts Blvd., Lake Buena Vista. www.swandolphin.com. ☎ **407/934-4000.** Swan: 756 units. $241–$505 non-club standard. Dolphin: 1,509 units. $221–$579 non-club doubles. Extra person $25. Children 17 and younger stay free in parent's room. Parking $23/night (self), $33/night (valet). Resort fee (both) $28/night. **Amenities:** 12 restaurants; cafe; character meals; babysitting; free domestic phone calls; kids' program (2 hrs. free if parents eat in one of its restaurants); game room; health club & spa; 5 heated outdoor pools; room service; 4 lighted tennis courts; Wi-Fi included with resort fee.

Wyndham Grand Orlando Resort Bonnet Creek ★

This resort caps off a crowded development of more than 1,000 timeshare villas around a pretty 10-acre lake at the south end of Disney property. When you stay here, you can roam the campus, dipping into pools themed after Caribbean fortresses and pirate ships, barbecuing on public grills. It's a sweet setup, and the fact that it's well-located among Disney's parks makes it better, but ho-hum rooms, aggressive timeshare sales, and a noticeably disaffected staff keep it from being a favorite. ***Resort fee warning:*** $28/night.

14651 Chelonia Pkwy., Orlando. www.wyndhamgrandorlando.com. ☎ **407/390-2300.** 400 units. $143–$249 standard room. Parking $22/night (self), $29/night (valet). Resort fee $28/night. **Amenities:** 4 restaurants; coffee bar; pool with access to 5 others; 2 lazy rivers; spa; fitness center; kids' activities; gift shop; jogging trail; game room; free Wi-Fi.

MODERATE

B Resort & Spa ★★

The onetime Royal Plaza Hotel (built in 1972), convenient to both I-4 and Disney Springs, completed a gut renovation in 2014. New threads and surfaces were laid on the old, finicky 17-story tower, and in place of a tired bed bunker you now have an airy Miami-flavored resort that smells great and is suffused in whites and clean lines. King rooms are much larger than double-queen ones, but all are sizable, and higher-floor "Stunning" (that's the name) rooms claim views. Ringing the zero-entry pool, "Chic" rooms come with bunk beds. The B stands apart from the others in Disney Springs for providing a grown-up stay that's family-friendly and affordable but that doesn't feel too much like a machine, so the fact it comes with Extra Magic Hours is just gravy. The ground-floor restaurant, American Kitchen, has a Ford F1 pickup truck parked in the center. The B often offers 3-for-2 deals on its website. ***Resort fee warning:*** $34/night.

1905 Hotel Plaza Blvd., Lake Buena Vista. www.BResortLBV.com. ☎ **407/828-2828.** 394 units. Typically $101–$186 doubles. Parking $22/night (self), $28/night (valet). Resort fee $34/night. **Amenities:** Restaurant; heated pool; pool bar; tennis courts; spa; 24-hr. fitness center; sundries shop; free Disney shuttle; access to Extra Magic Hours; 60-day advance Fastpass+ booking; free Wi-Fi.

Best Western Lake Buena Vista—Disney Springs Resort Area ★

Another motel-grade tourist machine on Hotel Plaza Boulevard nearly beside Disney Springs, this 18-story creaker (built in 1971) could use a brush-up (rooms are dark as caves, there are few electrical sockets, and the pool is punier than what they'd build today). But it distinguishes itself by having a small balcony for every room, which is better than some of the other joints on this strip. It's a fair mid-budget option if you can score a deal online (to pay three digits would be a stretch), and if you're lucky, your room will be high enough to offer fireworks views. *The biggest bonus:* You get Extra Magic Hours. *Resort fee warning:* $14/night.

2000 Hotel Plaza Blvd., Lake Buena Vista. www.lakebuenavistaresorthotel.com. ✆ **407/ 828-2424.** 325 units. $69–$125 2-queen rooms, $10 sleeper sofa. Parking $8/night (self), $12/night (valet). Resort fee $14/night. **Amenities:** 2 restaurants; snack bar; pool with children's pool; arcade; fitness center; sundries shop; frequent Disney shuttle; access to Extra Magic Hours; 60-day advance Fastpass+ booking; free Wi-Fi.

DoubleTree Suites By Hilton Orlando—Disney Springs Area ★

One of the rabble lining the road leading to Disney Springs, this decent corporate choice offers standard rooms measuring 540 square feet, including a living area with pullout couch, microwave, minifridge, and small dining table, plus a bedroom with a king bed or two queens; not a bad setup for families, and not bad for the price. It also bestows blatantly preferential treatment upon Hilton Honors members—higher-floor rooms, $5 cooked breakfast upgrades from the included continental, free Wi-Fi. So just join that for free before you arrive.

2305 Hotel Plaza Blvd., Lake Buena Vista. ✆ **407/934-1000.** www.hilton.com. 229 units. $110–$222. Parking $22/night (self), $27/night (valet). No resort fee. **Amenities:** Restaurant; pool; bar; tennis court; fitness center; playground; regular Disney shuttles; access to Extra Magic Hours; 60-day advance Fastpass+ booking; free Wi-Fi.

Wyndham Lake Buena Vista ★

Packaged as a tower (232 of its rooms) and the separate Garden (394 rooms in an echoing five-story courtyard building), Wyndham gets passing, but not flying, marks. You check in here because of its proximity (a 5-minute walk to Disney Springs), the Extra Magic Hours access (at a rate lower than the Mouse's hotels), and the only sanctioned Disney character breakfast on Hotel Plaza Boulevard (three mornings a week). The polished lobby makes everything seem more luxurious than it is—rooms are uninspired and motel-style, sometimes reeking of cleaning chemicals, in the Garden the sole window faces an outdoor corridor—but the kid-friendly if overworked staff boosts the value, which is undeniable. Ask for a Tower Room on the west side (floors 9–19) for a limited view of Lake Buena Vista. *Resort fee warning:* $25/night.

1850 Hotel Plaza Blvd., Lake Buena Vista. ✆ **407/209-3126.** www.wyndhamlake buenavista.com. 626 units. $84 doubles with courtyard view, $115 doubles in tower. Parking $10/night. Resort fee $25/night. **Amenities:** Restaurant; 3 lounges; character breakfast (Tues, Thurs, Sat); babysitting; children's activity program; health club; spa tub; 2 outdoor heated pools; 2 lighted tennis courts; free bus service to WDW parks; transportation to non-Disney parks for a fee; access to Extra Magic Hours; 60-day advance Fastpass+ booking; free Wi-Fi.

Inside Universal Orlando

By 2020, there will be eight hotels on Universal property totaling 9,000 rooms operated by the Loews hotel group, and for the first time, it has created a

"Value" category that means some of them come cheaper than comparable hotels just blocks away. There are strong advantages that come with the higher-priced ones. First, most hotels are within 15 minutes' walk of the parks, and three are connected by a free boat that runs continuously into the wee hours. Guests can use their room key to make charges throughout the resort, they get into Harry Potter an hour early, and at three hotels, they can join the Express line at the two parks' best attractions—that perk has the effect of freeing up a vacation schedule. Guests can also drink and dine all night at CityWalk next door without having to drive or wait for a bus. Use the hotels' website to find Hot Deals, which grants discounts of 20% to 30% on specified nights; the website also posts floor plans of all room types.

The Universal property is hemmed in by lots of real-world restaurants where prices are realistic, and free shuttles to SeaWorld are provided once a day. So unlike cloistered Disney, when you're at Universal, you're linked to the real Orlando, and there's more food flexibility. At Easter and during the December holidays, rates are, of course, higher. But there are no resort fees!

EXPENSIVE

Hard Rock Hotel ★★★   Besides being the city's most convenient hotel for any theme park—the two parks are both a 10-minute walk away—the Hard Rock, which is miles ahead of any other Hard Rock hotel in America, has more perks for the money than most of the city's similarly priced hotels. Rooms have genuinely funky furniture, tons of mirrors, two sinks (one in and one out of the bathroom), two big beds, and music systems. The ginormous pool, which imitates a beach gently descending to depth, has not only a substantial waterslide but also underwater speakers through which you can hear the party music. (They really bring out the finger cymbals in "Livin' on a Prayer.") Halls are lined with rock memorabilia (Whoa! Outfits worn by Lady Gaga AND Elvis). The Hard Rock truly walks the rock walk: The last Thursday of the month, the lobby is taken over by the rollicking Velvet Sessions (www.velvetsessions.com) concert series for classic acts, like Howard Jones, John Waite, and Survivor.

5000 Universal Blvd., Orlando. www.hardrockhotels.com/orlando. © **888/832-7155** or 407/503-7625. 650 units. Rooms $254–$394. Parking $22/night (self), $29/night (valet). **Amenities:** 3 restaurants; cocktail lounge; ice cream shop; babysitting; supervised children's program; Club Level rooms; fitness center; pool with activities and bar; free Wi-Fi.

Loews Portofino Bay Hotel ★★★   Universal's priciest and most romantic option faithfully re-creates the famous Italian fishing village, down to the angle of the boat docks, the bolted-down Vespas, and live opera music nightly along the waterfront. Beyond that spectacular gimmick (said to have been Steven Spielberg's idea, like much at Universal), rooms are of a particularly high standard—standard ones are a generous 450 square feet and have top-end beds. Because the resort is the farthest on property from the parks (but still only about 5 minutes by quick-loading boat or 15 minutes by foot), it tends to appeal to couples; however, a few suites are decked out in a *Despicable Me* theme to please your minions. Restaurants here—including upscale Bice and family-favorite Mamma Della's—are worth staying in for, plus there are a

Starbucks, an upscale pizzeria, and a gelateria on property. Choose from two enormous pools—one with a sand beach, zero entry, and waterslides, the other with palm trees, bocce, and a Mediterranean vibe—or a small third option for a cool break in your day.

5601 Universal Blvd., Orlando. www.universalorlando.com. ℰ **888/430-4999** or 407/503-1000. 750 units. Double queen or king rooms $279–$474. Parking $22/night (self), $29/night (valet). **Amenities:** 3 restaurants; ice cream shop; Starbucks; supervised children's programs; Club Level rooms; fitness center; Mandara spa; 3 pools with activities and bar; nightly opera show; free Wi-Fi.

Loews Royal Pacific Resort ★★★

The least expensive luxury option at Universal does an apt impression of the South Seas in the 1930s, and rooms were just renovated in 2016 with muted cream colors dominated by giant flowers on the walls. It's more luxurious yet cheaper than the Disney Polynesian, with a lush pool area (sandy beach, winding garden paths, interactive water play area) and a sophisticated, wood-and-wicker look. The standard is high: very soft robes, cushy beds with fat pillows, and marble-top chests. It's right over the road from Islands of Adventure; many rooms have a panorama of it. In any other city, the Royal Pacific might be everyone's favorite resort. Here, though, its subtler charms get lost in the crowd.

6300 Hollywood Way, Orlando. www.universalorlando.com. ℰ **888/430-4999** or 407/503-3000. 1,000 units. Rooms $224–$329. Parking $22/night (self), $29/night (valet). **Amenities:** 3 restaurants; sushi bar; cocktail lounge; pool with activities and bars; free Wi-Fi.

MODERATE

Universal's Cabana Bay Beach Resort ★★ Cabana Bay plays the role of a family vacation escape by kitsching it up as a tacky 1950s beach hotel. Geometric fabrics, teals and lemons, swooping Space Age architecture, a Jack LaLanne–branded gym, and a 10-lane bowling alley all wink at the midcentury

---

ENDLESS SUMMER: UNIVERSAL HOTELS go budget

Universal is smashing the three-digit hotel room price barrier! But this time, downward. Starting in August, its two-hotel **Endless Summer** complex begins opening on the old Wet 'n Wild lot. When finished, the Loews-run hotels (**Surfside Inn and Suites,** open 2019, and **Dockside Inn and Suites,** open 2020) will have 2,800 simple, beach-themed rooms starting at $73 per night for a 7-night stay ($85 for 4 nights) and 1,450 two-bedroom suites sleeping six starting at $111 ($131 for 4 nights). Yes—Universal's family suites will cost

just $1 more than Disney's cheapest *standard* rooms, 15 minutes south. Endless Summer won't give you room service, but it will grant a grab-and-go counter, a bar, pizza delivery, and early entry to its parks. Guests must connect to the rest of Univeral by shuttle bus because the resort is actually right on I-Drive; that also means guests benefit from not being trapped on resort property paying resort prices for food and activities. *7000 Universal Blvd., Orlando.* ℰ *888/273-1311; www.universal orlando.com.*

era. Things may *look* old but they're decidedly modern, down to the ample outlets in the bedrooms, gated parking, and air-conditioning that's whisper quiet. On the north end of the complex, where a motor court theme prevails, you'll find 600 family suites with kitchen areas (microwave, no stove) that sleep six somewhat tightly, two on a sofa bed. The music never stops in the two ginormous pool areas, which have Universal's only lazy river, and guests get a special side entrance to Volcano Bay next door (some rooms added in 2017 look right into the park and at its iconic volcano). But there's a trade-off: There's no Express pass privileges (you do get into the parks early), no room service, and to reach the action, you'll have take a shuttle to CityWalk—there is no water taxi to this hotel. (Sapphire Falls, priced a notch higher, has that.)

6550 Adventure Way, Orlando. www.universalorlando.com. ✆ **888/430-4999** or 407/ 503-4000. 2,200 units. Standard rooms from $119–$134, family suites $174–$284, with discounts for stays longer than 4 nights. Parking $12/night. **Amenities:** Food court; 10-lane bowling alley with food; 2 pools; 2 pool bars; waterslide; lazy river; fitness center; free standard-speed Wi-Fi (full-speed $15/day).

Loews Sapphire Falls Resort ★★★

The Modern Caribbean-inspired Sapphire Falls is clean and understated. It's also my favorite of Universal's moderate options because the service is strong, parking is sheltered, and you can take ferries or walks to the parks (the more crowded Cabana Bay only has buses). Most rooms have either a king or two queens (321 sq. ft.), but for $100 more you can have a King Suite with a separate sitting area (595 sq. ft.), and for $200 more there are Kids Suites with a separate double-twin bedroom for children. Quick-service food options are short, but the 16,000-square-foot pool area, which catches sun until sunset, is a world unto itself. A stay comes with early entry to The Wizarding World of Harry Potter, but not Express entry.

6601 Adventure Way, Orlando. www.universalorlando.com. ✆ **888/430-4999.** 1,000 units. Double queen or king rooms $179–$250. Covered parking $22/night (self parking), $29/night (valet parking). **Amenities:** 2 restaurants; 2 bars; fitness center; pool with activities and bar; free standard-speed Wi-Fi (full-speed $15/day).

Universal's Aventura Hotel ★★

New as of August 2018, Universal's sixth hotel, a lower-priced choice, is different from its sisters—it's a 16-story tower with a sort of mild modern Miami, sleeker urban aesthetic. Tucked down by Sapphire Falls and Volcano Bay, it has Bar 17 Bistro, an open-air rooftop bar and grill with fantastic views, plus rooms in which bedside tablets control things like the TV, the temperature, and pizza delivery. Guests won't receive Express privileges and they'll have to link with the parks by bus, but they will be allowed early park entry in the mornings. Standard rooms (258 sq. ft.—not giant, but enlived by decorative glass panels and floor-to-ceiling windows) have either two queen beds or a single king plus a pull-out couch, so they fit four. Deluxe rooms, starting at $30 more, are high enough for city views or to peer into Volcano Bay. A food hall promises fresh ingredients and quick global cuisine.

6725 Adventure Way, Orlando. www.universalorlando.com. ✆ **888/273-1311.** 600 units. Double queen or king rooms start at $116–$144 ($169 with the best views), with discounts for longer stays, Kids suite rooms sleeping 5 from $216. Covered parking $14/night. **Amenities:** Food court; 2 bars; fitness center; pool with bar; free standard-speed Wi-Fi (full-speed $15/day).

U.S. 192 Area Accommodations

West of Disney along U.S. 192 is quickly becoming a choice area where you'll find the highest density of vacation homes (p. 264), for starters. And at the Western Way and State Route 429, out Disney's back door, four new hotels totaling 998 rooms are being constructed in the Flamingo Crossings development: a Residence Inn, a Fairfield Inn, a Homewood Suites, and one more Hilton-branded moderate property.

But on U.S. 192 East across the I-4 dividing line is the lowest rung in the Orlando tourist ladder, both in price and class. Most of the stuff here was built in the 1970s boom in an outdated concrete motel style, and now it's settled into a category that could charitably be called ultra-budget—if you saw the 2017 movie *The Florida Project*, you saw the decay into which some of these forgotten inns have sunk (the movie's setting, the lavender Magic Castle, is a real motel at 5055 West 192, though it's not as desperate and grotty as the film version). Those places are technically located in the town of Kissimmee, which posts deals at **www.experiencekissimmee.com**. In this region, shuttles are often available to Disney, but not always to SeaWorld or Universal.

EXPENSIVE

Gaylord Palms ★ The Gaylord, run by fee-mad Marriott, is geared to captive audiences attending meetings, so although its scenery is extravagant, so are its incidental charges. Beneath its mighty glass atrium is a 4½-acre Florida-themed ecosystem of gator habitats, caves, indoor ponds, sand sculptures, restaurants, and a full-size sailboat—all of that makes for an attraction unto itself, and to face it, you'll pay about $25 extra. Rooms sleep five and sport unusually nice granite-lined bathrooms. If Disney weren't right outside, you might never leave, what with the on-site Cypress Springs mini water park, adults-only pool, and the Relâche Spa & Salon. It also schedules family activities and an annual holiday ICE! extravaganza (p. 276). Until 2021, it's undergoing expansion that will add 303 rooms, so get a room away from the construction zone. *Resort fee warning:* $22/night.

6000 W. Osceola Pkwy., Kissimmee. www.gaylordhotels.com/gaylord-palms. *℘* **800/ 429-5673** or 407/586-2000. 1,406 units. $169 king or double-queen rooms. Parking $22 (self), $33 (valet). Resort fee $22/night. **Amenities:** 5 restaurants; sports bar; 2 pools with splash zone; fitness center; spa; arcade; room service; free local phone calls; park shuttles (Disney free, others charged); free bottled water; Wi-Fi $15/day (fast $22/day).

The Grove Resort & Spa Orlando ★★

Just before the Great Reccession, a British developer took $200 million of other people's money, began constructing a massive 900-room lakeside resort on 106 acres by a conservation area west of Disney—and then fled the country. It sat grimly half-built for 7 years, a white elephant in the swamp, but finally, the saga has a happy ending. New owners have finished and expanded it, and now it's a full-service moderate resort that feels if not quite luxurious, then surely more expensive than it is. It's a fully equipped resort comprised of huge comfortable apartments, each with a fully equipped kitchen, washer/dryer, tub, and screened-in balcony; even the smallest are 975 sq. ft. There's only every-other-day cleaning, but to sweeten the pot, the grounds face a small Old Florida lake (only electric or human-powered boats, available for rent, are allowed, and so is fishing). Families are also drawn to the small private water park, separate from the adult pools, with a little slide tower and lazy river. Don't let the Winter Garden address scare you; I've timed it, and the drive to Disney's gate on Western Way via backroads is 7 minutes. In fact, the semirural location sets it apart from competitors, like a resort oasis in a wide wilderness of green. *Resort fee warning:* $25/night.

14501 Grove Resort Ave., Winter Garden. www.groveresortorlando.com. *℘* **844/203-0209** or 407/545-7500. 1,170 units. 1-bedroom, 1-bath units from $179; 2-bedroom, 2-bath units from $199; 3-bedroom, 2-bath units from $229. Lake view with distant Disney fireworks view about $65 more. Covered parking $10. Resort fee $25/night. **Amenities:** Restaurant; water park with 2 slides, FlowRider, and lazy river; 3 pools; 2 pool bars with grills; indoor cocktail lounge; fishing; electric boats; coffee bar and sundries shop; 24-hr. fitness center; free local and toll-free calls; business center; free Wi-Fi.

Hyatt Regency Grand Cypress Resort ★★★

Probably the most complete resort campus near Disney, the stepped tower packs every conceivable amenity into a lush 1,500-acre campus located practically inside Walt Disney World. There are 45 holes of golf, an unforgettable waterfall-and-cavern-studded lagoon pool system (for my money, it's the best pool of any Orlando resort), lush trails wrapping around a private pond, Lake Windsong, horses, and top-floor views of the fireworks at Epcot and the Magic Kingdom. With so many extras (kayaks, paddleboats, minigolf), it feels like what resorts used to be. Contrary to its decidedly 1980s atrium construction (and a snippy parrot, Merlot, who was allowed to remain in the lobby long after the previous tropical decor was retired), rooms—maximum guests: four; 360 square feet—have an almost Asian sleekness with rain showers, chaise lounges, and adapter panels to play multimedia on the 37-inch HDTV. Each year the resort gets a

Kissimmee Area Hotels

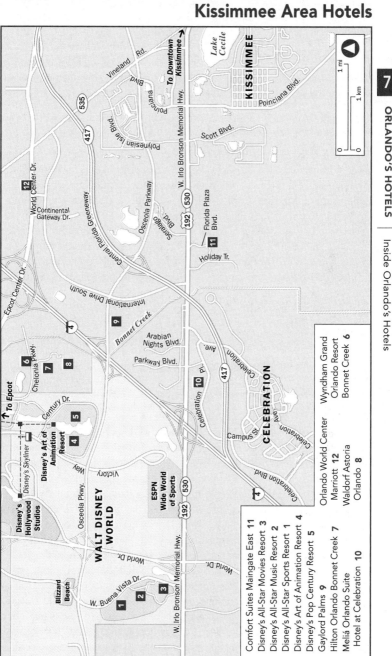

Comfort Suites Maingate East **11**
Disney's All-Star Movies Resort **3**
Disney's All-Star Music Resort **2**
Disney's All-Star Sports Resort **1**
Disney's Art of Animation Resort **4**
Disney's Pop Century Resort **5**
Gaylord Palms **9**
Hilton Orlando Bonnet Creek **7**
Meliá Orlando Suite
Hotel at Celebration **10**

Orlando World Center
Marriott **12**
Waldorf Astoria
Orlando **8**
Wyndham Grand
Orlando Resort
Bonnet Creek **6**

little better; the signature restaurant, Hemingway's, is in its own romantic courtyard pavilion and newly opened LakeHouse does clean, fresh ingredients and gorgeous sushi. I've seen $85 Priceline bids accepted—such a steal for a place that deserves to be packed. *Resort fee warning:* $30/night.

1 Grand Cypress Blvd., Lake Buena Vista. www.hyattgrandcypress.com. ℂ **800/233-1234** or 407/239-1234. 815 units. $135–$369 king or double queen. Parking $20 (self), $29 (valet). Resort fee $30/night. **Amenities:** 2 year-round restaurants; 3 cocktail bars; coffee bar; pool; babysitting; kids' club; business center; gift shop; game room; tennis courts; golf course; biking; trails; rock climbing wall; 24-hr. fitness center; salon; beach; free park shuttles; free throttled Wi-Fi (full-speed $5/day).

Orlando World Center Marriott ★

Mighty large, mighty busy, and mighty impersonal, the 200-acre World Center rises like a citadel over I-4, a straight shot into Disney on Epcot Center Drive. Although handsome and appointed as a Marriott resort should be—the pool and slide tower are among the best in town—but it's the infrastructure that does all the work. If you need more than that, any service whatsoever, expect waiting in line, inflated prices for food, and even to pay a fee for Wi-Fi, which by now should stamped out by mass revolt. The World Center mostly has what I call "points appeal"—it's a fine place to cash in rewards, but it will never be your favorite. Spring for the valet, because the parking structure is unforgivably far from the building—it requires a shuttle, which leaves a sour taste. *Alert:* "Resort View" rooms often mean "Parking View." *Resort fee warning:* $28/night.

8701 World Center Dr., Orlando. www.worldcentermarriott.com. ℂ **800/380-7931** or 407/239-4200. 2,009 units. $175–$369 king or double queen. Parking $22 (self), $35 (valet). Resort fee $28/night. **Amenities:** 6 restaurants; 3 bars; 2 pools with 3-waterslide tower and bar/grill; 18-hole golf course; golf school; 24-hr. fitness center; spa; 4 tennis courts; 2 sand volleyball courts; kids' activities; throttled Wi-Fi $15/day (high-speed $20).

The Villas of Grand Cypress Resort ★★★

This is what you envision when you dream of a Florida vacation: well-appointed, condo-like villa units under softly drooping trees—travel in February, when they bloom in multiple colors. Off the sunken living rooms, doors open to a private patio, which itself cascades down to your own deck on a glassy lake. Some open onto a Jack Nicklaus golf course; it's one of its main draws (nearly 100,000 rounds are played annually), and it surrounds the units, which makes a stay here feel like you're a world away from Disney even though you're so near—about 3 miles east from Cinderella Castle—that guests can see the fireworks. Villas are rich: full kitchens, huge leather couches, big dining table, washer/dryer, luxury bathrooms with a TV hidden behind the mirror, room service delivered by goft cart, and they encircle an easygoing pool complex. You can keep adding bedrooms with connecting doors; a 4-bedroom would sleep 10. (Bilevel "Club Suites" are just as nice, more like standard rooms but a huge 650 sq. ft. with 150-sq.-ft. terraces.) A stay here is like gaining access to two resorts, because guests have full access to the long list of amenities at the neighboring Hyatt Regency Grand Cypress (p. 252), home to one of Orlando's most epic pools. For all that you get, especially solitude so simple you can

Son of a Son of a Timeshare

This is not what you call wasting away. The $750-million Margaritaville Resort Orlando (8118 W. Irlo Bronson Memorial Hwy./U.S. 192, Kissimmee; www. margaritavilleresortorlando.com; ℂ 855/995/9099), a Jimmy Buffett–themed development, is being built on 320 acres on the south side of U.S. 192, 1 mile southwest of Disney's Animal Kingdom (but a circuitous 10-minute drive away). By late 2019, it will include a 184-room hotel (from $199), 900 conch house–style vacation cottages from 1 to 8 bedrooms, 300 timeshare units, and a 14-acre water park (3 slide towers, wave pool; open to the public spring 2019). Its SunsetWalk entertainment district is already open, including a 12-screen multiplex; Rock & Brews restaurant by KISS members Gene Simmons and Paul Stanley; a restaurant by country group Rascal Flatts; and a GameTime family arcade complex.

hear the night frogs sing, the price is incredibly good. There aren't many Orlando hotels that I would gladly live in. *Resort fee warning:* $30/night.

1 North Jacaranda, Lake Buena Vista. www.grandcypress.com. ℂ **877/330-7370** or 407/239-4700. 119 units. Club Suites from $179, 1-bedroom villas from $277, 2-bedroom villas from $389, discounts of 25% for advance purchase. Free parking. Resort fee $30/night per bedroom. **Amenities:** Pool with bar/grill; lounge; free local calls; free loaner bikes; free shuttle to Magic Kingdom, Disney Springs, and Tibet-Butler Nature Preserve; fitness center; catch-and-release fishing; daily activities; free shuttle to the Hyatt Regency Grand Cypress with free use of all its facilities; free Wi-Fi.

MODERATE

Meliá Orlando Suite Hotel at Celebration ★★

Suites (but not standard rooms) in this cloistered 240-room hotel have fully equipped kitchens including full-size fridges plus dishwashers. Many units, which are slightly stark, also have a little patio, and a queen-size pullout to sleep more people. Protected by the hotel's four curving buildings, a perfectly round vanishing-edge pool ringed with funky red pyramid umbrellas recalls South Beach style, so it's not the best choice for rambunctious kids. Getting a pool view adds about $20. It's in the low-rent jungle of U.S. 192, where it doesn't quite fit, but it's super close to Disney. *Resort fee warning:* $20/night.

225 Celebration Place, Celebration. www.meliaorlando.com. ℂ **407/964-7000** or 888/956-3542. 240 units. $89–$219 1-bedroom suites sleeping 4, 2-bedroom suites sleeping 8 $30 more, $135–$269 family suites sleeping 8. Free parking. Resort fee $20/night. **Amenities:** Restaurant with bar; pool; sauna; fitness center (offsite); free park shuttles; shuttles to Celebration village; free continental breakfast; free Wi-Fi.

INEXPENSIVE

Comfort Suites Maingate East ★★

My only recommendation on this stretch of U.S. 192, with attentive management, it's tucked just off the main drag a few miles east of Disney, with the restaurants and carnival-style amusements of Fun Spot and Old Town steps from the door—but not so near that the noise is truly annoying. The best rates are for "standard rooms" with either a king or queen bed, but you can get a "deluxe" two-bedroom one for

And Now, Two Warnings...

If you use a **debit card** (instead of a credit card) as collateral against any purchases you may make during your stay, your card may be temporarily charged $50 to $250 (or more) *per day,* whether or not you actually charge anything to your room. This policy can seriously deplete your account, leaving you with fewer funds than you might realize—and you won't see a credit back to your account until *up to 10 days after* you have checked out of your resort. Ask about your hotel's policy.

Also, Orlando police perennially fight the **pizza flyer scam,** in which shady outfits put menus under your hotel room door and then rip you off if you order. If you want to order food in, ask your hotel for its preferred vendors.

---

about $30 more, and all rooms are on the large side with minifridges, pullout couches (to up your occupancy, if needed) and microwaves for basic meal preparation. The elevators can be overwhelmed when it's at capacity.

2775 Florida Plaza Blvd., Kissimmee. www.comfortsuitesfl.com. ⓒ**888/784-8379.** 198 units. $89–$179 1-room suites. Free parking. **Amenities:** Pool with poolside bar; 24-hr. fitness center; sundries shop; game room; business center; free park shuttles; free hot breakfast buffet; free Wi-Fi.

Destiny Palms Hotel Maingate West ★ "Value for money" is the watchphrase in this rambling, old-style motel building on U.S. 192 west of Disney. The decor could use reviving (it could be termed "Early '80s Beige"), but the staff keeps things spotless, and that's what you want. Rooms come stocked with a toaster oven and minifridge; also included are free Wi-Fi and a continental breakfast upgraded with eggs, oatmeal, pancakes, and waffles. King rooms face the north parking lot and are on the small side; double queen rooms look south on some pleasing old-growth Florida woods. The east-facing pool (it, too, is motel-simple) also faces the trees, which keeps this place from feeling hemmed in. *Resort fee warning:* a puny $4.50/night. Why bother charging it?

8536 W. Irlo Bronson Memorial Hwy./U.S. 192, Kissimmee. www.destinypalmsmaingate. com. ⓒ**407/396-1600.** 104 units. $50–$70 doubles. Free parking. Resort fee $4.50/night. **Amenities:** Pool; free continental breakfast; free local calls; free Wi-Fi.

Quality Inn & Suites by the Parks ★★★ Scrupulously clean with fresh furniture and a professional staff, this three-level 1989 motel with elevators and outdoor corridors is top of the class for a budget choice. The courtyard pool is plain but immaculate, the beds made as tight as drums, and at breakfast it even does Mickey-face waffles. More expensive rooms have sleeper sofas and mini-kitchens. It's directly south of Disney's Animal Kingdom.

2945 Entry Point Blvd., Kissimmee. www.qualityinnbytheparks.com. ⓒ**855/849-1513** or 407/390-0204. 111 units. Doubles from $85. Free parking. No resort fee. **Amenities:** Pool; fitness center; free breakfast buffet; free Wi-Fi.

SpringHill Suites Orlando Flamingo Crossings/TownePlace Suites Orlando Flamingo Crossings ★★★ This area, a half-mile out its little-used western gate past Coronado Springs, is slowly being developed into Flamingo Crossings, a hub for lower-cost hotels. Getting to I-4 and the other attractions of Orlando requires driving across the busy Disney resort, but it's worth it for two new pristine Marriott-flagged hotels (opened 2016) with no parking or resort fees, tip-top management, and yet still undiscovered enough to yield very low prices. SpringHill offers doubles and queens with a desk partition (hence the "suites"), plus small fridges and microwaves, while TownePlace bumps up to a full-sized fridge. They share a big central pool area with a bar. For food options, take the toll expressway (State Road 429, $1.25) less than a mile south to U.S. 192.

13279 Flamingo Crossings Blvd., Winter Garden. www.marriott.com. © **407/507-1200.** SpringHill: 248 units. TownePlace: 250 units. Rooms from $87, 1-bedrooms from $105. No resort fee. Free parking. **Amenities:** Pool; spa; gym; sundries shop; free buffet breakfast; Magic Kingdom shuttle ($5); free Wi-Fi.

Lake Buena Vista

Roughly speaking, Lake Buena Vista is the area where the eastern end of Walt Disney World around Disney Springs meets exit 68 off I-4. LBV, as it's nicknamed, is more compact and higher-class than the comparable cluster of Kissimmee hotels along U.S. 192, a few miles south near Disney's southern gate. For breathing room, the best part of Lake Buena Vista is Palm Parkway, a lightly trafficked, winding, tree-lined avenue that's a secret shortcut to Universal skirting I-4. Drive north on it and you'll pass a turnoff for SeaWorld, a Walmart, a Whole Foods, and the restaurants of Sand Lake Road.

LBV has the highest occupancy rate in town, so you'll often pay higher prices (and meet lazier staff) than in Kissimmee or on I-Drive, and traffic stinks. Free shuttles around here tend to go to Disney but not to Universal or SeaWorld.

See the map on p. 232 for locations of the properties below.

MODERATE

Staybridge Suites Lake Buena Vista ★★ Close to lots of restaurants and Disney Springs, you'll find these apartment-like quarters (there are two TVs and the kitchens even have dishwashers). The three-level buildings don't have elevators, but overlook that fact and avoid the ground-floor rooms, which are darker and less private. The full breakfast is free and plentiful, and you can eat it indoors or out. There's also a well-used pool in one of the courtyards. It's for people who want a condo rental experience, including laundry, without renting an actual condo.

8751 Suiteside Dr., Orlando. www.sborlando.com. © **407/238-0777.** 150 units. $105–$145 1-bedrooms sleeping 4, $120–$176 2-bedrooms sleeping 8. Free rollaways and cribs. Free parking. No resort fee. **Amenities:** Full breakfast; heated pool; spa tub; business center; sundries shop; free Disney shuttle; free Wi-Fi.

INEXPENSIVE

Hawthorn Suites Lake Buena Vista ★ The decor is a touch dated (built in 2000, renovated in 2014), but the management is attentive and hard-working, so this L-shaped property, arranged around a quiet and uncomplicated kidney-shaped pool, is a safe budget pick. The special appeal of this place is its full kitchens, standard in all rooms, with dishwashers, stoves, cookware—everything you need to cook for yourself and save. All suites are one-bedroom suites, and the cheapest ones have two queen beds. There's no restaurant, but there are choices nearby, and access to both Disney and Universal is a 10-minute drive away—SeaWorld's even closer.

8303 Palm Pkwy., Orlando. www.hawthornlakebuenavista.com. ✆ **866/756-3778** or 407/597-5000. 120 suites. $89–$159 doubles. Free parking. No resort fee. **Amenities:** Pool; hot tub; small fitness center; free breakfast buffet; free Disney shuttle, $10 shuttle to other parks; game room; business center; sundries shop; free beer and wine at weekday manager receptions; free local calls; free Wi-Fi.

Hyatt Place Lake Buena Vista ★★

Opened in late 2016 and still well-run, it has the earmarks of the business-focused brand, which also happen to be useful for vacationers: large rooms divided into sleeping and sitting areas (with pullout couch) like low-cost junior suites, a kiosk for food, free breakfast, and free Wi-Fi. The pool's a little plain, but so what? Many other properties in the area date to the 1980s, so it's rare to find something so new out the side door to Disney Springs. You can walk to many places to eat.

8688 Palm Pkwy., Orlando. http://orlandolakebuenavista.place.hyatt.com. ✆ **407/778-5500.** 196 units. $90–$149 doubles. Free parking. No resort fee. **Amenities:** Pool; free buffet breakfast; business center; 24-hr. fitness center; free Wi-Fi.

International Drive, Universal

I-Drive is a good place to stay if you don't have a car because it's full of places to eat. It's also the only hotel zone with a semblance of street life. If you stay here, you'll be in the thick of the family-friendly come-ons, midway rides, souvenir hawkers, minigolf, and theme bars. You'll need wheels to reach Disney (most hotels offer shuttles, but not always to Disney, and not always free), although Universal is just across I-4 to the north and the dirt-cheap I-Ride Trolley (p. 271) links you with SeaWorld. Car traffic can clog I-Drive, but there's a workaround: Universal Boulevard, a block east, bypasses the mess.

EXPENSIVE

Hyatt Regency Orlando ★★ Hyatt's double skyscraper surpasses the expectations of a typical convention-center hotel, which it is, and delivers a luxurious if vaguely decorated stay above the gridlock of I-Drive. Expect space (415 sq. ft. is the norm but the maximum is 3–4 guests), an echoing lobby of white stone and marble, sculptural waterfalls, richly appointed bathrooms, ankle-level lights that switch on when they sense your movement, and other high-end touches that appeal to business travelers who come for its massive meeting halls. The free-form pool is pretty but not as frenetic as some other kid-focused ones, the fitness center is extremely well-stocked, and a collection of business-expense restaurants (an "Italian steakhouse," seafood) and a 24-hr. diner-style joint round out the well-balanced menu of options. The windows in the newer Regency Tower are larger, so ask for a View room

International Drive Hotels

Avanti Palms Resort and Conference Center **9**

Drury Inn Suites **11**

Fairfield Inn & Suites Orlando International Drive/Convention Center **12**

Hard Rock Hotel **2**

Holiday Inn Express & Suites —Orlando at SeaWorld **17**

Hyatt House Across from Universal Orlando Resort **4**

Hyatt Regency Orlando **14**

Loews Portofino Bay Hotel **1**

Loews Royal Pacific Resort **6**

Loews Sapphire Falls Resort **5**

Residence Inn Marriott Universal Studios **3**

Rosen Shingle Creek **15**

Sonesta ES Suites Orlando—International Drive **13**

TownePlace Suites Orlando at SeaWorld **16**

Universal's Cabana Bay Beach Resort **7**

Universal's Endless Summer Resort—Surfside Inn and Suites **10**

Universal's Aventura Hotel **8**

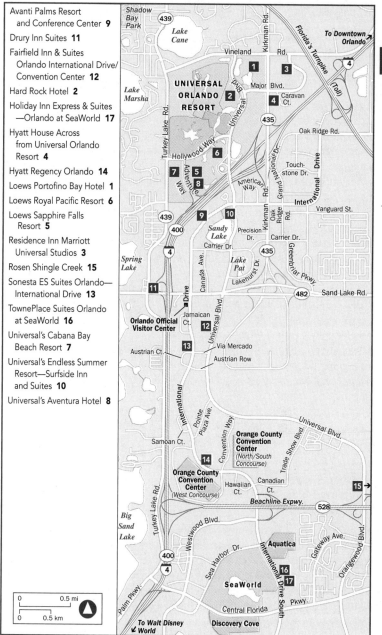

there—you'll spy the distant Disney fireworks. All in all, it's not cozy, but it's a solid hotel. *Resort fee warning:* $25/night.

9801 International Dr., Orlando. http://orlando.regency.hyatt.com. ℂ **407/284-1234.** 1,639 units. $139–$425 doubles or kings for up to 4. Parking $22 (self), $35 (valet). Resort fee $25/night. **Amenities:** 3 restaurants; cocktail bar; pool with children's area and activities; hot tub; babysitting; spa; bike rental; 24-hr. fitness center; tennis court; free Wi-Fi.

JW Marriott Grande Lakes Orlando/Ritz-Carlton Grande Lakes Orlando ★★

The two towers form a busy city unto themselves in a 500-acre plot east of SeaWorld. If you stay in one, you can use the main amenities of the other. The JW's 24,000-sq.-ft. pool area, landscaped with fake rocks, jungle greens, and a ¼-mile lazy river, is deservedly jammed on hot days, while the Ritz's water area is formal and refined. The JW's rooms' Florida-style furnishings (wicker, creamy greens and tans) won't be setting any trends, but the palatial beds and bathrooms might. The food is top-notch; restaurants by Melissa Kelly (**Primo**) and Norman Van Aken (**Norman's**) have earned plaudits for years; even the casual choices are delicious, and the property even grows some of its own ingredients. But none of it is cheap, and the remote location means you'll have to drive somewhere every time your stomach rumbles if you want to escape resort pricing. (It's a flaw; you'll spot guests coming back from local pizza joints and Wawa with cheaper provisions.) The 40,000-sq.-ft. Ritz-Carlton spa is one of the city's best and in its guest rooms, the pampering and quality are a notch higher than in the JW. Both have unobstructed views over a Greg Norman–designed golf course and a connected nature reserve (it's much larger than you'd think—you could get lost during an evening wander) where every diversion, from fishing to biking, is offered. It's truly full-service. Rates fluctuate wildly if there's a conference. *Resort fee warning:* $35/night.

4040 Central Florida Pkwy., Orlando. www.grandelakes.com. ℂ **800/576-5760** or 407/206-2400 for the Ritz; ℂ **800/576-5750** or 407/206-2300 for the JW Marriott. JW: 1,000 units, Ritz: 584 units. JW: From $179 doubles, Ritz: From $273 doubles. Parking (both) $28 (self), $35 (valet). Resort fee (both) $35/night. **Amenities:** 6 restaurants; 2 cafes; babysitting; 2 daily hr. of kids' club (Ritz only); spa; Club Level rooms; health club; golf course (normally membership-only); 2 outdoor heated pools; kids' pool; 3 tennis courts; kayaking; Starbucks; free local calls; free park shuttles; throttled Wi-Fi $15/day, video-speed Wi-Fi $20/day.

Rosen Shingle Creek ★★

It's not often you find a full-scale resort that isn't controlled by some corporate office far away. The Shingle Creek is the flagship of Harris Rosen, de facto Orlando tourism royalty who controls nine hotels and an incredble 6,705 rooms in town. So although it's massive and well-manicured, it feels a little different. I wouldn't quite call the room furnishings dated—they just feel resolutely beige and homey—but standard rooms have more space than usual and most of them have a great view since the hotel stands on its own (5 miles to Universal, 9 to Disney) with nothing blocking it. And miracles of miracles, there's no resort fee, which is reason enough to support it even if its does result in a few optional fees here and there to do some things. Conferences regularly take it over, and the fascinating mini–mall of restaurants and focus on golf (p. 187) are squarely aimed at them, but could be useful for you. There's even a little supermarket in the basement so you don't have to go out to buy a bottle of wine (and it's not priced to rip you off).

9939 Universal Blvd., Orlando. www.rosenshinglecreek.com. ✆ **866/966-6338.** 1,501 units. $139–$425 doubles or kings for up to 4. Parking $18 (self), $26 (valet). No resort fee. **Amenities:** 8 restaurants; 2 cocktail bars; 4 pools with bar; spa; coffee bar; ice cream and sandwich shop; nature trail; 24-hr. fitness center ($10/use); tennis; basketball; sand volleyball; arcade; mini supermarket; free shuttles to Universal and SeaWorld; babysitting (fee); free Wi-Fi (throttled), $10–$15 (video speed).

MODERATE

Drury Inn & Suites ★★★ A top pick. The popular, privately owned Missouri-based hotel group has an ideal plot—drive around the corner to Universal, down Palm Parkway to Disney, or go on foot to the restaurants of I-Drive or Sand Lake Road. Design is fresh in rust browns and greens, rooms are wider than the industry average, and there are tons of free extras. So friendly is this brand that every day at 5:30pm, it hosts a "kickback" with free food, beer, and wine—some cheapskates treat it as a free dinner. The king-bed category has only a shower; the others have tubs.

7301 W. Sand Lake Rd., Orlando. www.druryhotels.com. ✆ **407/354-1101.** 238 units. $100–$155 1-king or 2-queen rooms. Free parking. No resort fee. **Amenities:** Indoor/outdoor pool; free hot breakfast; free soda and popcorn; 24-hr. fitness room; business center; free local calls; pets permitted for free; free Universal shuttle; free Wi-Fi.

Holiday Inn Express & Suites—Orlando at SeaWorld ★★ One of the newer builds (summer 2017) in the tourist zone, and therefore one of the crisper choices, is this six-story hotel on the east side of SeaWorld, with a panoramic view roller-coaster nuts will swoon over. No restaurant, but there's a fair selection of franchise choices within walking or close driving distance, and you split the difference between resorts: Univeral is a 10-minute drive north while Disney parks are 15 minutes southwest. Rooms are typical of the brand, nothing unique, sort of sterile, but exactly what you need, and new. The shuttle offerings aren't strong.

10771 International Dr., Orlando. www.igh.com/holidayinnexpress. ✆ **407/996-4100** or 407/351-2100. 181 units. $93–$111 doubles. Free parking. No resort fee. **Amenities:** Free breakfast; pool; fitness center; business center; free Wi-Fi.

Hyatt House Across from Universal Orlando Resort ★★ It's not technically across from it—more like a 30-second drive around a bend—but it is brand-stinking new, having opened midway through 2018, and at 8 stories tall, west-facing rooms have a good peek at some of its rooftops. Hyatt House, if you don't know, is the hotel giant's "extended stay" product, which means it's ideal for families who like to be able to cook for themselves. Rooms and suites come with a microwave and cube fridge, and most suites have fully equipped kitchens and a living room. Studios have a floating divider but not an actual wall (easier for keeping an eye on little kids); bump up $20 or so if you want a bedroom door that shuts. But even studios can sleep 6. (Den rooms are like standard hotel rooms.) It looks great, is fully modern, and hits the value buttons.

5915 Caravan Ct., Orlando. http://acrossfromuniversalorlando.house.hyatt.com. ℭ **407/352-5660.** 168 units. Rooms $139–$189 with 2 double beds, $20 more for king bed. Free parking. No resort fee. **Amenities:** Heated pool; bar; sundries shop; 24-hr. fitness center; free Universal shuttle; free breakfast buffet; free Wi-Fi.

Sonesta ES Suites Orlando—International Drive ★★
This well-managed all-apartment hotel, across the street from the ICON Orlando and near plenty of places to eat, was recently lavished with a gut renovation, so there are fewer mid-priced properties as current. All units (most one-bedrooms are arranged around a courtyard pool, two-bedrooms face out) have new kitchens with new appliances, fresh furniture, fresh carpeting and bedding, a booth for family meals, and lots of added electrical outlets for recharging. Suddenly a dowdy 1980s holdover has again become family vacation darling. The staff is unusually dedicated, and some have been caring for this property for years. And when you come home after a long day, you can walk to dozens of restaurants.

8480 International Dr., Orlando. www.sonesta.com/orlando. ℭ **407/352-2400.** 146 units. 1-bedrooms $129–$189, 2-bedroom/2-bath $30–$40 more. Free parking. No resort fee. **Amenities:** Free breakfast; pool; spa tub; bar; sundries shop; small fitness center; free park shuttles (for Disney, connect via Epcot); free Wi-Fi.

INEXPENSIVE

Avanti Palms Resort and Conference Center ★
Let's be frank: This is just a 1972 property that got an extreme makeover. But they did a great job, and now it's one of the prime budget choices on I-Drive. It still has the creaky bones of a motel (older AC units, older pipes), but rooms aren't old-fashioned (they have laminate floors, for one). You definitely want to pass on a low-to-the-ground Garden room (324 sq. ft./30 sq. m) in favor of a room in the 14-story Tower (413 sq. ft/38 sq. m). Not just because they're bigger, but also because many of them look right at the gorgeous mountain of Volcano Bay, just a few hundred feet away, across I-4. All rooms have mini-fridges, which Disney won't do at its lowest price level. Because you'll be on I-Drive, there are heaps of places to eat, buy staples, and find cheap fun all around. All in all, you're doing quite well here for the low price. Pay attention that you book here and not at the sister Avanti down the road. ***Resort fee warning:*** $13.50/night.

6515 International Dr., Orlando. www.avantipalmsresort.com. ℭ **866/994-3157** or 407/996-0900. 653 units. $67–$109 doubles. Free parking. Resort fee $13.50/night. **Amenities:** Quick-service cafe; pool with hot tub and bar; Starbucks; fitness room; sundries shop; shuttles to Disney, Universal, and SeaWorld; free Wi-Fi.

Fairfield Inn & Suites Orlando International Drive/Convention Center ★★★
A 2013 new build, it has a terrific location by the ICON Orlando, which you can walk to. Expect large rooms in yellows and oranges, outlets galore, and large counters and desks to spread out on. On the east, rooms face nothing but greenery. True, the elevators and breakfast buffet can

get a tad overwhelmed in the mornings and you have to ask for a room with a minifridge or you may not get one, but overall, it's all you could wish for an affordable hotel. The top rate is for an Executive Kitchen Suite, which has a whopping 625 square feet and a fully equipped kitchen.

8214 Universal Blvd., Orlando. www.marriott.com. ℂ **407/581-9001.** 160 units. $94–$159 doubles. Free parking. No resort fee. **Amenities:** Pool; free breakfast buffet; sundries shop; free Wi-Fi.

Residence Inn Marriott Universal Studios ★★★ It's recommended because it's brand new (2018) and up-to-date (room doors will even open using the Marriott app), and yet it's still affordable. You're probably familiar with the corporate brand standard here. Rooms have real kitchens with stoves, ovens, pans, and utensils—save cash that way, too. The smallest unit, studios, are quite spacious (471 sq. ft./42 sq. m) and sleep three, but if you want a door to close while someone else sleeps on the pull-out sofa bed, you must upgrade. Staff is cheerful and the pool is uncomplicated. The parking garages of Universal are a 2-minute drive away and there are few chain places to eat within walking distance, but the area is by no means noisy or too busy.

5616 Major Blvd., Orlando. www.marriott.com. ℂ **407/313-1234.** 195 units. Studios $101–$141, 1-bedrooms $120–$174, 2-bedrooms $136–$209. Free parking. No resort fee. **Amenities:** Pool; fitness center; free Universal shuttle; sundries shop; putting green; free breakfast; free Wi-Fi (throttled; video speed $5/day).

TownePlace Suites Orlando at SeaWorld ★★★ You won't get much crisper than this one, which has only been open since the summer of 2017. Rooms, full of basic and durable furnishings, are larger than the hotel norm and have fully equipped kitchens with granite counters, pots and pans, and even dishwashers (good thing, since there's no on-site restaurant). Even the cheapest room, a "Studio" (325 sq. ft.) sleeps five if you use its living area and sleeper sofa. It's right beside SeaWorld, near plenty of things to eat.

10731 International Dr., Orlando. www.marriott.com. ℂ **407/996-3400.** 188 units. Rooms with 2 doubles or king from $89. Free parking. No resort fee. **Amenities:** Free hot breakfast buffet; pool; park shuttles; fitness center; free Wi-Fi.

Around Downtown Orlando

Because it's a 30-minute ride north of Disney on I-4 (yes, you should have a car for these), a hotel would have to be pretty special to convince a tourist to choose it over one that's nearer. Orlando has a few, where you can find respite from the hurdy-gurdy and plastinated smiles—or a breather from children.

EXPENSIVE

The Alfond Inn ★★ In 2013, Rollins College opened this boutique hotel in upscale Winter Park using a $12.5-million donation; its income will endow a scholarship program. Isn't that nice? So is the hotel. Its restaurant and cocktail bar, planted courtyard, and modern rooms striped in teal, wood, and lime, are designed to appeal to sophisticated palates, something that its fantastic public art collection, which is curated by the surprisingly well-stocked Cornell Fine Art Museum, underscores. These gleaming facilities are 3 blocks from the dignified shopping of Park Avenue and the Morse Museum (p. 170), making it an instant keystone of the Winter Park scene. It's probably too far if you've got a heavy theme park schedule, but it's ideal for love-nesting and grown-up explorations of the brick streets and '20s mansions of Winter Park.

300 E. New England Ave., Winter Park. www.thealfondinn.com. © **407/998-8090.** 112 units. $199–$259 doubles. Valet parking $20/night; no self-parking. No resort fee. **Amenities:** Restaurant; lounge; pool; fitness center; pets permitted; free Wi-Fi.

MODERATE

Courtyard at Lake Lucerne ★★
Orlando just doesn't have inns this individual anymore. South of downtown, literally beaneath highways (at least they go everywhere), you'll find a rare B&B, and rarer still, it preserves the feeling of Old Florida. There's a reason local couples favor it for weddings: Under Spanish moss, this hideaway of adult calm preserves four homey buildings of varied historic styles. Top of the line is the city's oldest documented house, 1883's Norment Parry Inn, which believe it or not has the cheapest rates here because not everyone likes sleigh beds and claw-footed tubs; you'll sleep in an elegant four-poster bed among Victorian-era European antiques. I. W. Phillips House recalls Key West because its wooden wrap-around verandah overlooks tropical plantings. Wellborn Suites is Art Deco, less elegant, but with kitchenettes. All rooms have TVs, phones, and private bathrooms. *Note:* There is no pool here.

211 N. Lucerne Circle E., Orlando. www.orlandohistoricinn.com. © **407/648-5188.** 30 units. $130–$225 doubles. Some rooms do not permit kids. Free parking. No resort fee. **Amenities:** Free breakfast; free Wi-Fi.

Home Rentals

In most destinations, you contact the owner directly. This is an option in Orlando, and the prominent online databases operate here, including **Airbnb. com, FabVillas.com, FlipKey.com, HomeAway.com, Housetrip.com,** and **Vacation Rentals by Owner** (www.vrbo.com). But in Orlando, many people who live far away keep homes as investments, so it's a lot better, for

Legoland Hotels

In 2015, Legoland opened the 152-room **Legoland Hotel ★★★**, and it's a wonder—a fabulous, candy-colored property crammed with Lego models and structures, with Lego play areas, character breakfasts, a heated pool, and rooms with elaborately executed themes ranging from pirates to medieval times. It's also just "132 kid steps," as the owners put it, from the front gates of the park (p. 158). It was such a smash that in 2017, the park opened a slightly cheaper, second hotel, the **Legoland Beach Retreat** (83 "beach bungalows" with 166 units sleeping up to 5). Those make for a dream trip to Legoland, but they're too distant to use as a base for the rest of Orlando, which can be an hour away depending on traffic. www.legolandhotel.com; © **877/350-5346.** *Rooms start at $135–$165 in low season, $349 in peak season, and often come with a second day of park tickets free. $20–$25/night resort fee.*

accountability's sake, to use a rental company. They inspect your potential home and give you support on the ground, unlocking the front door from miles away with the tap of a keyboard, and they can come fix things.

You'll find most homes or just south or west of Disney World in the towns of Clermont, Kissimmee, and Davenport—about a 10-minute drive. Nearly all were specifically built to have one bathroom for nearly every bedroom, and you'll have everything from an equipped kitchen to laundry. Generally, the older the house, the cheaper it is. Three-bedroom condo units sleeping up to eight, with a themed kids' room, start around $129 a night, or half what it costs to squeeze eight into two Disney Value rooms. Or you could have a whole three-bedroom house from $209. In addition to being selected for their reputations, longevity, and inventory, all of the companies listed in Frommer's **had an A+ rating** with the Better Business Bureau of Central Florida (www. bbb.org/central-florida) at press time, and most are accredited.

Your credit card will usually be charged a deposit ($200–$300 or 1 night's rent is standard) a month or two ahead of time, and if you cancel, you're unlikely to see that again. You'll also have to pay a one-time fee that goes toward insurance or cleaning; $50 to $80 is normal, which makes short stays less economical. Perks like a pool or grills may incur a surcharge, which is also normal. Also ask what supplies you'll need to buy. Clean bath towels and sheets are supplied, but maid service won't be unless you pay extra.

Global Resort Homes ★★   Founded in 1993, this solid and responsible moderate-price choice manages more than 300 properties, mostly around Disney, in one of nine gated vacation-home communities with clubhouses for activities and swimming. The people who own the homes are responsible for decor, but GRH nudges them to make sure everything meets a high standard— all include Wi-Fi, a pool (either communal or private), dishwasher and a laundry room, and crisp furnishings—and staff is on call 24/7. It's not unusual to find homes that sleep 10 going for as low as $231 a night in peak summer. Usefully, the website offers virtual tours of nearly every room in each property.

7796 W. Irlo Bronson Memorial Hwy./U.S. 192, Kissimmee. www.globalresorthomes. com. © **888/426-0472** or 407/387-3030. No pets.

IPG Florida Vacation Homes ★★   IPG began by serving British vacationers before branching out into Florida; now it's among the largest, dealing in dozens of home developments south and west of Disney, particularly Bella Piazza, Highlands Reserve, Windsor Hills, and the Villas at Island Club. Two-bedroom condos run $120 to $160, often less; six bedrooms can cost a mere $143.

9550 W. U.S. 192, Clermont. www.ipgflorida.com. © **800/311-7105** or 863/547-1050. Pets with $400 fee.

Magical Vacation Homes ★★   An area renter since 2007, it represents about 200 properties hosting from 2 to 14 people, most of them clustered in three high-quality developments (Reunion Resort, Windsor Hills, and

ChampionsGate) right south of Disney. You don't need keys since your entry is handled by coded keypad. There's a 4-night minimum at many of its homes.

7555 Osceola Polk Line Rd, Davenport. www.magicalvacationhomes.com. ℂ **866/991-3158** or 407/552-6155. No pets.

Orlando Vacation Homes 360 ★★ A specialist in the Orlando market, meaning it doesn't represent homes anywhere else, it focuses on 16 developments between 2 and 7 miles from Disney. Three-bedroom condos sleeping eight start at around $89 a night if it's a condo unit, but they represent homes of up to 8 bedrooms. It allows vacationers to pay on installment as long as everything is paid 30 days before arrival.

424 E. Central Blvd., 137/B, Orlando. www.ovh360.com. ℂ **888/826-0551** or 407/966-4144. Most homes don't allow pets.

Tropical Escape Resort Homes ★ Founded in 2006, the company deals in the major developments south of Disney, including ChampionsGate, Reunion, and West Haven. Homes start at 3 bedrooms and go up, but deals are easy to find among them; one of its 7-bedroom homes starts at just $200 a night—that's value.

8320 ChampionsGate Blvd., ChampionsGate. www.tropicalescapevacationhomes.com. ℂ **866/409-8598.** Some homes allow pets.

PLANNING YOUR TRIP TO ORLANDO

Orlando hosts some 68 million visitors a year, and the people who run the airports, hotels, and theme parks are specialists in moving them from one location to another. You'll always find someone eager to sell you what you need. You will, however, need to take care of some nitty-gritty details yourself, from flights to transportation.

GETTING THERE

BY PLANE Orlando is served by 37 airlines, so thankfully, competition keeps airfares among the lowest on the East Coast. More than 40 million people use **Orlando International Airport** (MCO; www.orlandoairports.net) each year, and airfare deals are common. Strategies for finding a good airfare include the following.

Primary websites that collect quotes from a variety of sources (whether they be airlines or other websites) include **CheapOAir. com**, **Expedia.com**, **Kayak.com**, and **Momondo.com**. Each has odd gaps in its coverage because of the way they obtain their quotes. Some sites have small booking fees of $5 to $10, and many force you to accept nonrefundable tickets for the cheapest prices. You can often save money by booking between roughly 7 weeks in advance if you're flying domestically and 3 to 4 months ahead from abroad.

MCO is mostly a pleasure. Current security wait times are listed on its home page and if, on the way home, you realize you neglected to buy any park-related souvenirs, fear not, because Disney, Sea-World, Kennedy Space Center, and Universal all maintain lavish stores (located before the security checkpoint, so leave time). The airport, 25 miles east of Walt Disney World, was built during World War II as McCoy Air Force Base, which closed in the early 1970s but bequeathed the airport with its deceptive code, MCO. Its on-time rate is 80%, one of the best in the country, even though the airport is America's 14th busiest. Midmornings and midafternoons can be crowded for outgoing passengers, weekends can be clogged with cruise passengers. Midafternoon summer thunderstorms sometimes create delays, so try to avoid that time.

The main terminal is divided into two sides, A and B, so if you can't find the desk for your airline or transportation service open on one side, it may be on the other side. Most major rental car companies are in a connected garage, no shuttles required.

Rental car companies at MCO:

Advantage: www.advantage.com; ☏ **800/777-5500**
Alamo: www.alamo.com; ☏ **800/327-9633**
Avis: www.avis.com; ☏ **800/831-2847**
Budget: www.budget.com; ☏ **800/527-0700**
Dollar: www.dollar.com; ☏ **800/800-4000**
Enterprise: www.enterprise.com; ☏ **800/325-8007**
E-Z Rent-A-Car: www.e-zrentacar.com; ☏ **800/266-5171**
Hertz: www.hertz.com; ☏ **800/654-3131**
National: www.nationalcar.com; ☏ **800/227-7368**
Payless: www.payless.com; ☏ **407/856-5539**
Thrifty: www.thrifty.com; ☏ **800/367-2277**

Very few airlines use **Orlando Sanford International Airport** (www.orlandosanfordairport.com), or SFB, which despite the Orlando in its name is 42 miles northeast of Disney. It's connected to the Disney area by the Central Florida GreeneWay, or S.R. 417—the trip takes about 40 minutes and there are tolls, so new arrivals should have U.S. money on them—preferably quarters. European visitors might fly into **Tampa International Airport** (www.tampaairport.com), or TPA, 90 minutes southwest.

BY TRAIN Amtrak's (www.amtrak.com; ☏ **800/872-7245**) Silver Service/Palmetto route serves Orlando and Kissimmee. Trains go direct between New York City, Washington, D.C., Charleston, and Savannah. The privately funded **Brightline** service (www.gobrightline.com) has been announced to connect Orlando International Airport with West Palm Beach, Fort Lauderdale, and Miami in 3 hours, but not until 2021 at the earliest.

Transportation to & from MCO

BY RENTAL CAR Get a car. Otherwise, theme park resorts conspire to hold you prisoner. If you intend to experience the "real" Orlando or its rich natural wonders, get a car. If you want to save huge amounts of money on meals, if you ever want to take a breather from the theme parks' relentless plastic personalities—get a car.

Economy rental cars start around $25–$30 a day. Test the waters at a site such as Kayak, Orbitz, or Travelocity, which compare multiple renters with one click. Priceline and Hotwire have been known to rent for as little as $20 a day.

If you rent a car, be alert as you **exit the airport**—you must decide whether to use the south exit (marked for Walt Disney World) or the north exit (for SeaWorld, Universal, the Convention Center, and downtown Orlando). Whichever route you take, you will pay a few dollars in tolls, and some booths are automated and don't accept bills, so have loose change. Also, at tollbooths, stay to the right, where the cash windows are; the left lanes are for e-passes. (You can rent e-passes from your rental car company, but if you're staying within Orlando, you won't use it enough to warrant the expense.)

If you're staying on Disney turf, an economical solution is to rent a car for only the days you'd like to venture off property. To that end, **Alamo** (www. alamo.com; ✆ 800/462-5266) and **National** (www.nationalcar.com; ✆ 800/227-7368) operate satellite agencies within the Walt Disney World Resort: at the Car Care Center near the parking lot of the Magic Kingdom and at the Dolphin hotel by Epcot. Many giant resorts host a rental car desk from one of the major names. Renting away from the airport incurs taxes of around half of those charged by renting (or even merely returning) a car at the airport, where they're more than 20%. Always fill up *before* heading back to MCO, because gas stations near the airport's entrance have been nabbed for gouging. Stations inside Walt Disney World charge a competitive price, but one not as low as outside the tourist zone.

Agencies might not rent to those under 25. **Action Car Rental** (3719 McCoy Rd., Orlando; www.actionrac.com; ✆ 407/240-2700) has awful service but goes as low as 18-year-olds. It's not as cheap as the major renters. Most companies won't rent to anyone older than 85.

BY AIRPORT SHUTTLE **Mears Transportation** (www.mearstransportation. com; ✆ 407/423-5566 or 855/463-2776) is the 800-pound gorilla of shuttles and taxis; it sends air-conditioned vans bouncing to hotels every 15 to 20 minutes. Round-trip fares for adults are $33 ($25 for kids 4–11, kids 3 and under free) to the International Drive area, or $37 per adult ($28 for kids) to Walt Disney World/U.S. 192/Lake Buena Vista. You'll probably make several stops (it'll take up to 90 minutes) because the vans are shared with other passengers.

If you have more than four or five people, it's more economical to reserve a car service (do it at least 24 hr. ahead) and split the lump fee; an SUV for up to 7 would be $100 to $190 round-trip from MCO (zooming to $225 from SFB). Try Mears, **Tiffany Towncar** (www.tiffanytowncar.com; ✆ 888/838-2161 or 407/370-2196), or **Quicksilver Tours** (www.quicksilver-tours.com; ✆ 888/468-6939; starting at $50), which often volunteers to toss in a free 30-minute stop at a grocery store so you can stock up on supplies.

If you have a reservation at a Disney-owned hotel, you have the right to take the company's free airport motorcoaches (also known as **Disney's Magical Express,** run by Mears). The Mouse mails you tags for your luggage, which you affix before leaving home, and tells you everything will be taken care of from there. But by the time you even board the bus to the resort, you may have already have waited in two long lines (one to check into Magical Express, then another for your hotel motorcoach) at the airport—the first of many, many lines you'll endure, so get used to it—and then you may stop at up to five other hotels first. Your bags may not meet up with you again for 6 to 8 hours, so hitting a park right away may be difficult (pack swimsuits in your carry-on). When you depart for home, you must be ready 3 to 4 hours before your flight. Magical Express is free, but you can see how it also costs you. It also lulls you into not renting a car, which means you'll probably never leave Disney property. Universal Orlando has its own small system, **Universal SuperStar Shuttle Service** (© **866/604-7557**), that's a $36 adults and $26 kids 3–9 (kids 2 and under free) add-on to its vacation packages, and you can't buy it without a package. Obviously, it doesn't go to Disney and Magical Express won't visit Universal.

BY RIDESHARE **Uber** and **Lyft** are available. Meet them at the Express Pickup Tunnel by the rental car counters. You should pay $55–$60 to the tourist zones outside of surge periods. The airport tacks on a $5.80 fee, one of the highest such fees in the nation.

BY TAXI It'll be about $70 to the Disney hotels, $60 to Universal, not including a tip, which is cheaper than a town car but not than rentals or Uber.

Traveling from Orlando to Other Parts of America

Orlando, while not an important air hub, is well connected to the cities that are, particularly New York, Atlanta, and Chicago. For advice on how to find cheap airfare, see "Getting There," p. 267.

The **USA Rail Pass** is the American equivalent of the Eurail Pass in Europe—although our national rail system, **Amtrak** (www.amtrak.com; © **800/872-7245** or 215/856-7953), hardly compares to the European system. It barely compares to freight. The pass allows travel within the U.S. The cheapest pass is a 15-day pass, which grants eight trips ($459; $230 kids 2–12); the most expensive offers 45 days of travel over 18 trips ($899; $450 kids). Those on a grand tour of America may benefit from those rates compared to flying.

From April to early June, some car renters redistribute inventory by offering **"drive-out"** deals for one-way rentals that originate in Florida and drop off elsewhere in the country. Rates can start at $10/day, so ask about those.

For bus travel, Orlando is served by **Greyhound** (www.greyhound.com; © **800/231-2222**), **Megabus** (www.megabus.com; © **877/462-6342**), and RedCoach (www.redcoachusa.com; © **877/733-0724**). Long-distance bus travel in the United States is a purgatorial experience. Don't.

GETTING AROUND

BY CAR Probably 90% of what a tourist wants to do lies within a 10-minute drive of Interstate 4, or I-4, as it's called. That free highway runs diagonally from southwest to northeast, connecting Walt Disney World, SeaWorld, the Convention Center, Universal Orlando, and downtown Orlando. I-4 is technically an east-west road linking Florida's coasts, so directions are listed as either west (toward Tampa and the Gulf of Mexico) or east (toward Daytona Beach and the Atlantic Ocean). Once you've got that down, you'll be set. Exits are numbered according to the mile marker at which they're found.

Therefore, the Disney World exits (62, 64, 65, and 67) are roughly 10 miles from Universal Orlando's (74 and 75), which are about 9 miles from downtown (83). If you know the exit number, you can figure out distance.

If you stray much onto minor roads, it's a good idea to carry a map or turn on the Waze app or Google Maps. Roads can go by several names and be confusing. Disney World is a particular disaster, since its signage is intentionally incomplete to funnel traffic. Don't rely on free maps; laughably, some maps provided by Universal don't acknowledge that Disney exists at all. **Visit Orlando** (www.visitorlando.com/mapexplorer) has free marked maps.

Some Florida toll roads are cashless and require a transponder to pay. Fortunately for tourists, in Orlando only the Florida Turnpike and parts of 528 have gone cashless. Rental cars will lend you a transponder for about $4 a day, even if you don't use it, plus the cost of tolls. Better to avoid the Turnpike instead.

SHUTTLES   Universal is easy: You walk, bus, or take a free boat everywhere. At Disney, though, hoofing it is impossible. It's so big, it requires a fleet of more than 400 buses, the **Disney Transportation System (DTS),** which anyone may use for free. Find out about getting around Disney on p. 30.

There are also **hotel theme park shuttles,** which go from independent hotels and are often free (or paid for by resort fees). Yes, you can save money by using them, but there are strong downsides, including wildly inadequate scheduling (you might miss fireworks) and rambling routes. These only go to the park gates, not to restaurants or the many worthwhile smaller attractions.

Another option is the **I-Ride Trolley** (www.iridetrolley.com; ☎ **866/243-7483;** adults $2 per ride, seniors over 65 25¢, kids 3–9 $1; day pass $5, 3-day pass $7, 5-day pass $9; free transfers; passes not sold on board; daily 8am–10:30pm), an excellent shuttle bus with plenty of clearly marked and well-maintained stops, benches to wait on, and genuinely useful routes—except it doesn't go to Disney. Its **Red Line** (every 20 min.) plies International Drive from the shops and restaurants just north of I-4's exit 75 all the way to Orlando Premium Outlets, near Disney; along the way it touches down at SeaWorld and the Orlando Eye. The second route, the **Green Line** (every 30 min.), takes in SeaWorld, too, but heads down Universal Boulevard, making it more of an express route, and turns around at Orlando Premium Outlets. It comes within a long block of the entrance to Universal Orlando. Visitors without cars may find it feasible to stay on I-Drive, use this dirt-cheap shuttle to see nearly everything, and then tack on the hated hotel shuttle or a city bus for Disney days.

BY PUBLIC TRANSIT   Ultimately, Orlando is a car city, not a public transit city. Buses are infrequent (usually one or two an hour), shelters are often nonexistent, and when the sun's strong, the combination is dangerous. Distances are also fairly great, so journeys can take a while. The Central Florida Regional Transportation Authority runs the **LYNX system** (www.golynx.com), on which one-way fares are $2, day passes cost $4.50, week passes are $16, and transfers between lines are free. Up to three kids 6 and under ride with adults free, and you have to pay with exact change. In

Mouse-Clickers: The Best Planning Websites

If you really want to be intense about planning (for your sanity and relaxation, don't), there are obsessive resources that go into granular detail. My choices:

o **AllEars.net** offers encyclopedic compendiums of everything Disney, down to the menus, what's under renovation, and which rooms are best.

o **EasyWDW.com** tracks the minutiae of how to navigate moment-to-moment.

o **OrlandoInformer.com** comprehensively reports Universal, including deals.

o **WDWmagic.com** and **WDWinfo.com** (and its **DISBoards.com**) host some of the most active message forums for news, but their tone is defensively Disney-positive.

o The independently run **Party ThroughTheParks.com** rates drinking and nightlife and **DisneyFood Blog.com** keeps track of meals.

o **MouseSavers.com** and **TheMouse ForLess.com** post current Disney deals.

o **OrlandoAttractions.com**, **TheDisney Blog.com**, and **JimHillMedia.com** professionally stay on top of Disney Parks news and history.

---

downtown Orlando, there's the free **LYMMO** (www.golynx.com; Mon–Thurs 6am–10:45pm, Fri 6am–midnight, Sat 10am–midnight, Sun 10am–10pm) bus service, three lines that loop every 10 to 15 minutes.

For tourists, here are the most convenient routes, many of which stop at Disney Springs where you can transfer to Disney's free bus system:

o **Route 56** connects Kissimmee to the front gates of the Magic Kingdom, where you can catch DTS to the other parks. Buses run every 30 minutes, but the last one leaves at 10:53pm.

o **Route 8** does most of International Drive, including the Convention Center and SeaWorld. It duplicates the service offered by the I-Ride Trolley (see above).

o **Route 50** goes from downtown Orlando to Disney Springs and to the gates of the Magic Kingdom. It stops at SeaWorld where passengers can connect to I-Drive on Route 8.

o The lesser Disney areas are served by the 300-series lines: **300** goes to Hotel Plaza Boulevard from downtown; **301** to Epcot and Disney's Animal Kingdom from Pine Hills; **302** to the Magic Kingdom from Rosemont; and **303** to Hollywood Studios from the Washington Shores area. Bus **304** is the only one that connects with another tourist zone; it trawls Sand Lake Road, which bisects I-Drive. Buses 301 and 302 pass within a few blocks of Universal Orlando, on Kirkman Road, so if you toss in about 15 minutes of walking, they could technically be used for Universal, too, but it wouldn't be fun.

o **Route 42** starts at the Convention Center on International Drive, and 75 minutes later, reaches the airport.

Orange County has **SunRail** (www.sunrail.com; ℂ **855/724-5411**; $2 one-way, $3.75 round-trip), running from DeBary, north of Sanford, to an obscure spot on E. Sand Lake Road near S. Orange Avenue. Tourists only care about

the 16-minute jaunt between downtown Orlando and Winter Park, but as departures are widely scattered in the morning or evening, targeting commuters, you won't see the point.

BY TAXI   Given so many alternatives, taxis are not a natural choice. **Uber** and **Lyft** operate in Orlando, and increasing numbers of tourists rely on them. Uber trips within Disney World are about $10–$14 (much cheaper than Disney's in-house Minnie Vans, operated via Lyft, which cost a flat $25). To go between Disney and Universal you'll pay a little under $20. You will still almost always find a cluster waiting within range of the theme parks' gates.

Many companies accept major credit cards, but ask when you summon a ride, because your payment may need to be processed by phone. Companies are not carefully monitored, so only choose a recommended carrier. Call your own:

- **Diamond Cab Company** (www.diamondcabco.com): ℭ **407/523-3333**
- **Transtar** (mytranstar.com): ℭ **407/857-9999**
- **Yellow** (www.mearstransportation.com): ℭ **407/422-2222**

WHEN TO GO

The main consideration when it comes to selecting dates is balancing good weather with thin crowds. Crowds keep you from seeing everything. In the peak season (such as spring break or the week after Christmas), the Magic Kingdom's turnstiles spin like propellers. None of the theme parks close on **public holidays.** In fact, they do better business then. In late December, Disney parks sometimes hit capacity and seal gates. But in September and the week after Thanksgiving, you can do nearly everything in a day. Light crowds do not automatically mean shorter waits, because on quieter days, rides run at lower capacity.

So when are the **peak seasons?** Put simply: when American kids are out of school. That means mid-spring, summer until late August, and the holidays. Hotel rates rise then, too. If you want to **save cash,** early January, early May, late August, all of September, and the first half of December are prime. The flipside of low season is that the theme parks trim services when it's quieter. January is a particularly tough month for missing out on rides due to rehabs. And especially in the winter months, you may find it too chilly to enjoy the rides that get you wet, which is a shame since Orlando has some of the best water rides in the world.

Which Day of the Week?

The busiest days at all parks are generally Saturday and Sunday. Seven-day guests are often traveling on these days, and weekends are when locals come to play. Beyond that: Tuesday and Thursday see an uptick in the Magic Kingdom; Tuesday and Friday (and evenings) at Epcot; Wednesday is a tad busier at Disney's Hollywood Studios; and Monday, Tuesday, and Wednesday can be a zoo (forgive the pun) at the Animal Kingdom. Crowds tend to thin later in the day.

CLIMATE   June to September is the heaviest season for excruciating sun and brief torrential rain. Every afternoon, another heavy storm rolls in and shuts rides temporarily—pretty much everything outdoors or on water will temporarily shut down if lightning is detected within range. Those deluges usually roll out within an hour but scare away a significant percentage of guests, so for shorter lines, it almost always pays to wait out the rain. Central Florida suffers more lightning strikes than any other American locale. During that season, bring along a cheap poncho from home.

Orlando Average Temperature & Rainfall

	JAN	FEB	MAR	APR	MAY	JUNE	JULY	AUG	SEPT	OCT	NOV	DEC
HI/LOW DAILY TEMPS (°F)	72/49	73/50	78/55	84/60	88/66	91/71	92/73	92/73	90/73	84/65	78/57	73/51
HI/LOW DAILY TEMPS (°C)	22/10	23/10	26/13	29/16	31/19	33/22	33/23	33/23	32/23	29/19	26/14	23/11
INCHES OF PRECIPITATION	2.25	2.82	3.32	2.43	3.30	7.13	7.27	6.88	6.53	3.16	1.98	2.25

Orlando's Calendar of Events

Check the special events pages at the theme park websites to see if any themed weekends or smaller events are in the works. In addition, the events listings at **Visit Orlando** (www.visitorlando.com), **Orlando Weekly** (www.orlandoweekly.com), and the **Orlando Sentinel** (www.orlandosentinel.com) are comprehensive. You will also find a few listings at **Orlando magazine** (www.orlandomagazine.com).

JANUARY

Citrus Bowl. Now stickered by the Overton's marine supply company—can *anyone* keep track of the square-dancing corporate naming rights anymore? Held New Year's Day at the Florida Citrus Bowl Stadium (Camping World Stadium), it pits the second-ranked teams from the Big Ten and SEC conferences against one another. www.floridacitrussports.com.

Pro Bowl. Love it or hate it, the late-season all-star AFC/NFC game is no longer held in Hawaii. In 2017, it signed a three-year deal to join the other tourist attractions in a city players' families would rather visit. Late Jan. www.nfl.com/probowl.

Walt Disney World Marathon. The route goes through all four theme parks, or just do the Half, which hits Epcot and the Magic Kingdom. Close to 80,000 runners come for at least one of the five events. Other half-marathon events pop up over the rest of the year. First week of January. www.disneyworld.com.

ZORA! Festival. The folklorist and writer Zora Neale Hurston (1891–1960) was from Eatonville (a 30-min. drive north of Orlando), the country's oldest incorporated African-American town. This weeklong event includes lectures and an art fair. www.zorafestival.org; ✆ **407/647-3307.**

Epcot International Festival of the Arts. The newest and least focused of Epcot's four major annual festivals is about performance, visual art, and food. In addition to Broadway-style performances and kiosks selling gourmet mini-dishes throughout World Showcase, on many days there are free talks or short workshops with artists who share their disciplines. Begins mid-January. www.disneyworld.com; ✆ **407/939-3378.**

FEBRUARY

Winter Park Bach Festival. This annual event at Rollins College began in 1935 and has evolved into one of the country's better choral fests. Although it has stretched to include other composers and guest artists (Handel, P.D.Q. Bach), at least one concert is devoted to Johann. It takes place mid-February to early March, with scattered one-off guest performances throughout the year. www.bachfestivalflorida.org; ✆ **407/646-2182.**

Silver Spurs Rodeo. Lest you doubt Central Florida is far removed from the American Deep South, it hosts the largest rodeo east of the Mississippi (with bareback broncs, barrel racing horses, rodeo clowns, and athletes drawn from the cowboy circuit) over 3 days on the third weekend in February in an indoor arena off U.S. 192. 2019 marks its 142nd event. 1875 Silver Spur Lane, Kissimmee. www.silver spursrodeo.com; ℭ **321/697-3495.**

Rock the Universe. Universal's festival of top-flight Christian rock bands, which perform on stages inside Universal Studios park. Rides and performances continue past midnight, after regular patrons go home. It's separately ticketed. www.rocktheuniverse.com.

Mardi Gras at Universal Studios. On Saturday nights, Universal books major acts (Bonnie Raitt, Hall & Oates, LL Cool J, Diana Ross, Ne-Yo) and mounts a family-friendly parade complete with stilt-walkers, jazz bands, Louisiana-made floats, and bead tossing—although here, what it takes to win a set of beads is considerably less risqué than it is in the Big Easy. It's included with admission. www.universalorlando.com/mardigras; ℭ **407/224-2691.**

Spring Training. See p. 167 for a rundown of which Major League Baseball teams play where. Mid-February through March.

MARCH

Epcot's International Flower & Garden Festival. This spring event, which lasts 75 days from March through May, transforms Epcot with some 30 million flowers, 70 topiaries, a screened-in butterfly garden, presentations by noted horticulturalists, and a lineup of "Flower Power" concerts (Chubby Checker, the Pointer Sisters). It's free with standard entry. www.disneyworld.com; ℭ **407/934-7639.**

APRIL

Epcot's International Flower & Garden Festival. See March for full listing, above.

Florida Music Festival. Some 250 bands over 4 days give exposure to up-and-coming musicians—at a pace of 50 per night, all over town. April or May. www.floridamusicfestival. com.

Florida Film Festival. This respected event showcases films by Florida artists and has featured past appearances by the likes of Ellen Burstyn, William H. Macy, Christopher Walken, and Sissy Spacek. www.floridafilm festival.com; ℭ **407/629-1088.**

MAY

Orlando International Fringe Festival. This theatrical smorgasbord, the longest-running fringe fest in America, spends 14 days mounting some 950 performances of more than 160 newly written, experimental performances in Loch Haven Park. Some 72,000 attended in 2018. www.orlandofringe.org; ℭ **407/648-0077.**

Epcot's International Flower & Garden Festival. See March for full listing, above.

SEPTEMBER

Epcot International Food & Wine Festival. The World Showcase makes amends with the countries it ignores by installing temporary booths selling tapas-size servings of foods and wines from many nations. That's supplemented with chef demonstrations, seminars, "Eat to the Beat" concerts by known acts, and tastings by at least 100 wineries. In short, it's a sensation. A few of the more extravagant events are charged, but most are free. The festival, which tends to more crowded on weekends, lasts 90 days from late September to mid-November and the hotly awaited details are posted by Disney in the summer. www.disneyworld.com/foodand wine; ℭ **407/939-3378.**

AUGUST

Gay Days. What started as a single day for gay and lesbian party-minded visitors in 1991 has bloomed into a full week of some 40 events managed by a host of promoters. It's said that attendance goes as high as 150,000. Until last year, it was held in early June, but starting in 2019 it moves to August, when hotel rates are cheaper. Gay Days are a blow-out party with group visits to the city's parks (wearing red shirts as a gentle reminder of visibility), an ongoing bash at Parliament House (p. 182), concerts (En Vogue, LeAnn Rimes), a marketplace, several dance events, and more than a dozen pool parties. 2019: Aug 13–19 at host hotel Wyndham Orlando Resort International Drive. www.gaydays.com.

OCTOBER

Mickey's Not-So-Scary Halloween Party. The best of the Magic Kingdom's separately ticketed evening events, this one mounts a special parade with fiendishly catchy theme song, a few special shows, a fireworks display that surpasses the usual one, and stations where you can pick up free candy. Kids even show up in costume, although it's not required. The event happens on scattered evenings from mid-August through the end of October. Unfortunately, it's so over-sold that you will barely be able to move. Target audience: people who like lolli-pops. www.disneyworld.com/halloweenparty; ✆ **407/934-7639.**

Halloween Horror Nights. Unquestionably Universal's biggest event, HHN is the equiva-lent of a whole new theme park that's designed for a year but only lasts a month. After dark, the Studios are overtaken by gro-tesque "scareactors" who terrorize crowds with chain saws, gross-out shows, and seven or eight big, well-made, walk-through haunted houses that are created from scratch each year. The mayhem lasts into the wee hours. Wimps need not apply; children are discouraged by the absence of kids' ticket prices. On top of all this, most rides remain open. HHN has legions of fans. Target audi-ence: people who like to poop themselves in fright. (Busch Gardens' Howl-o-Scream event's scariness is somewhere between Uni-versal's and Disney's.) www.halloweenhorror nights.com.

SeaWorld's Halloween Spooktacular. Sea-World throws a sweet, toddler-approved weekend Halloween event of its own, with trick-or-treating (kids dress up), a few encoun-ters with sea fairies and bubbles, and show starring Count von Count from *Sesame Street*. Target audience: people who have a naptime. It's included in admission.

Orlando Film Festival. Like all festivals worth their salt, this one presents mostly mainstream and independent films in advance of their wider release dates, plus cool events like workshops on writing and pitching. It lasts about a week in October or early November, screening at various down-town venues. www.orlandofilmfest.com; ✆ **407/843-0801.**

NOVEMBER

ICE! It debuted in 2003 at the Gaylord Palms hotel and has quickly become a holiday perennial. The hotel brings in nearly 2 million pounds of ice, sculpts it into a walk-through city, keeps it chilled to 9°F (–13°C), and issues winter coats to visitors. Add synchronized light shows and you've got an event that charges $29 adults, $17 kids for entry—and sells out. www.gaylordpalms.com; ✆ **407/ 586-0000.**

DECEMBER

Mickey's Very Merry Christmas Party. This crowded night, which occurs on various nights starting even before Thanksgiving, is probably Disney's most popular special annual event. It requires a separate ticket from regular admission. What you get is a tree-lighting ceremony, a few special holiday-themed shows, a special fireworks display (very green and red), an appearance by Santa Claus, a special parade, and *huge* crowds. Meanwhile, Disney's warehouse for holiday decorations (it exists) empties out and its hotels deck the halls: The Grand Floridian erects a life-size house made of gingerbread. www.disneyworld.com/christmasparty; ✆ **407/934-7639.**

Epcot International Festival of the Holi-days. This 75-day event features holiday customs of many nations and a host of cos-tumed storytellers, but its real showpiece is the daily, 40-minute candlelight processional, a retelling of the Christmas Nativity story by a celebrity narrator (regular names include Sigourney Weaver, Gary Sinise, Edward James Olmos, and Neil Patrick Harris) accom-panied by a 50-piece orchestra and a full Mass choir. The processional is a WDW tradi-tion going back to its earliest days—Cary Grant did it! www.disneyworld.com/holidays.

Grinchmas & The Macy's Holiday Parade. Usual holiday traditions include a musical version of *How the Grinch Stole Christmas* and daily parades by Macy's, which brings some balloons and floats to Universal when

Before Magic Your Way made ticket expiration standard, pretty much every Disney ticket was good forever. That means there are a lot of unused days floating around. It's illegal to sell them, but that doesn't stop people. When you see a sign on the side of U.S. 192 promising discounted tickets, guess what may be for sale? Buying a ticket like this is a gamble, particularly if you don't have the expertise to recognize a fake or a spent ticket. Often, only a Disney laser scan can tell for sure.

Other organizations, such as timeshare developers, offer legit tickets to theme parks and dinner shows, but to get them, you will have to endure heavy-duty sales presentations that may last several hours. The requirements for attendance can be tight: Married couples must attend together (gay couples are often discriminated against—that's still legal in Florida), you both must swear your combined annual income is above a certain amount ($50,000, for example, for Westgate branded resorts—owned by the timeshare baron in the film *The Queen of Versailles*), that you are in a given age range (23–68 is common), and that you commit to staying for at least 90 minutes, although being pitched for as long as 4 hours is also common. Even if you're willing, an entire morning of your hard-earned vacation time is worth more than whatever discount is being promised. After all, how many days of working did it take for you to accrue those 4 or 5 hours? You also may not arrive at the parks until lunchtime, missing (in some cases) a third of the opening hours. Don't be so cheap and discount-obsessed that you throw away your time at an aggressive timeshare pitch.

Thanksgiving is over. That's included in the ticket price. Holiday events kick in then, too. www.universalorlando.com.

Camping World Bowl. An ACC team battles a Big Ten team, usually a few days before New Year's and always at the Camping World Stadium, once called the Citrus Bowl. Going since 1990, the game has had many faces, including the Champs Sports Bowl, Carquest Bowl, Tangerine Bowl, Russell Athletic Bowl, and its very first sponsor, the doomed videocassette giant Blockbuster. www.campingworldbowl.com.

New Year's Eve. Yahoo.com reports that Orlando regularly makes its list of top five most-searched New Year's Eve destinations. There's no shortage of places to party. At the parks: **CityWalk** throws its EVE bash with outdoor dance floor and light shows. The **Disney parks** stay open until the wee hours and may have live DJs. **SeaWorld** brings in big-band music or jazz, plus fireworks.

Getting Attraction Discounts

For a full breakdown of Disney's ticketing, how it works, and how to guard against overspending, see p. 22.

Universal and SeaWorld discount the gate price if you book online, and all the parks discount per-day entry if you buy multiple days. SeaWorld and Busch Gardens also offer courtesy admission for members of the military and their families. Check www.wavesofhonor.com to see if you are eligible. You will also find coupons through the discount circular **HotelCoupons.com**.

A few outfits (such as, occasionally, local AAA chapters) sell faintly discounted tickets. **Maple Leaf Tickets** (www.mapleleaftickets.com; ℗ 800/841-2837) and **The Official Ticket Center** (www.officialticketcenter.com; ℗ 877/406-4836), both accredited by the Better Business Bureau. So is **Undercover Tourist** (www.undercovertourist.com; ℗ 800/846-1302), which also publishes a marvelous calendar that guesses, using as many statistics as possible, at what the best touring plans are for the days you're visiting. No Disney deals ever seem deep enough to offset shipping fees or the hassle of picking up your tickets at some third-party office; however, multiple purchases, stays of a week or longer, and third-tier diversions such as dinner shows ($10–$15 off) may be worth it. Tickets are nontransferable. If you don't want the hassle of pre-planning, a desk at the Orlando Official Visitor Center (p. 286) furnishes similar discounts on tickets you can trust.

One to be wary of is the **Go Orlando Card** (www.goorlandocard.com; ℗ 800/887-9103), which offers admission to secondary attractions. The catch is you get an obscenely short time to use it. Rare is the person who can move fast enough to make the price (a 2-day card is $149 for adults, $129 kids) pay off unless one of the days is used at an expensive attraction such as Legoland and the other day is crammed from morning to bedtime with lesser diversions.

[FastFACTS] ORLANDO

Accessible Travel

Nearly everything is accessible. This situation predates the Americans with Disabilities Act of 1990; as multigenerational attractions, the parks have always worked to be inclusive, and in response, guests with mobility issues have long embraced them in return.

Disney's full descriptions of its support facilities are posted under the "Services" section at www.disneyworld.disney.go.com/guest-services. Upon arrival at Disney, anyone with a disability heads to Guest Relations to obtain a **Disability Access Service Card** that designates you as requiring consideration. No doctor's letter is required. Parties with wheelchairs will be given a reservation time

that accounts for the current wait time (you can come back later as long as the time has passed, but you can't get another reservation until you've used the first one). Or part of your group might be asked to pass through the standard line while you wait in a special area and reunite with them before riding. There will usually be a place for you to wait for the special wheelchair-ready ride vehicle to come around. You might have to transfer to a manual wheelchair; the park maps indicate which rides will require you to leave your **wheelchair or ECV.** A very few, pre-ADA attractions, such as Tom Sawyer Island and the Swiss Family Treehouse, require you to be

ambulatory. Those are marked, too. Companions of guests with cognitive disabilities such as autism also obtain ride reservations that correspond to the current wait time; cast members can also direct them to "break areas" for easing stimulation. Oxygen tanks may not be permitted on rides. There is a special parade-viewing area for those with mobility issues so you can have good sightlines; arrive early and ask any cast member where it is. At Universal, go to the Guest Relations desk after the turnstiles for an **Attractions Assistance Pass.** If a ride's wait is less than 30 minutes, you'll scoot right on, and if it's longer, you'll be issued a time to return but you cannot get a new reservation time until that one is fulfilled. If that system won't work for you, Universal may choose to issue a **Guest Assistance Pass,** which grants Express access to all attractions, no appointment required. (Universal publishes a **ride guide** to accessibility: www.universalorlando.com/rg). Similarly, SeaWorld offers the **Ride Accessibility Pass.**

Theme park hotels all can lend door knock and phone alerts, amplifiers, bed shakers, strobes, and TTY phones. For off-property stays, consider renting a house, which provides much more room; most home-rental companies also comply with ADA requirements.

All the parks have a full range of in-park services for guests of every need, including at least a half-dozen TTY phones scattered around and sign-language interpreters on scheduled days of the week. Universal marks the times for its ASL shows on its guide map. Service animals are permitted but aren't always allowed to ride attractions. Disney maintains a Special Services hotline to answer all accessibility needs, including full arrangements for blind guests and captioning for hearing-impaired guests with devices requiring a $25 refundable deposit (✆ **407/824-4321** (voice) and TTY ✆ 407/827-5141; Disability.services@disneyparks.com). Universal Orlando can be reached at ✆ **800/447-0672** (TDD) or 407/224-4233 (voice) (www.universalorlando.com); SeaWorld Orlando's number is ✆ **407/363-2400** (www.

seaworld.com); Kennedy Space Center is at ✆ **321/449-4443** (www.kennedyspacecenter.com). Try to contact those a few weeks ahead. Most parks can arrange sign-language interpreters with a few weeks' notice; all furnish assisted listening devices or scripts for some, but not all, of the biggest attractions. There are plenty of accessible parking spots.

Medical Travel, Inc. (www.medicaltravel.org; ✆ **866/322-4400** or 407/438-8010) specializes in the rental of mobility equipment, ramp vans, and supplies such as oxygen tanks (be aware that many rides do not allow tanks). Electric scooters and wheelchairs can be delivered to your accommodation through these established companies: **Orlando Medical Rentals** (www.orlandomedicalrentals.com; ✆ **877/356-9943**) also supplies oxygen, scooters, and the like. **Buena Vista Scooter Rentals** (www.buenavistascooters.com; ✆ **866/484-4797** or 407/938-0349), **Scootaround** (www.scootaround.com; ✆ **888/441-7575**), **CARE Medical Equipment** (www.caremedicalequipment.com; ✆ **800/741-2282** or 407/856-2273), and **Walker Medical & Mobility Products** (www.walkermobility.com; ✆ **888/726-6837** or 407/518-6000). All the theme parks, except the water parks, rent ECVs for about $50 a day and wheelchairs for about $12 a day. If your own wheelchair is wider than 25 inches, think about switching to the park model,

because it is guaranteed to navigate tight squeezes such as hairpin queue turns. If you wear a prosthetic limb, you may have to remove it for the most aggressive rides. A few coasters (like SeaWorld's Mako) have restraint systems that won't be effective if you use certain prosthetics, so always ask the operators what's safe for you.

Organizations that offer assistance to travelers with disabilities include the **American Federation for the Blind** (www.afb.org; ✆ **800/232-5463**) and **Society for Accessible Travel & Hospitality** (www.sath.org; ✆ **212/447-7284**).

Area Codes The area code for the Orlando area is **407** (if you're dialing locally, a preceding 1 is not necessary, but the 407 is), although you may encounter the less common **321** code, which is also used on the Atlantic Coast. The **863** area code governs the land between Orlando and Tampa, and the Tampa area uses **813** and **727.** The region west of Orlando uses **352.**

Business Hours Offices are generally open weekdays between 9am and 5pm, while banks tend to close at 4pm. Typically, stores open between 9 and 10am and close between 6 and 7pm Monday through Saturday, except malls, which stay open until 9pm. On Sunday, stores generally open at 11am and close by 7pm.

Car Rentals This topic is perhaps the most hotly debated issue in all of Disneydom. The bottom line is there's only one reason to do without a car: You never intend to leave Disney. If you plan to fan out, such as visiting Harry Potter or the Space Shuttle, get wheels.

Disney guests often justify forgoing a car by saying they can't afford one. This is a fallacy. Disney hotels charge as much as twice what you'll pay to stay at a hotel of similar quality off-site. If you stay at a non-Disney property, you can afford a car and *still* pay less. A large inventory means rentals are cheaper here than in other American cities: $25 a day is common for a compact car.

One caveat is that **parking charges** can add up. Valet is often free in town, but the theme parks charge $22 a day for a space (Universal is free after 6pm). If you stay at a Disney resort, it is free. Also, if you pay for parking once at any Disney park, you won't have to pay again for another park on the same day. The bigger hotels now slap on $20-plus nightly fees for parking. In the rest of Orlando, parking is free, plentiful, and off the street.

Make sure your rental car locks by remote control fob; use it to make your vehicle honk and locate it in those confusing theme park parking pastures.

Crime   Disney may advertise itself as "the Happiest Place on Earth," but it's still on Earth. As we are all too aware, that means bad things happen. Never open your hotel room door to a stranger, never order anything off a flyer you find

under your door, and never give your personal details or credit card number to anyone who calls your room, even if they claim to work for the hotel. **Pickpockets** are virtually unheard of, but they exist. Be vigilant about bags; you're going to be bumped and jostled many times—one of those bumps could be a nimble-fingered thief. The theme parks all have metal detectors and bag checks.

Customs   Rules change. For details regarding current regulations, consult **U.S. Customs and Border Protection** (www.cbp.gov; ✆ **877/227-5511**).

Doctors   There are first-aid centers in all of the theme parks. There's also a 24-hour number for the **Poison Control Center** (✆ **800/222-1222**). To find a dentist, contact the **Dental Referral** (www.dentalreferral.com; ✆ **800/235-4111**). **DOCS** (www.doctorsoncallservice. com; ✆ **407/399-3627**) makes house and room calls. If you don't have a car, **East-Coast Medical Network** (www.themedicalconcierge. com; ✆ **855/932-5252**) makes "hotel room calls" to area resorts or rental homes for $150 to $275 for most ailments. It's available at all hours, accepts most insurance, and brings a portable pharmacy, although prescriptions cost more. Do not bring **medical marijuana** through Orlando's MCO airport; despite the fact carrying it is legal in Florida, the airport management has gone rogue and heeds

federal rules instead. Also see "Hospitals."

Drinking Laws   The legal drinking age is 21. Proof of age is always requested, even if you look older, so carry photo ID. It's illegal to carry open containers of alcohol in any car or public area that isn't zoned for alcohol consumption (as CityWalk and Disney Springs are), so outside of the resorts, the police may ticket you on the spot.

Driving Rules   Americans drive on the right. In Florida, you may turn right on red only after making a full stop unless the signal is an illuminated arrow, in which case you must wait for green. Many intersections are equipped with traffic cameras that will take a photo of your license plate, and rental car companies pass on fines along with hefty fees. If your plans take you outside the Orlando area, some toll roads (in Miami and Tampa, for example) are cashless and can only be paid by a SunPass sensor that must be rented, for an extra daily fee, from your rental agency, otherwise you will incur large penalties. Last, Florida is full of visitors who don't know where they're going or maybe have never even driven on the right before. These wandering souls will halt, cross three lanes of traffic, and barrel into the wrong lane without thinking. Keep a safe distance from the car in front of you.

Electricity   The United States uses 110 to 120 volts

AC (60 cycles), compared to the 220 to 240 volts AC (50 cycles) that is standard in Europe, Australia, and New Zealand. If your small appliances use 220 to 240 volts, buy an adapter and voltage converter before you leave home, because these can be difficult to come by in Orlando.

Embassies & Consulates The nearest embassies are located in the nation's capital, Washington, D.C. Some consulates are located in major U.S. cities, and most nations have a mission to the United Nations in New York City. Call for directory information in Washington, D.C. (© **202/555-1212**), or log on to **www.embassy.org/embassies**.

Emergencies Call © **911** for the police, to report a fire, or to get an ambulance. If you have a medical emergency that does not require an ambulance, you should be able to walk into the nearest hospital emergency room (see "Hospitals," below).

Family Travel All parks have a cool **baby care center** for heating formula, nursing, and so on, and diaper changing tables in the restrooms. But think carefully about whether your child is ready for the theme parks. I agree with many parenting experts who say that about 3 years old is the minimum age. Younger children get wigged out by costumed characters and get turned away from rides they have

their hearts set on. Some experts say kids are not truly ready for the rigors of theme parks until they can walk on their own all day. Whether or not very young children are *advisable*, they are *possible*: Scarier rides have what's called a **child swap.** That provides an area where one adult can wait with a child while their partner rides and then switch off so the other gets a chance without having to wait all over again. Many rides also have a bypass corridor where chickens can do their chicken-out thing.

Your **stroller** will not be allowed inside most attractions, and it will not be attended in parking sections, so never leave anything valuable in it. Come prepared with a system for repeatedly unloading valuables. Also have something that covers the seat; like in parked cars, they get sizzling hot in the Florida sun. Finally, tie an identifying marker (like a white flag, as in "I surrender") to yours so you can identify it amid the sea of clones. Some outfits deliver nicer models than Disney's to hotels: **Magic Strollers** (www.magicstrollers.com; © **866/866-6177**) and **Baby Wheels** (www.babywheelsorlando.com; © **800/510-2480**) among them.

If you want to lose $100 a day, you can rent a hand-made wire-frame stroller that looks like Cinderella's carriage from **Princess Carriage Rentals** (www.princesscarriagerentals.com; © **407/990-1844**).

Family Travel Tips

o **To avoid tears, familiarize yourself with height restrictions in advance.** They are posted at the parks' websites and listed on the maps. Universal also keeps physical gauges in front of both its parks. Everything is measured in inches, so if your child is usually measured in centimeters, multiply by 0.393.

o **Bring supplies to kidproof your hotel room.**

o **Slather your kids in sun lotion.** Florida sun is stronger than you think.

o **Dress kids in bright colors.** You'll spot them faster if you're separated. Some parents even put their phone number on their kids with temporary tattoos. You might also want to wear a distinctive hat or shirt yourself so they can spot you.

o **Dress to get wet.** There are water playgrounds, plus frequent rains.

o **Baby changing tables are in both women's and men's rooms.** No sexism here. At least in this. All those princesses hunting for men is another matter.

o **Hotels offer "kids eat free" programs.** Ask.

o **Theme park strollers are easy, but basic;** they don't recline, and they won't secure kids younger than toddlers. Folding "umbrella" strollers have distinct advantages. They make getting onto trams, monorails, and into other tight spaces easier (not just for you—also for people waiting for you).

o **Bring a picture of your child** or keep one on your mobile phone in case you get separated. Teach your child to go straight to the nearest employee if they get separated from you. Everyone is well trained in reuniting families.

Health Your biggest concern is the **sun,** which can burn you even through gray skies on cloudy days. You will be spending a lot more time outdoors than you might suspect—rides take 3 minutes, but some lines will have you waiting outside for an hour. Hats are your friends. If you see a wide roach about an inch and a half long, it's not necessarily due to uncleanliness at your hotel—those are waterbugs, which thrive in the damp Florida environment and are always hunting for food. As for mosquitos, the resorts' spraying regimes keep them in check, but if you're worried, any Disney cast member can tell you where to obtain free repellant.

Holidays Banks close on the following holidays: January 1 (New Year's), the third Monday in January (Martin Luther King, Jr., Day), the third Monday in February (Presidents' Day), the last Monday in May (Memorial Day), July 4 (Independence Day), the first Monday in September (Labor Day), the second Monday in October (Veterans Day), the fourth Thursday in November

(Thanksgiving Day), and December 25. The theme parks are open every day of the year.

Hospitals Dr. P. Phillips Hospital (9400 Turkey Lake Rd., Orlando; ℂ **407/351-8500**) is a short drive north up Palm Parkway from Lake Buena Vista. To get to **Florida Hospital Celebration Health** (400 Celebration Place, Celebration; ℂ **407/764-4000**), from I-4, take the U.S. 192 exit; then at the first traffic light, turn right onto Celebration Avenue, and at the first stop sign, make another right. Clinics: **Centra Care Walk-In Care** in Lake Buena Vista (12500 Apopka-Vineland Rd., ℂ **407/934-2273;** www.centracare.org; Mon–Fri 8am–midnight, Sat–Sun 8am–8pm); near the vacation homes south of Disney (8201 W. U.S. 192, Kissimmee; ℂ **407/465-0846;** Mon–Fri 8am–8pm, Sat–Sun 8am–5pm); and northwest of Universal (8014 Conroy-Windermere Rd., Suite 104; ℂ **407/291-8975;** Mon–Fri 8am–8pm, Sat–Sun 8am–5pm). In addition, each theme park has its own infirmary capable of handling a range of medical emergencies.

Insurance Among many options, you could try **UnitedHealthcare Global** (www.UHCsafetrip.com; ℂ **800/732-5309**) or **Travel Assistance International** (www.travelassistance.com; ℂ **800/821-2828**) for overseas medical insurance coverage.

So what else may you want to insure? You may want special coverage for **apartment stays,** especially

if you've plunked down a deposit, and any **valuables,** since airlines are only required to pay up to $2,500 for lost luggage domestically, less for foreign travel.

If you do decide on insurance, compare policies at **InsureMyTrip.com** (ℂ 800/487-4722) or **SquareMouth. com**.

Internet & Wi-Fi Getting online isn't hard. Wi-Fi is now considered an essential amenity, like running water. Most hotels will have free access—sometimes in common areas, sometimes in guest rooms, and sometimes in both places. Walt Disney World's hotels have free Wi-Fi, and so do all the theme parks in town. Hotel connections aren't always fast enough to stream movies, but they're usually fast enough for standard uses. Nearly all home rentals come with Internet-connected computers and free Wi-Fi.

LGBT Travelers
Orlando still has a conservative streak, but the Pulse massacre has made its citizens feel much more protective of its gay population. Most hotels aren't troubled in the least by gay couples, and gay people can be themselves anyplace. The most intolerant attitudes will come from other guests at the theme parks, who, of course, mostly aren't from Orlando. Public displays of affection are not likely to be attacked, but don't expect a warm reception, either. Then again, sexual affection is not celebrated in the parks if you're straight, either. Use

your intuition, your manners, and your common sense.

Mail At press time, domestic postage rates were 35¢ for a postcard and 50¢ for a letter. For international mail, a first-class letter of up to 1 ounce costs $1.15; a first-class international postcard costs the same as a letter. The post office most convenient to Disney and Universal is at 10450 Turkey Lake Rd. (© **407/351-2492;** Mon–Fri 8am–7pm, Sat 9am–5pm). If all you need is to buy stamps and mail letters, you can do that at most hotels. For more information, including locations nearest you, go to **www. usps.com** and click on "Calculate a Price." Ask at the theme park Guest Relations desks if mailing your items there will entitle you to a novelty postmark.

Mobile Phones Your phone will work in Orlando; it may not work is you drive far from commercial areas, such as in some remote vacation home developments (although in those cases you'll probably have Wi-Fi for Internet calling). To buy a pay-as-you-go SIM card, ask for a "no-contract" SIM card.

The theme parks' new reliance on programming your schedule via apps drains devices quickly. To have enough juice for a 13-hour day, carry a **portable charger or battery.** The theme parks' photo stores, located near the front gate, have FuelRod (www.fuel-rod. com) machines selling $30 pre-filled booster batteries,

adapter included; when it's depleted (they're not very powerful—your own would be better), you pop it into any other FuelRod vending machine elsewhere at Disney or anywhere in the world and swap for a fresh one at no charge. (FuelRods are about $10 cheaper if you buy one at home.) Disney will also charge your phone for free at Guest Relations if you have the required cord. At the Magic Kingdom, there's a public charger in a fake tree stump among the benches across from Peter Pan's Flight and in the big tent beside the Fantasyland railroad station; bring your own cord.

Money This town exists to rake in money. Consequently, it places few obstacles between you and the surrender of it. Most ATMs are run by third parties, not your bank (Disney's are by Chase), which means that you'll be slapped with fees of around $2.50 per withdrawal (around $5 for international visitors). Machines accept pretty much anything you can stick into them. Citibank customers can avoid the usage fee by using the fancy Citibank machines located at most 7-Eleven convenience stores. International visitors should make advance arrangements with their banks to ensure their cards will function in the United States. Also ask your bank if it has reciprocal agreements for free withdrawals anywhere.

Credit cards are nearly universally accepted. In fact,

you *must* have one to rent a car without a hassle. Most places accept the Big Four: American Express, MasterCard, Visa, and Discover. Very few places add Diners Club, and some family-owned businesses subtract American Express because of the pain of dealing with it.

Before you leave home, let your issuer know that you're about to go on vacation. Many of them get antsy when they see unexpectedly large charges start appearing so far from your home, and sometimes they freeze your account in response.

Try not to use credit cards to withdraw cash. You'll be charged interest from the moment your money leaves the slot. Universal sells its own private scrip, Wizarding Bank Notes, at Gringotts Money Exchange in Universal Studios. It's charged as a purchase, not a withdrawal, sparing you extra charges, and can be used to buy things inside Universal's parks.

Because ATM withdrawals give better deals, old-fashioned exchange desks are rare. One is Travelex Currency Exchange at Lake Buena Vista Factory Stores (p. 191; Mon–Sat 10am–9pm, Sun 10am–7pm), but you'll get better rates at a bank during regular banking hours.

Newspapers & Magazines A decreasing number of business hotels distribute that shallow McNewspaper, *USA Today*, to use as your morning doormat. The local paper, the *Orlando Sentinel* (www. orlandosentinel.com) is less widely available but much better for discovering local happenings. *Orlando Weekly* (www.orlandoweekly.com), free around town, covers trends, events, and restaurants. Also see the box on amateur-run websites covering the theme parks on p. 272; those are better for park goings-on.

Packing For the latest rules on how to pack and what you will be permitted to bring as a carry-on, consult your airline or the **Transportation Security Administration** (www.tsa.gov). Also be sure to find out from your airline what your checked-baggage weight limits will be;

maximums of around 50 pounds per suitcase are standard. Anything heavier will incur a fee. Paying for the luggage at the airport is often more expensive than online.

If you forget something, there's nothing you can't buy in Orlando. It's hardly Timbuktu. But bring the basics for sunshine (lotion of at least 30 SPF, wide-brimmed hat, bathing suit, sunglasses), for rain (a compact umbrella or a plastic poncho, which costs $10 if you wait until you get into the parks), for walking (good shoes, sandals for wet days), and for memories (camera, storage cards, chargers). Theme parks are too crowded for the safe use of large

umbrellas. Gum also isn't sold at any theme park resort because it makes the night cleaners cry.

Pets None of the Disney resorts allows animals (except service dogs) to stay (the only exception being Disney's Fort Wilderness Campground, where you can have your pet at the full-hook-up campsites). Disney offers **overnight animal boarding,** usually for about $30–$40 per day. Disney uses a single facility, **Best Friends Pet Care,** on the Bonnet Creek Parkway (www.wdw.bestfriendspetcare.com; ☏ **407/209-3126**). Overnight prices start at $41 for dogs and $26 for cats. For **daytime dog and cat boarding,** Universal charges

---

Stuff You Never Thought to Bring (But Should)

Besides the usual toiletries, recharging cords, and medications, you might not have thought of these good ideas, too:

- **Earplugs.** Orlando flights are swinging with kids going insane with excitement.

- **Hand sanitizer.** Turnstiles. Safety bars. Handrails. Furry mice. You're going to be handling a lot of dirty things.

- **Sole inserts.** You will be walking for miles and standing for hours, with few benches in sight. Even hardy feet need all the comfort you can provide.

- **Dark-colored clothing.** On almost all flume rides, the seating doubles as a step, so you're bound to stain your butt with a slightly muddy footprint. Also, it's hot and you'll be in lots of photos—and colored shirts show sweat marks.

- **Sandals that fasten.** Water-based rides soak regular shoes and cause

pruning. Flip-flops won't always do because they're not hardy and they won't stay on.

- **Skin-tight underwear.** Florida humidity can cause chafing even in people who rarely experience it. Under Armour or nonpadded bike shorts preempt that.

- **Sunscreen, a hat, and sunglasses.** Okay, so you probably thought of these, but it bears repeating.

- **A mobile phone battery recharger.** Between the My Disney Experience app, Wi-Fi, photos, and social media updating, you'll drain your battery quickly.

- **A superabsorbent shammy.** For lenses and wet children.

- **Pocket-size games.** People talk about rides, but they neglect to mention the hour in line before those exciting 3 minutes. Orlando *is* lines. Bring diversions.

$15 per pet at its first-come, first-served kennel (📞 **407/ 224-9509**) in the parking structure; there, owners must feed and walk their own dogs, but water is provided. You don't have to stay at a resort property to use Universal's service. Off-property, there's **VIPet Resort** (📞 **407/355-3594**; www. vipet.net; $50 overnight, $26 daytime), near where Sand Lake Road meets Florida's Turnpike. For all these services, your must have written proof of current vaccinations.

Universal's resorts (minus Cabana Bay) allow pets for a fee, and the hotels also provide welcome amenities. Also pet-friendly: Drury Hotels (p. 263) and the Marriott at Flamingo Crossings (p. 258). Expect a daily fee. To find more pet-friendly hotels, two solid resources are **www.petswelcome.com** and **www.dogfriendly.com**.

Pharmacies The tourist area hosts mostly national chains. **Walgreens** (7650 W. Sand Lake Rd. at Dr. Phillips Blvd., Orlando; 📞 **407/370-6742**), which has a round-the-clock pharmacy, could, at a stretch, be deemed an outfit with local roots; back in the day, Mr. Walgreen spent the cold months in Winter Park. **Turner Drugs** (1530 Celebration Blvd., Suite 105-A, Celebration; www.turnerdrug.com; 📞 **407/828-8125**) is not a 24-hour pharmacy, but it delivers prescriptions to most Disney-area accommodations.

Police Call 📞 **911** from any phone in an emergency.

Safety Calculated in fatalities per mile, the 132 miles of I-4 through Orlando is the deadliest highway in the United States, so drive it with extreme caution. Train kids to approach the nearest park employee in case of **separation.** Never dress kids in clothing that reveals their name, address, or hometown, and unless it's a travel day, remove any luggage tags where this information will be visible. If people can read your address off a tag while you're in line at Toy Story Land, then they'll know you're not at home. Stay out of lakes at night—Florida belonged to alligators for thousands of years before we were here, and evening is often when they get hungry. Attacks are extraordinarily rare, but one did happen in June 2016 on Disney's Seven Seas Lagoon when a gator mistook a 2-year-old child for small prey. Don't leave valuables visible when you park your car. Also, please keep your arms and legs inside the vehicle at all times. Thank you.

Senior Travel Just about every secondary attraction offers a special price for seniors, but the theme parks offer precious little. If you're over 50, you can join **AARP** (601 E. Street NW, Washington, DC 24009; www.aarp. org; 📞 **888/687-2277**) to find out what's being offered in terms of discounts for hotels, airfare, and car rentals. Before you bite, be sure that the AARP discount you are offered actually undercuts others that are out there. Elderhostel's well-respected **Road Scholar** (www.roadscholar.org; 📞 **800/454-5768**) runs classes and programs, both inside the theme parks and around the Orlando area, designed to delve into literature, history, the arts, and music. Packages last from a day to a week and include lodging, tours, and meals. Most are multigenerational; bring the grandkids.

Smoking Smoking is prohibited in public indoor spaces, including offices, restaurants, hotel lobbies, and most shops. Some bars permit it. In general, if you need to smoke, you must go outside into the open air, and in the theme parks smokers are comically quarantined to strictly enforced areas like bad kids in detention.

Taxes A 6.5% to 7% sales tax is charged on all goods with the exception of most edible grocery items and medicines. Hotels add another 2% to 5% in a resort tax, so the total tax on accommodations can run up to 12%. The United States has no VAT, but the custom is to not list prices with tax, so the final amount that you pay will be slightly higher than the posted price.

Telephones Generally, hotel surcharges on long-distance and local calls are astronomical, so you're better off using your **cellphone** or a **public pay telephone.**

Many convenience groceries and packaging services sell **prepaid calling cards** in denominations from $10 to $50; for international visitors these can be the least expensive way to call home. Many public phones at airports now accept American Express, MasterCard, and Visa credit cards. **Local calls** made from public pay phones in most locales cost either 35¢ or 50¢. Pay phones do not accept pennies, and few will take anything larger than a quarter. Make sure you have roaming turned on for your cellphone account.

If you will have high-speed Internet access in your room, save on calls by using **Skype** (www.skype. com), WhatsApp, or another Web-based calling app.

For calls within the United States and to Canada, dial 1 followed by the area code and the seven-digit number. **For other international calls,** first dial 011, then the country code, and then proceed with the number, dropping any leading zeroes.

Calls to area codes **800, 888, 877,** and **866** are toll-free. However, calls to area codes **700** and **900** can be very expensive—usually a charge of 95¢ to $3 or more per minute, and they sometimes have minimum charges that can run as high as $15 or more.

For **reversed-charge or collect calls,** and for person-to-person calls, dial the number 0, then the area code and number. If your operator-assisted call is international, ask for the overseas operator.

For **local directory assistance** ("information"), dial ☏ **411;** for long-distance information, dial 1, then the appropriate area code and 555-1212.

Time   Orlando is on Eastern Standard Time, so when it's noon in Orlando, it's 11am in Chicago (CST), 10am in Denver (MST), and 9am in Los Angeles (PST). Daylight saving moves the clock 1 hour ahead of standard time. Clocks change the second Sunday in March and the first Sunday in November.

Tipping   Tips are customary and should be factored into your budget. Waiters should receive 15% to 20% of the cost of the meal (depending on the quality of the service), bellhops get $1 per bag, bartenders get $1 per drink, chambermaids get $1 to $2 per day for straightening your room (although many people don't do that last one), and cab drivers should get 15% of the fare. The Disney Dining Plan automatically includes gratuity. Don't be offended if you are blatantly reminded to tip—it's usually to remind international visitors, who don't participate in the custom back home.

Toilets   Each theme park has dozens of restrooms that are clean (at least at opening time). Outside the parks, every fast-food place—and there are hundreds—should have a restroom you can use. Lobbies of large hotels also have some.

Visas   Citizens of western and central Europe, Australia, New Zealand, and Singapore need only a valid machine-readable passport and a round-trip air ticket or cruise ticket to enter the United States for stays of up to 90 days. Canadian citizens may enter without a visa with proof of residence.

Citizens of all other countries will need to obtain a tourist visa from the U.S. consulate. Depending on your country of origin, there may or may not be a charge attached (and you may or may not have to apply in person). Be sure to check with your local U.S. embassy or consulate for the very latest in entry requirements, because these continue to shift. Full information can be found at the **U.S. State Department**'s website, www. travel.state.gov.

Visitor Information
Orlando has one of the friendliest visitors' bureaus in America and it operates the **Orlando Official Visitor Center** (8102 International Dr.; www.visitorlando.com; ☏ **407/363-5872;** daily 8am–9pm), on the west side of I-Drive just south of Sand Lake Road. It's stocked from carpet to rafter with free brochures. Although many, many places in town claim to offer "official" tourist information, this is the only *truly* official place. Its ticket desk has the inside line on discounts, or use its free app

for find them or communicate with a city expert.

Kissimmee, the town closest to Walt Disney World, maintains its own tourist bureau (www.experience kissimmee.com; © **800/333-5477**). The Kissimmee CVB works with the Orlando bureau, so you won't have to make two trips.

Water   A powerful sense memory you will always carry after an Orlando vacation is the smell of the water. Tap water has a distinct mineral taste and aroma. Your hotel's pipes are not to blame. Rather, think of Central Florida as an island floating over a cushion of deep mineral water. In fact, most of the city's lakes started as sinkholes. Drinking water is drawn from the aquifer, hence the specific flavor and odor. Don't worry. It's safe. Likewise, your hotel pool smells of chlorine. And the water-based rides at the theme parks have an odor all their own: It's bromine, a cleaning agent that's favored in amusement rides because it's longer-lasting and easier to maintain than chlorine. (Bet you didn't know that. Aren't you glad you bought this book?)

Index

See also Accommodations and Restaurant indexes, below.

General Index

A

Accessible travel, 278–279
Accommodations, *see also* Accommodations Index
 amenities, 234
 discounts, 230
 Disney property, 234–235
 "Good Neighbor," 243
 Orlando, best, 5–6
 rates, 228
 rentals, homes, 264–266
 resorts, 235–243
 seasons, 230–234
 shuttles, 228
Adventureland, 43–46
Adventurers Outpost, 86
The Affection Station, 91
Africa, 90–91
After-dark activities, 59, 80, 93, 112
Air travel, 267–270
AirHeads, 165
Akershus Royal Banquet Hall, 74
Alien Swirling Saucers, 104
Amazing Adventures of Spider-Man, 3, 9, 135
American Adventure, 66, 77
American dream, 1–2
America's Escape Game, 169
Andretti Indoor Karting & Games, 161
Animal Actors on Location!, 129
Animal Connections, 148
Animal Guide, 32
Animal Kingdom, *see* Disney's Animal Kingdom
Animation Courtyard, 105–106
Antarctica: Empire of the Penguin, 153
Aquarium: The Beautiful Ocean, 151
Aquatica, 3, 146, 157
Area codes, 279
Arnold Palmer's Bay Hill Club & Lodge, 187
Asia, 91–93
Astro Orbiter, 38, 57
Astronaut Training Experience, 179–180
Atlanta Braves, 167
Authentic experiences, Orlando, 5
Aux Vins de France, 79
Avatar Flight of Passion, 3, 88–89

B

Babysitting, 204
Backstage Magic, 114
Badges, 40

Banana Beach, 157
The Band, 173
Barnes & Noble, 194
Barnstormer, 55
Baseball, 167
Base ticket, 22–23
The Beat Builders, 123
The Beatles, 173
Be Our Guest, 10
Beauty and the Beast—Live on Stage, 100, 103
Beer, 34
Behind-the-scenes tours, 5
BetterBidding.com, 251
Bibbidi Bobbidi Boutique, 10, 43, 192–194
BiddingForTravel.com, 251
BiddingTraveler.com, 251
Big Thunder Mountain Railroad, 38–39, 47–48
Bijutsu-kan Gallery, 4, 78
BK Adventure, 185
Blackfish documentary, 148
Blizzard Beach, 3, 109–110
Blue Man Group, 225
Blue Spring State Park, 5, 183
The Blues Brothers, 122
BoardWalk, 204–205, 225
Boardwalk Baseball, 160
Boat tours, 185–186
Bob Marley—A Tribute to Freedom, 225
Boggy Creek Airboat Rides, 185
Bok Tower Gardens, 5, 172
The Boneyard, 93
Bon Voyage, 222
Boop Oop A Doop, 136
Boutique de Cadeaux, 79
The Brass Bazaar, 78
Breakfast with Elmo and Friends, 156
Breakout Escape Rooms, 169
British Revolution band, 79
Bruce's Shark World, 71
Busch Gardens Tampa Bay, 159–160
Business hours, 279
Busy times, 273–274
Butterbeer, 139
Buzz Lightyear's Space Ranger Spin, 38–39, 56–57
Bypass, 40

C

Camp Jurassic, 138
Camping World Bowl, 277
Canada, 79–80
Canaveral cruises, 194–195
Cape May Café, 222
Capone's Dinner & Show, 218
Captain Jack Sparrow's Pirate Tutorial, 46
Car rentals, 268–269, 279–280
Car travel, 270–271
Carkitt Market, 124–125
Carnival Cruise Lines, 195
Caro-Seuss-el, 142
Carrousel, 38
Casablanca Carpets, 78

Casey Jr. Splash 'N' Soak Station, 55
Cassadaga, 4, 11, 171
Castaway Creek, 111
Castle Couture, 51
The Cat in the Hat, 142–143
Celebration Golf Course, 188
Central Florida Nature Adventures, 185
ChampionsGate Golf Resort, 187
Character greetings, 33
Character meals, 6, 112, 220–223
Character Party Zone, 128
Characters in Flight, 111
Charles Hosmer Morse Museum of American Art, 5, 170–172
Chase Disney Rewards Visa credit card, 26
Cheetah Hunt, 160
Chef Mickey's, 222
China, 75–76
Chocolate Kingdom, 161–162
Cinderella Castle, 37, 42–43
Cinderella's Happily Ever After Dinner, 222
Cinderella's Royal Table, 7, 10, 37, 43, 221
Cinematic Celebration, 120
The Circle of Life, 72
Circus World, 160
Cirque du Soleil, 111
Citrus Bowl, 274
City Hall, 40
CityWalk, 226
CityWalk's Rising Star, 226
Classic attractions, 46
Climate, 274
Closing time, 35
Clothing, 33
Clyde & Seamore's Sea Lion High, 150–151
Coastersaurus, 159
Cobra's Curse, 160
Colby, George P., 171
Cold War, 19
Comfort, 19
Comic Book Shop, 134
Commissary Lane, 103
Congo River Adventure Golf, 177
Consulates, 281
Contact numbers, 32
Conventions, tickets, 24
Cornell Fine Arts Museum, 5, 172
Costs, basics, 34
Country Bear Jamboree, 46
Crayola Experience, 162
Crime, 280
Cross Country Creek, 110
Crown & Crest, 79
Cruises, from Port Canaveral, 194–195
Crush 'n' Gusher, 110
Crystal Palace, 221
Culture, Disney, 44
Curious George Goes to Town, 130
Customs, 280
Cypress Gardens Historic Botanical Garden, 159

D

Dapper Dans, 40
A Day in the Park with Barney, 129–130
Deals, tickets, 26
De Leon Springs State Park, 5, 11, 183–184
Der Teddybär, 76
Despicable Me Character Breakfast, 223
Despicable Me Minion Mayhem, 121
Detroit Tigers, 167
Devish and Banges, 139
Diamond Bellas, 122
Dining, see also Restaurant Index
  Animal Kingdom, 94–97
  Downtown Orlando, 214–217
  Epcot, 80–85
  Hollywood Studios, 106–108
  International Drive, 211–214
  Islands of Adventure, 143–145
  Lake Buena Vista, 207–211
  Little Vietnam, 217
  Magic Kingdom, 58–64
  on-site, 29
  plans, 30, 33, 132, 156
  Quick Service, 33
  reservations, 196
  savings tips, 61
  SeaWorld, 156–157
  Universal Orlando, 205–207
  Universal Studios Florida, 130–132
Dinnertainment, 217–220
DinoLand U.S.A., 93–94
Dinosaur World, 173
DINOSAUR, 88, 94
Disabled travellers, 278–279
DISBoards.com, 26
Discounts, 24, 26, 277–278
Discovery Cove, 3, 146, 157–158
Discovery Island Trails, 86
Discovery Island, 86–89
"Disco Yeti," 92
Disney, Elias, 1–2
Disney, Roy, 41
Disney, Walt, 19–20
Disney & Pixar, 72
Disney Cruise Line, 195
Disney culture, 44
Disney Dining Plan, 30, 33
Disney Imagineers, 221–222
Disney Junior Play 'N Dine, 222
Disney Junior—Live on Stage!, 100, 105
Disney Skyliner gondolas, 31
Disney Springs, 10, 111–113, 191–192, 201–204, 223–224
Disney Transportation System, 30–31
Disney Vacation Club, 7, 243–244
Disneyfication, 2
Disney's Animal Kingdom, 2, 3, 10–11, 85–97
  adults (without kids), 88
  Adventurers Outpost, 86
  The Affection Station, 91
  Africa, 90–91

after dark, 93
Asia, 91–93
Avatar: Flight of Passage, 88–89
best of, 86
The Boneyard, 93
Chester & Hester's Dino-Rama, 93–94
Conservation Station, 91
dining, 94–97
DinoLand U.S.A., 93–94
DINOSAUR, 88, 94
"Disco Yeti," 92
Discovery Island, 86–89
Discovery Island Trails, 86
entry, 85
Expedition Everest, 88, 91–92
"Festival of the Lion King," 88, 90–91
Finding Nemo—The Musical, 88, 93
Fossil Fun Games, 93
Gorilla Falls Exploration Trail, 88, 90
Habitat Habit!, 91
It's Tough to Be a Bug!, 86–89
Kali River Rapids, 88, 92
kid-friendly activities, 88
Kilimanjaro Safaris, 88, 90, 93
Maharajah Jungle Trek, 88, 92
Na'vi River Journey, 88, 90
Pandora—The World of Avatar, 88–90, 93
Primeval Whirl, 88, 93
quick-service restaurants, 94–96
Rafiki's Planet Watch, 88, 91
Rivers of Light, 88, 93
table-service restaurants, 96–97
The Tree of Life, 86, 93
TriceraTop Spin, 88, 93
UP! A Great Bird Adventure, 88, 92–93
Wilderness Explorers, 91
Wildlife Express Train, 91
Disney's Hollywood Studios, 2–3
Disney's Spirit of Aloha Show, 219
Disney's Winter Summerland, 177
Doctors, 280
Doldrick's Escape Room, 169
Dolphin Days, 151
Dolphin Encounter, 152
Dolphin Lagoon, 158
Dolphin Nursery, 152
Dolphin Plunge, 157
Donald's Dining Safari, 222
Donkey's Photo Finish, 121
Downhill Double Dipper, 109
Downtown Orlando, 16–17, 214–217
Dr. Doom's Fearfall, 135
Dr. Phillips Center for the Performing Arts, 180
Drinking laws, 280
Driving rules, 280
Driving School, 159
Dudley Do-Right's Ripsaw Falls, 3, 136
Duff Brewery's, 127
Dumbo the Flying Elephant, 37–38, 46, 53–54

DUPLO Valley, 159
DVC, see Disney Vacation Club

E

East of Orlando, 18
Eating on-site, 29
Echo Lake, 97–102
ECV (electric convenience vehicle), 34
The Edison, 224
Electrical Boat Parade, 112
Electricity, 280–281
Embassies, 281
Emergencies, 281
The Emporium, 37, 40
Enchanted Tales with Belle, 38, 53
Enchanted Tiki Room, 38–39, 44–46
Enoteca Castello, 77
Entry, 32, 35–37, 66–67, 85, 133
Enzian, 180–181
Epcot, 2–4, 8–10, 64–85
  after dark, 80
  Akershus Royal Banquet Hall, 74
  American Adventure, 66, 77
  Aux Vins de France, 79
  best of, 68
  Bijutsu-kan Gallery, 78
  Boutique de Cadeaux, 79
  The Brass Bazaar, 78
  British Revolution band, 79
  Bruce's Shark World, 71
  Canada, 79–80
  Casablanca Carpets, 78
  China, 75–76
  The Circle of Life, 72
  Crown & Crest, 79
  Der Teddybär, 76
  dining, 80–85
  Disney & Pixar, 72
  Enoteca Castello, 77
  entry, 66–67
  Fez House, 78
  France, 78–79
  Frozen Ever After, 66, 75
  Future World, 66–73
  Germany, 76
  Gran Fiesta Tour, 66, 74
  Guardians of the Galaxy ride, 68
  hedge maze, 79
  history, 67
  hours, 67
  House of Good Fortune, 75
  House of the Whispering Willow, 75
  IllumiNations: Reflections of Earth, 66, 80
  "Impressions de France," 79
  Innoventions, 69
  International Gateway, 67
  Italy, 76–77
  itinerary, 66
  Japan, 77–78
  Journey into Imagination with Figment, 72–73
  Karamell-Küche, 76
  Kidcot Fun Stops, 71

Epcot (continued)
kid-friendly activities, 71
La Gemma Elegante, 77
L'Esprit de la Provence, 79
Librairie et Galerie, 79
Living with the Land, 66, 72
Lords and Ladies, 79
Mdundo Kibanda, 76
Mexico, 74
Mission: Space, 66, 69
Mitsukoshi Department Store, 78
monorail, 66
Morocco, 78
Moroccan Style, 78
MouseGear, 69
Northwest Mercantile, 80
Norway, 74–75
"O Canada!" 80
Outpost, 76
Phineas and Ferb: Agent
  P's World Showcase
  Adventure, 71
Plume et Palette, 78
The Puffin's Roost, 75
quick-service restaurants, 80–82
Ratatouille ride, 68
"Reflections of China," 75–76
Royal Sommerhus, 75
The Seas with Nemo and
  Friends, 66, 70–71
Soarin', 66, 71–72
Spaceship Earth, 66, 68–69
Sportsman's Shoppe, 79
Stave Church Gallery, 74
table-service restaurants, 82–85
Tea Caddy, 79
Test Track, 66, 69–70
Toy Soldier, 79
Turtle Talk with Crush, 71
United Kingdom, 79
U.S.A., 77
The Wandering Reindeer, 75
Weinkeller, 76
wine tasting, 76
Wonders of Life, 70
World Fellowship Fountain, 69
World Showcase, 66–67, 73–80
Epcot Character Spot, 69
Epcot International Festival of the
  Arts, 274
Epcot International Festival of the
  Holidays, 276
Epcot International Food & Wine
  Festival, 275
Epcot's International Flower &
  Garden Festival, 275
The Escape Game, 169
Escape rooms, 169
Escapology, 169
E.T. Adventure, 129
Eternelle's Elixir of
  Refreshment, 125
E-tickets, 57
Events calendar, 274–277
Expedition Everest, 88, 91–92
Expedition SeaWorld VIP
  Tour, 149
Explorer's Aviary, 158
Express Plus, 117

F
Fairytale Hall, 38
Falcon's Fury, 160
Falcon's Fire Golf Club, 188
Family travel, 281–282
Fantasmic!, 95, 97, 100, 103, 112
Fantasyland Station, 55–56
Fantasyland, 50–56
Fast & Furious—Supercharged,
  4, 123
Fastpass+, 7, 10, 26–28, 35,
  37–39
Fear Factor Live, 127
Ferryboat, 35
Festival of Fantasy Parade, 47
"Festival of the Lion King," 88,
  90–91
Fez House, 78
Fievel's Playland, 129
Finding Nemo—The Musical,
  88, 93
Fire Station, 41
Fireworks, 8, 37, 39, 59, 112
Fireworks Dessert Party, 59
Flag retreat ceremony, 40
Flight of the Hippogriff, 140
Florida Film Festival, 275
Florida Mall, 190
Florida Music Festival, 275
Flying School, 159
Footwear, 8
Fossil Fun Games, 93
Fountain of Fair Fortune, 125
France, 78–79
Free activities, 63
Freshwater Oasis, 158
Frontierland, 46–49
Frontierland Shootin' Arcade, 39,
  48–49
Frontier Station, 48
Frozen Ever After, 3, 9, 66, 75
Frozen Sing-Along
  Celebration, 98
Fun Spot America—
  Kissimmee, 174
Fun Spot America—Orlando, 162
Future World, 9, 66–73

G
Gangplank Falls, 110
Garden Grill, 222
Garden Grove, 222
Gasoline Alley, 136
Gatorland, 3, 5, 174–175
Gay Days, 275
Germany, 76
Give Kids the World Village, 4,
  175–176
Global Resort Homes, 265
Golf, 186–189
Gone with the Wind, 42
Good Morning Breakfast with
  Goofy & Pals, 223
Gorilla Falls Exploration Trail,
  88, 90
Gospel Brunch, 220
Gran Fiesta Tour, 66, 74
The Grand Reef, 158
Great Depression, 19

The Great Escape Room, 169
The Great Lego Race, 159
Great Moments in American
  History, 49
Green Eggs & Ham Café, 142
Grinchmas, 276–277
the groove, 226
Guardians of the Galaxy ride, 68
Guest Relations, 32
Guest Services, 32
Guidemap, 32

H
Habitat Habit!, 91
The Hall of Presidents, 50
Halloween Horror Nights, 276
Happily Ever After, 59, 112
Hard Rock Live, 226
Harmony Barber Shop, 4–5,
  41–42
Harry P. Leu Gardens, 5, 184
Harry Potter and the Escape from
  Gringotts, 4, 9, 124
Harry Potter and the Forbidden
  Journey, 3, 140
Harry Potter roller coaster, 3
The Haunted Mansion, 3, 8,
  37–39, 46, 49–50
Hawk's Landing Golf Club, 188
Health, 282
Heat, 11
Hedge maze, 79
Hidden Mickeys, 106
High in the Sky Seuss Trolley Train
  Ride!, 142
Highlands Reserve Golf Club, 188
History, Epcot, 67
Hogsmeade, 9
Hogwart's Express train, 8–9, 126,
  140–141
Holidays, 282
Hollywood, 118, 128
Hollywood Boulevard, 97–102
Hollywood Character Zone, 128
Hollywood Drive-In Golf, 177
Hollywood Rip Ride Rockit,
  120–121
Hollywood Studios, 10–11, 95,
  97–108
  adults (without kids), 100
  Alien Swirling Saucers, 104
  Animation Courtyard, 105–106
  Beauty and the Beast—Live on
    Stage, 100, 103
  best of, 98
  Commissary Lane, 103
  dining, 106–108
  Disney Junior—Live on Stage!,
    100, 105
  Echo Lake, 97–102
  Fantasmic!, 95, 97, 100, 103
  Frozen Sing-Along
    Celebration, 98
  Hidden Mickeys, 106
  Hollywood Boulevard, 97–102
  Indiana Jones Epic Stunt
    Spectacular, 95, 98–101
  itinerary, 100
  Jedi Academy, 100

Jedi Training, 101–102
kid-friendly activities, 100
Lightning McQueen's Racing
    Academy, 100, 102
Mickey & Minnie's Runaway
    Railway, 101
Mickey Mouse meeting, 100
Muppets Courtyard, 103
Muppet*Vision 3-D, 100, 103
Pixar Place, 105–106
quick-service restaurants,
    106–107
Rock 'n' Roller Coaster, 95,
    100, 102
Slinky Dog Dash, 95, 100, 104
Star Tours—The Adventure
    Continues, 95, 100–101
Star Wars: A Galactic
    Spectacular, 95, 97, 100
Star Wars: Galaxy's Edge, 101
Star Wars Launch Bay, 105
Star Wars: Path of the Jedi, 98
Sunset Boulevard, 102–103
table-service restaurants,
    107–108
Toy Story Land, 104
Toy Story Mania!, 95, 100, 104
Twilight Zone Tower of Terror,
    95, 100, 102
Voyage of the Little Mermaid,
    100, 105
Walt Disney Presents, 105–106
Holy Land Experience, 168
Home rentals, 264–266
Honeydukes, 139
**Hoop-Dee-Doo Musical Revue, 8,
    10, 220**
The Hopping Pot, 125
Horizont Alley, 124–125
Hospitals, 282
Hot-air balloons, 189–190
Hotels, see also
    Accommodations Index
    amenities, 234
    discounts, 230
    Disney property, 234–235
    "Good Neighbor," 243
    Orlando, best, 5–6
    rates, 228
    resorts, 235–243
    seasons, 230–234
    shuttles, 228
House of Blues, 113
House of Good Fortune, 75
**House of the Whispering Willow,
    4, 75**
Houston Astros, 167
Howl at the Moon Saloon, 181

I

ICE!, 276
Icebar, 181
ICON Orlando, 4, 165
I-Drive NASCAR, 162–164
If I Ran the Zoo, 142
iFly, 164
Ihu's Breakaway Falls, 157
**IllumiNations: Reflections of
    Earth, 9, 66, 80**

Imagineers, 221–222
"Impressions de France," 79
Incredible Hulk Coaster, 3, 9, 134
**Indiana Jones Epic Stunt
    Spectacular, 95, 98–101**
Infinity Falls, 3–4, 154
Innoventions, 69
Insurance, 282
International Drive, 16, 161–177
    AirHeads, 165
    Andretti Indoor Karting &
        Games, 161
    Bok Tower Gardens, 172
    Charles Hosmer Morse
        Museum of American Art,
        170–172
    Chocolate Kingdom, 161–162
    Cornell Fine Arts Museum, 172
    Crayola Experience, 162
    dining, 211–214
    Dinosaur World, 173
    Fun Spot America—
        Kissimmee, 174
    Fun Spot America—
        Orlando, 162
    Gatorland, 174–175
    Give Kids the World Village,
        175–176
    Holy Land Experience, 168
    ICON Orlando, 165
    I-Drive NASCAR, 162–164
    iFly, 164
    Machine Gun America, 176
    Madame Tussauds, 164
    Magical Midway Thrill Park, 164
    Mennello Museum of American
        Art, 168
    Old Town, 176
    Orange County Regional
        History Center, 169–170
    Orlando Museum of Art, 170
    Orlando Science Center, 170
    Orlando SeaLife Aquarium, 165
    Orlando StarFlyer, 166
    Outer Limitz, 165
    Reptile World Serpentarium,
        176–177
    Ripley's Believe It or Not!
        Odditorium, 166
    Skeletons: Museum of
        Osteology, 166
    Titanic: The Artifact Exhibition,
        166–167
    Winter Park, 170–172
    WonderWorks, 167–168
    Zombie Outbreak, 165
International Gateway, 67
Internet, 282
IPG Florida Vacation Homes, 265
**Islands of Adventure, 2–3, 9,
    132–145**
    The Amazing Adventures of
        Spider-Man, 135
    best of, 135
    Boop Oop A Doop, 136
    Butterbeer, 139
    Camp Jurassic, 138
    Caro-Seuss-el, 142
    The Cat in the Hat, 142–143
    Comic Book Shop, 134

    Devish and Banges, 13?
    dining, 143–145
    Dr. Doom's Fearfall, 135
    Dudley Do-Right's Ripsa?
        Falls, 136
    entry, 133
    Flight of the Hippogriff, 140
    Gasoline Alley, 136
    Green Eggs & Ham Café, 142
    Harry Potter and the Forbidden
        Journey, 140
    High in the Sky Seuss Trolley
        Train Ride!, 142
    Hogwarts Express, 140–141
    Honeydukes, 139
    If I Ran the Zoo, 142
    Incredible Hulk Coaster, 134
    Jurassic Park, 137–138
    Jurassic Park Discovery
        Center, 138
    Jurassic Park River
        Adventure, 138
    localARTicles Boutique, 141
    The Lost Continent, 141
    The Magic Neep, 139
    Marvel Super Hero Island,
        134–135
    Me Ship, the Olive, 137
    Mystic Fountain, 141
    Nighttime Lights at Hogwarts
        Castle, 140
    Ollivanders, 140
    One Fish, Two Fish, Red Fish,
        Blue Fish, 142
    Popeye & Bluto's Bilge-Rat
        Barges, 136–137
    Poseidon's Fury, 141
    Pteranodon Flyers, 138
    Pumpkin Juice, 139
    Raptor Encounter, 138
    Seuss Landing, 141–143
    shopping, 134
    Skull Island: Reign of Kong, 137
    Storm Force Accelatron, 134
    Toon Lagoon, 135–137
    The Wizarding World of
        Harry Potter—Hogsmeade,
        138–141
Italy, 76–77
**"it's a small world," 3, 8, 37–39,
    46, 51**
It's Tough to Be a Bug!, 86–89

J

Japan, 77–78
Jedi Academy, 100
Jedi Training, 101–102
**Jimmy Buffett's
    Margaritaville, 226**
Johnson, LB, 173
**Journey into Imagination with
    Figment, 72–73**
Journey of the Little Mermaid, 38
Journey to Atlantis, 153
Jungle Cruise, 3, 38–39, 44, 46
JungleLand Zoo, 160
Jurassic Park Discovery Center, 138
Jurassic Park River Adventure, 138
Jurassic Park, 137–138

K

Kali River Rapids, 88, 92
Kang & Kodos' Twirl 'n' Hurl, 128
Karamell-Küche, 76
Kennedy Space Center, 4, 11, 178–180
Kennedy, John, 19
Kerouac, Jack, 173
Ketchakiddee Creek, 111
Kidcot Fun Stops, 71
Kid-friendly activities, 112
   Animal Kingdom, 88
   Epcot, 71
   Hollywood Studios, 100
Kids under 8, 38
Kilimanjaro Safaris, 88, 90, 93
Kings Bowl Orlando, 181
"Kiss Goodnight," 59
Kissimmee, 15–16
Knight Bus, 123
Knockturn Alley, 124
Ko'okiri Body Plunge, 145
Kopiko Wai, 145
Krakatau, 145
Kraken Unleashed, 4, 153
Kwik-E-Mart, 127

L

La Gemma Elegante, 77
Lake Buena Vista, 16, 191, 207–211
Lard Lad Donuts, 127
Layout, Orlando, 11–14
Leaky Cauldron, 8
Le Chapeau, 40
Legoland Florida, 3–5, 158–159
Lennon, John, 19
L'Esprit de la Provence, 79
Let the Magic Begin, 35
LGBT travelers, 282–283
Liberty Square Riverboat, 46, 50
Liberty Square, 49–50
Librairie et Galerie, 79
Liftoffs, 180
Lightning McQueen's Racing Academy, 100, 102
Line hopping, 117–118
Little Vietnam, 217
Living with the Land, 66, 72
localARTicles Boutique, 141
Lockbusters, 169
Lockers, 34
Loggerhead Lane, 157
Loose articles, 120
Lords and Ladies, 79
The Lost Continent, 141
Lost Kingdom Adventure, 159
Lunch with an Astronaut, 180

M

Machine Gun America, 176
Macy's Holiday Parade, 276–277
Madame Tussauds, 164
"Made with Magic" mouse ears, 59
Mad Tea Party, 39, 52–53
Magazines, 283–284

Magical Menagerie, 125
MagicBands, 25–28, 33, 42
Magic of Disney, 19–22
Magic Kingdom, 2–3, 8–10, 34–64
   adults only itinerary, 39
   Adventureland, 43–46
   after dark, 59
   Astro Orbiter, 38, 57
   badges, 40
   Barnstormer, 55
   best of, 37
   Bibbidi Bobbidi Boutique, 43
   Big Thunder Mountain Railroad, 38–39, 47–48
   Buzz Lightyear's Space Ranger Spin, 38–39, 56–57
   bypass, 40
   Carrousel, 38
   Casey Jr. Splash 'N' Soak Station, 55
   Castle Couture, 51
   Cinderella Castle, 37, 42–43
   Cinderella's Royal Table, 37, 43
   City Hall, 40
   closing time, 35
   Cosmic Dance Party, 56
   Country Bear Jamboree, 38–39, 48
   Crystal Arts, 40
   Crystal Palace, 37
   Dapper Dans, 40
   dining, 58–64
   Dumbo the Flying Elephant, 37–38, 53–54
   The Emporium, 37, 40
   Enchanted Tales with Belle, 38, 53
   Enchanted Tiki Room, 38–39, 44–45
   entering, 35–37
   Fairytale Hall, 38
   Fantasyland, 50–56
   Fantasyland Station, 55–56
   ferryboat, 35
   Festival of Fantasy Parade, 47
   Fire Station, 41
   fireworks, 37, 39, 59
   flag retreat ceremony, 40
   Frontierland, 46–49
   Frontierland Shootin' Arcade, 39, 48–49
   Frontier Station, 48
   Great Moments in American History, 49
   The Hall of Presidents, 50
   Happily Ever After, 59
   Harmony Barber Shop, 41–42
   Haunted Mansion, 37–39, 49–50
   "it's a small world," 37–39, 51
   Journey of the Little Mermaid, 38
   Jungle Cruise, 38–39, 44
   kids under 8, 38
   Le Chapeau, 40
   Let the Magic Begin, 35
   Liberty Square, 49–50
   Liberty Square Riverboat, 50
   "Made with Magic" mouse ears, 59

Mad Tea Party, 39, 52–53
   MagicBand, 42
   Magic Carpets of Aladdin, 38, 44
   Main Street, U.S.A., 37–39, 46
   Many Adventures of Winnie the Pooh, 37–39, 52
   Memento Mori, 50
   Mickey's PhilharMagic, 38–39, 52
   Mickey's Royal Friendship Faire, 43
   Monorail, 35
   Monsters, Inc. Laugh Floor, 58
   Move It! Shake It! Dance & Play It! Street Party, 47
   names, windows, 42
   Once Upon a Time, 59
   one-day itineraries, 38–39
   parade, 40, 47, 112
   peaceful places, 37
   PeopleMover, 57
   Peter Pan's Flight, 37–39, 51–52
   Pete's Silly Sideshow, 38, 54–55
   A Pirate's Adventure—Treasures of the Seven Seas, 46
   Pirates of the Caribbean, 37–39, 45–46
   Prince Charming Regal Carrousel, 52
   Princess Fairytale Hall, 52
   quick-service restaurants, 58–61
   Seven Dwarfs Mine Train, 37–39, 53
   shopping, 37
   Sorcerers of the Magic Kingdom, 41
   Space Mountain, 37–39, 56
   Splash Mountain, 37–39, 46–47–48
   Storybook Circus, 51
   strategy, 37
   Swiss Family Treehouse, 37, 43
   table-service restaurants, 61–64
   teens, 38–39
   Tomorrowland, 56–58
   Tomorrowland Speedway, 37, 38, 56
   Tomorrowland Transit Authority, 39, 57
   Tom Sawyer Island, 48
   Town Square Theater, 38, 42
   Transportation and Ticket Center (TTC), 35
   TRON Lightcycle Power Run, 56
   Under the Sea—Journey of the Little Mermaid, 54
   Walt Disney's Carousel of Progress, 37, 39, 57–58
   Walt Disney World Railroad, 41, 47, 55–56
   window names, 42
Magical Midway Thrill Park, 164
Magical Vacation Homes, 265–266
The Magic Neep, 139
Magic Sunrise Ballooning, 189
Magic Your Way, 22–26
Maharajah Jungle Trek, 88, 92

Mail, 283
Main Street, U.S.A., 37–39, 46
Mako, 4, 154
Maku Puihi, 145
Mall at Millenia, 190
Manatee Rehabilitation, 152
Mango Market, 157
Mango's Tropical Café, 181–182
Manta, 4, 151–152
Many Adventures of Winnie the
    Pooh, 37–39, 52
Mardi Gras at Universal
    Studios, 275
Marilyn Monroe, 122
Marvel Character Dinner, 223
Marvel Super Hero Island,
    134–135
Mayday Falls, 110
Mdundo Kibanda, 76
MDX, 25–28, 33
Me Ship, the Olive, 137
Medieval Times, 218
Melt Away Bay, 109
Memento Mori, 50
Memory Maker, 10, 34
Men in Black: Alien Attack, 126
Mennello Museum of American
    Art, 168
MetroWest Golf Club, 188
Mexico, 74
Mickey & Minnie's Runaway
    Railway, 2, 101
Mickey ice cream bars, 34, 37
Mickey Mouse meeting, 100
Mickey's Not-So-Scary Halloween
    Party, 276
Mickey's Royal Friendship
    Faire, 43
Mickey's Very Merry Christmas
    Party, 276
Mickey's Backyard BBQ, 220
Mickey's PhilharMagic, 38–39, 52
Mills Fifty, 10, 217
Miniature golf, 177
Miniland USA, 4
Minnie Vans, 31
Minus5° Icebar, 181
Miss Adventure Falls, 111
Mission: Space, 66, 69
Mistakes, planning, 8
Mitsukoshi Department Store, 78
Mobile ordering, tickets, 28
Mobile phones, 283
Moe's Tavern, 127
Money, 283
Monorail, 8, 35, 46, 66
Monsters, Inc. Laugh Floor, 58
Moroccan Style gallery, 4, 78
Morocco, 78
Morse Museum, 11
MouseGear, 69
MouseSavers.com,, 26
Move It! Shake It! Dance & Play It!
    Street Party, 47
Munchies, savings, 61
Muppet*Vision 3-D, 100, 103
Muppets Courtyard, 103
My Disney Experience, see MDX

My Universal Photos, 118
MyMagic+, 25
Mystic Dunes Golf Club, 187
Mystic Fountain, 141

N

Names, windows, 42
NASA, 179
Na'vi River Journey, 88, 90
NBC Media Center, 129
Neighborhoods, Orlando, 14–18
    Downtown, 16–17
    East of Orlando, 18
    International Drive, 16
    Kissimmee, 15–16
    Lake Buena Vista, 16
    North of Orlando, 17
    South of Orlando, 17–18
    U.S. 192, 15–16
    Walt Disney World Resort,
        14–15
    West of Orlando, 18
    Winter Park, 17
New Year's Eve, 277
New York, 118, 122–123
Newspapers, 283–284
Nightlife, 180–183, 223–226
Nighttime Lights at Hogwarts
    Castle, 140
Nixon, Richard, 173
Non-tourist locations, 173
North of Orlando, 17
Northwest Mercantile, 80
Norway, 74–75
Norwegian Cruise Lines, 195

O

"O Canada!" 80
Official Universal Orlando Resort
    App, 118
'Ohana Character Breakfast, 223
Ohno slide, 145
Ohyah slide, 145
Old Town, 176
Ollivanders, 125–126, 140
Once Upon a Time, 59
One-day itineraries, 7–8, 38–39
One Fish, Two Fish, Red Fish, Blue
    Fish, 142
One Ocean, 150
One-week itinerary, 10–11
On-site eating, 29
Optional services, 33–34
Options, ticket, 23
Orange County National Golf
    Center and Lodge, 189
Orange County Regional History
    Center, 169–170
Orange World, 194
Orlando
    authentic experiences, 5
    best of, 1–6
    hotels, best, 5–6
    layout, 11
    neighborhoods, 14–18
    overlooked experiences, 4–5
    restaurants, best, 6
    rides, best, 3–4

    shows, best, 3–4
    theme parks, best experiences,
        2–3
Orlando Balloon Rides, 189
Orlando Brewing and
    Taproom, 182
Orlando Film Festival, 276
Orlando International Fringe
    Festival, 275
Orlando International Premium
    Outlets, 190
Orlando Museum of Art, 170
Orlando Science Center, 170
Orlando SeaLife Aquarium, 165
Orlando StarFlyer, 4, 166
Orlando Tree Trek Adventure,
    189–190
Orlando Vacation Homes
    360, 266
Orlando Vineland Premium
    Outlets, 191
Outdoor activities, 183–190
    Arnold Palmer's Bay Hill Club &
        Lodge, 187
    BK Adventure, 185
    Blue Spring State Park, 183
    boat tours, 185–186
    Boggy Creek Airboat
        Rides, 185
    Celebration Golf Course, 188
    Central Florida Nature
        Adventures, 185
    ChampionsGate Golf
        Resort, 187
    De Leon Springs State Park,
        183–184
    Falcon's Fire Golf Club, 188
    golf, 186–189
    Harry P. Leu Gardens, 184
    Hawk's Landing Golf Club, 188
    Highlands Reserve Golf
        Club, 188
    hot-air balloons, 189–190
    Magic Sunrise Ballooning, 189
    MetroWest Golf Club, 188
    Mystic Dunes Golf Club, 187
    Orange County National Golf
        Center and Lodge, 189
    Orlando Balloon Rides, 189
    Orlando Tree Trek Adventure,
        189–190
    Reunion Resort & Club, 187
    The Ritz-Carlton Golf Club, 187
    Royal St. Cloud Golf Links, 189
    Scenic Boat Tour, 186
    Shingle Creek Golf Club, 187
    Tibet-Butler Preserve, 184
    Timacuan Golf and Country
        Club, 189
    Tranquilo Golf Club at Four
        Seasons Resort Orlando, 187
    Villas of Grand Cypress, 187
    Wallaby Ranch, 190
    Walt Disney World Golf
        Course, 188
    Wekiwa Springs State Park,
        184–185
Outer Limitz, 165
Outlet malls, 190–191

Outpost, 76
The Outta Control Magic Comedy Dinner Show, 218–219
Overlooked experiences, Orlando, 4–5
Overplanning, 8
Overpurchasing tickets, 8

P

Pacific Point Preserve, 154
Packages, tickets, 24–26
Packing, 284
Pandora—The World of Avatar, 2, 9, 88–90, 93
Parade, 40, 47, 112
Park Hopper, 23
Park Hopper Plus, 23–24
Parking, 31–32, 34
Parliament House Orlando, 182
Pat O'Brien's, 226
Peaceful places, Magic Kingdom, 37
Peak season, 273
PeopleMover, 57
Peter Pan's Flight, 3, 37–39, 46, 51–52
Pete's Silly Sideshow, 38, 54–55
Pets, 284–285
Pets Ahoy!, 151
Pharmacies, 285
Phineas and Ferb: Agent P's World Showcase Adventure, 71
PhotoPass, 34
Pins, 194
A Pirate's Adventure—Treasures of the Seven Seas, 46
Pirates of the Caribbean, 3, 8, 37–39, 45–46
Pirate's Cove, 177
Pirates' Cove Live Water Ski Show, 159
Pirates Dinner Adventure, 219
The Pirates League salon, 46
Pirates and Pals Fireworks Voyage, 59
Pixar Place, 105–106
Planning, vacation, 7–10, 267–287
busy times, 273–274
climate, 274
discounts, 277–278
events calendar, 274–277
fast facts, 278–287
packing, 284
temperature, 274
timeline, 10
websites, 272
Play Disney Parks app, 49
Player 1 Orlando, 182
Plume et Palette, 78
Police, 285
Popeye & Bluto's Bilge-Rat Barges, 3, 136–137
Poseidon's Fury, 141
Presley, Elvis, 5
Prices, tickets, 23
Primeval Whirl, 88, 93
Prince Charming Regal Carrousel, 52

Princess Fairytale Hall, 52
Princess Storybook Dining, 222
Pro Bowl, 274
Production Central, 118, 120–122
Psychics, 171
Pteranodon Flyers, 138
Public transit, 271–273
The Puffin's Roost, 75
Pulse nightclub, 12
Pumpkin juice, 139
Punga Racers, 145

Q

The Quest for Chi, 159
Quick Queue Unlimited, 149
Quick-service restaurants
Animal Kingdom, 94–96
Epcot, 80–82
Hollywood Studios, 106–107
Magic Kingdom, 58–61

R

Race Through New York Starring Jimmy Fallon, 122
Rafiki's Planet Watch, 88, 91
Rain, 11
Raptor Encounter, 138
Ratatouille ride, 68
Ray Feeding, 158
Ray Rush, 157
Red Coconut Club, 226
"Reflections of China," 75–76
Regional History Center, 194
Rentals, homes, 264–266
Reptile World Serpentarium, 176–177
Restaurants, best of, 6, see also Restaurants Index
Reunion Resort & Club, 187
Revenge of the Mummy, 123
Ride Reservations, 117
Rideshare, 270
Rides, Orlando's best, 3–4
Ripley's Believe It or Not! Odditorium, 166
The Ritz-Carlton Golf Club, 187
River Country, 160
Rivers of Light, 88, 93, 112
Roa's Rapids, 157
Rock 'n' Roller Coaster, 95, 100, 102
Rock the Universe, 275
Royal Caribbean International cruises, 195
Royal Joust, 159
Royal Sommerhus, 75
Royal St. Cloud Golf Links, 189
Runoff Rapids, 110

S

Safari Trek, 159
Safety, 285
SAK Comedy Lab, 183
San Francisco, 120, 123
Saturn V rocket, 4
Scenic Boat Tour, 5
Sea of Delight, Sea of Mystery, 154–155

Sea of Legends, Sea of Ice, 153
Sea of Power, Sea of Fun, 155–156
Sea of Shallows, 151–152
The Seas with Nemo and Friends, 66, 70–71
SeaVenture, 158
SeaWorld Discovery Guide app, 149
SeaWorld Orlando, 3–4, 9–10, 146–158
Animal Connections, 148
Antarctica: Empire of the Penguin, 153
Aquarium: The Beautiful Ocean, 151
Aquatica, 146
best of, 149, 150–151
Blackfish documentary, 148
Breakfast with Elmo and Friends, 156
Clyde & Seamore's Sea Lion High, 150–1561
costs, basics, 154
dining plans, 156
dining, 156–157
Discovery Cove, 146
Dolphin Days, 151
Dolphin Encounter, 152
Dolphin Nursery, 152
Expedition SeaWorld VIP Tour, 149
Infinity Falls, 154
Journey to Atlantis, 153
Kraken Unleashed, 153
Mako, 154
Manatee Rehabilitation, 152
Manta, 151–152
One Ocean, 150
Pacific Point Preserve, 154
Pets Ahoy!, 151
Quick Queue Unlimited, 149
Sea of Delight, Sea of Mystery, 154–155
Sea of Legends, Sea of Ice, 153
Sea of Power, Sea of Fun, 155–156
Sea of Shallows, 151–152
seating, 150
SeaWorld Discovery Guide app, 149
Sesame Street at SeaWorld Orlando, 155
Shamu Stadium, 155
Shark Encounter, 155
show schedule, 149
Sky Tower, 155
soak zone, 150
Stingray Lagoon & Feeding, 152
timing, 149
tours, 157
trainers, 152
TurtleTrek, 152
Up-Close Dining at Shamu Stadium, 156
Wild Arctic, 155–156
SeaWorld's Halloween Spooktacular, 276
Security, 32

Senior travel, 285
Serenity Bay, 158
Sesame Street at SeaWorld Orlando, 155
Seuss Landing, 141–143
Seven Dwarfs Mine Train, 37–39, 53
Scenic Boat Tour, 186
Shamu Stadium, 155
Shark Encounter, 155
Shark Swim, 158
SheiKra, 160
Shingle Creek Golf Club, 187
Shopping, 190–194
  Barnes & Noble, 194
  Bibbidi Bobbidi Boutique, 192–194
  Disney Springs, 191–192
  Florida Mall, 190
  Lake Buena Vista Factory, 191
  Mall at Millenia, 190
  Orange World, 194
  Orlando International Premium Outlets, 190
  Orlando Vineland Premium Outlets, 191
  Outlet malls, 190–191
  Regional History Center, 194
Shows, Orlando's best, 3–4
Shrek 4-D, 121
Shutterbutton's, 125
Shuttles, 269–271
Silver Spurs Rodeo, 274–275
The Simpson's Ride, 4, 127–128
The Singing Sorceress: Celestina Warbeck and the Banshees, 124
Sing It!, 122
Size restrictions, 32–33
Skeletons: Museum of Osteology, 166
Ski Patrol, 110
Skull Island: Reign of Kong, 3, 9, 137
Sky Tower, 155
Sleuth's Mystery Dinner Shows, 219
Slinky Dog Dash, 2, 95, 100, 104
Slush Gusher, 109
Smoking, 285
Snow Stormers, 109
Soak zone, 150
Soarin', 3, 66, 71–72
Soarin' Around the World, 9
Soda, 34
Sorcerers of the Magic Kingdom, 41
South of Orlando, 17–18
Spaceship Earth, 9, 66, 68–69
Space Shuttle orbiter *Atlantis*, 4
Spirit Encounters Night Photography Tour, 171
Splendid China, 160
Splitsville Luxury Lanes, 113
SpongeBob StorePants, 128
Sportsman's Shoppe, 79
Springfield, 120, 127–128
Spring training, 167, 275

Star Tours—The Adventure Continues, 95, 100–101
Star Wars: A Galactic Spectacular, 95, 97, 100, 112
Star Wars: Galaxy's Edge, 2, 101
Star Wars Launch Bay, 105
Star Wars: Path of the Jedi, 98
Steamboat Springs, 109
Stingray Lagoon & Feeding, 152
Storm Force Accelatron, 134
Storm Slides, 110
Storybook Circus, 51
Strollers, 33–34
Studios park, 8
Sugarplum's, 125
Summit Plummet, 109
Sunscreen, 8
Sunset Boulevard, 102–103
Supercalifragilistic Breakfast, 223
Superstar Parade, 120
Surf Pool, 110
Space Mountain, 3, 8, 37–39, 56
Stave Church Gallery, 4, 74
Splash Mountain, 3, 8, 37–39, 46–47–48
The Swiss Family Robinson, 43
Swiss Family Treehouse, 37, 43

T

Table-service restaurants
  Animal Kingdom, 96–97
  Epcot, 82–85
  Hollywood Studios, 107–108
  Magic Kingdom, 61–64
The Tales of Beedle the Bard, 124
Taxes, 285
Taxis, 270, 273
Tea Caddy, 79
Teens, 38–39
Telephones, 285–286
Temperature, 274
Terminator-themed movie, 128
Test Track, 66, 69–70
Theme parks, best experiences, 2–3
TheMouseForLess.com, 26
Three-day itinerary, 9–10
Tibet-Butler Preserve, 184
Tickets, 8, 22–28
  base ticket, 22–23
  Chase Disney Rewards Visa credit card, 26
  conventions, 24
  deals, 26
  DISBoards.com, 26
  discounts, 24, 26
  Fastpass+, 26–28
  MagicBands, 25–28
  Magic Your Way, 22–26
  MDX, 26–28
  mobile ordering, 28
  MouseSavers.com,, 26
  My Disney Experience, *see also* MDX, 25–26
  MyMagic+, 25
  options, 23
  overpurchasing, 8
  packages, 24–26

Park Hopper, 23
Park Hopper Plus, 23–24
  prices, 23
  TheMouseForLess.com, 26
  Universal Orlando, 116–118
Tike's Peak, 110
Timacuan Golf and Country Club, 189
Time, 286
Timeline, planning, 10
Times Guide, 32, 46, 73
Timeshare pitches, 277
Tipping, 286
Titanic: The Artifact Exhibition, 166–167
Toboggan Racers, 109
Toilets, 286
Toll-free numbers, 32
Tom Sawyer Island, 46, 48
Tomorrowland, 56–58
Tomorrowland Speedway, 37, 38, 46, 56
Tomorrowland Transit Authority, 39, 46, 57
Toon Lagoon, 135–137
Topgolf Orlando, 177
Tours, 113–114, 157
  boat tours, 185–186
  Kennedy Space Center, 179–180
Town Square Theater, 38, 42
Toy Soldier, 79
Toy Story Land, 2, 104
Toy Story Mania!, 3, 95, 100, 104
Trader Sam's Grog Grotto, 225
Trainers, SeaWorld, 152
Train travel, 268, 270
Tranquilo Golf Club at Four Seasons Resort Orlando, 187
Transformers: The Ride—3D, 9, 121–122
Transportation Center, 29
Transportation and Ticket Center (TTC), 35
Transportation System, 30–31
The Tree of Life, 86, 93
TriceraTop Spin, 88, 93
TRON Lightcycle Power Run, 56
Tropical Escape Resort Home, 266
Turtle Talk with Crush, 71
TurtleTrek, 152
Twilight Zone Tower of Terror, 95, 100, 102
Two-day itinerary, 8–9
Two parks, one day, 95
Typhoon Lagoon, 3, 110–111

U

Uber, 29
Underplanning, 8
Under the Sea—Journey of the Little Mermaid, 54
United Kingdom, 79
Universal Dining Plan—Quick Service, 132
Universal Express Pass, 117
Universal Horror Make-Up Show, 128

ACCOMMODATIONS INDEX

Universal Orlando, 2–4, 8–10, 115–146
  clothing, 118
  contact information, 117
  costs, basics, 118
  dining, 205–207
  Express Plus, 117
  Islands of Adventure, 132–145
  line hopping, 117–118
  My Universal Photos, 118
  Official Universal Orlando Resort App, 118
  Ride Reservations, 117
  tickets, 116–118
  Universal Express Pass, 117
  Universal Studios, 118–132
  VIP Experience, 117
  Volcano Bay, 145–146
Universal Studios Florida, 2–3, 118–132
  Animal Actors on Location!, 129
  The Beat Builders, 123
  best of, 122
  The Blues Brothers, 122
  Carkitt Market, 124–125
  Character Party Zone, 128
  Cinematic Celebration, 120
  Curious George Goes to Town, 130
  A Day in the Park with Barney, 129–130
  Despicable Me Minion Mayhem, 121
  Diamond Bellas, 122
  dining, 130–132
  dining plans, 132
  Donkey's Photo Finish, 121
  Duff Brewery's, 127
  E.T. Adventure, 129
  Eternelle's Elixir of Refreshment, 125
  Fast & Furious—Supercharged, 123
  Fear Factor Live, 127
  Fievel's Playland, 129
  Fountain of Fair Fortune, 125
  Harry Potter and the Escape from Gringotts, 124
  Hogwarts Express, 126
  Hollywood, 118, 128
  Hollywood Character Zone, 128
  Hollywood Rip Ride Rockit, 120–121
  The Hopping Pot, 125
  Horizont Alley, 124–125
  Kang & Kodos' Twirl 'n' Hurl, 128
  Knight Bus, 123
  Knockturn Alley, 124
  Kwik-E-Mart, 127
  Lard Lad Donuts, 127
  Magical Menagerie, 125
  Marilyn Monroe, 122
  Men in Black: Alien Attack, 126
  Moe's Tavern, 127
  NBC Media Center, 129
  New York, 118, 122–123
  Ollivanders, 125–126

Production Central, 118, 120–122
Race Through New York Starring Jimmy Fallon, 122
Revenge of the Mummy, 123
San Francisco, 120, 123
Shrek 4-D, 121
Shutterbutton's, 125
The Simpsons Ride, 127–128
The Singing Sorceress: Celestina Warbeck and the Banshees, 124
Sing It!, 122
SpongeBob StorePants, 128
Springfield, 120, 127–128
Sugarplum's, 125
Superstar Parade, 120
The Tales of Beedle the Bard, 124
Terminator-themed movie, 128
Transformers: The Ride—3D, 121–122
Universal Dining Plan—Quick Service, 132
Universal Horror Make-Up Show, 128
Universal Studios Store, 120
Weasleys' Wizard Wheezes, 125
Williams of Hollywood, 127
The Wizarding World of Harry Potter—Diagon Alley, 120, 123–126
Woody Woodpecker's Kidzone, 120, 128–130
Woody Woodpecker's Nuthouse Coaster, 130
World Expo, 120, 126–127
Universal Studios Store, 120
UP! A Great Bird Adventure, 88, 92–93
Up-Close Dining at Shamu Stadium, 156
U.S. 192, 15–16
U.S.A., Epcot, 77
utilidor system, 113

V

Vacation planning, 7–10
  timeline, 10
Villas of Grand Cypress, 187
VIP Experience, 117
VIP Tours, 34
Visas, 286
Visitor information, 286–287
The Void/Star Wars: Secrets of the Empire, 112
Volcano Bay, 2, 10, 145–146
Voyage of the Little Mermaid, 100, 105

W

Wait times, 54–55
Wallaby Ranch, 190
Walt Disney's Carousel of Progress, 37, 39, 46, 57–58
Walt Disney Presents, 105–106
Walt Disney World, 2–3

Walt Disney World Golf Course, 188
Walt Disney World Marathon, 274
Walt Disney World Railroad, 41, 46–47, 55–56
Walt Disney World Resort, 14–15
Walt Disney World Tours, 113–114
The Wandering Reindeer, 75
Wantilan Luau, 220
Water, 8, 34, 287
Water parks, 108–111
  Blizzard Beach, 109–110
  food, 109
  lockers, 108
  preparation, 109
  timing, 109
  Typhoon Lagoon, 110–111
Waturi Beach, 145
Weasleys' Wizard Wheezes, 125
Websites, planning, 272
Weinkeller, 76
Wekiwa Springs State Park, 5, 184–185
West of Orlando, 18
Wheelchairs, 34
Wild Arctic, 155–156
Wilderness Explorers, 91
Wildlife Express Train, 91
Williams of Hollywood, 127
Williams, Esther, 5, 159
Wind-Away River, 158
Window names, 42
Wine tasting, Epcot, 76
Winter Park Bach Festival, 274
Winter Park, 11, 17, 170–172
Wishes, 3
The Wizarding World of Harry Potter, 3, 8
The Wizarding World of Harry Potter—Diagon Alley, 3, 9, 120, 123–126
The Wizarding World of Harry Potter—Hogsmeade, 138–141
Wonders of Life, 70
WonderWorks, 167–168
Woody Woodpecker's Kidzone, 120, 128–130
Woody Woodpecker's Nuthouse Coaster, 130
World Expo, 120, 126–127
World Fellowship Fountain, 69
World Showcase, 9, 66–67, 73–80

X

Xanadu, 160

Z

Zombie Outbreak, 165
ZORA! Festival, 274

Accommodations

The Alfond Inn, 263–264
Avanti Palms Resort and Conference Center, 262
Aventura Hotel, 5, 250–251
B Resort, 6, 246

Best Western Lake Buena Vista, 246–247

Comfort Suites Maingate East, 255–256

Courtyard at Lake Lucerne, 264

Destiny Palms Hotel Maingate West, 256

Disney's All-Star Movies/Disney's All-Star Music/Disney's All-Star Sports, 242

Disney's Animal Kingdom Lodge, 236

Disney's Art of Animation Resort, 242–243

Disney's Beach Club/Disney's Yacht Club, 236–237

Disney's BoardWalk Inn, 237

Disney's Caribbean Beach Resort, 239–240

Disney's Contemporary Resort, 5, 6, 8, 237–238

Disney's Coronado Springs Resort, 240

Disney's Fort Wilderness Resort & Campground, 240

Disney's Grand Floridian Resort & Spa, 238

Disney's Polynesian Village Resort, 238–239

Disney's Pop Century Resort, 243

Disney's Port Orleans and French Quarter, 241

Disney's Wilderness Lodge, 239

Dockside Inn and Suites, 249

DoubleTree Suites By Hilton Orlando, 247

Drury Inn & Suites, 261

Endless Summer Resort, 5–6, 249

Fairfield Inn & Suites Orlando, 262–263

Four Seasons Resort Orlando, 6, 244

Gaylord Palms, 6, 251–252

The Grove Resort & Spa Orlando, 252

Hard Rock Hotel, 248

Hawthorn Suites Lake Buena Vista, 257–258

Hilton Orlando Bonnet Creek, 245

Holiday Inn Express & Suites—Orlando at SeaWorld, 261

Hyatt House, 6, 261–262

Hyatt Place Lake Buena Vista, 258

Hyatt Regency Grand Cypress, 6, 252–254

Hyatt Regency Orlando, 258–260

JW Marriott, 6, 260

Legoland Beach Retreat, 264

Legoland Hotel, 264

Loews Portofino Bay Hotel, 248–249

Loews Royal Pacific Resort, 249

Loews Sapphire Falls Resort, 250

Margaritaville Resort, 255

Meliá Orlando Suite Hotel at Celebration, 255

Orlando World Center Marriott, 254

Quality Inn & Suites by the Parks, 256

Residence Inn, 6, 263

Ritz-Carlton, 6, 260

Rosen Shingle Creek, 260–261

Sapphire Falls Resort, 5

Shades of Green, 241

Sonesta ES Suites Orlando—International Drive, 262

SpringHill Suites and TownePlace Suites Orlando Flamingo Crossings, 6, 256–257

Staybridge Suites Lake Buena Vista, 257

Surfside Inn and Suites, 249

TownePlace Suites Orlando, 263

Universal's Aventura Hotel, 4, 250–251

Universal's Cabana Bay Beach Resort, 249–250

The Villas of Grand Cypress Resort, 254–255

Waldorf Astoria Orlando, 245

Walt Disney World Swan and Dolphin, 245–246

Wyndham Grand Orlando Resort Bonnet Creek, 246

Wyndham Lake Buena Vista, 247

Restaurants

ABC Commissary (Commissary Lane), 106

Adventureland, 37

Agave Azul, 212

Aloha Isle Refreshments (Adventureland), 60

Antojitos Authentic Mexican Food, 206

Arepas el Cacao, 213

Backlot Express (Echo Lake), 107

Baseline Tap House (Commissary Lane), 107

Be Our Guest Restaurant (Fantasyland), 64

Beverly Hills Boulangerie (Hollywood), 132

Biergarten Restaurant (Epcot, Germany), 76, 83

Blondie's (Toon Lagoon), 143

The Boathouse (Disney Springs), 201–202

Bob Marley—A Tribute to Freedom, 206, 225

Boma, 6, 197

Boulangerie Pâtisserie (France), 82

Bruno's Italian Restaurant, 6, 208

Bubbalou's Bodacious Bar-B-Que, 213–214

Bumblebee Man's Taco Truck, 132

The Burger Digs (Jurassic Park), 144

Cafe 4 (Marvel Super Hero Island), 143

Café Tu Tu Tango, 212

California Grill, 6, 197

Captain America Diner (Marvel Super Hero Island), 143

Captain Pete's Island Hot Dogs (SeaWorld), 157

Casey's Corner (Main Street, U.S.A.), 59

Catalina Eddie's (Sunset Boulevard), 106

Ceviche, 215–216

Chef Art Smith's Homecomin', 6, 202

Chefs de France, 84

Christini's, 211

Cinderella's Royal Table (Fantasyland), 63–64

Circus McGurkus Cafe Stoo-pendous (Seuss Landing), 145

Citrus Swirl, 37

Classic Monsters Café (Production Central), 130

Cletus' Chicken Shack, 131

Columbia Harbour House (Liberty Square), 60

Columbia Restaurant, 207–208

Comic Strip Café (Toon Lagoon), 143

Confisco Grille (Islands of Adventure), 143

Coral Reef Restaurant (The Seas with Nemo & Friends), 82

Cosmic Ray's Starlight Café (Tomorrowland), 60

The Cowfish Sushi Burger Bar, 206

Croissant Moon Bakery (Islands of Adventure), 143

The Crystal Palace (Main Street, U.S.A.), 62

Dandelion Communitea Café, 6, 216

Dawa Bar (Africa), 96

Deep Blu Seafood Grille, 197–200

The Diamond Horseshoe (Liberty Square), 62

Dino-Bites kiosk, 96

Doc Sugrue's Desert Kebab House (Lost Continent), 144–145

DoveCote, 216

El Tenampa, 208–210

Electric Umbrella (Innoventions East), 81

Ethos Vegan Kitchen, 216–217

Expedition Café (SeaWorld), 156

Fairfax Fare (Sunset Boulevard), 106

Fantasyland, 37

Fast Food Boulevard, 9, 131–132

50's Prime Time Café (Echo Lake), 107–108

Finnegan's Bar & Grill (New York), 130

Fire-Eater's Grill (Lost Continent), 145

Flame Tree Barbecue (Discovery Island), 94

Flamecraft Bar (SeaWorld), 156

Flying Fish, 205

The Friar's Nook (Fantasyland), 60

The Frying Dutchman, 131

The Garden Grill (The Land), 82

RESTAURANT INDEX

Gaston's Tavern (Fantasyland), 37, 60
Hanamizuki Japanese Restaurant, 214
Harambe Market (Africa), 96
Hard Rock Café, 206
Hash House A Go Go, 212
Havana's Cuban Cuisine, 6, 208
Hog's Head pub (Wizarding World), 144
Hollywood & Vine (Echo Lake), 107
Hollywood Brown Derby (Hollywood Boulevard), 107
Japan, 9
Jerusalem Restaurant, 210
Jiko—The Cooking Place, 200
Jimmy Buffett's Margaritaville, 206–207, 226
K Restaurant & Wine Bar, 214–215
Katsura Grill (Japan), 81
Kringla Bakeri Og Kafé (Norway), 81
Krusty Burger, 131
Kusafiri Coffee Shop & Bakery (Africa), 96
La Cantina De San Angel (Mexico), 81
La Hacienda de San Angel (Mexico), 83
Lard Lad Donuts, 131
The Leaky Cauldron (Diagon Alley), 131
Le Cellier Steakhouse (Canada), 85
Le Coq Au Vin, 215
LeFou's Brew, 37
Liberty Inn (American Adventure), 81
Liberty Tree Tavern, 62–63
Lisa's Teahouse of Horror, 131
Lisbon Portuguese Cuisine, 211
Lombard's Seafood Grille (San Francisco), 131
Lotus Blossom Café (China), 81
Louie's Italian Restaurant (New York), 130
Luigi's Pizza, 131
The Lunching Pad (Tomorrowland), 60
Mama Melrose's Ristorante Italiano (Streets of America), 107
Mango Joe's Café (SeaWorld), 157
Maxine's on Shine, 6, 216
Mel's Drive-In (Hollywood), 132
Merguez Restaurant, 210
Mexico, 9

Miller's Lake Buena Vista Ale House, 210
Mills Fifty, 6
Min & Bill's Dockside Diner (Echo Lake), 107
Moe's Tavern (Springfield), 132
Monsieur Paul (France), 84
Morimoto Asia, 6, 202
Morocco, 9
Mythos Restaurant (Lost Continent), 144
Nile Ethiopian Cuisine, 6, 214
Nine Dragons Restaurant (China), 83
Pat O'Brien's, 207, 226
Pecos Bill Tall Tale Inn and Café (Frontierland), 60
Pinocchio Village Haus (Fantasyland), 60
Pio Pio, 212
Pizza Predattoria (Jurassic Park), 144
Pizzafari (Discovery Island), 94
PizzeRizzo (Muppets Courtyard), 107
Plaza Ice Cream Parlor (Main Street, U.S.A.), 59
The Plaza Restaurant (Main Street, U.S.A.), 62
Polite Pig, 203–204
Princess Storybook Dining at Akershus Royal Banquet Hall (Norway), 83
Punjab Kitchen, 208
Q'Kenan, 6, 210–211
Raglan Road, 202
Rainforest Café (park entry), 96, 203
The Ravenous Pig, 215
Restaurant Marrakesh (Morocco), 84
Restaurantosaurus (DinoLand U.S.A.), 96
Richter's Burger Co. (San Francisco), 131
Rocco's Tacos, 213
Rose & Crown Pub & Dining Room (United Kingdom), 85
Rosie's All-American Café (Sunset Boulevard), 106
Royal Anandapur Tea Company kiosk (Asia), 96
San Angel Inn Restaurante (Mexico), 82–83
San Francisco Pastry Company, 131
Satu'li Canteen (Pandora), 94
Sci-Fi Dine-In Theater Restaurant (Commissary Lane), 108
The Seafire Grill (SeaWorld), 156

Sharks Underwater Grill & Bar (SeaWorld), 156
Skipper Canteen (Adventureland), 62
Sommerfest (Epcot, Germany), 76, 81
Spice Mill Burgers (SeaWorld), 156
Spice Road Table (Morocco), 84
STK Orlando, 203
Sunshine Seasons (The Land), 80–81
Sunshine Tree Terrace (Adventureland), 37, 59–60
Tamu Tamu Eats & Refreshment (Africa), 96
Tangierine Café (Morocco), 82
Taverna Opa, 213
Teppan Edo (Japan), 84
Thai Thani, 213
Three Broomsticks (Wizarding World of Harry Potter), 144
Thunder Falls Terrace (Jurassic Park), 144
Tiffins (Oasis), 96–97
Todd English's bluezoo, 200
Tokyo Dining (Japan), 84
The Tomorrowland Terrace, 60–61
Tony's Town Square Restaurant (Main Street, U.S.A.), 62
Toothsome Chocolate Emporium, 207
Tortuga Tavern (Adventureland), 60
Trattoria al Forno, 205
T-Rex, 203
The Trolley Car Café (Hollywood Boulevard), 106
Tusker House Restaurant (Africa), 97
Tutto Gusto (Italy), 81
Tutto Italia Ristorante (Italy), 83
Via Napoli (Italy), 83–84
Victoria & Albert's, 6, 10, 200–201
Vivo Italian Kitchen, 207
Voyagers Smokehouse (SeaWorld), 156
Waterstone Grill (Aquatica), 157
Waterway Grill (SeaWorld), 156
Wimpy's (Toon Lagoon), 143–144
Wine Bar George, 203
Woody's Lunch Box (Toy Story Land), 107
Yak & Yeti Local Food Cafes (Asia), 96
Yak & Yeti Restaurant (Asia), 97
Yorkshire County Fish Shop (United Kingdom), 82

Map List

Orlando at a Glance   13
Walt Disney World & Lake
   Buena Vista   20
The Magic Kingdom   36
Epcot   65
Disney's Animal Kingdom   87
Disney's Hollywood Studios   99
Universal Studios Florida   119
Islands of Adventure   133
SeaWorld   147

Orlando Area Attractions   163
Disney Springs   193
Walt Disney World & Lake Buena
   Vista Restaurants   198
Orlando Area Restaurants   209
Orlando Area Hotels   231
Walt Disney World & Lake Buena
   Vista Hotels   232
Kissimmee Area Hotels   253
International Drive Hotels   259

Photo Credits

Frommer's EasyGuide to Disney World, Universal & Orlando 2019, 6th Edition

Published by
FROMMER MEDIA LLC

Disney Springs map data copyright © OpenStreetMap contributors

ISBN 978-1-62887-414-3 (paper), 978-1-62887-415-0 (e-book)

Editorial Director: Pauline Frommer
Editor: Melissa Klurman
Production Editor: Lynn Northrup
Cartographer: Roberta Stockwell
Photo Editor: Meghan Lamb
Indexer: Kelly Henthorne
Cover Designer: Dave Riedy

For information on our other products or services, see www.frommers.com.

Frommer Media LLC also publishes its books in a variety of electronic formats. Some content that
appears in print may not be available in electronic formats.

Manufactured in the United States of America

5 4 3 2 1

ABOUT THE AUTHOR

Jason Cochran was twice awarded Guide Book of the Year by the Lowell Thomas Awards (Society of American Travel Writers) and once by the North American Travel Journalists Association. His voice has reached millions of travelers, from the mid-1990s when he wrote one of the world's first travel blogs, to his familiarity as a commentator on CBS and for AOL, to his work today as editor-in-chief of Frommers.com and co-host of the Frommer Travel Show on WABC. For this edition, he'd like to thank Alex Miranda, Andre Beermann, Kristin Harmel, Tracy Temple, Julie Morris, Jake Cochran, and Zachary Cochran.

ABOUT THE FROMMER'S TRAVEL GUIDES

For most of the past 50 years, Frommer's has been the leading series of travel guides in North America, accounting for as many as 24 percent of all guidebooks sold. I think I know why.

Though we hope our books are entertaining, we nevertheless deal with travel in a serious fashion. Our guidebooks have never looked on such journeys as a mere recreation, but as a far more important human function, a time of learning and introspection, an essential part of a civilized life. We stress the culture, lifestyle, history, and beliefs of the destinations we cover, and urge our readers to seek out people and new ideas as the chief rewards of travel.

We have never shied from controversy. We have, from the beginning, encouraged our authors to be intensely judgmental, critical—both pro and con—in their comments, and wholly independent. Our only clients are our readers, and we have triggered the ire of countless prominent sorts, from a tourist newspaper we called "practically worthless" (it unsuccessfully sued us) to the many rip-offs we've condemned.

And because we believe that travel should be available to everyone regardless of their incomes, we have always been cost-conscious at every level of expenditure. Though we have broadened our recommendations beyond the budget category, we insist that every lodging we include be sensibly priced. We use every form of media to assist our readers, and are particularly proud of our feisty daily website, the award-winning Frommers.com.

I have high hopes for the future of Frommer's. May these guidebooks, in all the years ahead, continue to reflect the joy of travel and the freedom that travel represents. May they always pursue a cost-conscious path, so that people of all incomes can enjoy the rewards of travel. And may they create, for both the traveler and the persons among whom we travel, a community of friends, where all human beings live in harmony and peace.

Arthur Frommer

Before, During, or After your use of a Frommer's guidebook... you'll want to consult

FROMMERS.COM

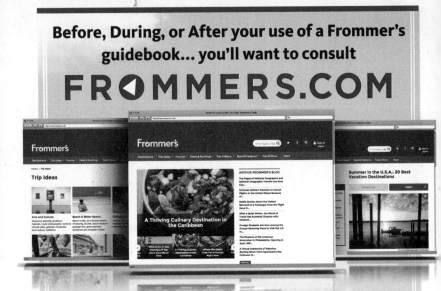

FROMMERS.COM IS KEPT UP-TO-DATE, WITH:

NEWS
The latest events (and deals) to affect your next vacation

BLOGS
Opinionated comments by our outspoken staff

FORUMS
Post your travel questions, get answers from other readers

SLIDESHOWS
On weekly-changing, practical but inspiring topics of travel

CONTESTS
Enabling you to win free trips

PODCASTS
Of our weekly, nationwide radio show

DESTINATIONS
Hundreds of cities, their hotels, restaurants and sights

TRIP IDEAS
Valuable, offbeat suggestions for your next vacation

*AND MUCH MORE!

Smart travelers consult Frommers.com